P9-CJR-538

THE WALLFLOWER
YAMATONADESHIKO SHICHIHENGE

7

Tomoko Hayakawa

TRANSLATED AND ADAPTED BY
David Ury

LETTERING BY
Dana Hayward

DEL REY

BALLANTINE BOOKS • NEW YORK

A Del Rey Trade Paperback Original

Copyright © 2002 by Tomoko Hayakawa.
English translation copyright © 2006 by Tomoko Hayakawa

All rights reserved.

Published in the United States by Del Rey Books, an imprint of The Random House Publishing Group, a division of Random House, Inc., New York.

DEL REY is a registered trademark and the Del Rey colophon is a trademark of Random House, Inc.

Publication rights arranged through Kodansha Ltd.

First published in Japan in 2002 by Kodansha Ltd., Tokyo, as *Yamatonadeshiko Shichihenge*.

Library of Congress Number: 2004095918

ISBN 0-345-48371-5

Printed in the United States of America

www.delreymanga.com

9 8 7 6 5 4 3 2 1

Translator and adapter—David Ury

Lettering—Dana Hayward

Cover design—David Stevenson

Contents

A Note from the Author   iv

Honorifics   v

The Wallflower, Volume 7   1

Bonus Manga   166

Four-panel Comics   170

About the Creator   174

Translation Notes   175

Preview of Volume 8   179

A Note from the Author

IT'S SIX FEET HIGH, AND IT'S HUGE!

MY...

...LIVING ROOM (JUST PART OF IT)

♥ Heh, heh, heh. It's the "Satan chair" or maybe the "devil chair." The thing in front is the "skeleton chair." I'd sure like to have a pentagon quilt hanging on the wall. ♥ . . . what am I . . . a witch or something? Well, that's my living room. It doesn't look like your ordinary house. But I wanna keep getting more of this stuff! ♥

—Tomoko Hayakawa

Honorifics

Throughout the Del Rey Manga books, you will find Japanese honorifics left intact in the translations. For those not familiar with how the Japanese use honorifics, and more important, how they differ from American honorifics, we present this brief overview.

Politeness has always been a critical facet of Japanese culture. Ever since the feudal era, when Japan was a highly stratified society, use of honorifics—which can be defined as polite speech that indicates relationship or status—has played an essential role in the Japanese language. When addressing someone in Japanese, an honorific usually takes the form of a suffix attached to one's name (example: "Asuna-san"), or as a title at the end of one's name or in place of the name itself (example: "Negi-sensei," or simply "Sensei!").

Honorifics can be expressions of respect or endearment. In the context of manga and anime, honorifics give insight into the nature of the relationship between characters. Many translations into English leave out these important honorifics, and therefore distort the "feel" of the original Japanese. Because Japanese honorifics contain nuances that English honorifics lack, it is our policy at Del Rey not to translate them. Here, instead, is a guide to some of the honorifics you may encounter in Del Rey Manga.

-san: This is the most common honorific, and is equivalent to Mr., Miss, Ms., Mrs., etc. It is the all-purpose honorific and can be used in any situation where politeness is required.

-sama: This is one level higher than "-san" and it is used to confer great respect.

-dono: This comes from the word "tono," which means "lord." It is an even higher level than "-sama," and confers utmost respect.

-kun: This suffix is used at the end of boys' names to express familiarity or endearment. It is also sometimes used by men among friends, or when addressing someone younger or of a lower station.

-chan: This is used to express endearment, mostly toward girls. It is also used for little boys, pets, and even among lovers. It gives a sense of childish cuteness.

Bozu: This is an informal way to refer to a boy, similar to the English term "kid" or "squirt."

Sempai/senpai: This title suggests that the addressee is one's "senior" in a group or organization. It is most often used in a school setting, where underclassmen refer to their upperclassmen as "sempai." It can also be used in the workplace, such as when a newer employee addresses an employee who has seniority in the company.

Kohai: This is the opposite of "sempai," and is used toward underclassmen in school or newcomers in the workplace. It connotes that the addressee is of lower station.

Sensei: Literally meaning "one who has come before," this title is used for teachers, doctors, or masters of any profession or art.

[blank]: Usually forgotten in these lists, but perhaps the most significant difference between Japanese and English. The lack of honorific means that the speaker has permission to address the person in a very intimate way. Usually, only family, spouses, or very close friends have this kind of permission. Known as *yobisute,* it can be gratifying when someone who has earned the intimacy starts to call one by one's name without an honorific. But when that intimacy hasn't been earned, it can be very insulting.

THE wallflower

YAMATONADESHIKO SHICHIHENGE

ヤマトナデシコ七変化♡

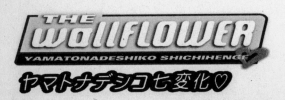

CONTENTS

Chapter 27   3
Oui Monsieur

Chapter 28   43
Little Lost Boy

Chapter 29   83
The Strongest Women in the World

Chapter 30   123
A Scary Winter Story

THE WALLFLOWER
YAMATONADESHIKO SHICHIHENGE

Chapter 27

♥ BOOK 7 ♥

Oui Monsieur

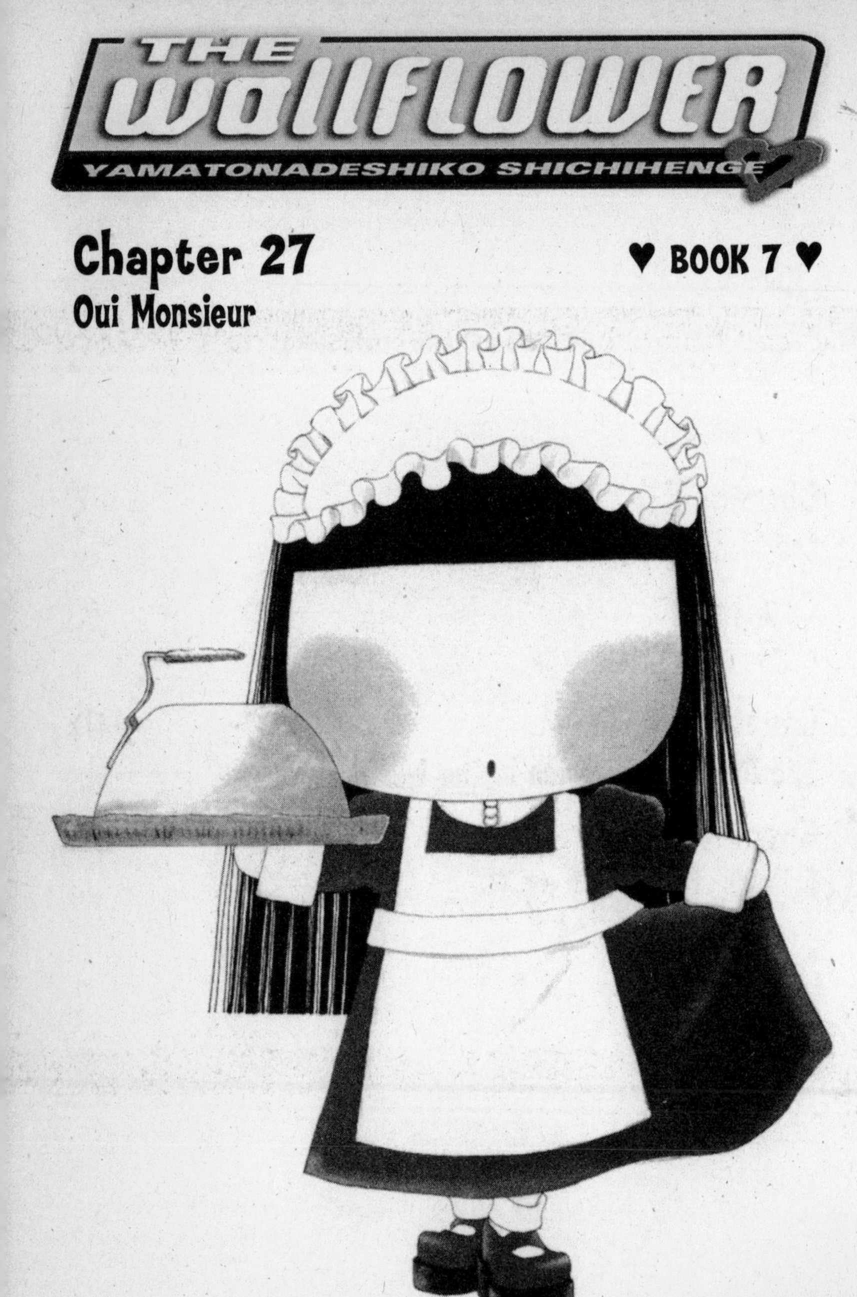

Wallflower's Beautiful Cast of Characters (?)

SUNAKO IS A DARK LONER WHO LOVES HORROR MOVIES. WHEN HER AUNT, THE LANDLADY OF A BOARDING HOUSE, LEAVES TOWN WITH HER BOYFRIEND, SUNAKO IS FORCED TO LIVE WITH FOUR HANDSOME GUYS. SUNAKO'S AUNT MAKES A DEAL WITH THE BOYS, WHICH CAUSES NOTHING BUT HEADACHES FOR SUNAKO. "MAKE SUNAKO INTO A LADY, AND YOU CAN LIVE RENT FREE."

AT FIRST THE FOUR GUYS TRIED THEIR HARDEST, BUT LATELY THEY SEEM TO HAVE FORGOTTEN ALL ABOUT THEIR GOAL. THE GUYS AND SUNAKO SOMEHOW MANAGE TO COEXIST IN HARMONY...OF COURSE SUNAKO WOULD PREFER IT IF THEY'D JUST LEAVE HER ALONE.

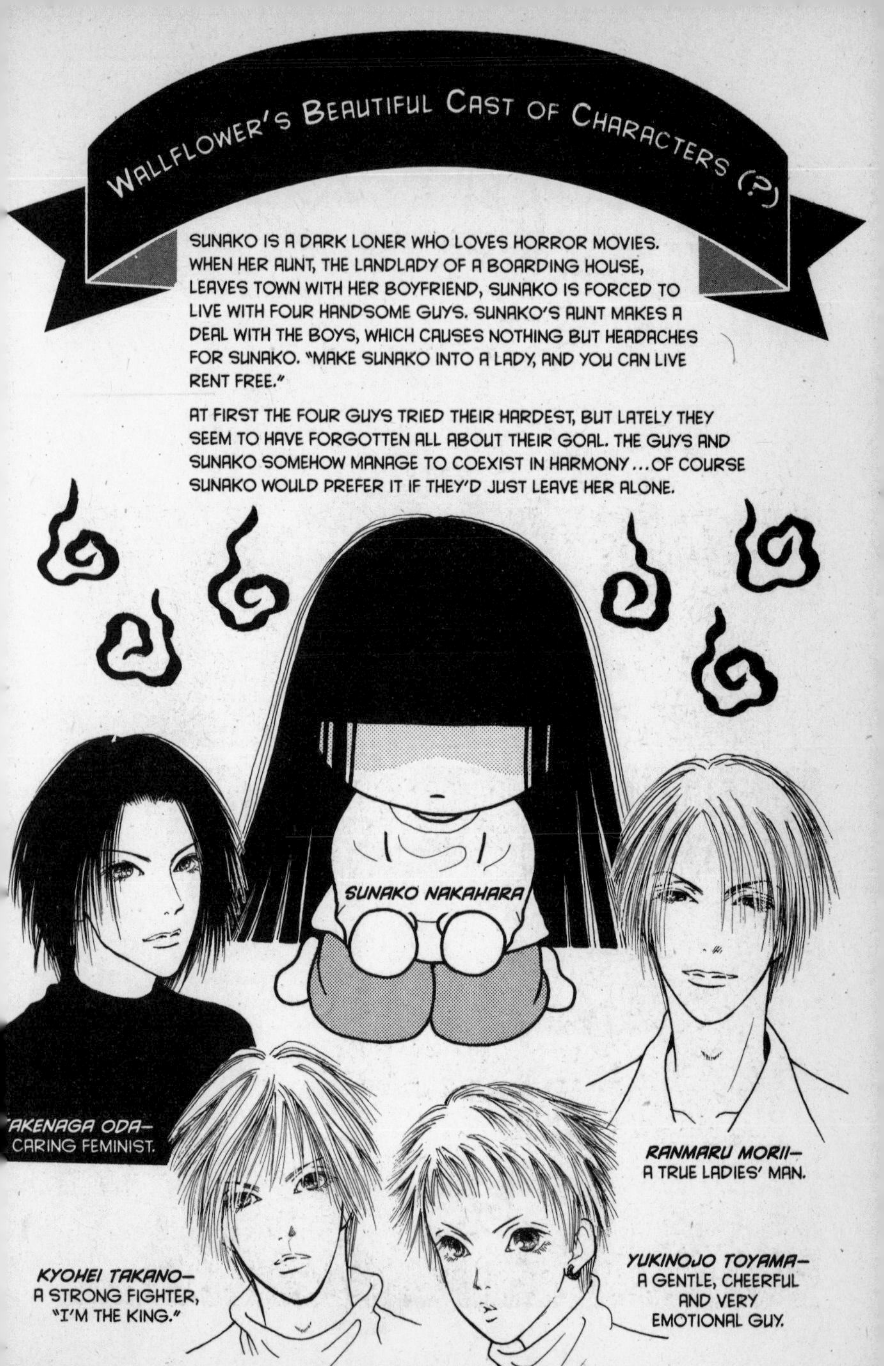
SUNAKO NAKAHARA
RANMARU MORII—
A TRUE LADIES' MAN.
AKENAGA ODA—
CARING FEMINIST.
YUKINOJO TOYAMA—
A GENTLE, CHEERFUL
AND VERY
EMOTIONAL GUY.
KYOHEI TAKANO—
A STRONG FIGHTER,
"I'M THE KING."

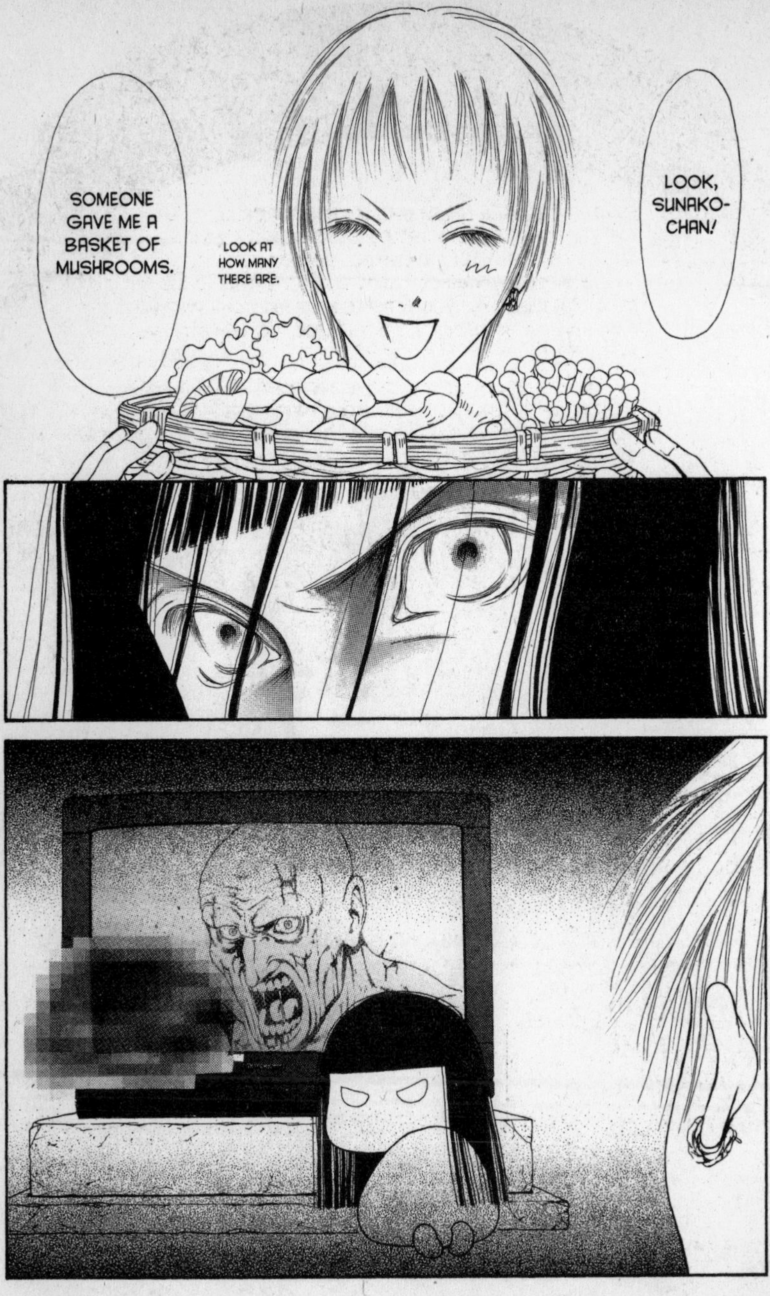
LOOK, SUNAKO-CHAN!
LOOK AT HOW MANY THERE ARE.
SOMEONE GAVE ME A BASKET OF MUSHROOMS.

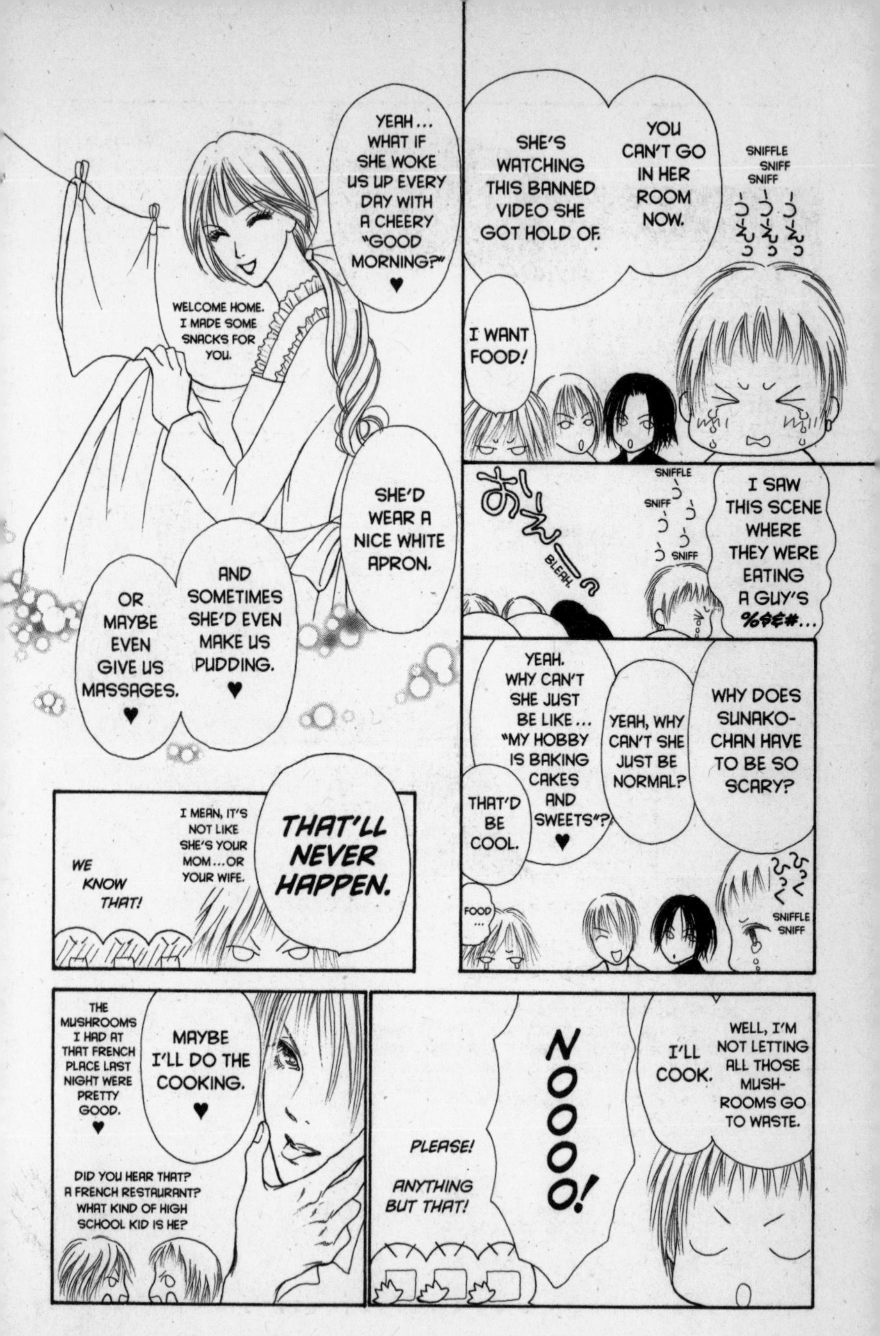
SNIFFLE
SNIFF
SNIFF
YOU CAN'T GO IN HER ROOM NOW.
SHE'S WATCHING THIS BANNED VIDEO SHE GOT HOLD OF.
I WANT FOOD!
I SAW THIS SCENE WHERE THEY WERE EATING A GUY'S %$¢#...
SNIFFLE
SNIFF
SNIFF
BLEAH.
WHY DOES SUNAKO-CHAN HAVE TO BE SO SCARY?
YEAH, WHY CAN'T SHE JUST BE NORMAL?
YEAH. WHY CAN'T SHE JUST BE LIKE... "MY HOBBY IS BAKING CAKES AND SWEETS"? ♥
THAT'D BE COOL.
SNIFFLE
SNIFF
FOOD...
YEAH... WHAT IF SHE WOKE US UP EVERY DAY WITH A CHEERY "GOOD MORNING?" ♥
WELCOME HOME. I MADE SOME SNACKS FOR YOU.
SHE'D WEAR A NICE WHITE APRON.
AND SOMETIMES SHE'D EVEN MAKE US PUDDING. ♥
OR MAYBE EVEN GIVE US MASSAGES. ♥
THAT'LL NEVER HAPPEN.
I MEAN, IT'S NOT LIKE SHE'S YOUR MOM...OR YOUR WIFE.
WE KNOW THAT!
WELL, I'M NOT LETTING ALL THOSE MUSH-ROOMS GO TO WASTE.
I'LL COOK.
NOOOOO!
PLEASE!
ANYTHING BUT THAT!
MAYBE I'LL DO THE COOKING. ♥
THE MUSHROOMS I HAD AT THAT FRENCH PLACE LAST NIGHT WERE PRETTY GOOD. ♥
DID YOU HEAR THAT? A FRENCH RESTAURANT? WHAT KIND OF HIGH SCHOOL KID IS HE?

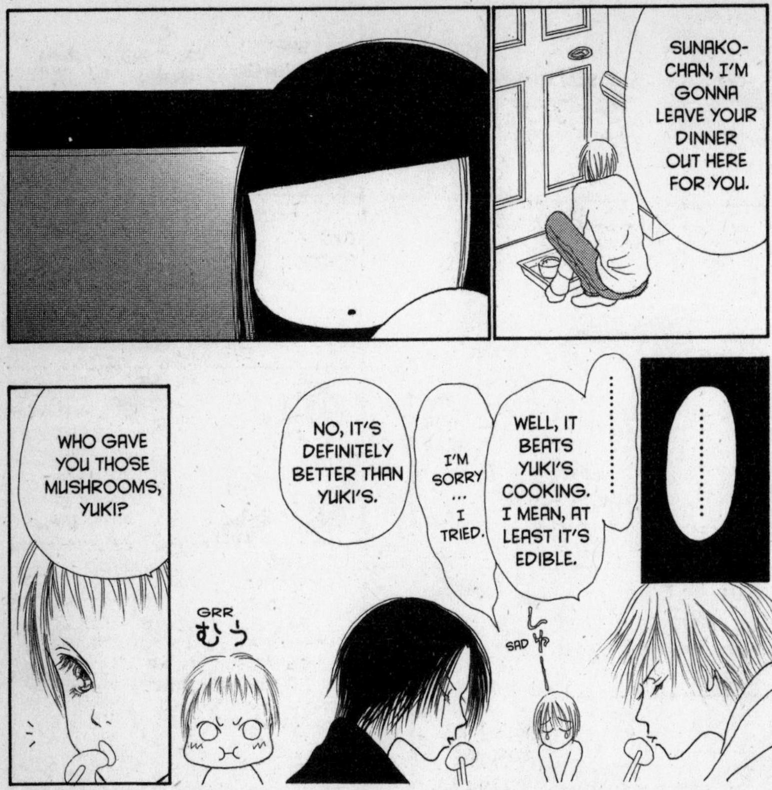
SUNAKO-CHAN, I'M GONNA LEAVE YOUR DINNER OUT HERE FOR YOU.
......
......
WELL, IT BEATS YUKI'S COOKING. I MEAN, AT LEAST IT'S EDIBLE.
SAD
I'M SORRY ... I TRIED.
NO, IT'S DEFINITELY BETTER THAN YUKI'S.
GRR むう
WHO GAVE YOU THOSE MUSHROOMS, YUKI?

BEHIND THE SCENES

IT WAS REALLY A PAIN DRAWING SUNAKO. I MEAN, IT TOOK TWICE AS LONG AS IT USUALLY DOES. SHOULDN'T THE MAIN CHARACTER BE EASIER TO DRAW? BUT IT WAS FUN DRAWING RANMARU IN COSPLAY. ♥ ... THAT TOOK A LONG TIME, TOO.

THE GENIUS ATSUKO NANBA SAVED THE DAY.

MY DEADLINE WAS THE SAME DAY AS THE BAROKKU CONCERT AT TOKYO KOUSEI HALL ... I STAYED UP ALL NIGHT, AND DANCED LIKE CRAZY.

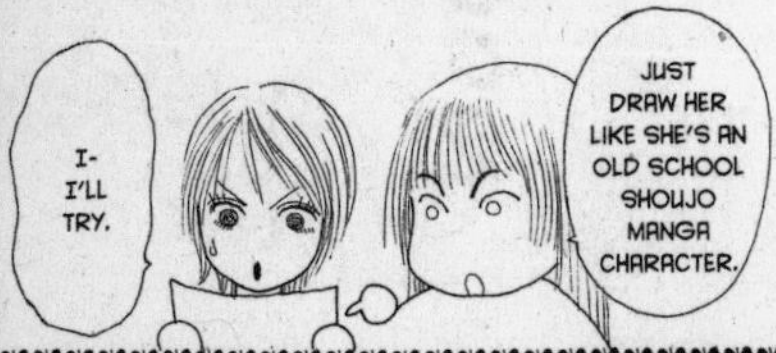
JUST DRAW HER LIKE SHE'S AN OLD SCHOOL SHOUJO MANGA CHARACTER.
I-I'LL TRY.

⇨ AND SHE DID A FABULOUS JOB! SHE DREW TWO PANELS ... SEE IF YOU CAN FIND THEM.

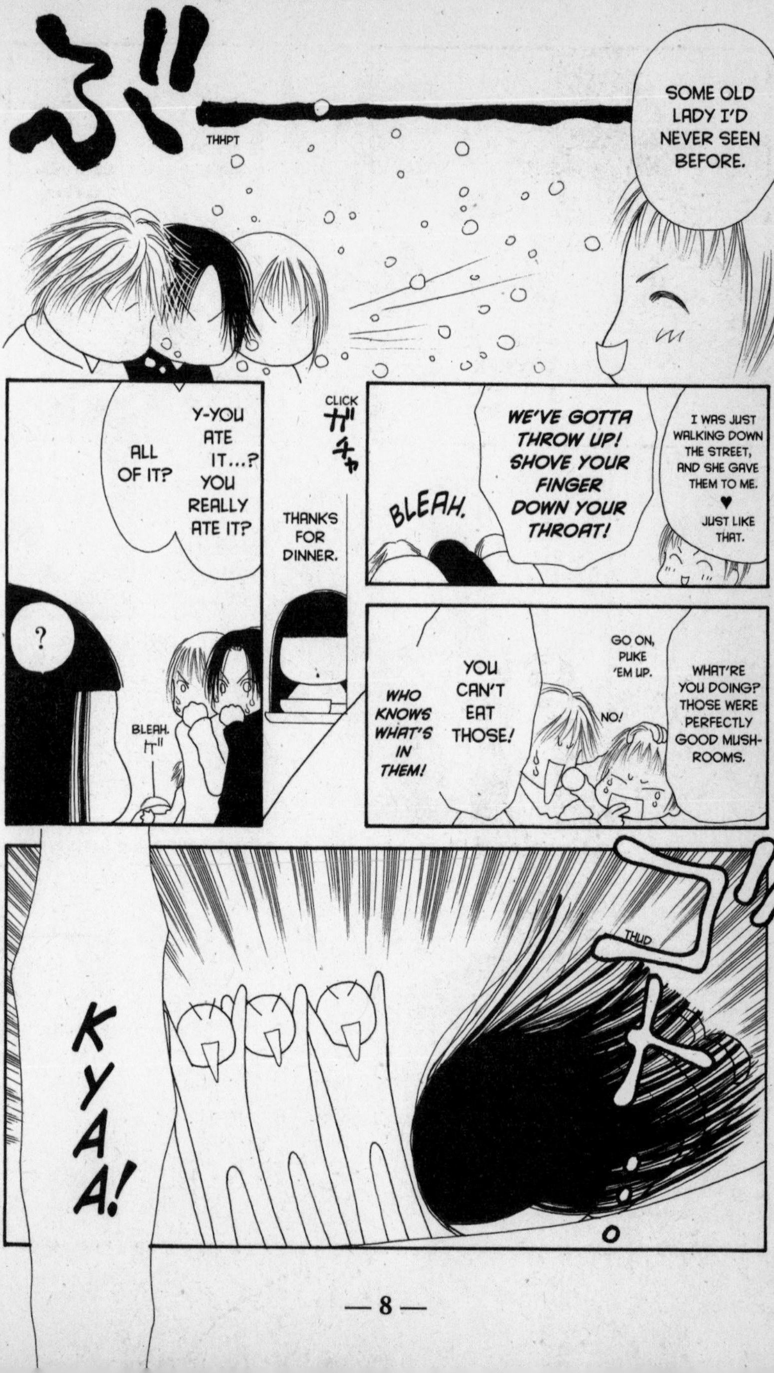

SOME OLD LADY I'D NEVER SEEN BEFORE.
ぶ
THHPT
I WAS JUST WALKING DOWN THE STREET, AND SHE GAVE THEM TO ME. ♥ JUST LIKE THAT.
WE'VE GOTTA THROW UP! SHOVE YOUR FINGER DOWN YOUR THROAT!
BLEAH.
WHAT'RE YOU DOING? THOSE WERE PERFECTLY GOOD MUSH-ROOMS.
GO ON, PUKE 'EM UP.
NO!
YOU CAN'T EAT THOSE!
WHO KNOWS WHAT'S IN THEM!
CLICK
ガチャ
THANKS FOR DINNER.
Y-YOU ATE IT...? YOU REALLY ATE IT?
ALL OF IT?
?
BLEAH.
ゲ"
THUD
KYAA!

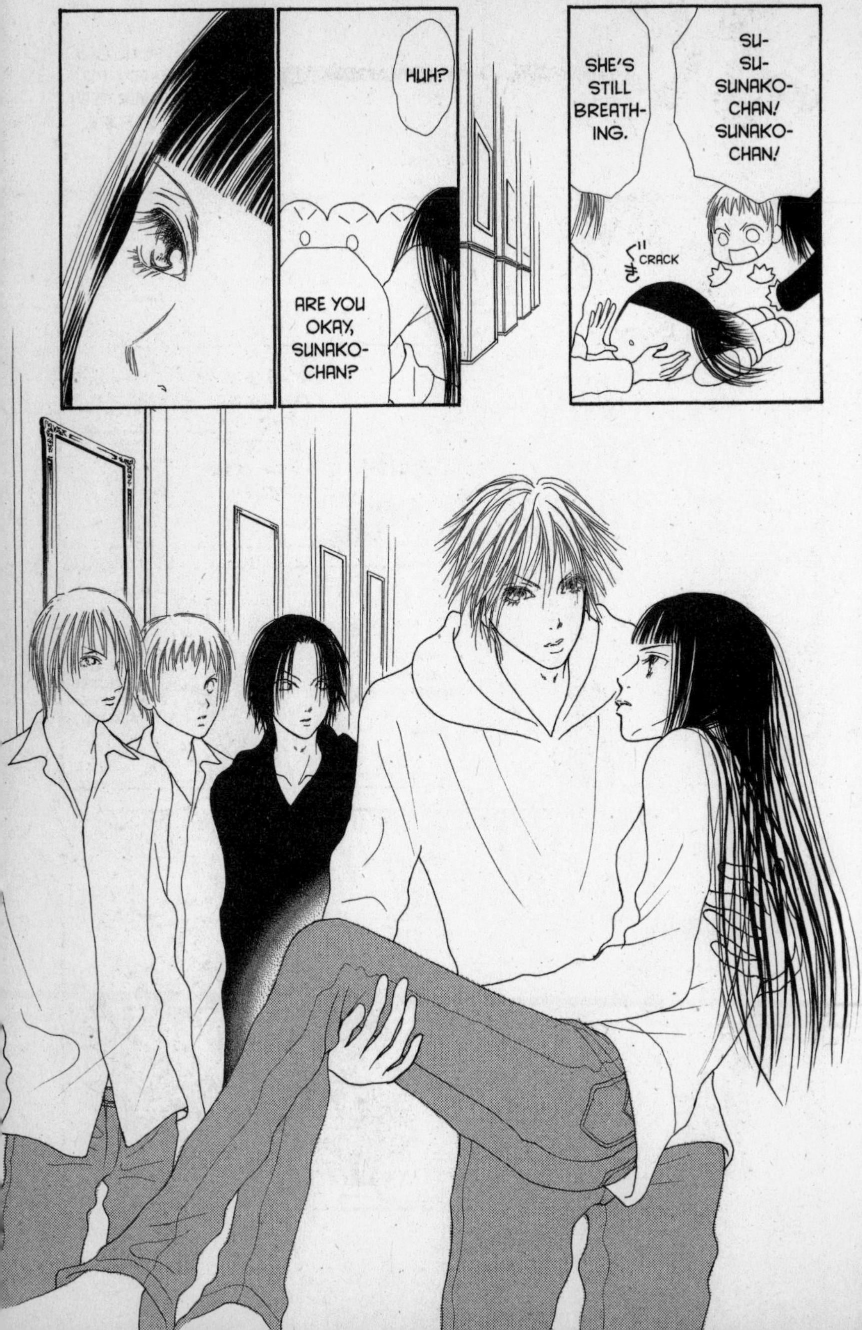
SU-SU-SUNAKO-CHAN! SUNAKO-CHAN!
SHE'S STILL BREATHING.
CRACK
HUH?
ARE YOU OKAY, SUNAKO-CHAN?

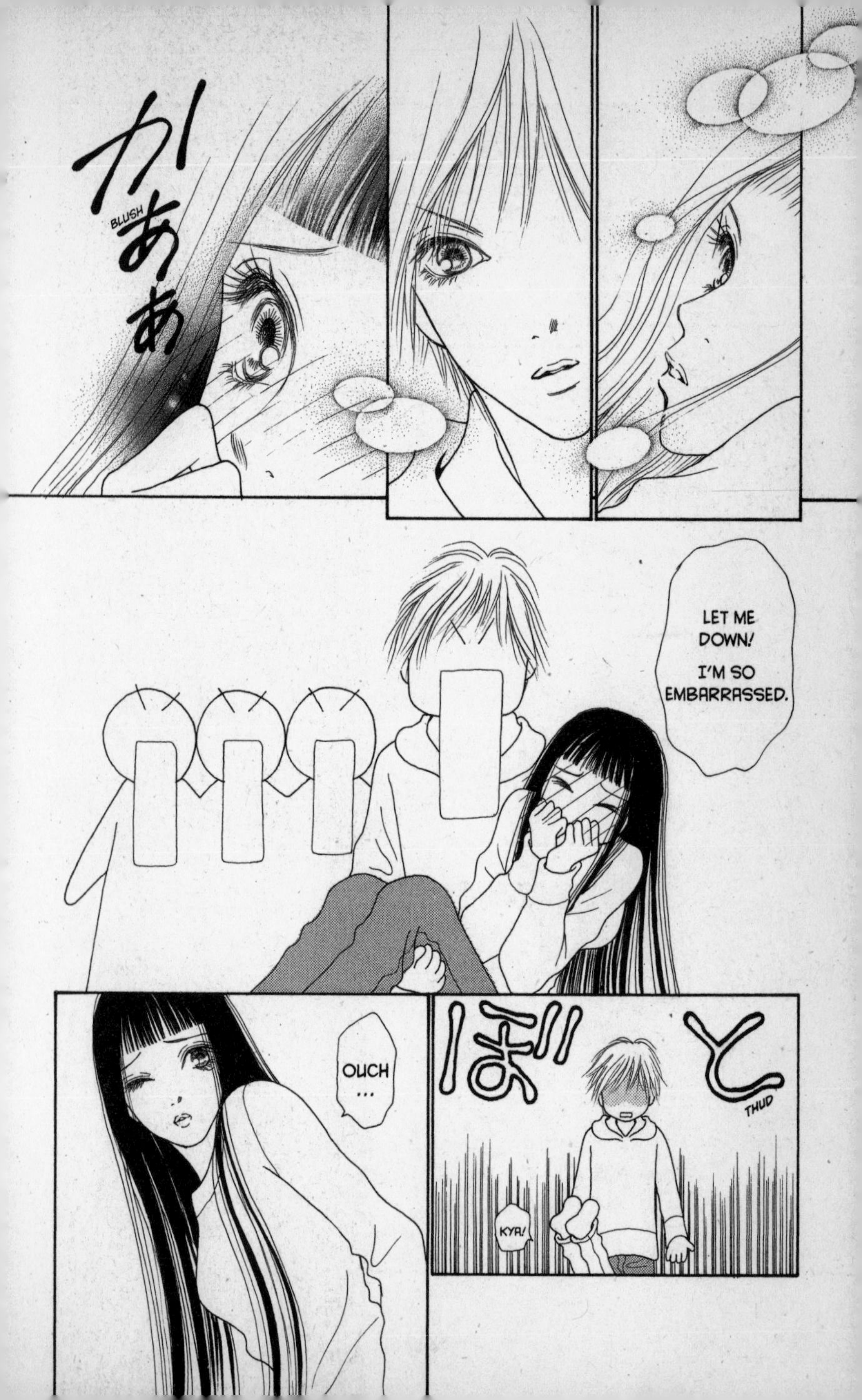
かぁぁ
BLUSH
LET ME DOWN!
I'M SO EMBARRASSED.
ぼっと
THUD
KYA!
OUCH ...

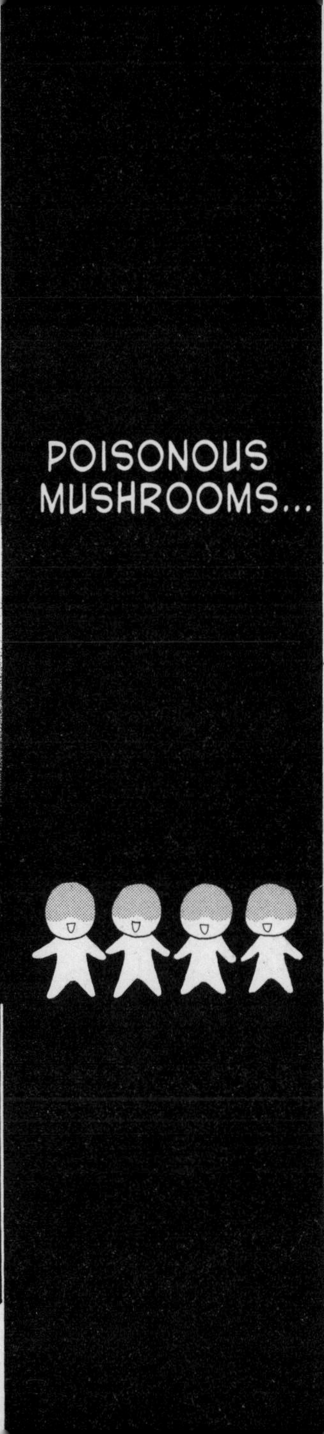
POISONOUS MUSHROOMS...

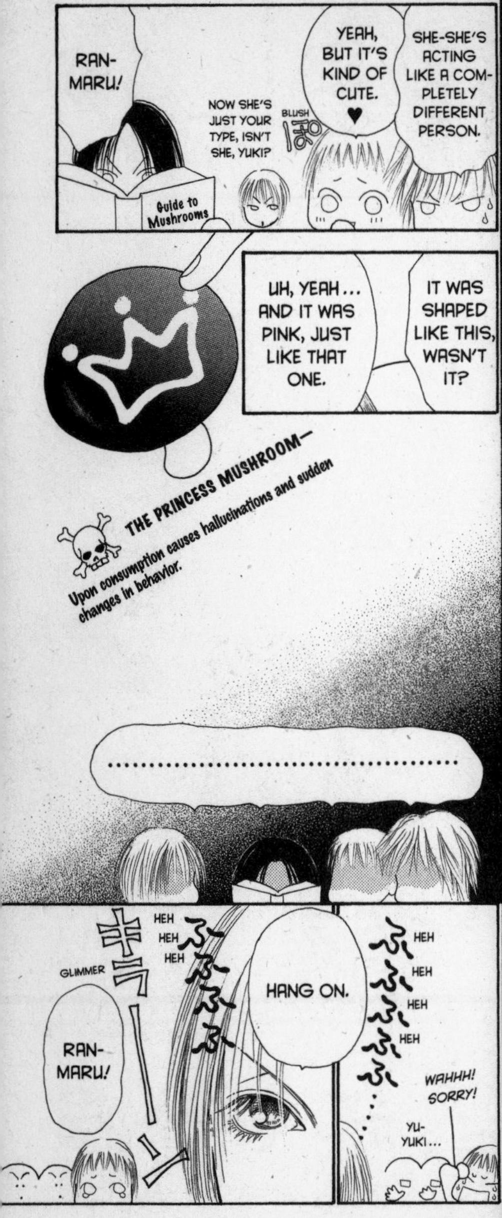
SHE-SHE'S ACTING LIKE A COMPLETELY DIFFERENT PERSON.
YEAH, BUT IT'S KIND OF CUTE. ♥
BLUSH
NOW SHE'S JUST YOUR TYPE, ISN'T SHE, YUKI?
RAN-MARU!
Guide to Mushrooms
IT WAS SHAPED LIKE THIS, WASN'T IT?
UH, YEAH... AND IT WAS PINK, JUST LIKE THAT ONE.
THE PRINCESS MUSHROOM—
Upon consumption causes hallucinations and sudden changes in behavior.
....
HEH HEH HEH HEH
WAHHH! SORRY!
YU-YUKI...
HANG ON.
HEH HEH HEH
GLIMMER
RAN-MARU!

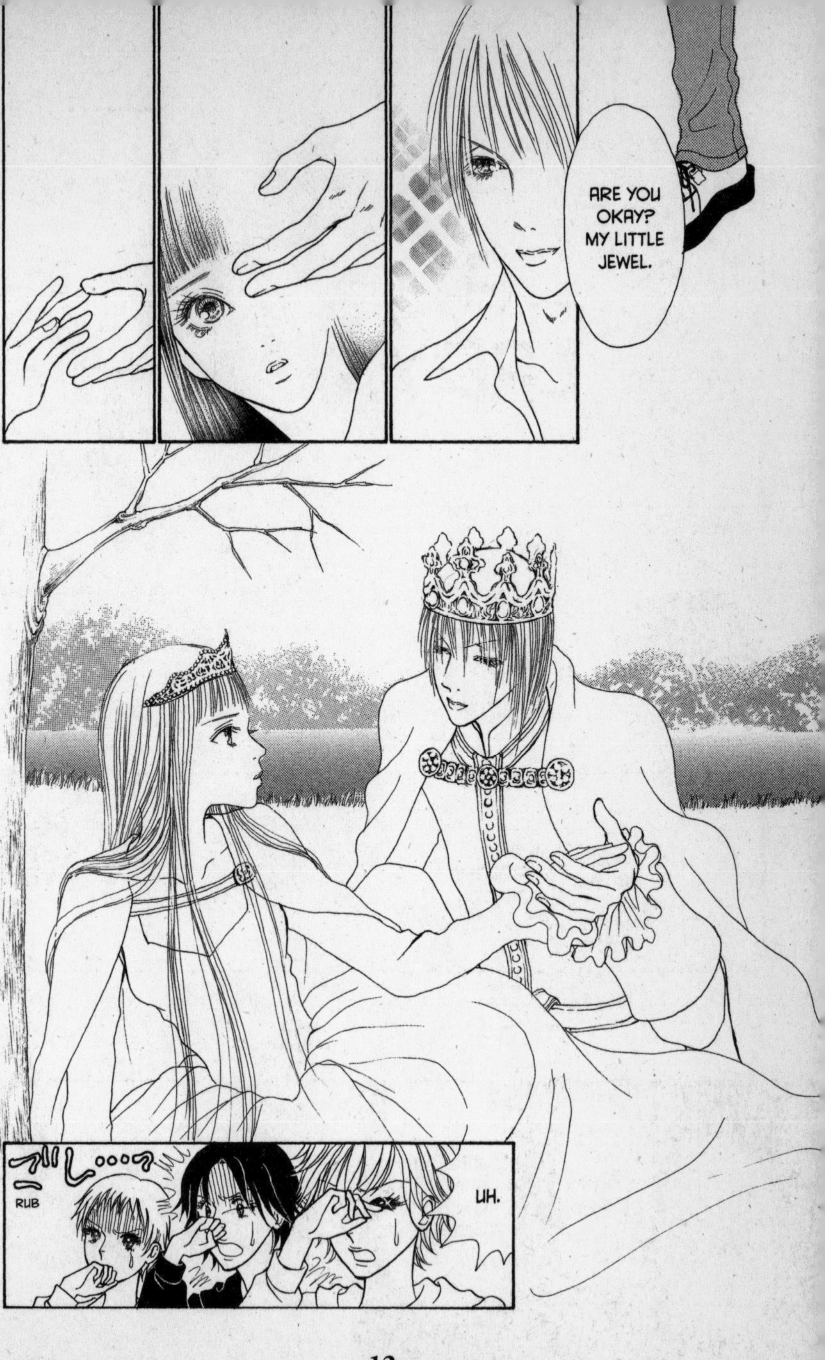
ARE YOU OKAY? MY LITTLE JEWEL.
UH.
RUB

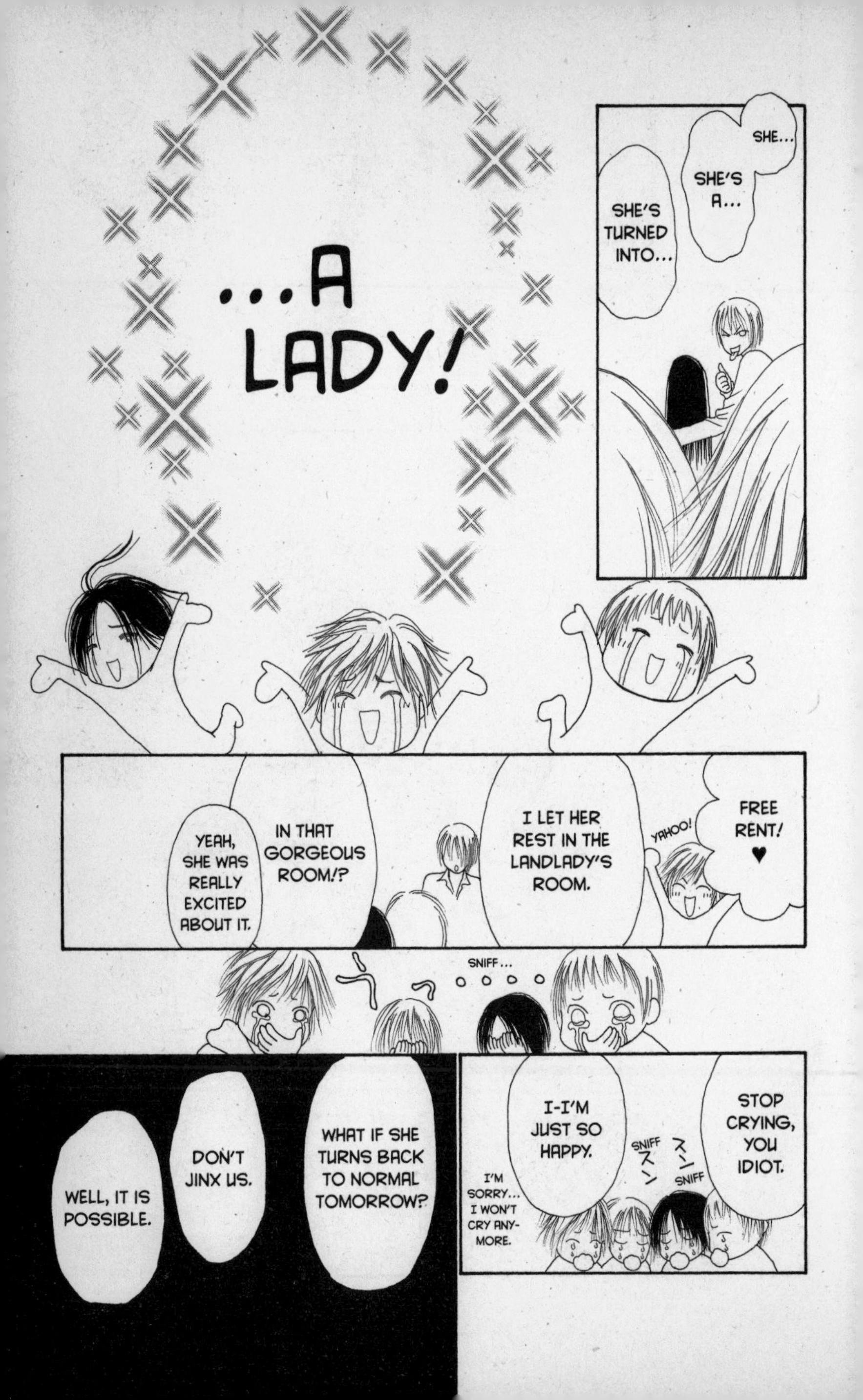
SHE...
SHE'S A...
SHE'S TURNED INTO...
...A LADY!
FREE RENT! ♥
YAHOO!
I LET HER REST IN THE LANDLADY'S ROOM.
IN THAT GORGEOUS ROOM!?
YEAH, SHE WAS REALLY EXCITED ABOUT IT.
SNIFF...
STOP CRYING, YOU IDIOT.
SNIFF
スン
スン
SNIFF
I-I'M JUST SO HAPPY.
I'M SORRY... I WON'T CRY ANY-MORE.
WHAT IF SHE TURNS BACK TO NORMAL TOMORROW?
DON'T JINX US.
WELL, IT IS POSSIBLE.

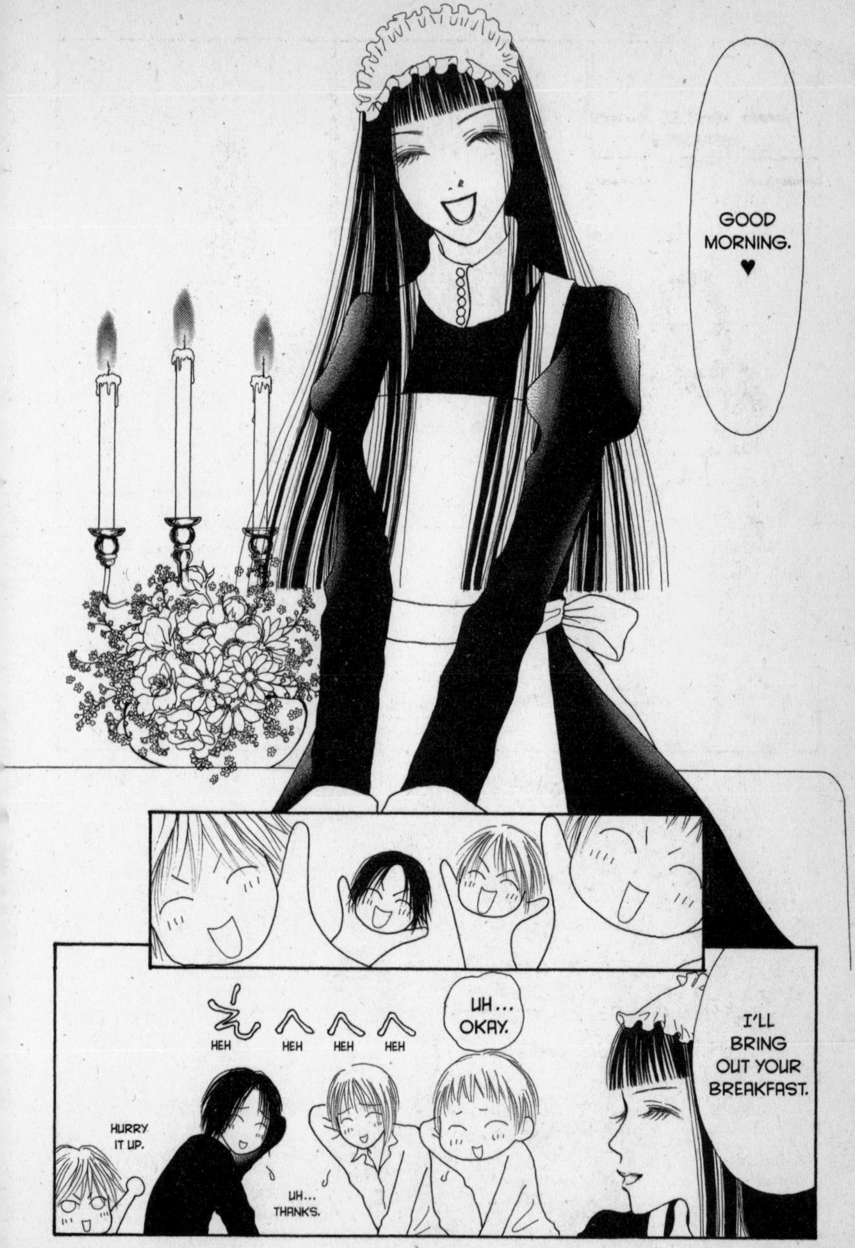
GOOD MORNING. ♥
I'LL BRING OUT YOUR BREAKFAST.
UH... OKAY.
えへへへ
HEH HEH HEH HEH
UH... THANKS.
HURRY IT UP.

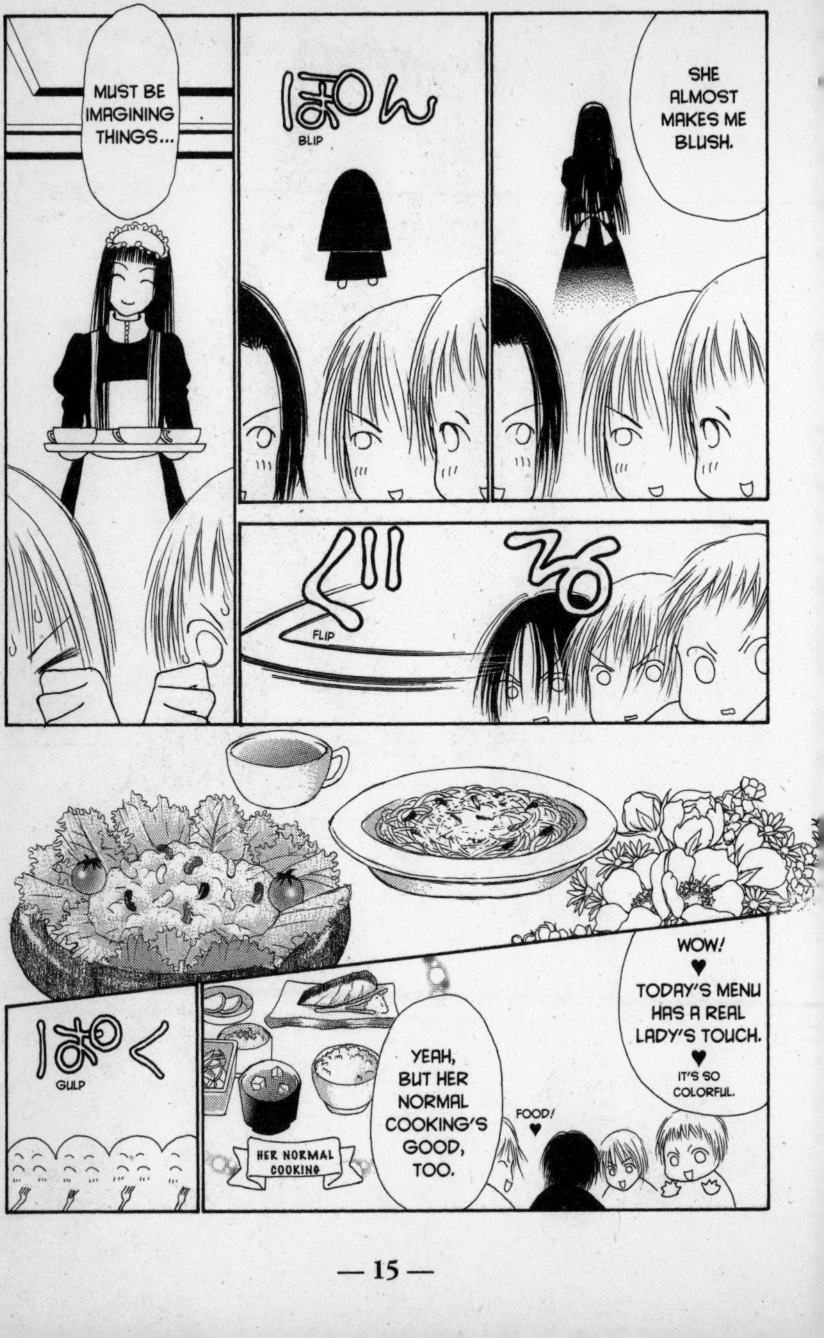
SHE ALMOST MAKES ME BLUSH.
BLIP
FLIP
MUST BE IMAGINING THINGS...
WOW! ♥ TODAY'S MENU HAS A REAL LADY'S TOUCH. ♥
IT'S SO COLORFUL.
FOOD! ♥
YEAH, BUT HER NORMAL COOKING'S GOOD, TOO.
HER NORMAL COOKING
GULP

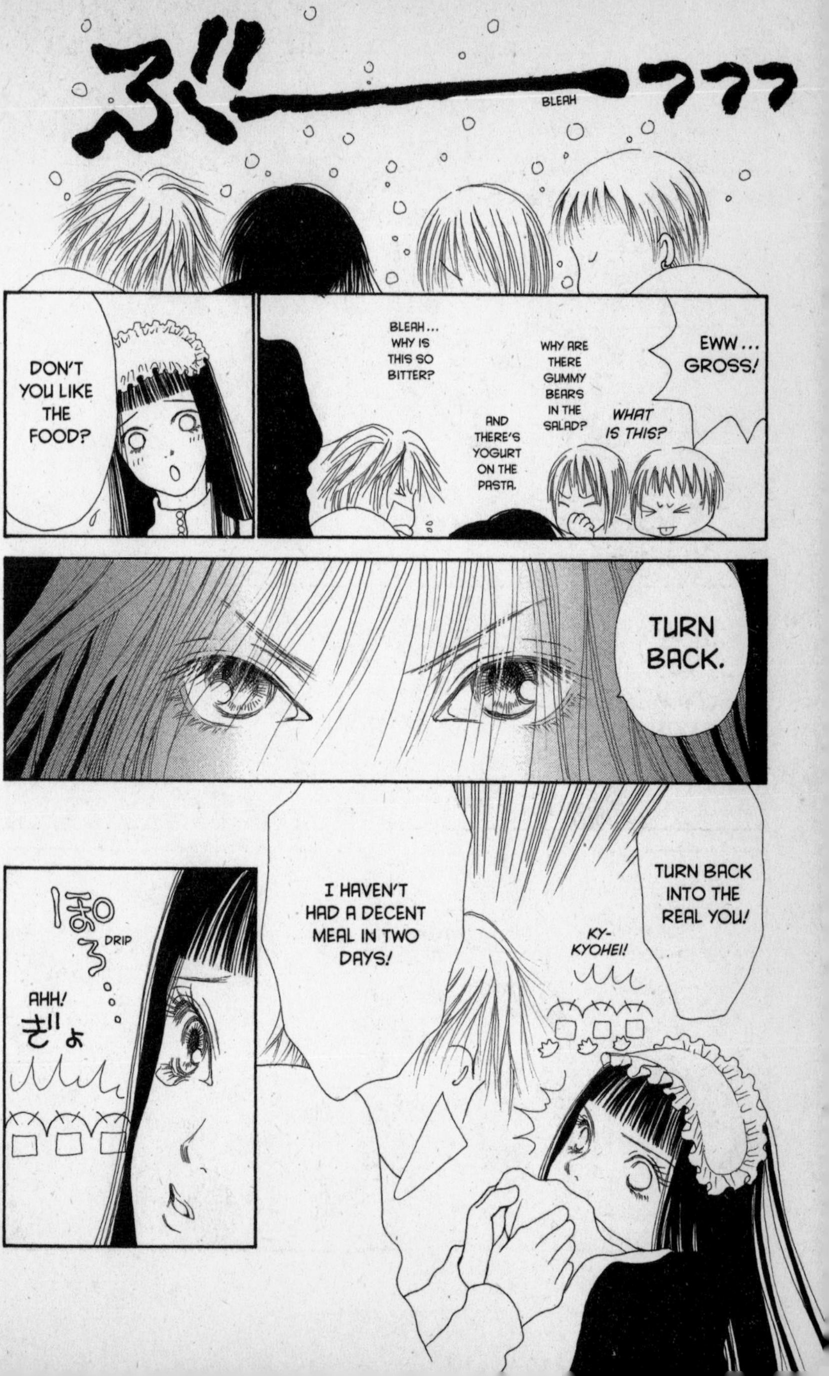

ぶーっっっ
BLEAH
EWW... GROSS!
WHAT IS THIS?
WHY ARE THERE GUMMY BEARS IN THE SALAD?
AND THERE'S YOGURT ON THE PASTA.
BLEAH... WHY IS THIS SO BITTER?
DON'T YOU LIKE THE FOOD?
TURN BACK.
TURN BACK INTO THE REAL YOU!
I HAVEN'T HAD A DECENT MEAL IN TWO DAYS!
KY- KYOHEI!
ぽろ
DRIP
AHH!
ぎょ

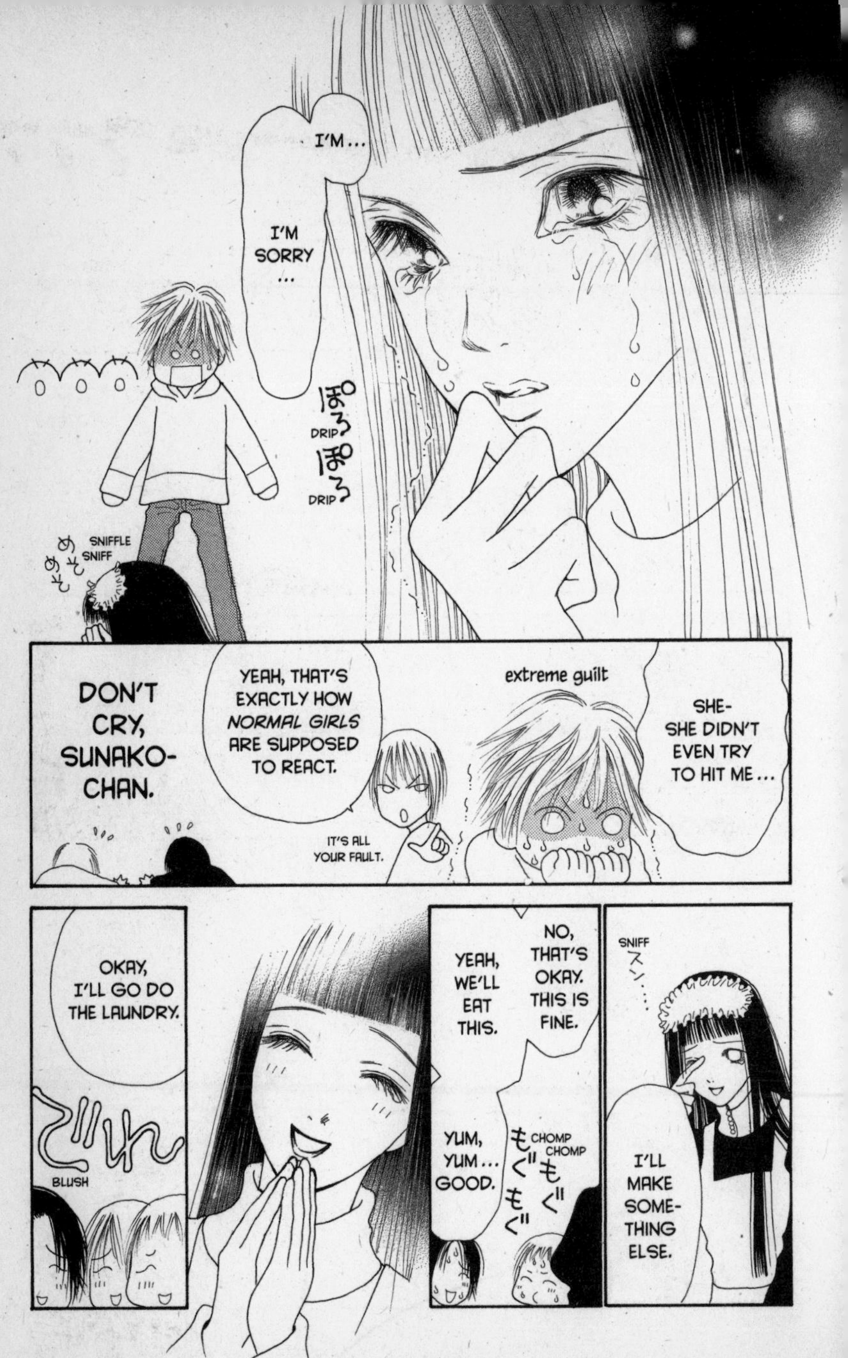

I'M...
I'M SORRY...
ぽろぽろ DRIP
ぽろぽろ DRIP
めそめそ SNIFFLE SNIFF
SHE- SHE DIDN'T EVEN TRY TO HIT ME...
extreme guilt
YEAH, THAT'S EXACTLY HOW *NORMAL GIRLS* ARE SUPPOSED TO REACT.
IT'S ALL YOUR FAULT.
DON'T CRY, SUNAKO-CHAN.
スン... SNIFF
I'LL MAKE SOME-THING ELSE.
NO, THAT'S OKAY. THIS IS FINE.
YEAH, WE'LL EAT THIS.
もぐもぐ CHOMP CHOMP
YUM, YUM... GOOD.
OKAY, I'LL GO DO THE LAUNDRY.
でれ BLUSH

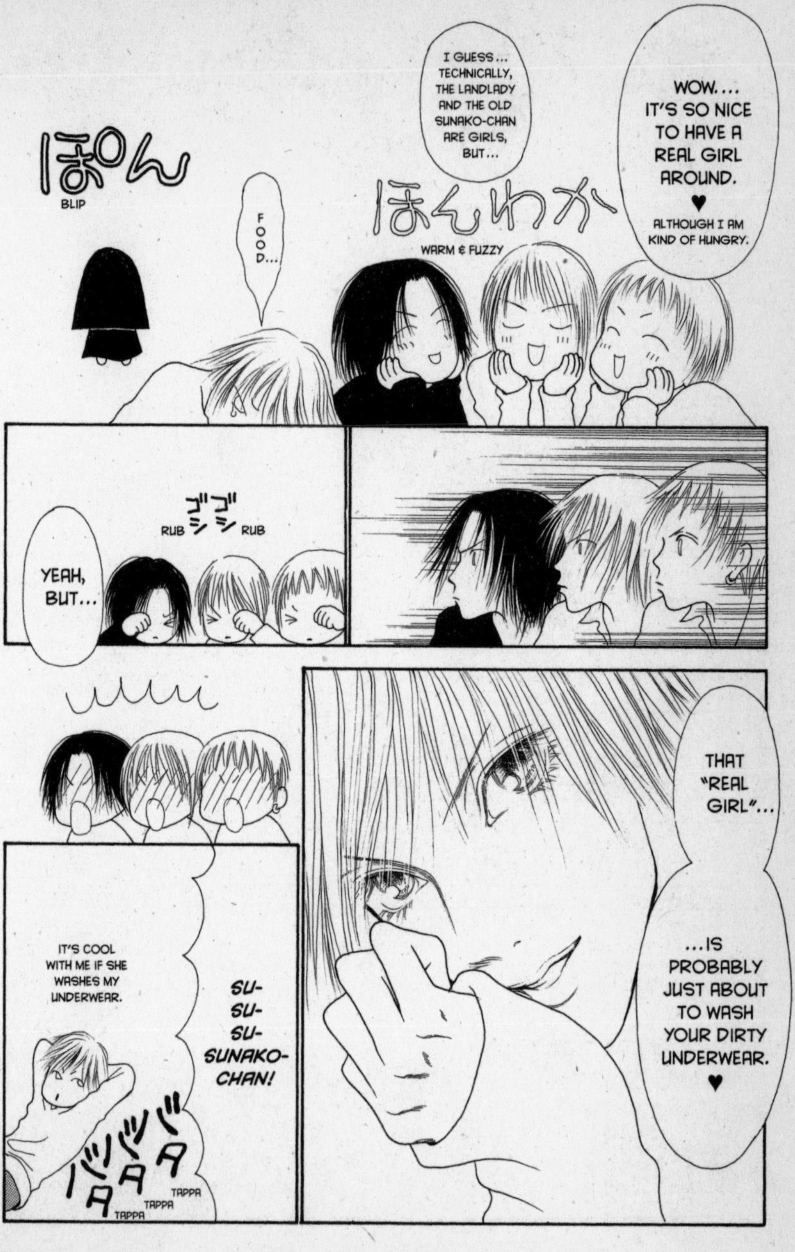
WOW.... IT'S SO NICE TO HAVE A REAL GIRL AROUND. ♥
ALTHOUGH I AM KIND OF HUNGRY.
I GUESS... TECHNICALLY, THE LANDLADY AND THE OLD SUNAKO-CHAN ARE GIRLS, BUT...
ほんわか
WARM & FUZZY
FOOD...
ぽん
BLIP
ゴシゴシ
RUB RUB
YEAH, BUT...
THAT "REAL GIRL"...
...IS PROBABLY JUST ABOUT TO WASH YOUR DIRTY UNDERWEAR. ♥
SU-SU-SU-SUNAKO-CHAN!
IT'S COOL WITH ME IF SHE WASHES MY UNDERWEAR.
バタバタ
TAPPA TAPPA TAPPA

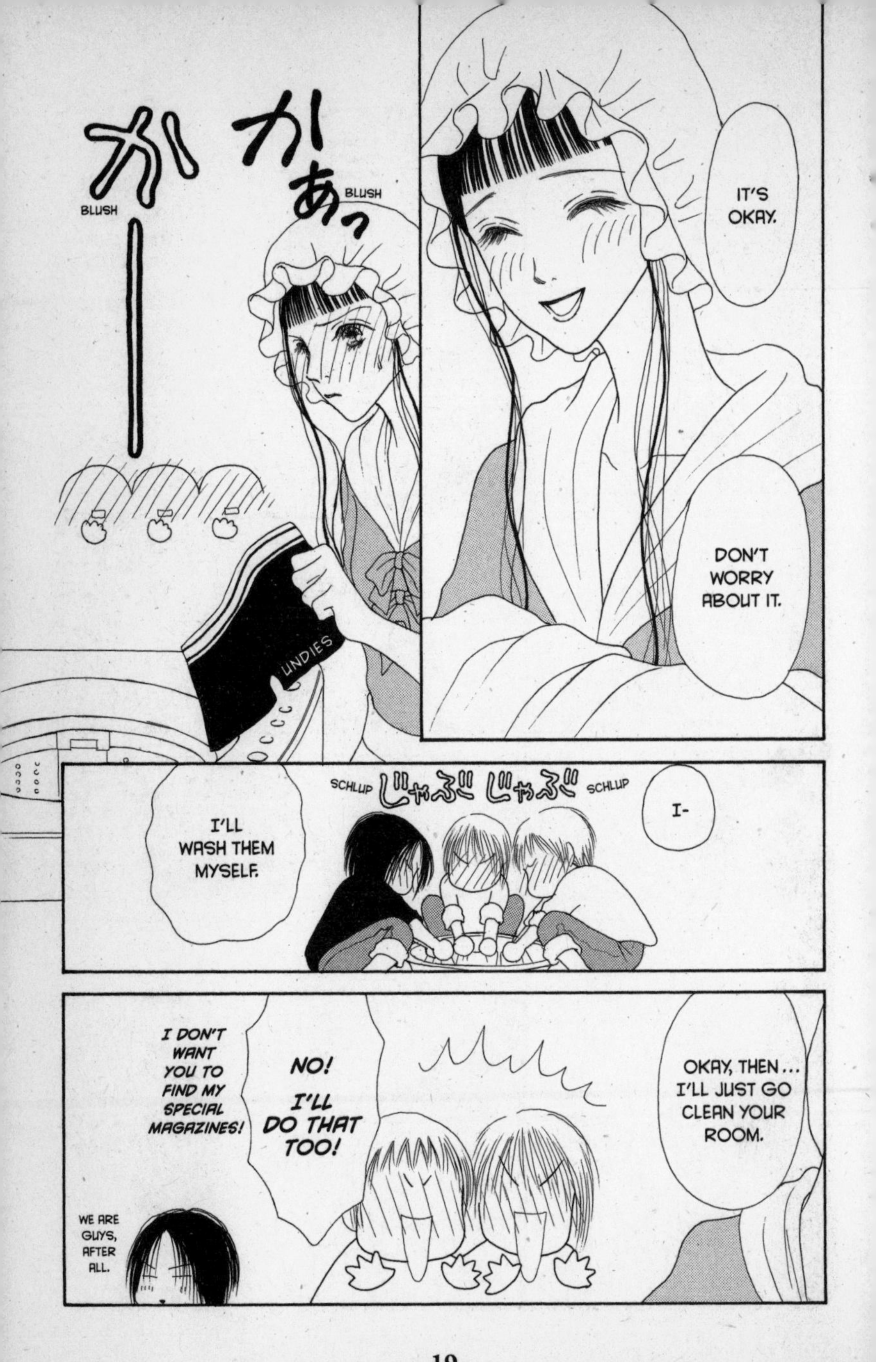
IT'S OKAY.
DON'T WORRY ABOUT IT.
かあっ
BLUSH
かー
BLUSH
UNDIES
I-
SCHLUP じゃぶじゃぶ SCHLUP
I'LL WASH THEM MYSELF.
OKAY, THEN... I'LL JUST GO CLEAN YOUR ROOM.
NO! I'LL DO THAT TOO!
I DON'T WANT YOU TO FIND MY SPECIAL MAGAZINES!
WE ARE GUYS, AFTER ALL.

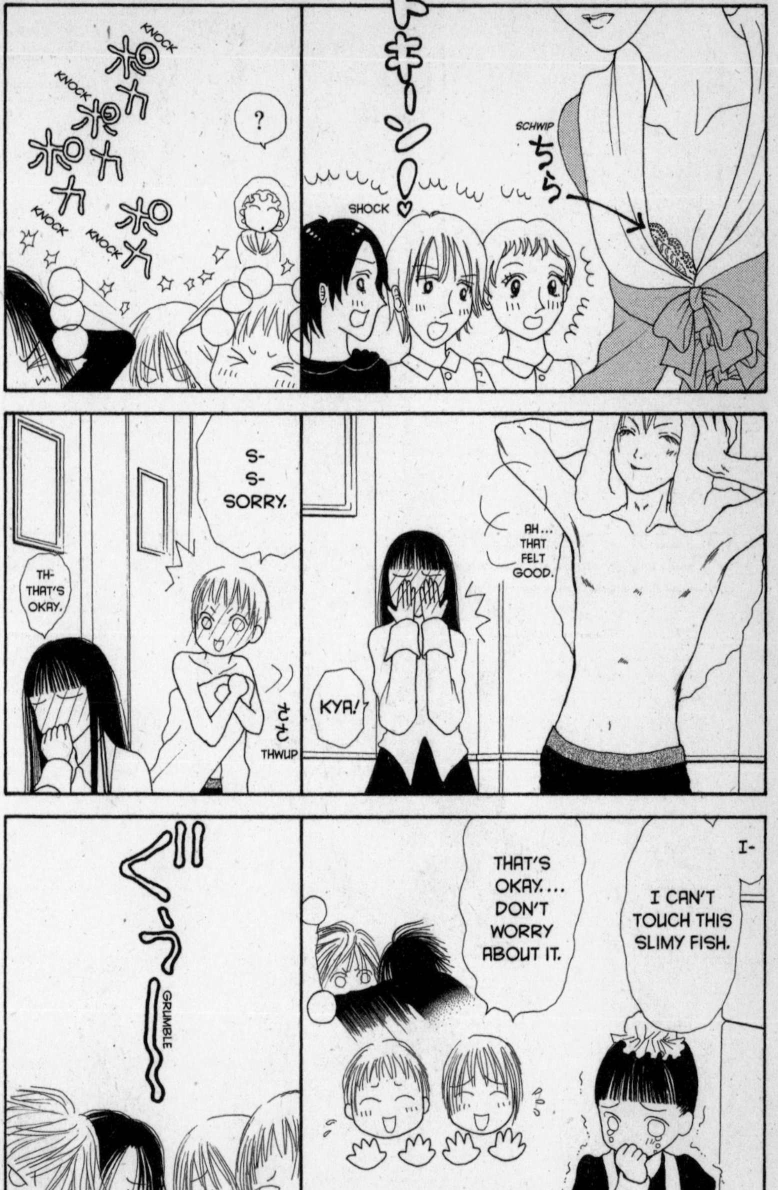
SCHWIP
ちら
ドキーン!♡
SHOCK
KNOCK
KNOCK
KNOCK
KNOCK
?
AH... THAT FELT GOOD.
KYA!
S- S- SORRY.
TH- THAT'S OKAY.
THWUP
I-
I CAN'T TOUCH THIS SLIMY FISH.
THAT'S OKAY.... DON'T WORRY ABOUT IT.
GRUMBLE

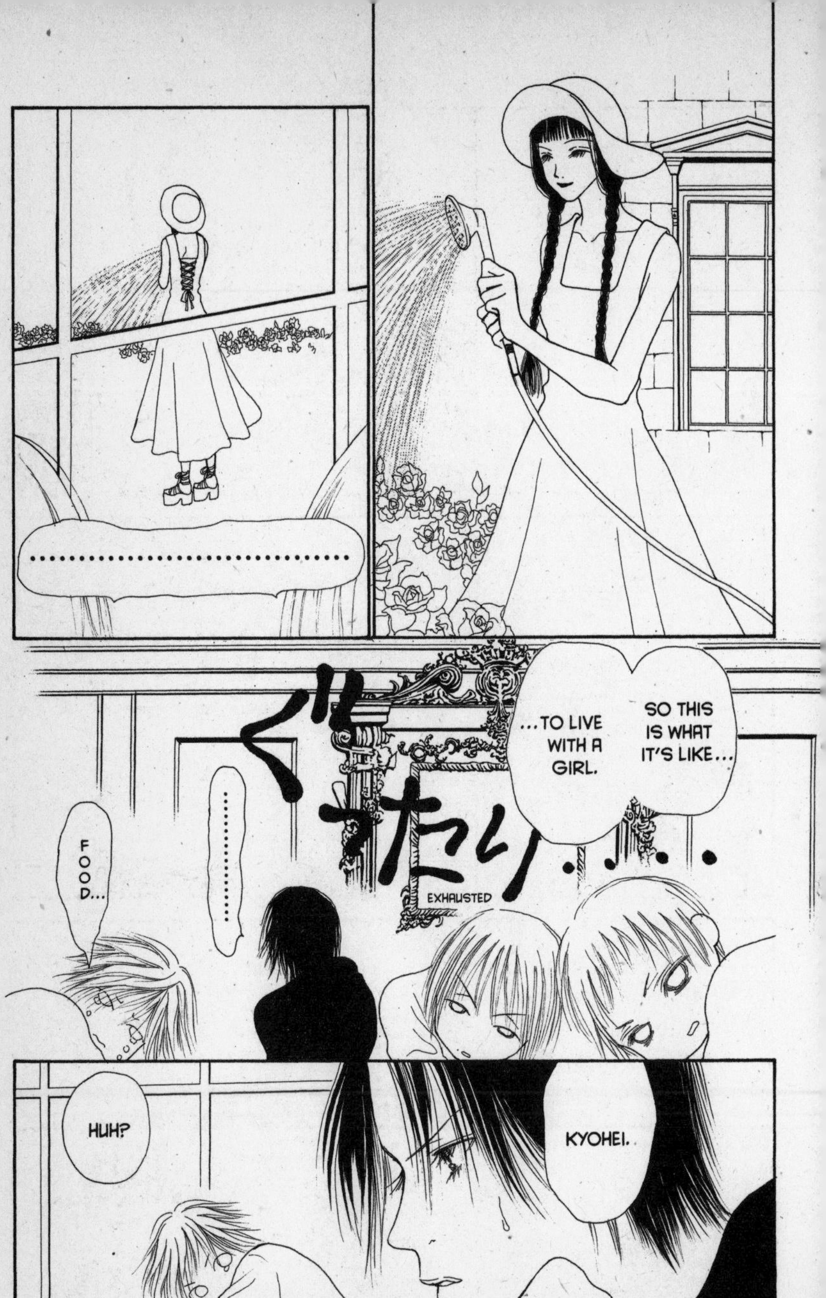
……………………………
SO THIS IS WHAT IT'S LIKE...
...TO LIVE WITH A GIRL.
ぐったり...
EXHAUSTED
……………
FOOD...
KYOHEI.
HUH?

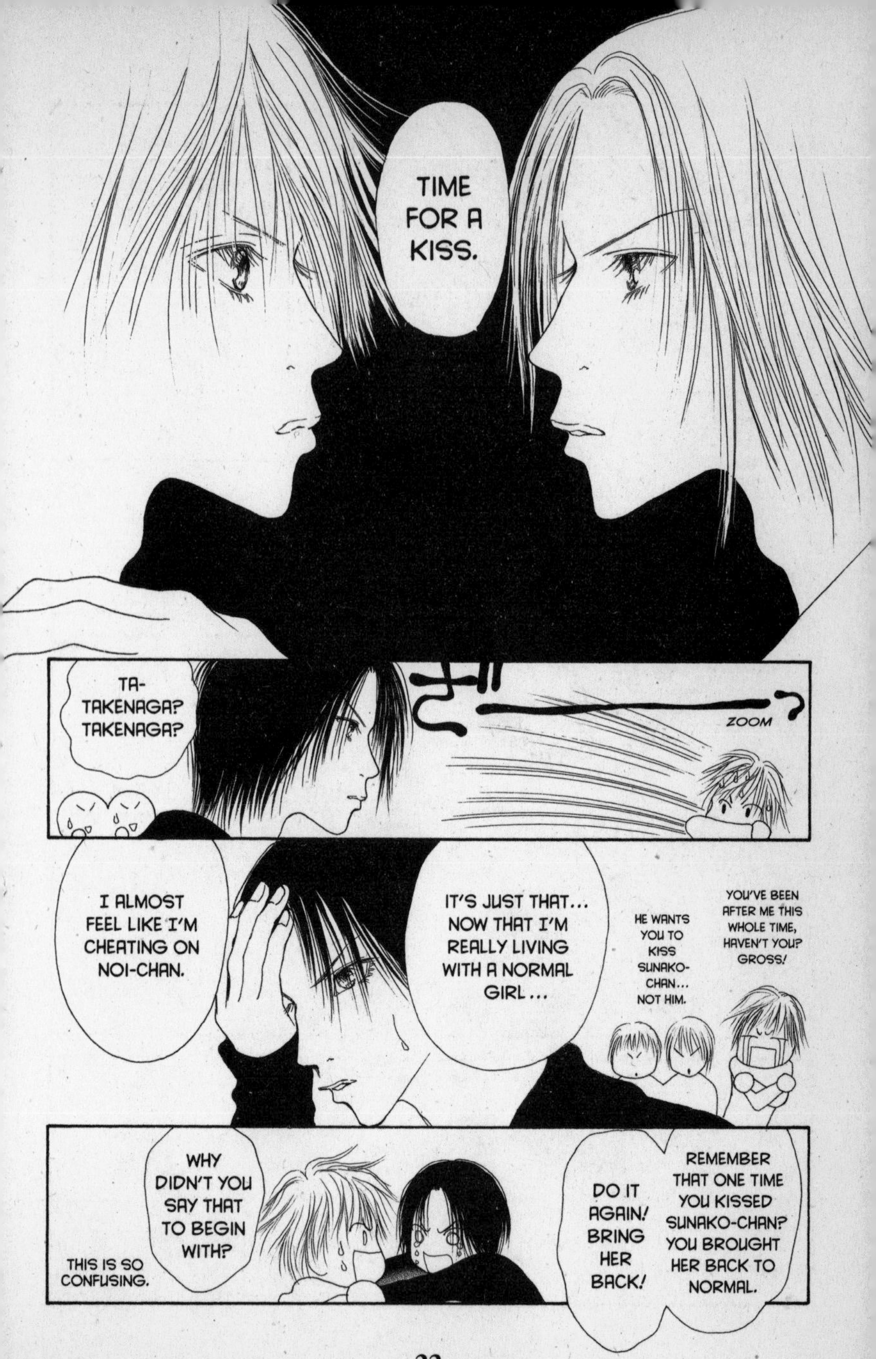
TIME FOR A KISS.
ZOOM
TA- TAKENAGA? TAKENAGA?
YOU'VE BEEN AFTER ME THIS WHOLE TIME, HAVEN'T YOU? GROSS!
HE WANTS YOU TO KISS SUNAKO-CHAN... NOT HIM.
IT'S JUST THAT... NOW THAT I'M REALLY LIVING WITH A NORMAL GIRL...
I ALMOST FEEL LIKE I'M CHEATING ON NOI-CHAN.
REMEMBER THAT ONE TIME YOU KISSED SUNAKO-CHAN? YOU BROUGHT HER BACK TO NORMAL.
DO IT AGAIN! BRING HER BACK!
WHY DIDN'T YOU SAY THAT TO BEGIN WITH?
THIS IS SO CONFUSING.

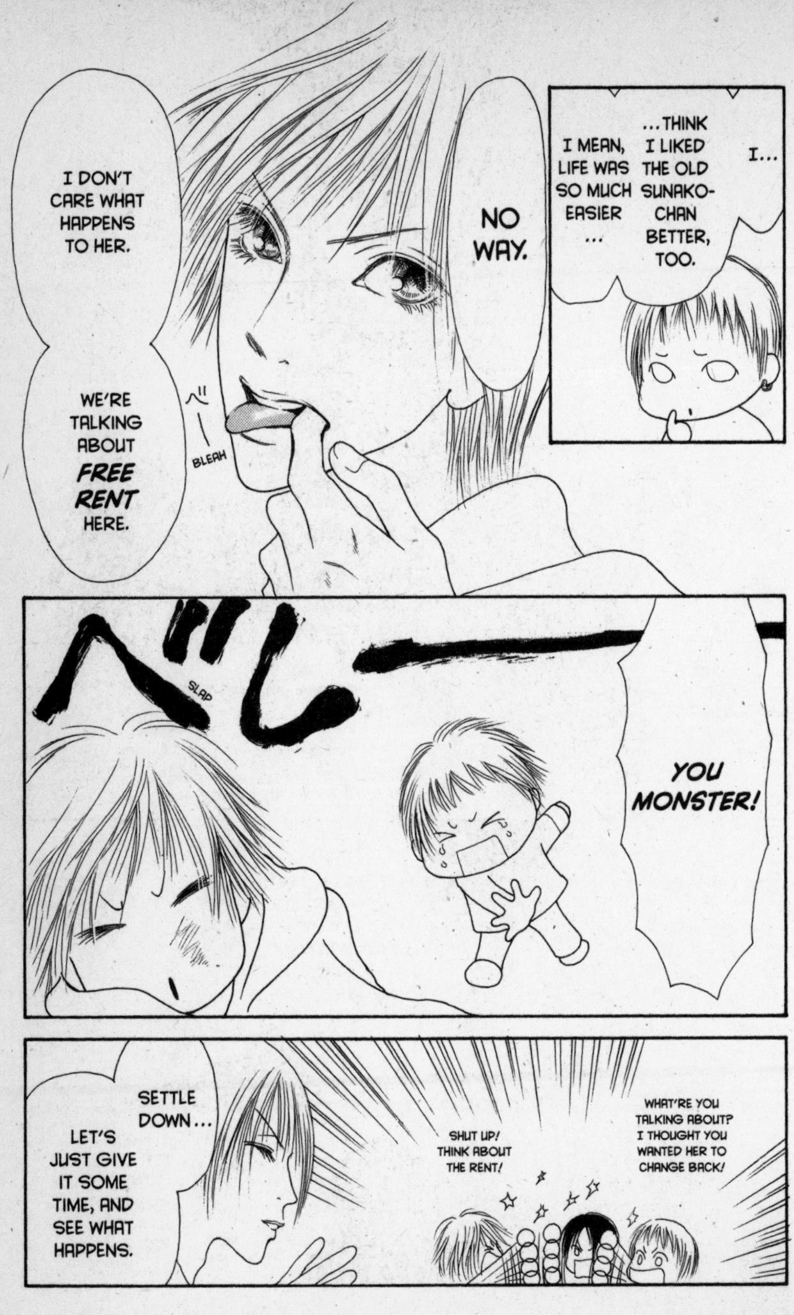
I...
...THINK I LIKED THE OLD SUNAKO-CHAN BETTER, TOO.
I MEAN, LIFE WAS SO MUCH EASIER ...
NO WAY.
I DON'T CARE WHAT HAPPENS TO HER.
WE'RE TALKING ABOUT FREE RENT HERE.
べー
BLEAH
YOU MONSTER!
べしー
SLAP
WHAT'RE YOU TALKING ABOUT? I THOUGHT YOU WANTED HER TO CHANGE BACK!
SHUT UP! THINK ABOUT THE RENT!
SETTLE DOWN...
LET'S JUST GIVE IT SOME TIME, AND SEE WHAT HAPPENS.

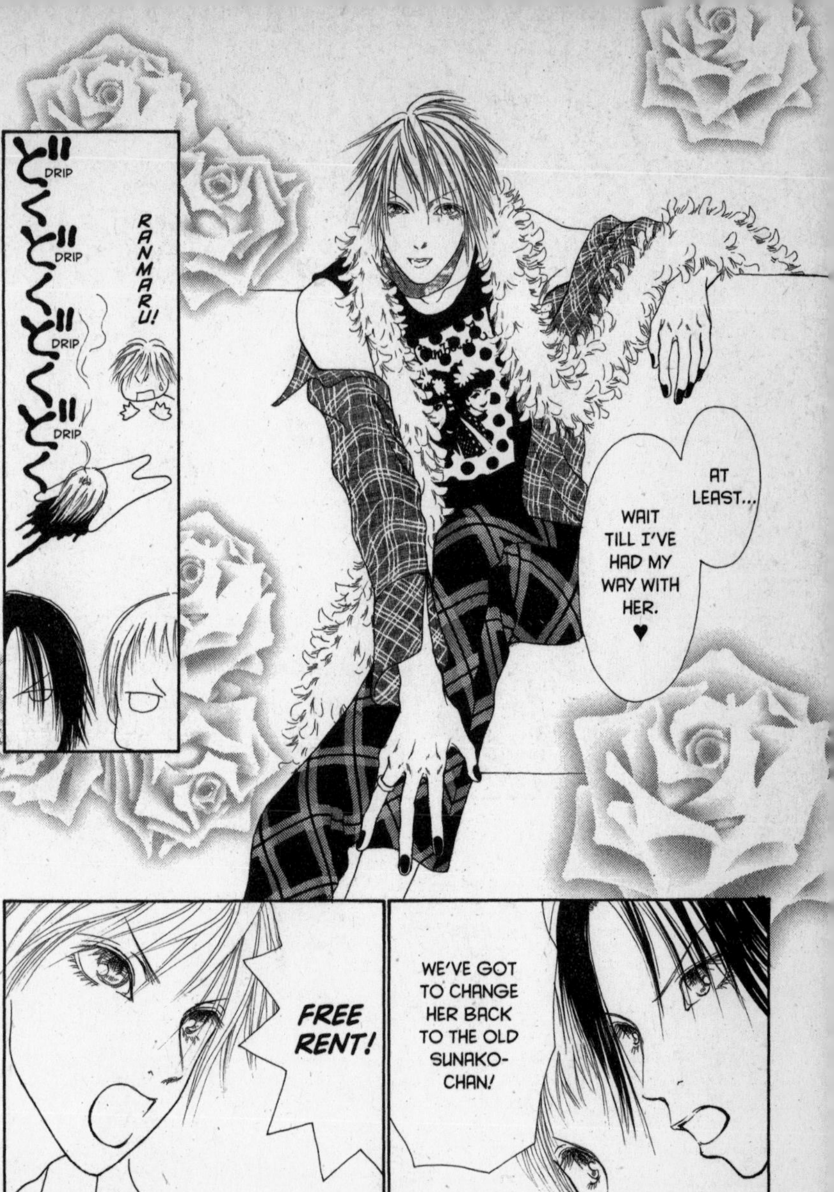
AT LEAST...
WAIT TILL I'VE HAD MY WAY WITH HER. ♥
RANMARU!
どくどくどくどく
DRIP DRIP DRIP DRIP
WE'VE GOT TO CHANGE HER BACK TO THE OLD SUNAKO-CHAN!
FREE RENT!

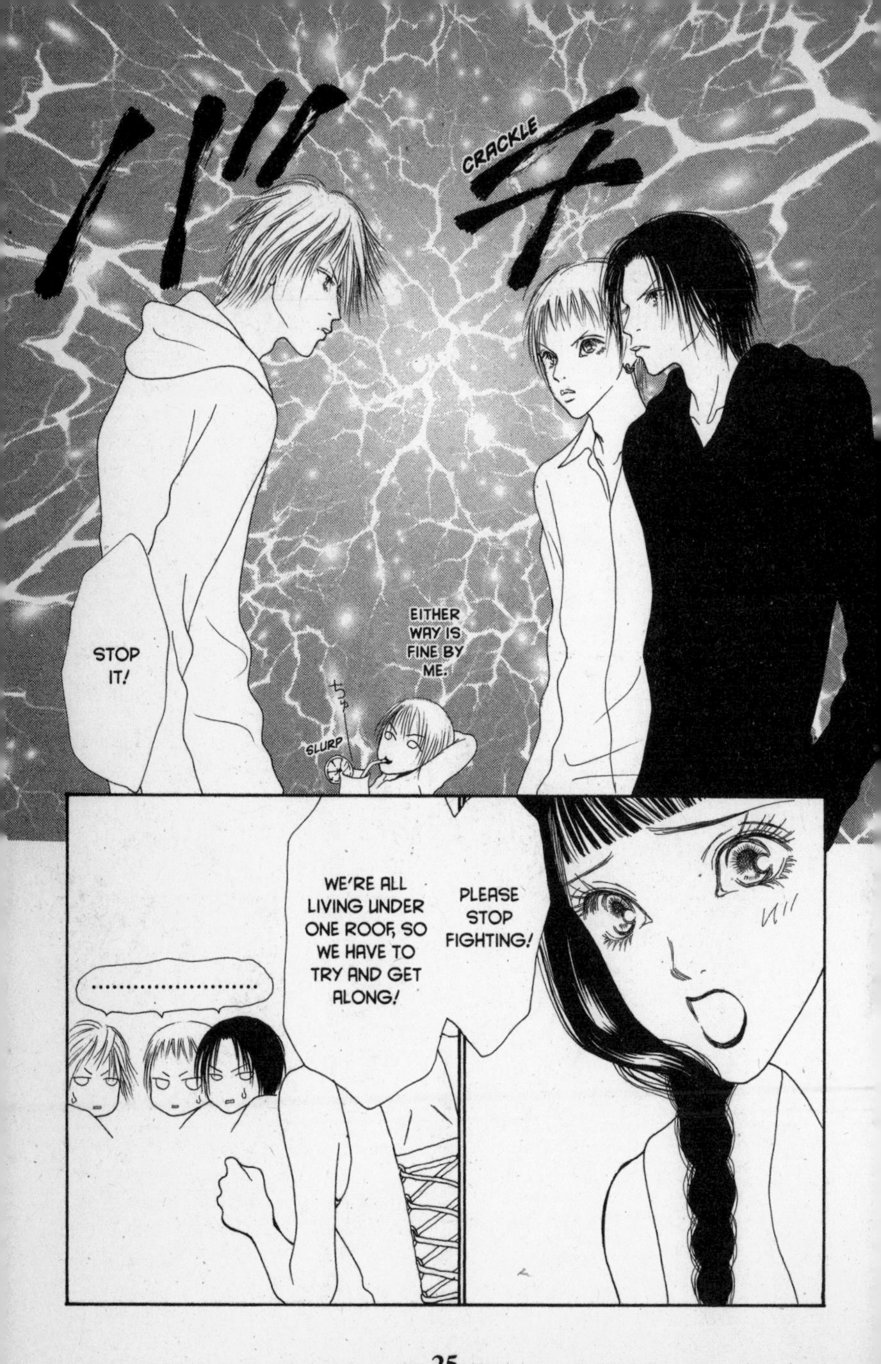
CRACKLE
EITHER WAY IS FINE BY ME.
STOP IT!
SLURP
PLEASE STOP FIGHTING!
WE'RE ALL LIVING UNDER ONE ROOF, SO WE HAVE TO TRY AND GET ALONG!
....

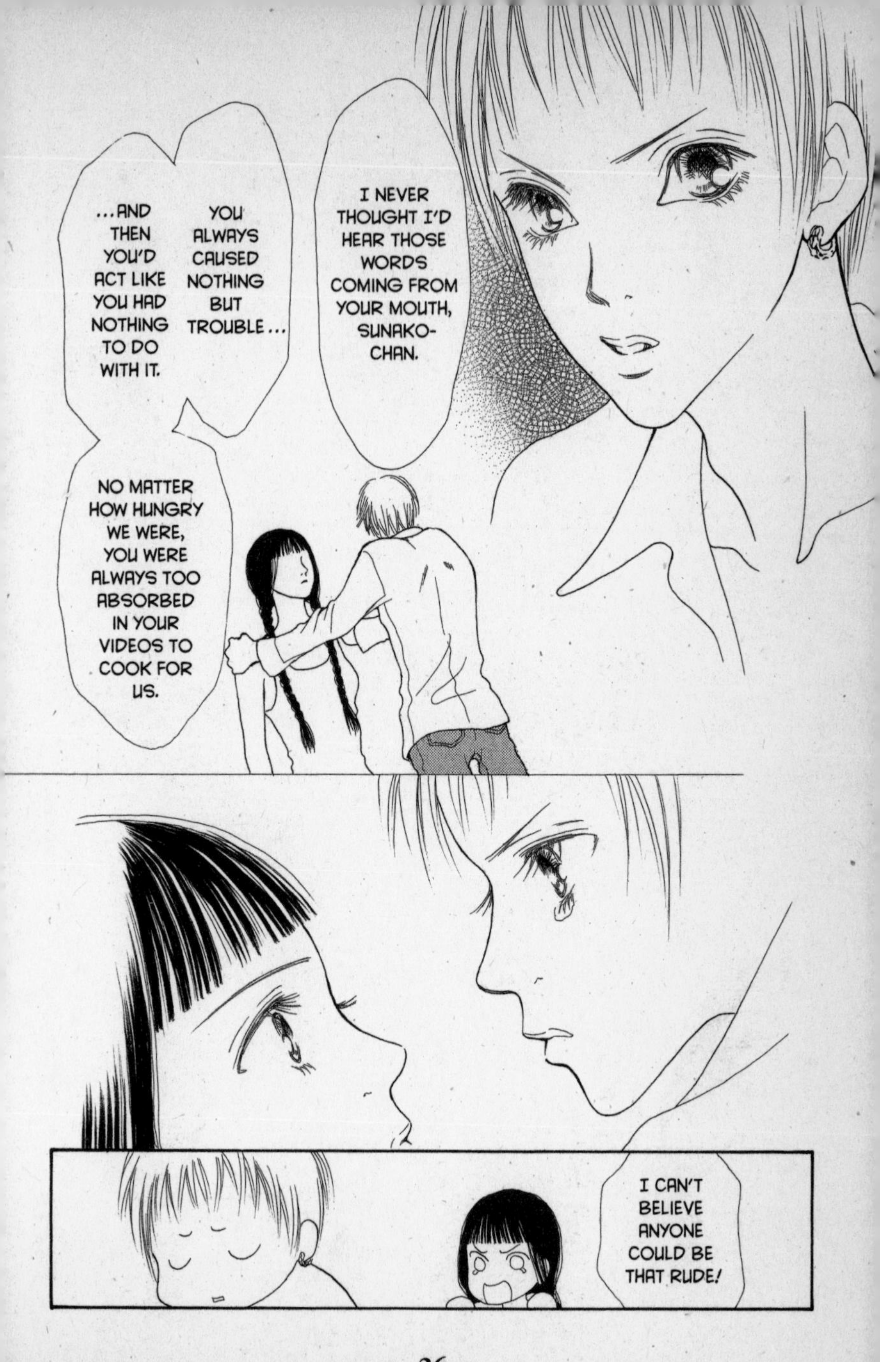
I NEVER THOUGHT I'D HEAR THOSE WORDS COMING FROM YOUR MOUTH, SUNAKO-CHAN.
YOU ALWAYS CAUSED NOTHING BUT TROUBLE...
...AND THEN YOU'D ACT LIKE YOU HAD NOTHING TO DO WITH IT.
NO MATTER HOW HUNGRY WE WERE, YOU WERE ALWAYS TOO ABSORBED IN YOUR VIDEOS TO COOK FOR US.
I CAN'T BELIEVE ANYONE COULD BE THAT RUDE!

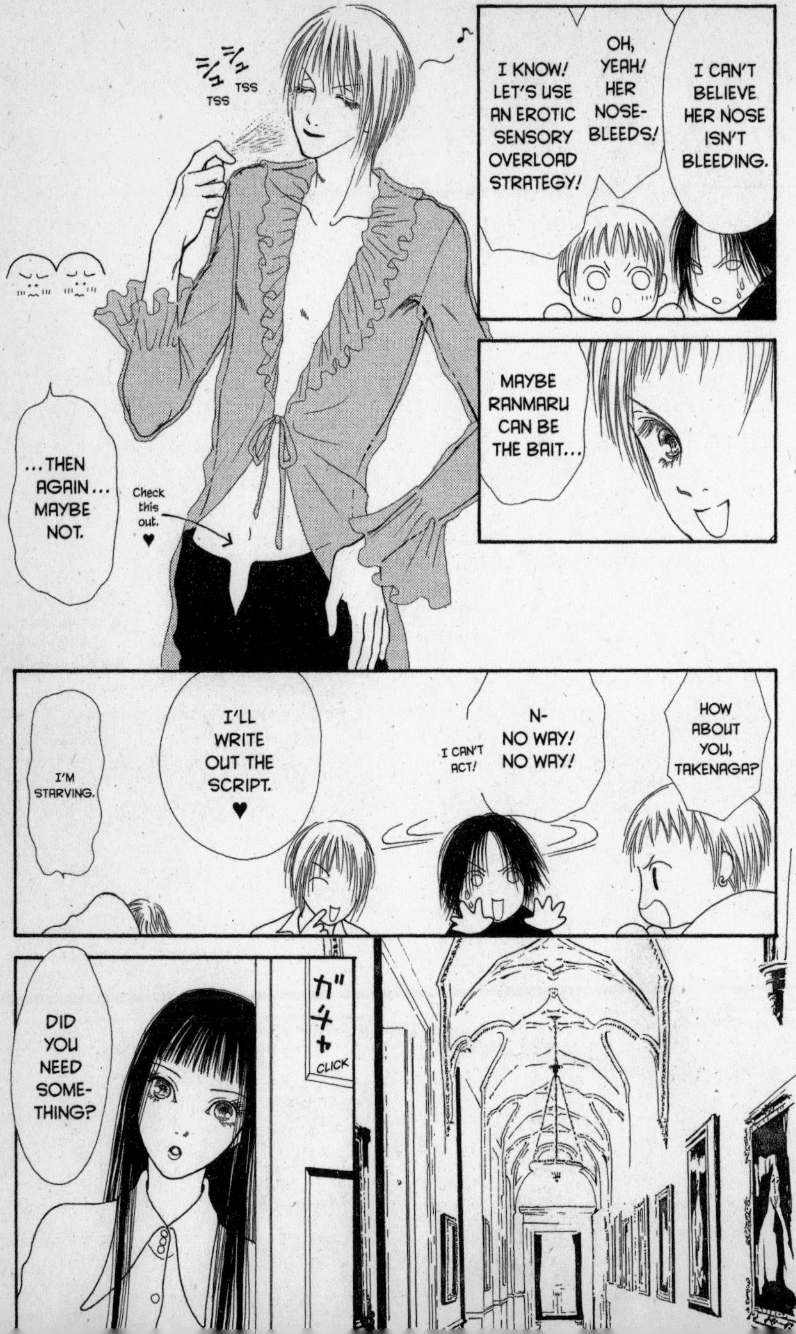
I CAN'T BELIEVE HER NOSE ISN'T BLEEDING.
OH, YEAH! HER NOSE-BLEEDS!
I KNOW! LET'S USE AN EROTIC SENSORY OVERLOAD STRATEGY!
MAYBE RANMARU CAN BE THE BAIT...
シュ シュ
TSS TSS
Check this out. ♥
...THEN AGAIN... MAYBE NOT.
HOW ABOUT YOU, TAKENAGA?
N- NO WAY! NO WAY!
I CAN'T ACT!
I'LL WRITE OUT THE SCRIPT. ♥
I'M STARVING.
ガチャ
CLICK
DID YOU NEED SOMETHING?

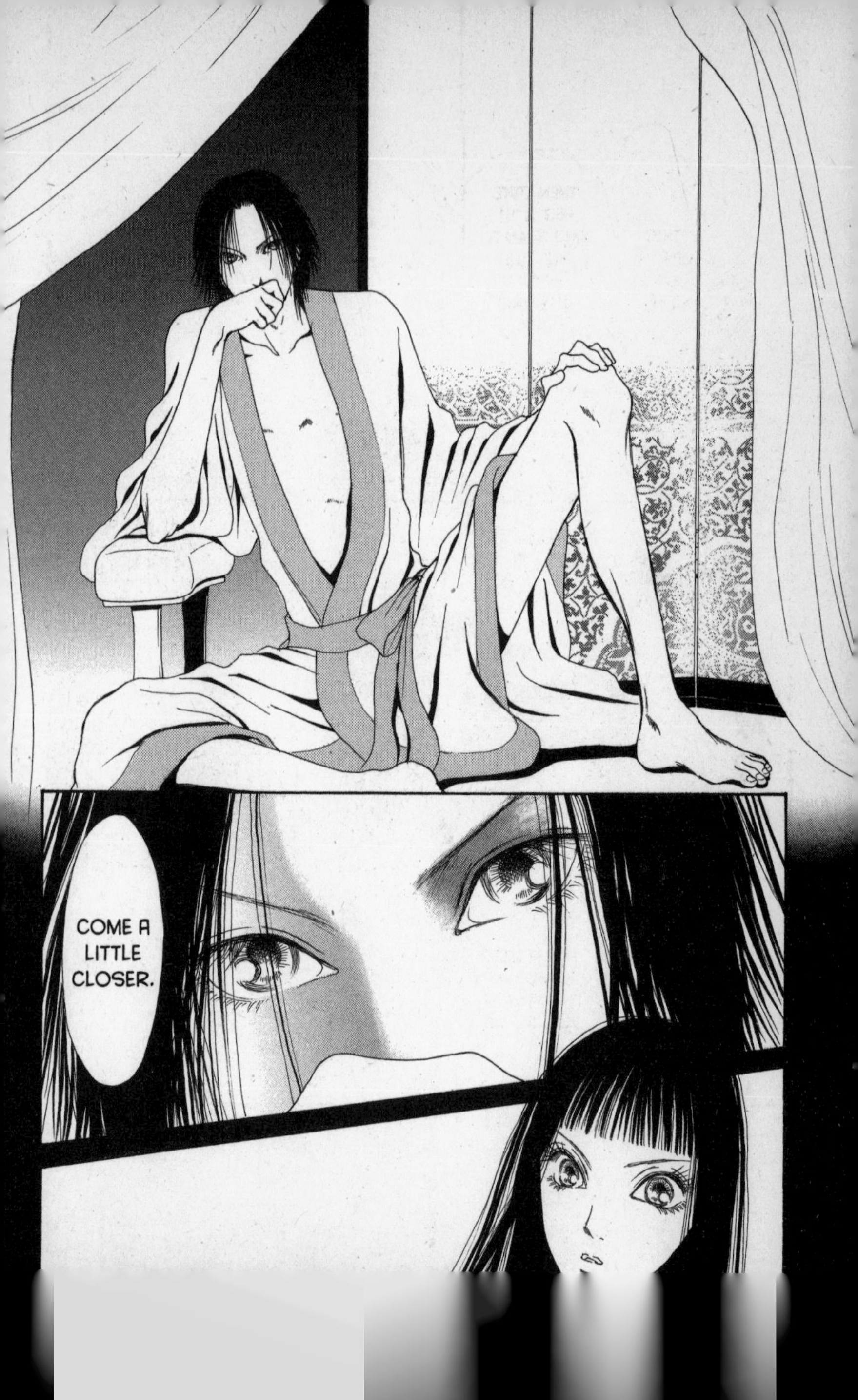
COME A LITTLE CLOSER.

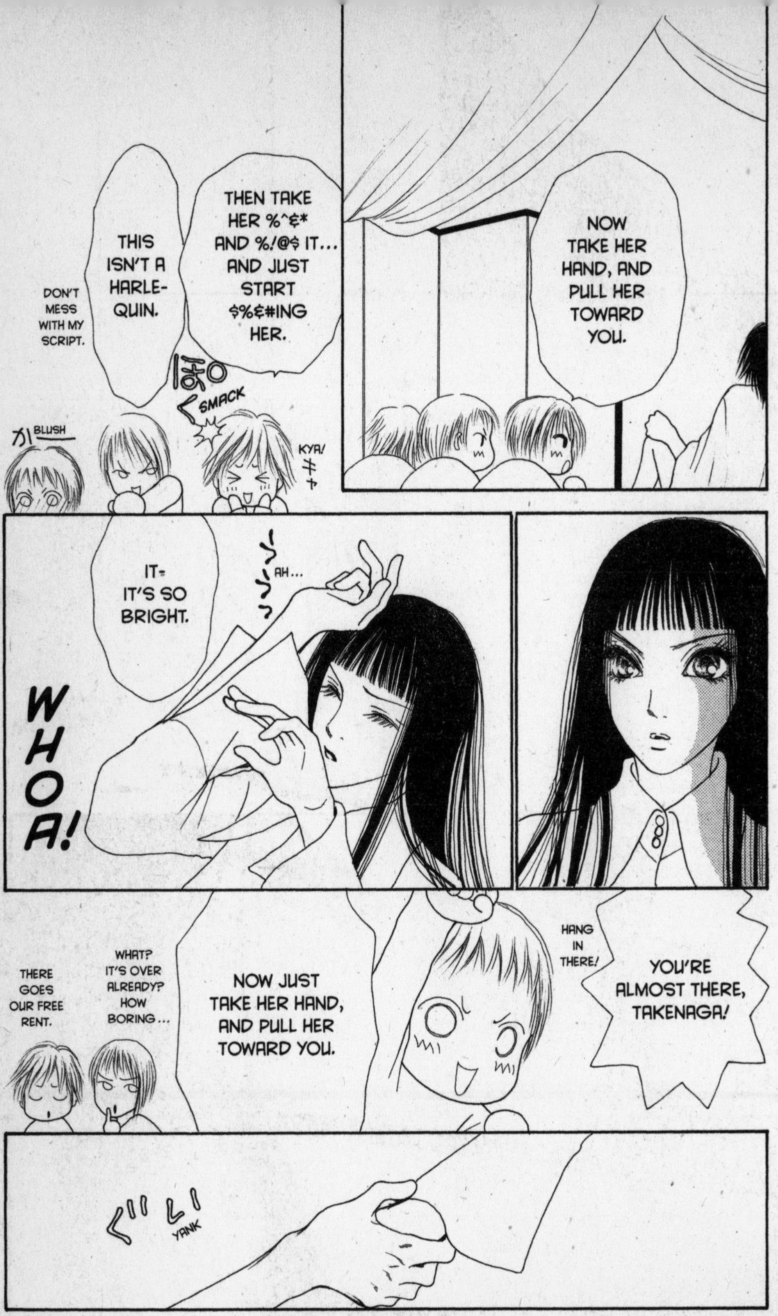
NOW TAKE HER HAND, AND PULL HER TOWARD YOU.
THEN TAKE HER %^&* AND %!@$ IT... AND JUST START $%&#ING HER.
THIS ISN'T A HARLEQUIN.
DON'T MESS WITH MY SCRIPT.
SMACK
KYA!
BLUSH
AH...
IT- IT'S SO BRIGHT.
WHOA!
YOU'RE ALMOST THERE, TAKENAGA!
HANG IN THERE!
NOW JUST TAKE HER HAND, AND PULL HER TOWARD YOU.
WHAT? IT'S OVER ALREADY? HOW BORING...
THERE GOES OUR FREE RENT.
YANK

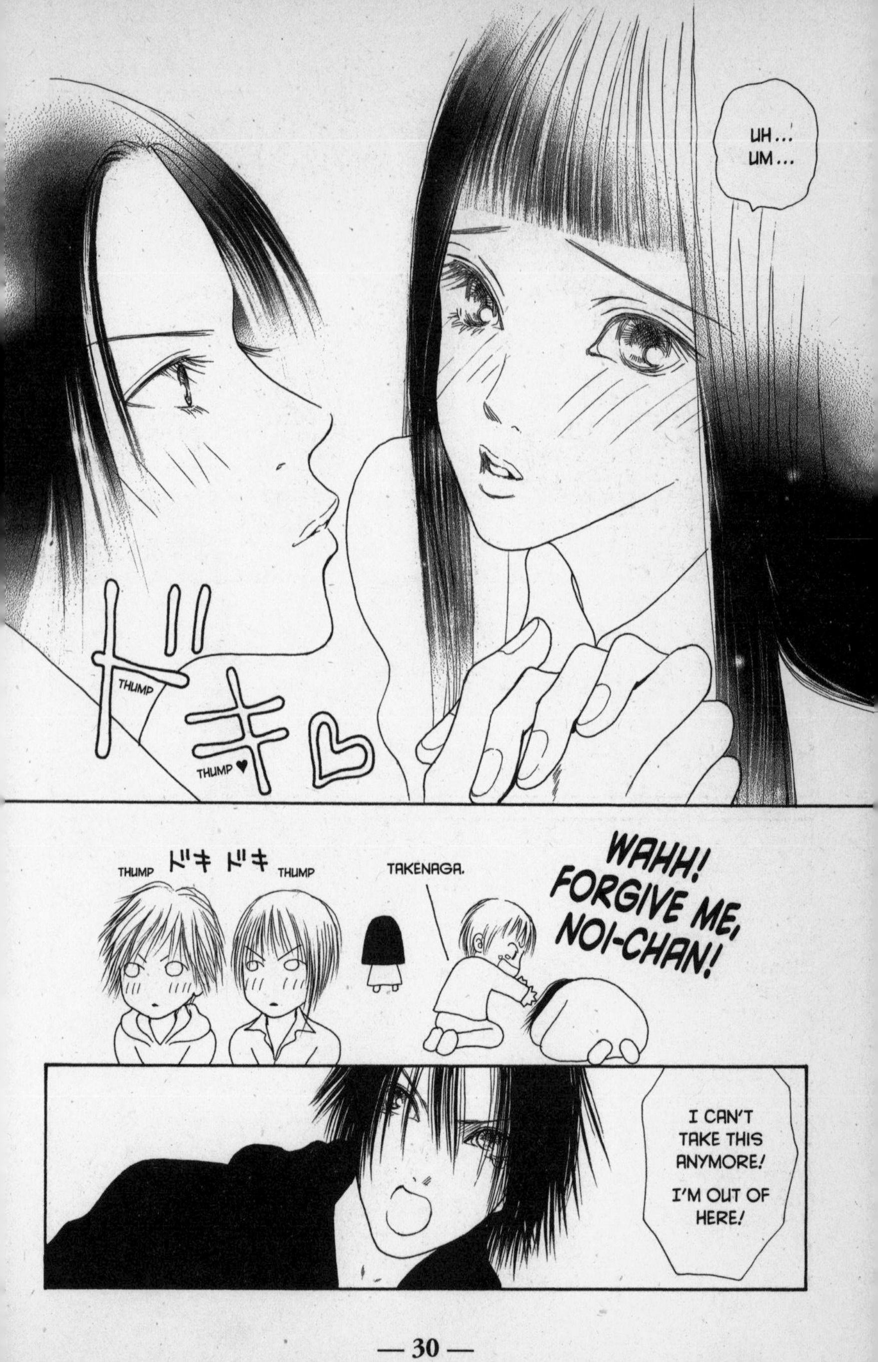
UH... UM...
ドキ♡
THUMP
THUMP♥
WAHH! FORGIVE ME, NOI-CHAN!
TAKENAGA.
ドキ ドキ
THUMP
THUMP
I CAN'T TAKE THIS ANYMORE!
I'M OUT OF HERE!

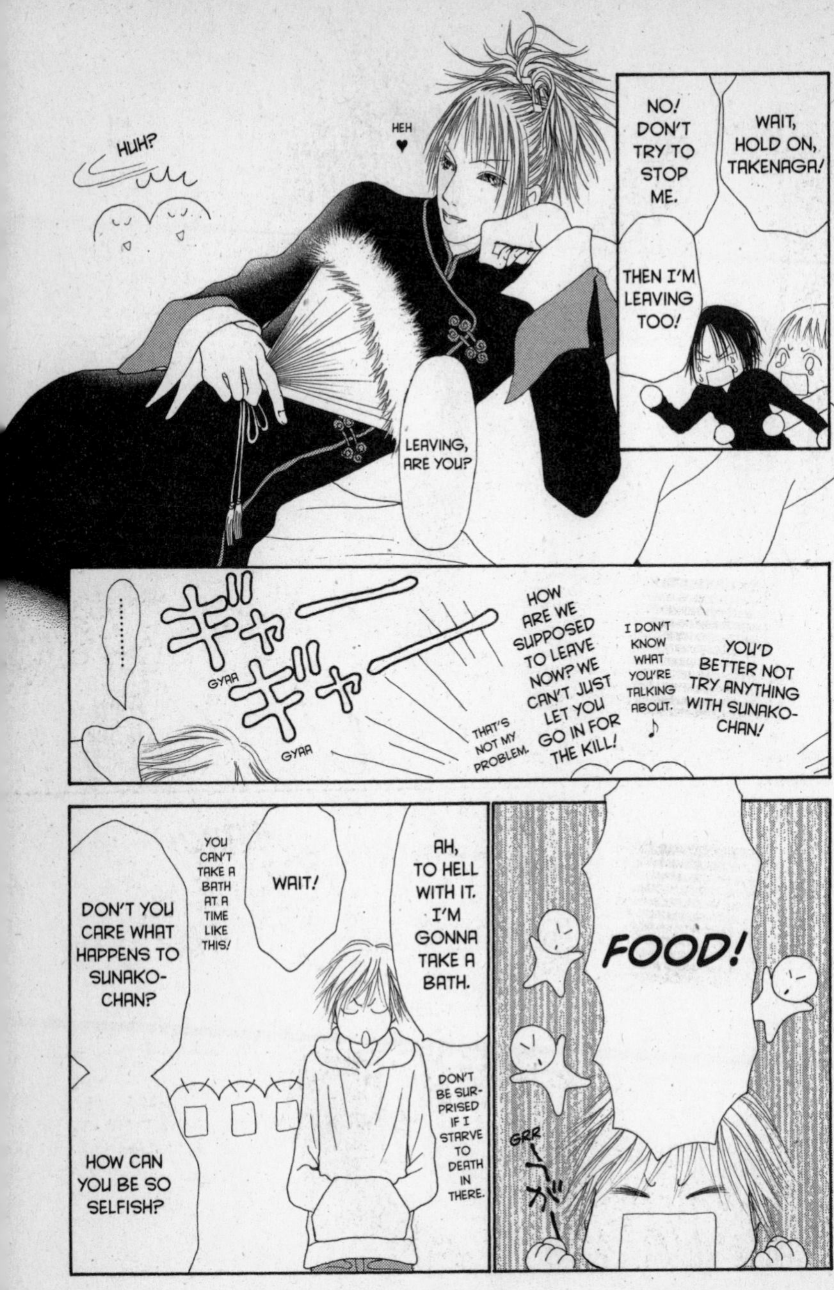
WAIT, HOLD ON, TAKENAGA!
NO! DON'T TRY TO STOP ME.
THEN I'M LEAVING TOO!
HEH ♥
LEAVING, ARE YOU?
HUH?
YOU'D BETTER NOT TRY ANYTHING WITH SUNAKO-CHAN!
I DON'T KNOW WHAT YOU'RE TALKING ABOUT. ♪
HOW ARE WE SUPPOSED TO LEAVE NOW? WE CAN'T JUST LET YOU GO IN FOR THE KILL!
THAT'S NOT MY PROBLEM.
GYAA
GYAA
......
FOOD!
GRR
AH, TO HELL WITH IT. I'M GONNA TAKE A BATH.
WAIT!
YOU CAN'T TAKE A BATH AT A TIME LIKE THIS!
DON'T YOU CARE WHAT HAPPENS TO SUNAKO-CHAN?
DON'T BE SURPRISED IF I STARVE TO DEATH IN THERE.
HOW CAN YOU BE SO SELFISH?

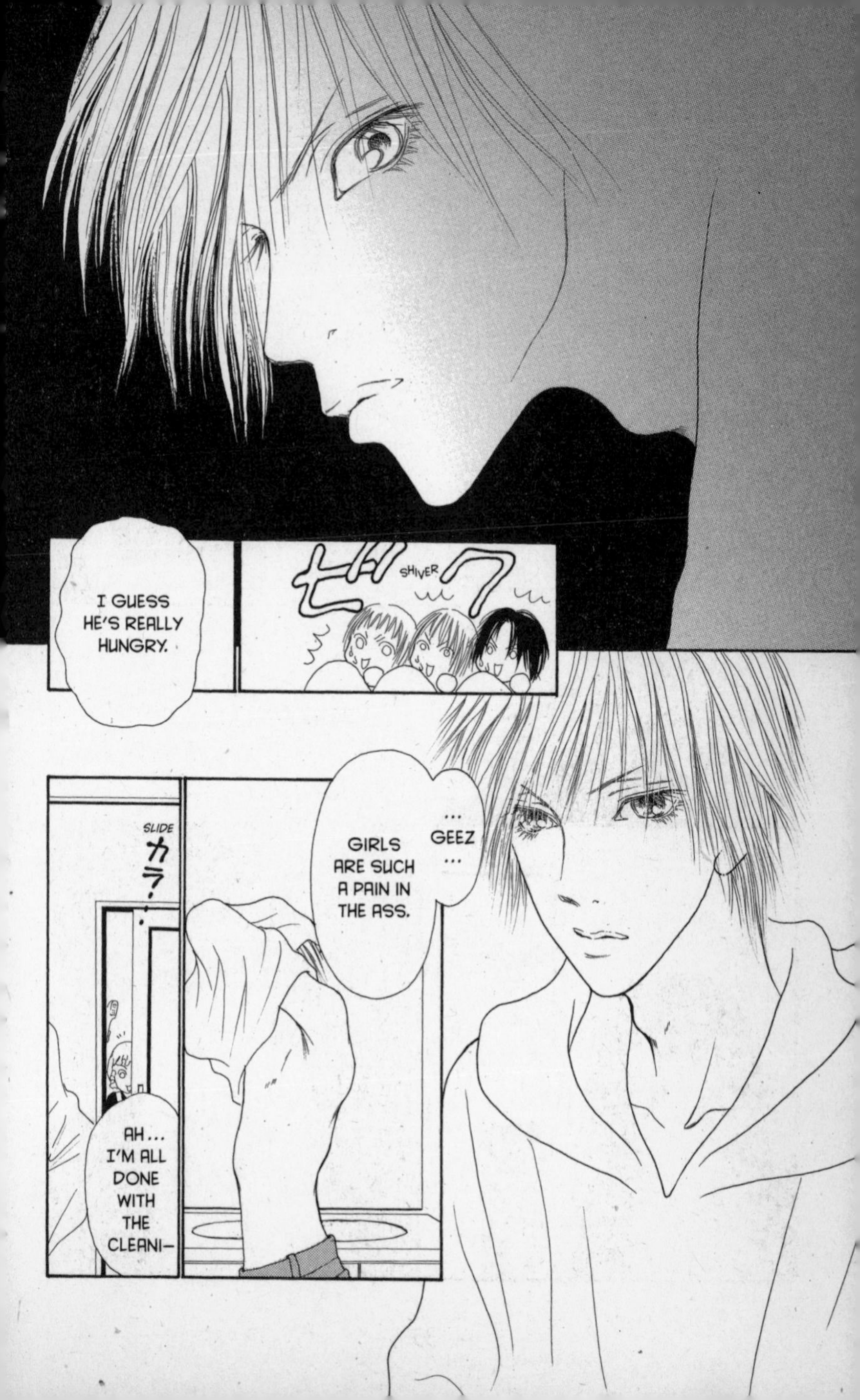
SHIVER
I GUESS HE'S REALLY HUNGRY.
... GEEZ ...
GIRLS ARE SUCH A PAIN IN THE ASS.
SLIDE
カラ
AH... I'M ALL DONE WITH THE CLEANI—

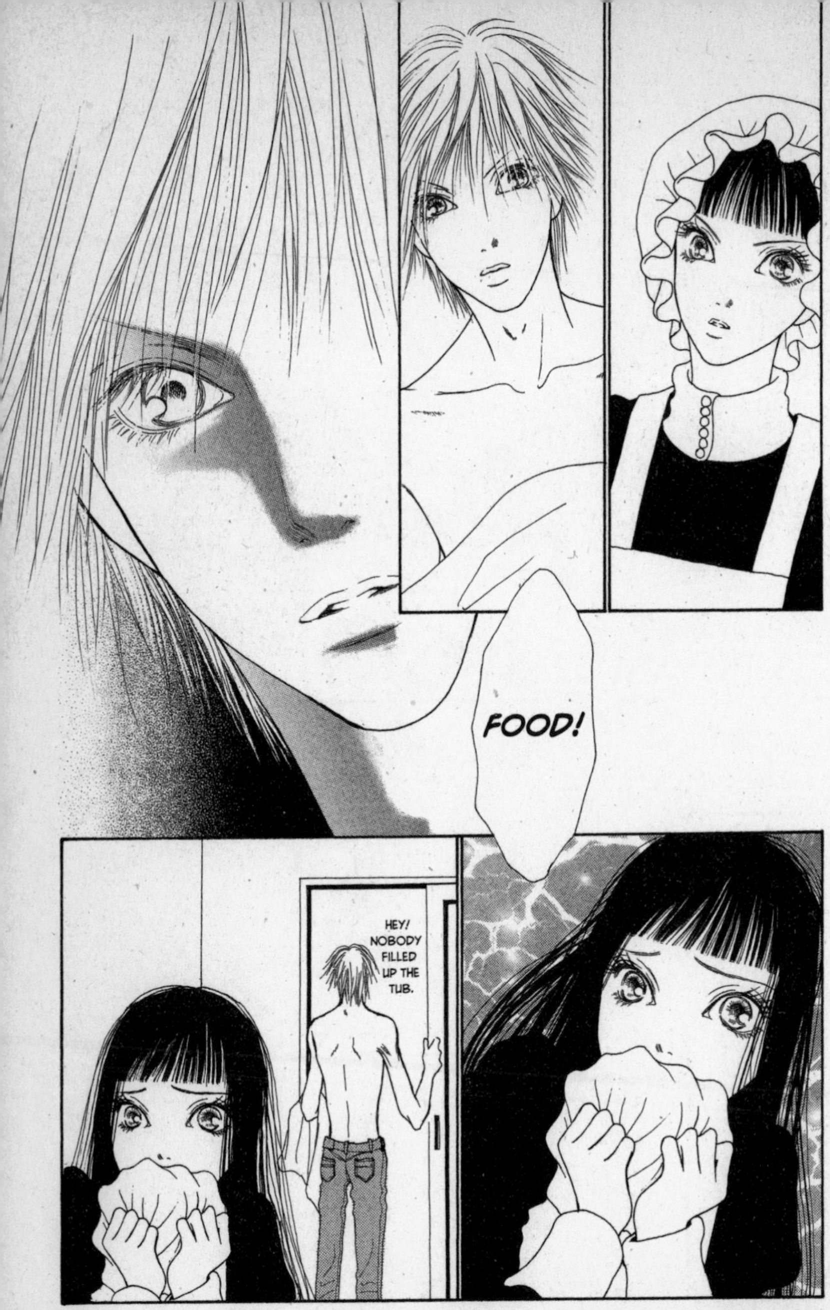
FOOD!
HEY! NOBODY FILLED UP THE TUB.

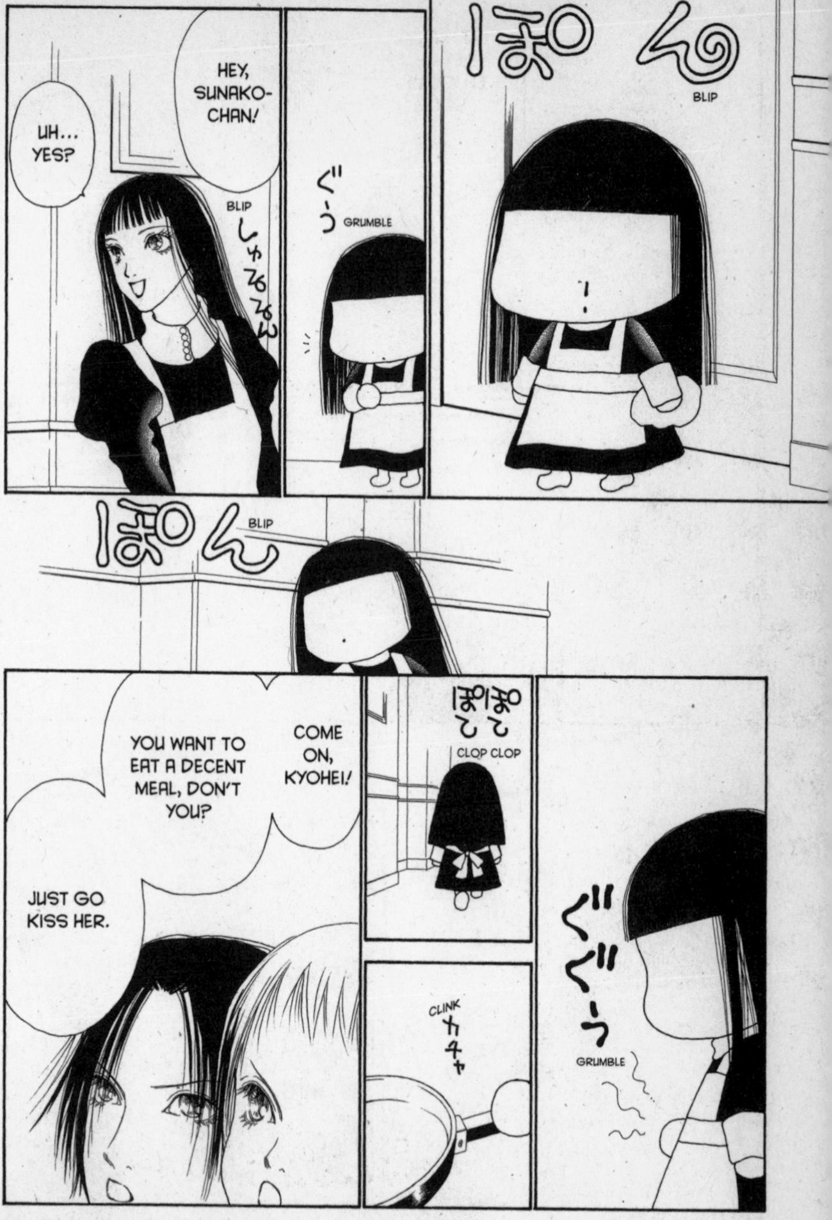
ぽん
BLIP
ぐ~う
GRUMBLE
HEY, SUNAKO-CHAN!
UH... YES?
BLIP
しゅるるるん
ぽん
BLIP
ぐ~ぐ~う
GRUMBLE
ぽてぽて
CLOP CLOP
カチャ
CLINK
COME ON, KYOHEI!
YOU WANT TO EAT A DECENT MEAL, DON'T YOU?
JUST GO KISS HER.

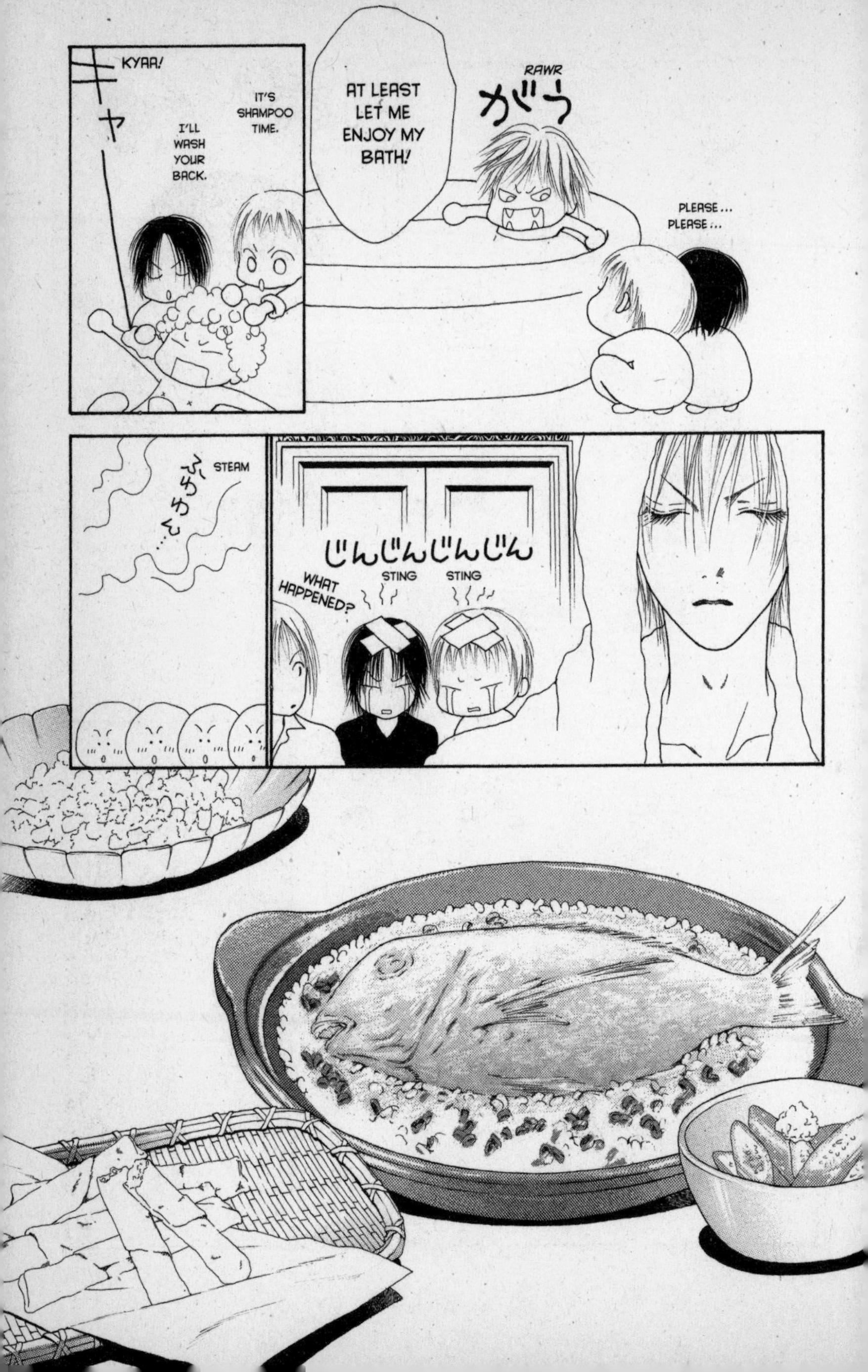
がう
RAWR
PLEASE ... PLEASE ...
AT LEAST LET ME ENJOY MY BATH!
キャー
KYAA!
IT'S SHAMPOO TIME.
I'LL WASH YOUR BACK.
じんじんじんじん
STING
STING
WHAT HAPPENED?
ふわわん…
STEAM

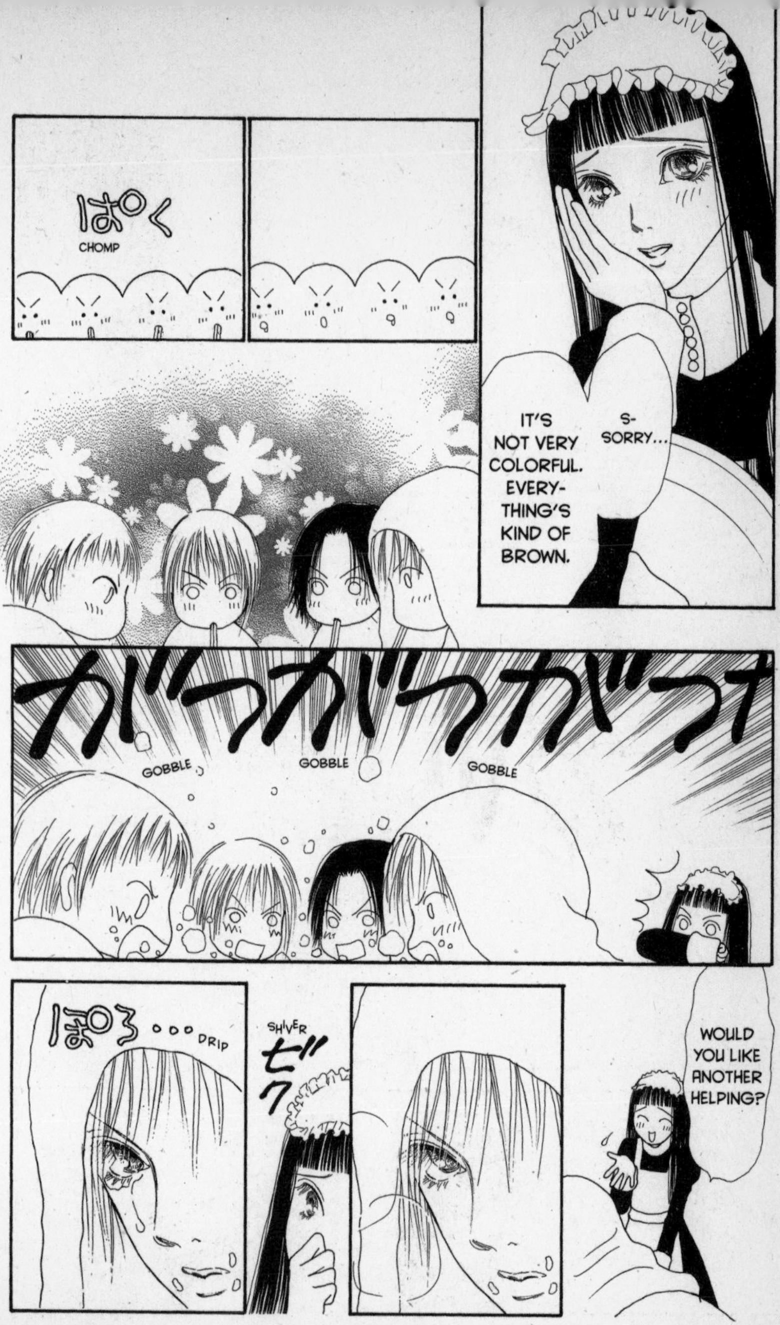
S-SORRY...
IT'S NOT VERY COLORFUL. EVERY-THING'S KIND OF BROWN.
ぱく
CHOMP
がつがつがつ
GOBBLE
GOBBLE
GOBBLE
WOULD YOU LIKE ANOTHER HELPING?
ビク
SHIVER
ぽろ
DRIP

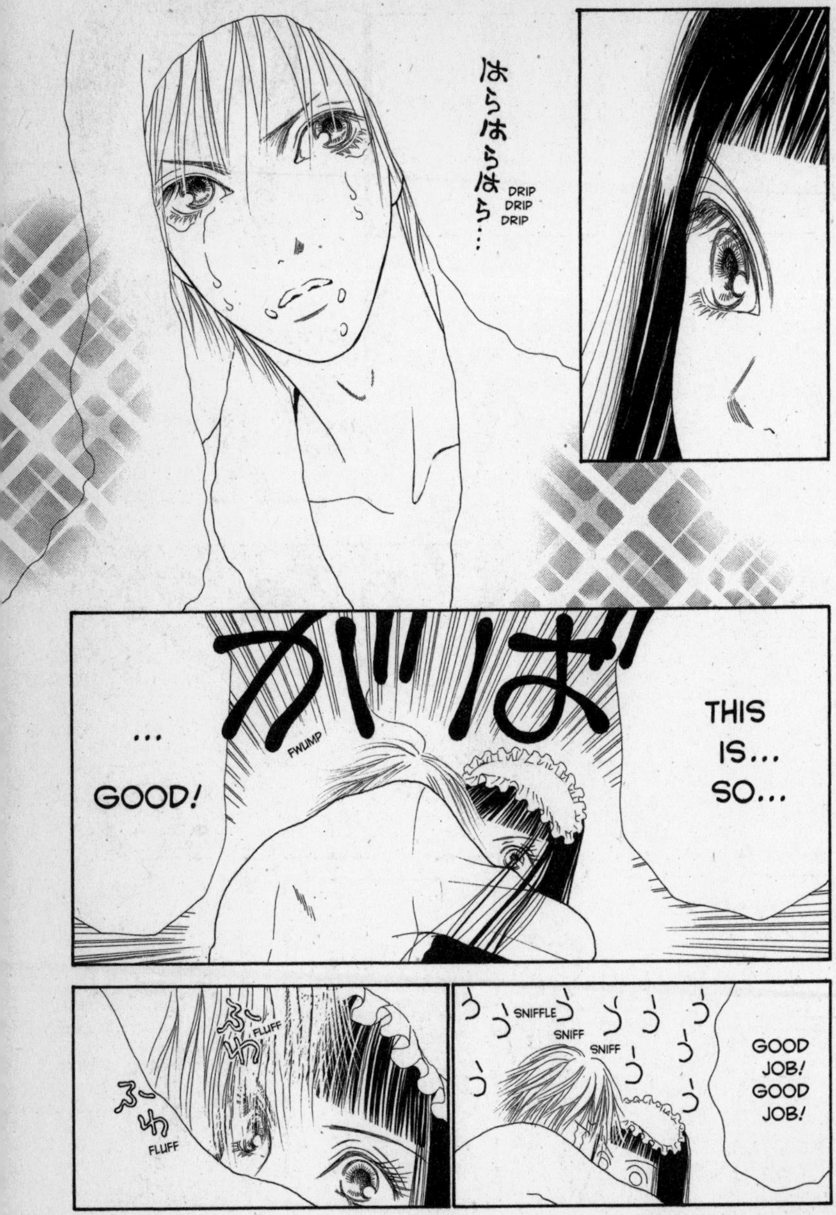

はらはらはら…
DRIP DRIP DRIP
THIS IS... SO...
FWUMP
... GOOD!
SNIFFLE
SNIFF
SNIFF
GOOD JOB! GOOD JOB!
ふわ
FLUFF
ふわ
FLUFF

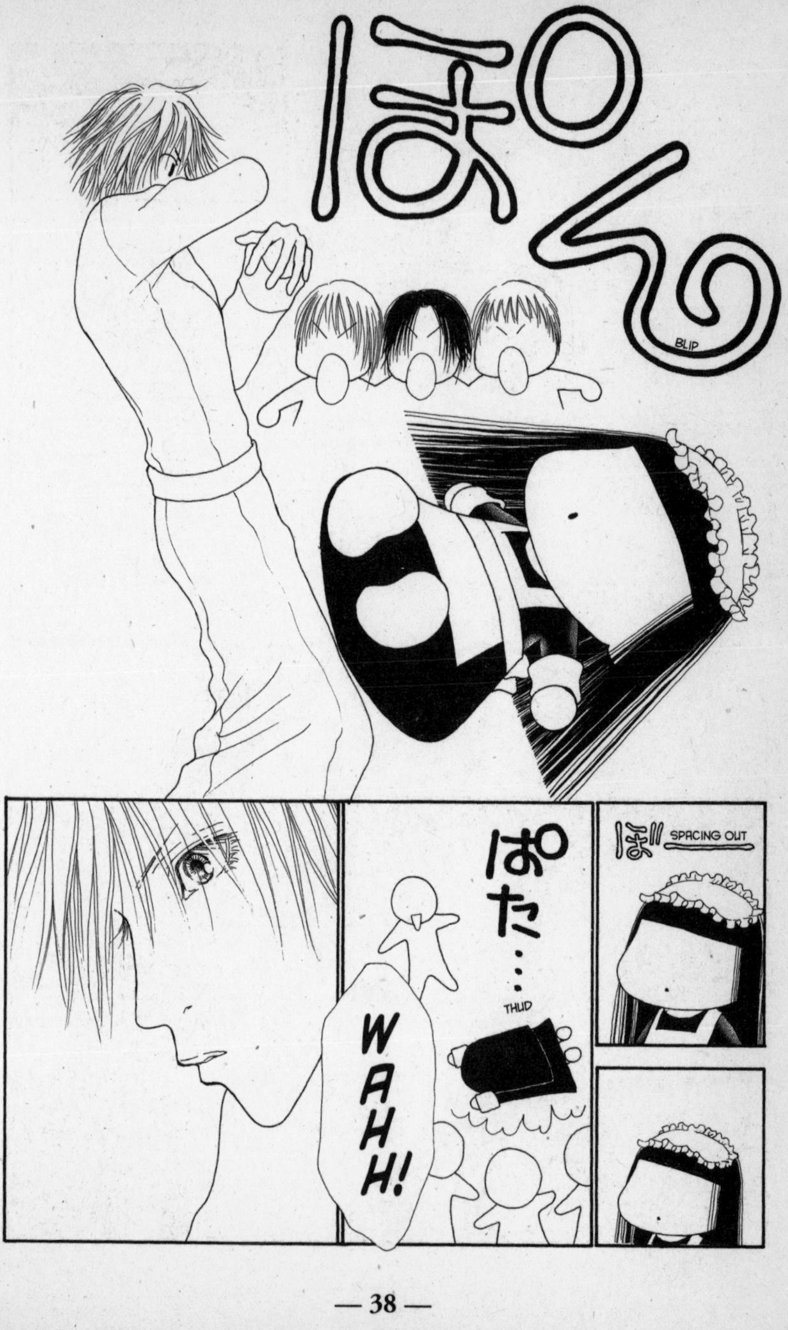
ぽん
BLIP
ぼ
SPACING OUT
ぱた…
THUD
WAHH!

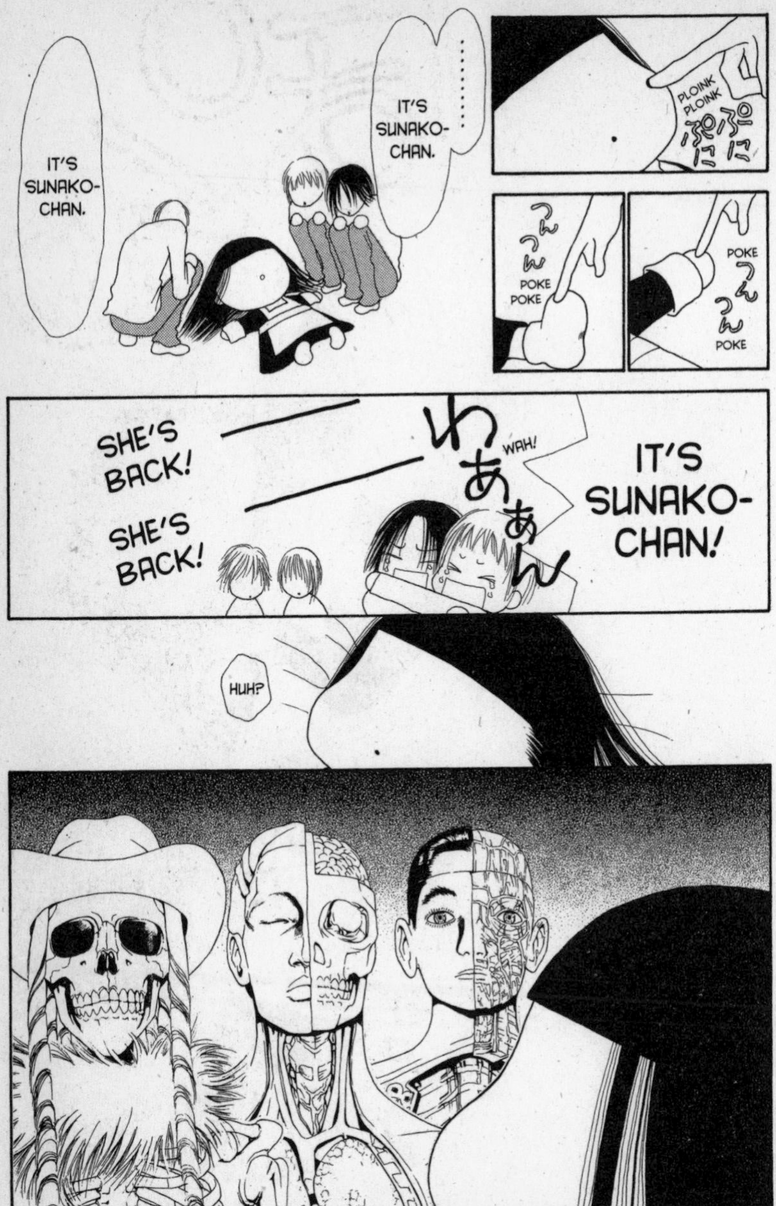

PLOINK PLOINK
ぷにぷに
POKE
つんつん
POKE
つんつん
POKE POKE
...... IT'S SUNAKO-CHAN.
IT'S SUNAKO-CHAN.
IT'S SUNAKO-CHAN!
わあああん
WAH!
SHE'S BACK!
SHE'S BACK!
HUH?

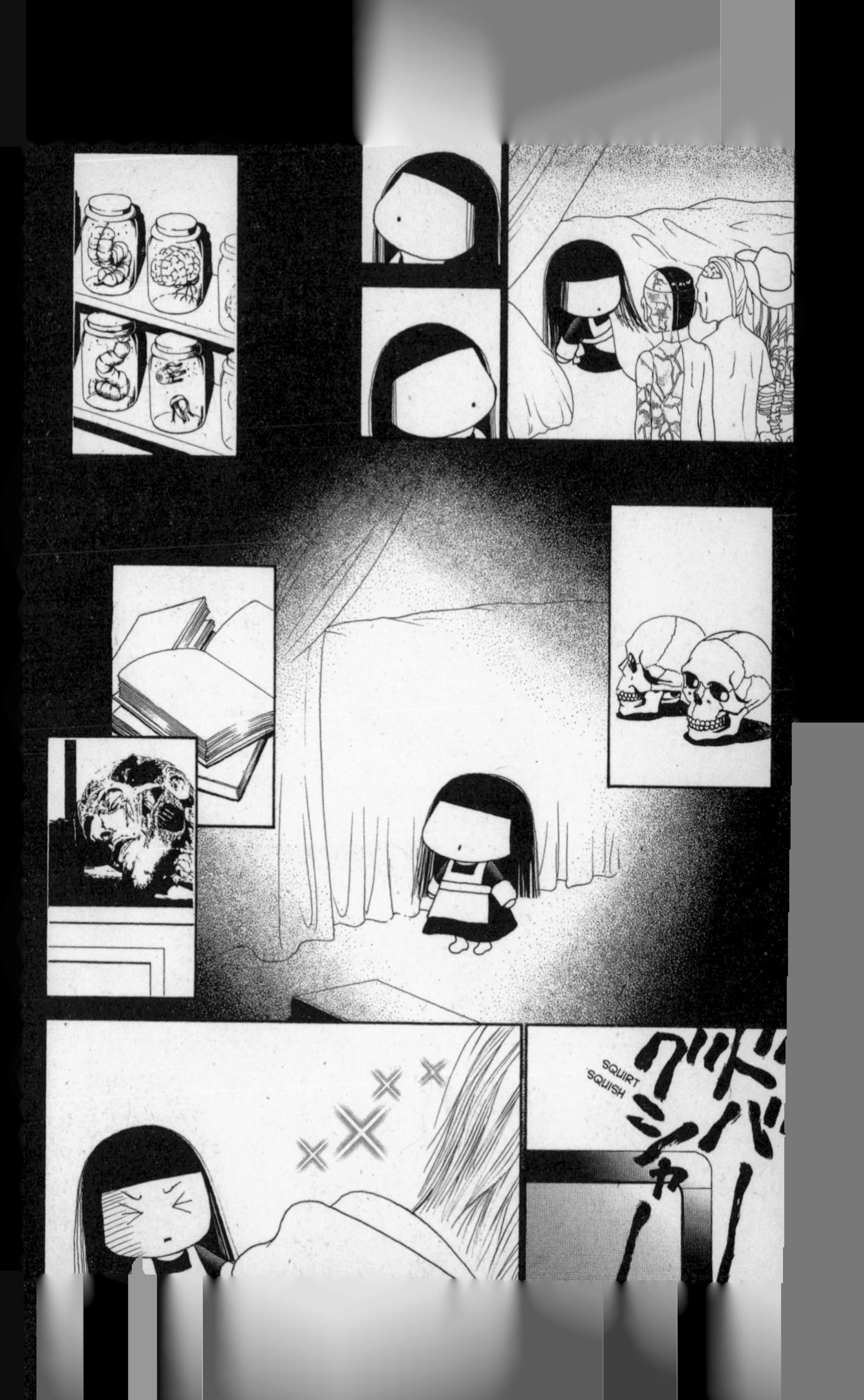
SQUIRT
SQUISH
グバシャーッ

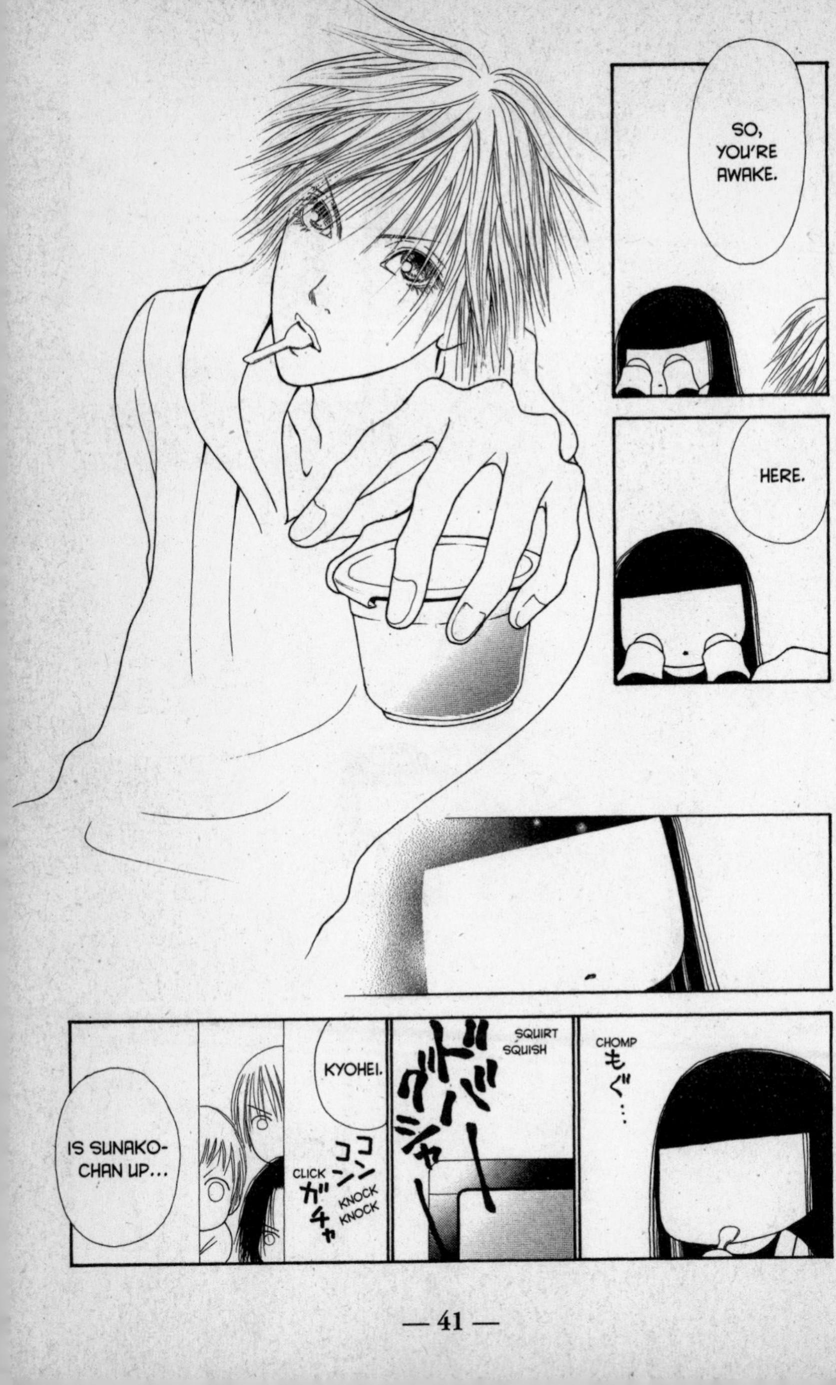
SO, YOU'RE AWAKE.
HERE.
CHOMP
もぐ…
SQUIRT SQUISH
ドバー
グシャー
KYOHEI.
コンコン
KNOCK KNOCK
ガチャ
CLICK
IS SUNAKO-CHAN UP…

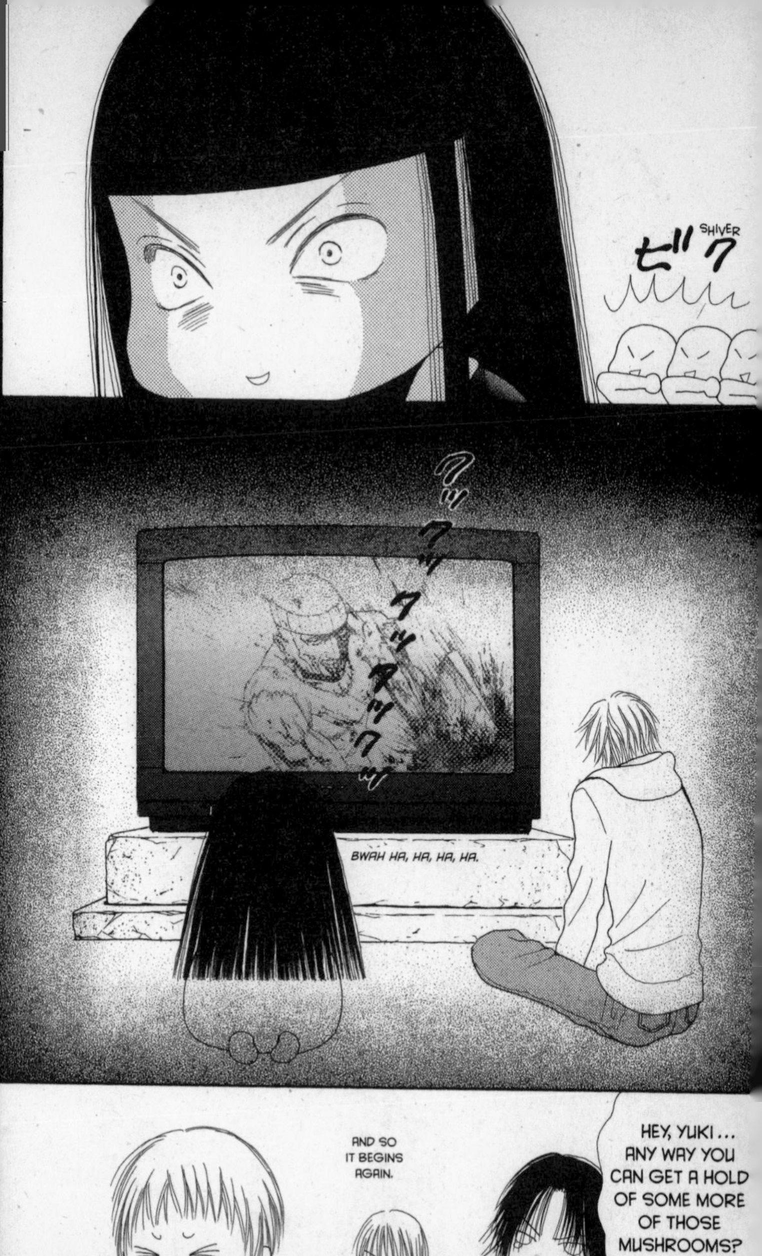
ビク
SHIVER
BWAH HA, HA, HA, HA.
HEY, YUKI... ANY WAY YOU CAN GET A HOLD OF SOME MORE OF THOSE MUSHROOMS?
AND SO IT BEGINS AGAIN.

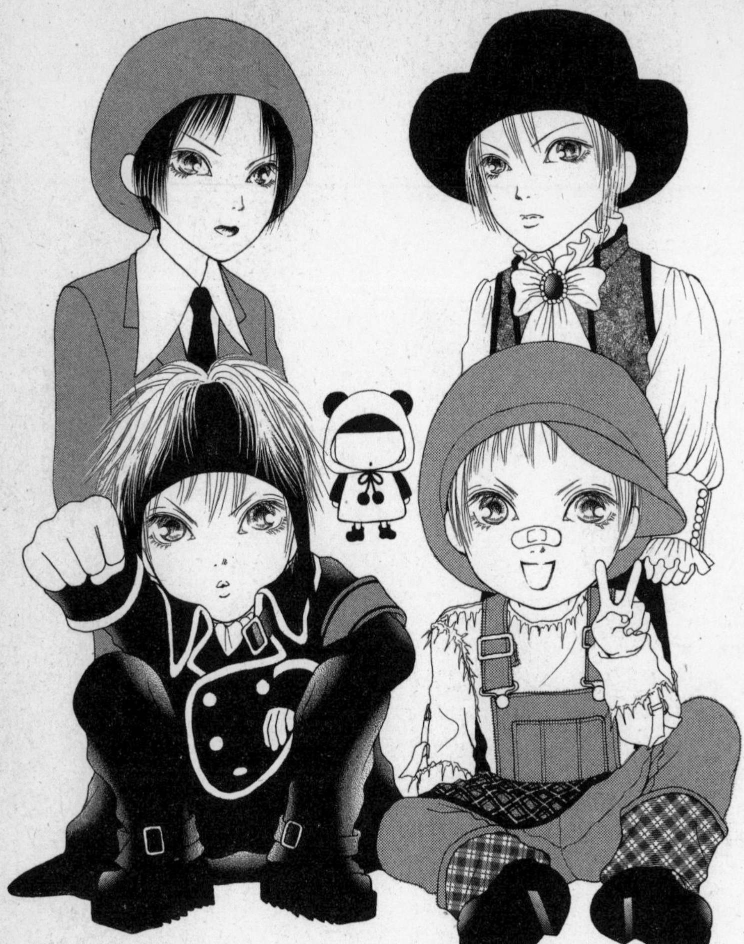

Chapter 28
Little Lost Boy

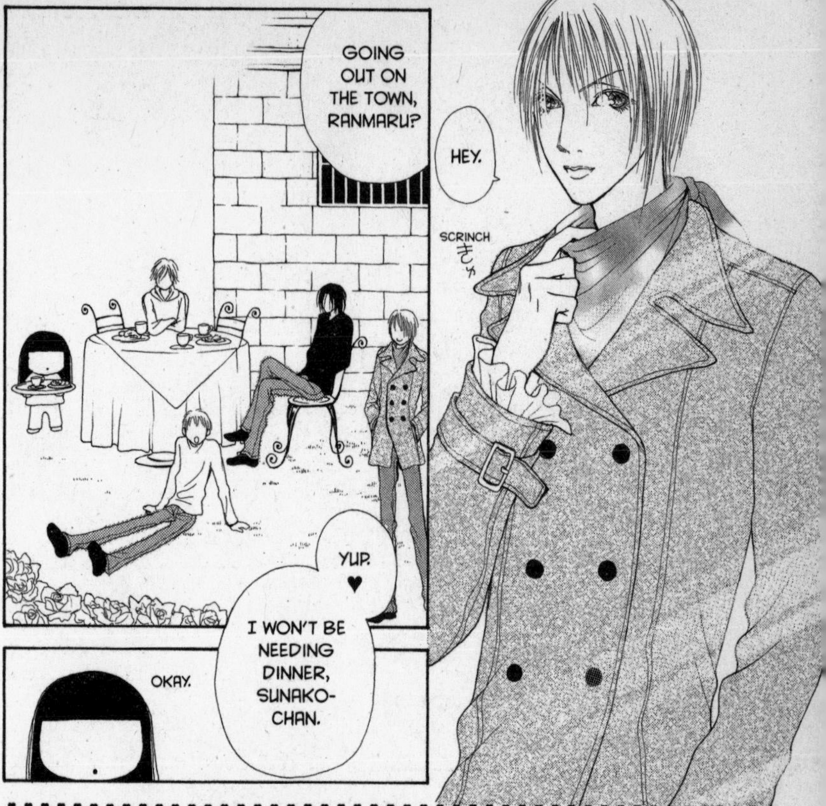
GOING OUT ON THE TOWN, RANMARU?
HEY.
SCRINCH
YUP. ♥
I WON'T BE NEEDING DINNER, SUNAKO-CHAN.
OKAY.

BEHIND THE SCENES

WHILE WRITING THIS CHAPTER, I WITNESSED A PECULIAR PHENOMENON. I WENT THREE WHOLE DAYS WITH HARDLY ANY FOOD OR SLEEP, BUT I DIDN'T FEEL TIRED OR HUNGRY AT ALL. AND I FELT PRETTY RELAXED. (USUALLY I FEEL CRANKY AND I LAUGH CONSTANTLY.)

I WAS JUST STARTING TO WONDER WHY, WHEN FOR SOME REASON A BUNCH OF WINGED ANTS SUDDENLY APPEARED OUT OF NOWHERE. AND AS SOON AS I FINISHED MY STORYBOARDS, THEY VANISHED. WHERE'D THEY GO?

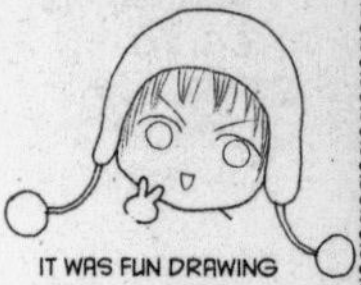

IT WAS FUN DRAWING THAT LITTLE KID. I'D LIKE TO DRAW HIM AGAIN SOMEDAY.

IT TOOK ME FIVE HOURS TO DRAW RANMARU IN COSPLAY.

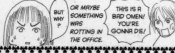

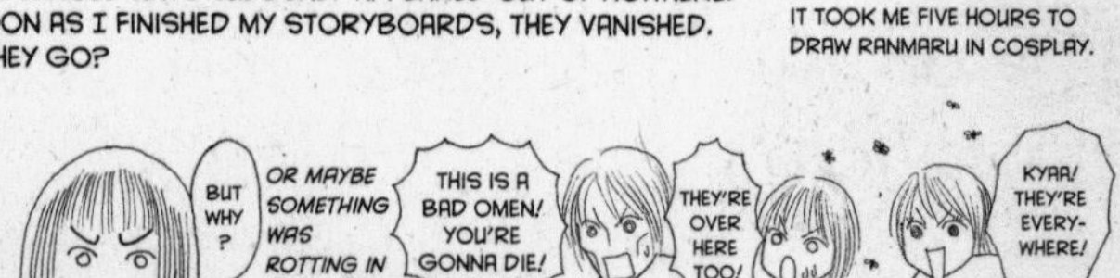
KYAA! THEY'RE EVERY-WHERE!
THEY'RE OVER HERE TOO!
THIS IS A BAD OMEN! YOU'RE GONNA DIE!
OR MAYBE SOMETHING WAS ROTTING IN THE OFFICE.
BUT WHY?
I WONDER IF THOSE ANTS CAME OUT OF MY BRAIN . . .

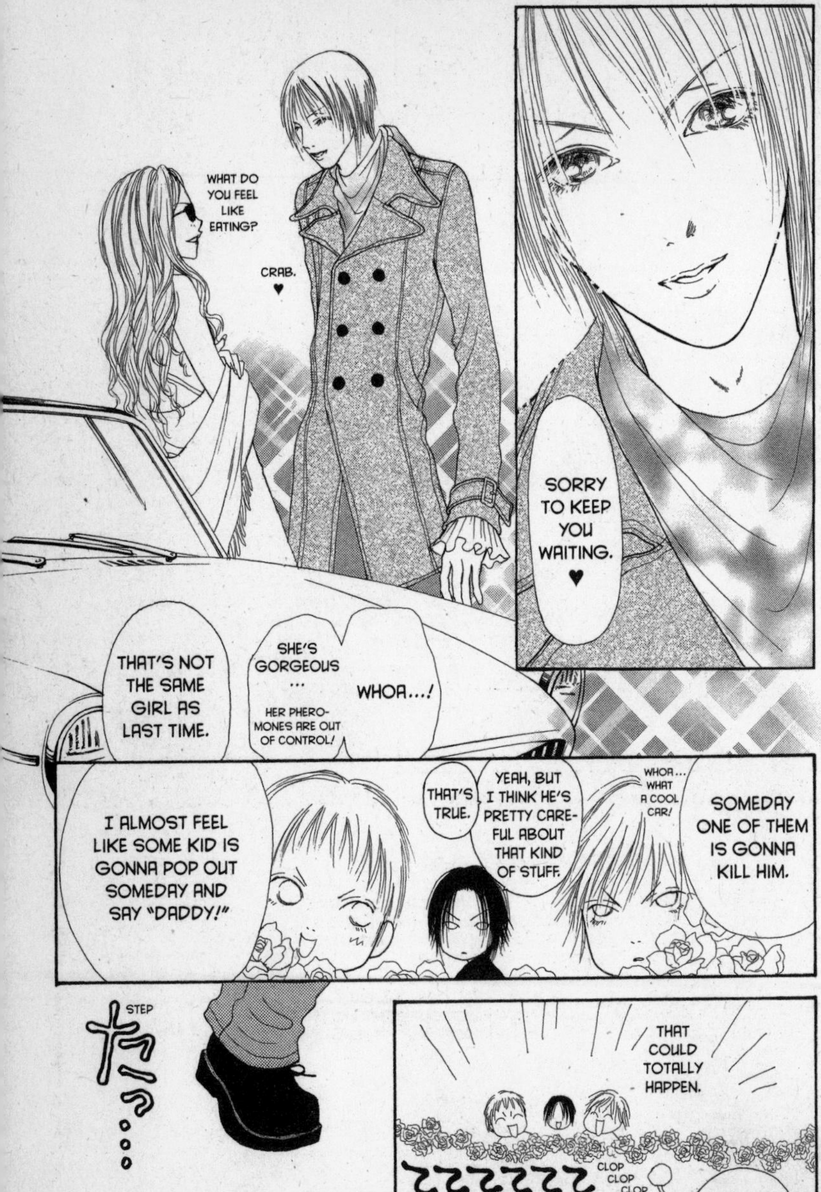
SORRY TO KEEP YOU WAITING. ♥
WHAT DO YOU FEEL LIKE EATING?
CRAB. ♥
WHOA...!
SHE'S GORGEOUS... HER PHEROMONES ARE OUT OF CONTROL!
THAT'S NOT THE SAME GIRL AS LAST TIME.
SOMEDAY ONE OF THEM IS GONNA KILL HIM.
WHOA... WHAT A COOL CAR!
YEAH, BUT I THINK HE'S PRETTY CAREFUL ABOUT THAT KIND OF STUFF.
THAT'S TRUE.
I ALMOST FEEL LIKE SOME KID IS GONNA POP OUT SOMEDAY AND SAY "DADDY!"
THAT COULD TOTALLY HAPPEN.
CLOP CLOP CLOP
STEP

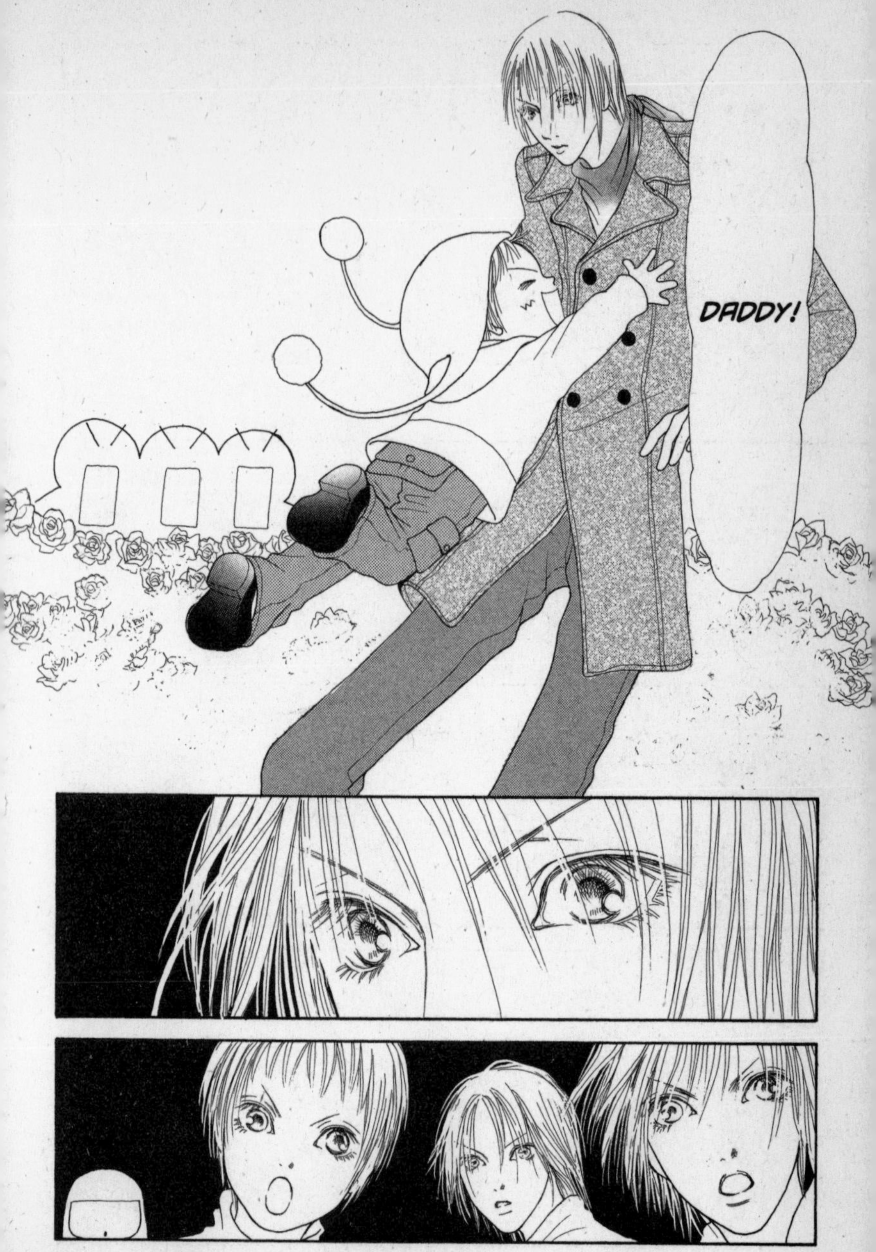
DADDY!

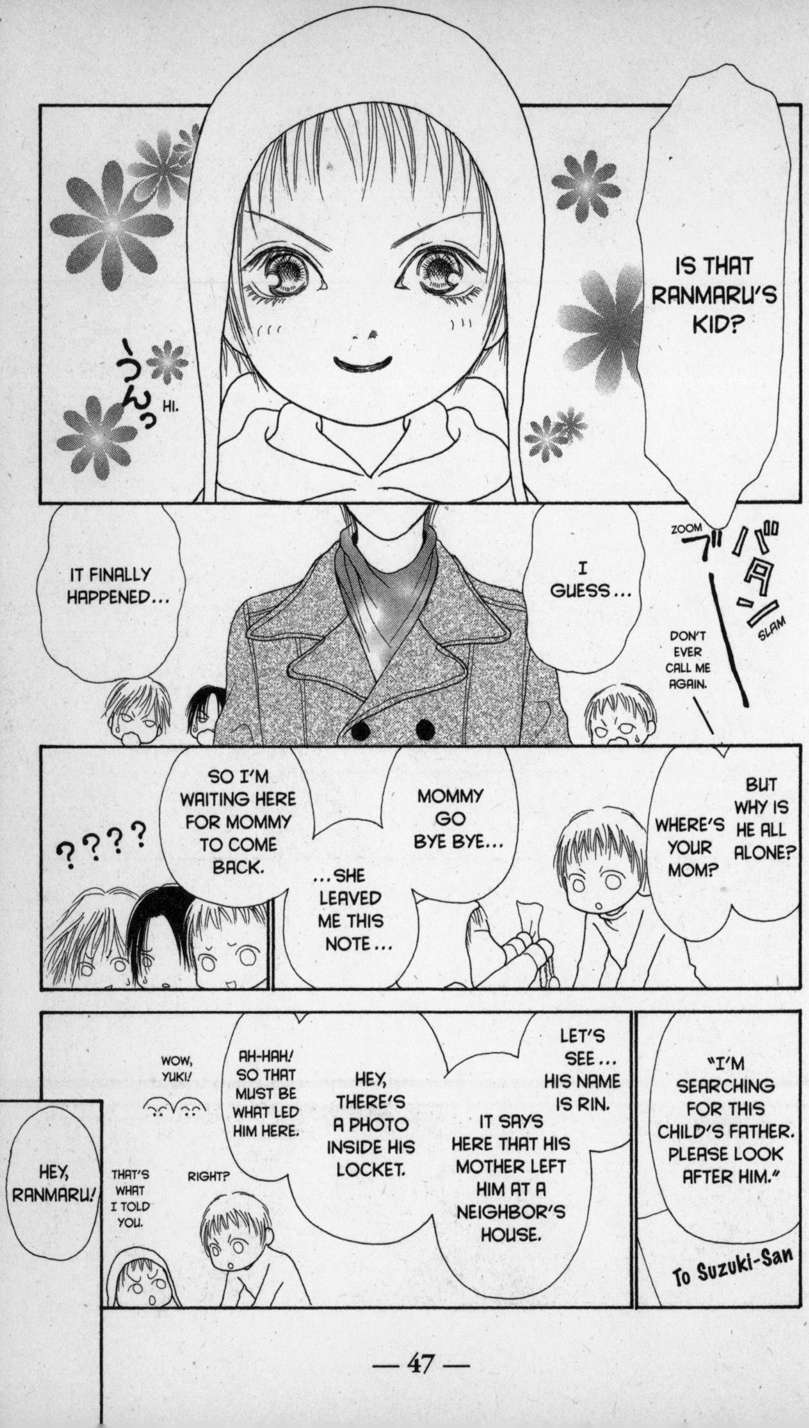
IS THAT RANMARU'S KID?
うんっ
HI.
ZOOM
ブバタン
SLAM
DON'T EVER CALL ME AGAIN.
I GUESS...
IT FINALLY HAPPENED...
BUT WHY IS HE ALL ALONE?
WHERE'S YOUR MOM?
MOMMY GO BYE BYE...
...SHE LEAVED ME THIS NOTE...
SO I'M WAITING HERE FOR MOMMY TO COME BACK.
????
"I'M SEARCHING FOR THIS CHILD'S FATHER. PLEASE LOOK AFTER HIM."
To Suzuki-San
LET'S SEE... HIS NAME IS RIN.
IT SAYS HERE THAT HIS MOTHER LEFT HIM AT A NEIGHBOR'S HOUSE.
HEY, THERE'S A PHOTO INSIDE HIS LOCKET.
AH-HAH! SO THAT MUST BE WHAT LED HIM HERE.
WOW, YUKI!
RIGHT?
THAT'S WHAT I TOLD YOU.
HEY, RANMARU!

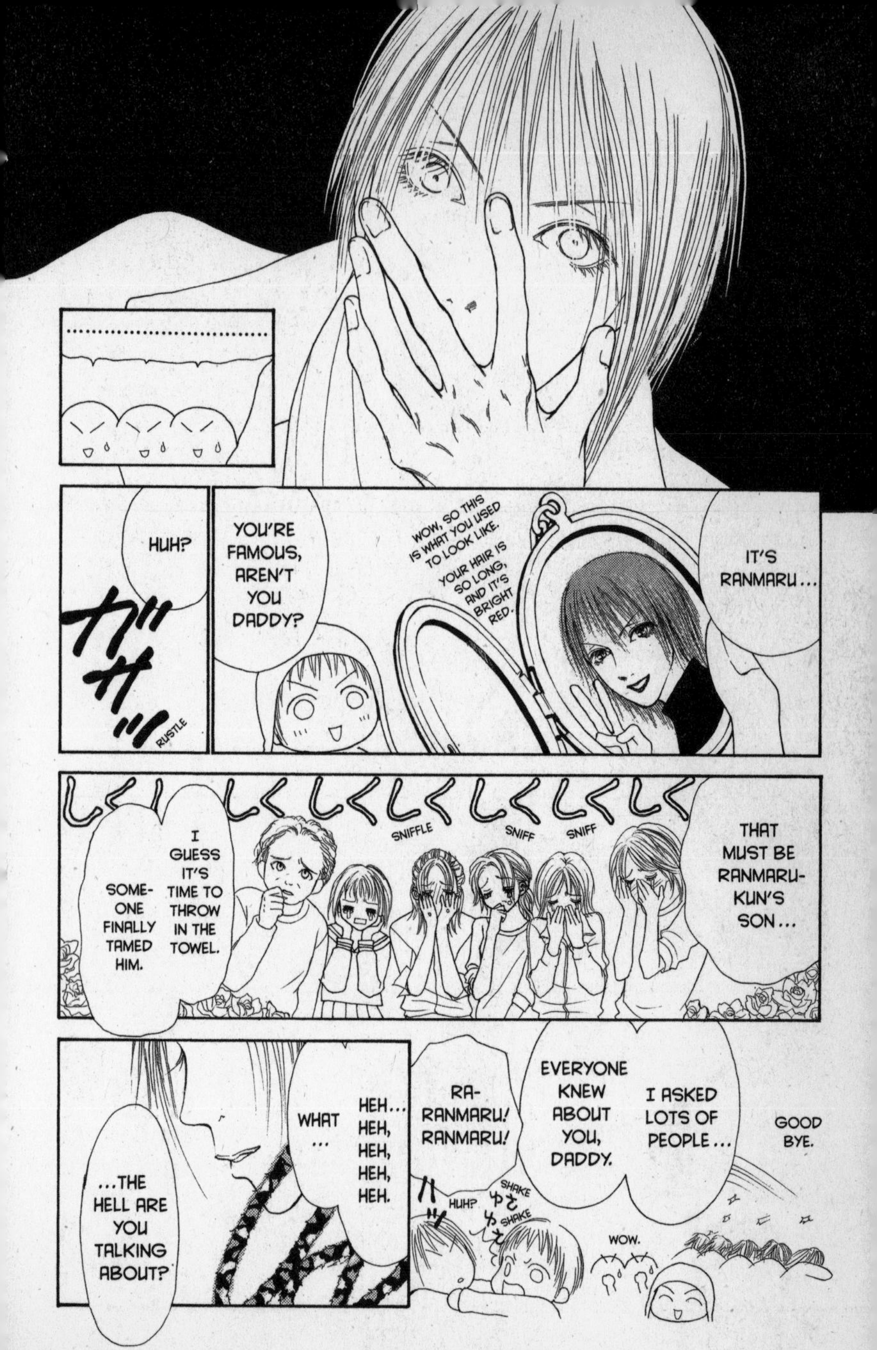
……………
IT'S RANMARU…
WOW, SO THIS IS WHAT YOU USED TO LOOK LIKE.
YOUR HAIR IS SO LONG, AND IT'S BRIGHT RED.
YOU'RE FAMOUS, AREN'T YOU DADDY?
HUH?
RUSTLE
THAT MUST BE RANMARU-KUN'S SON…
SNIFF
SNIFF
SNIFFLE
I GUESS IT'S TIME TO THROW IN THE TOWEL.
SOME-ONE FINALLY TAMED HIM.
GOOD BYE.
I ASKED LOTS OF PEOPLE…
EVERYONE KNEW ABOUT YOU, DADDY.
RA-RANMARU! RANMARU!
SHAKE
SHAKE
HUH?
WOW.
HEH… HEH, HEH, HEH, HEH.
WHAT …
…THE HELL ARE YOU TALKING ABOUT?

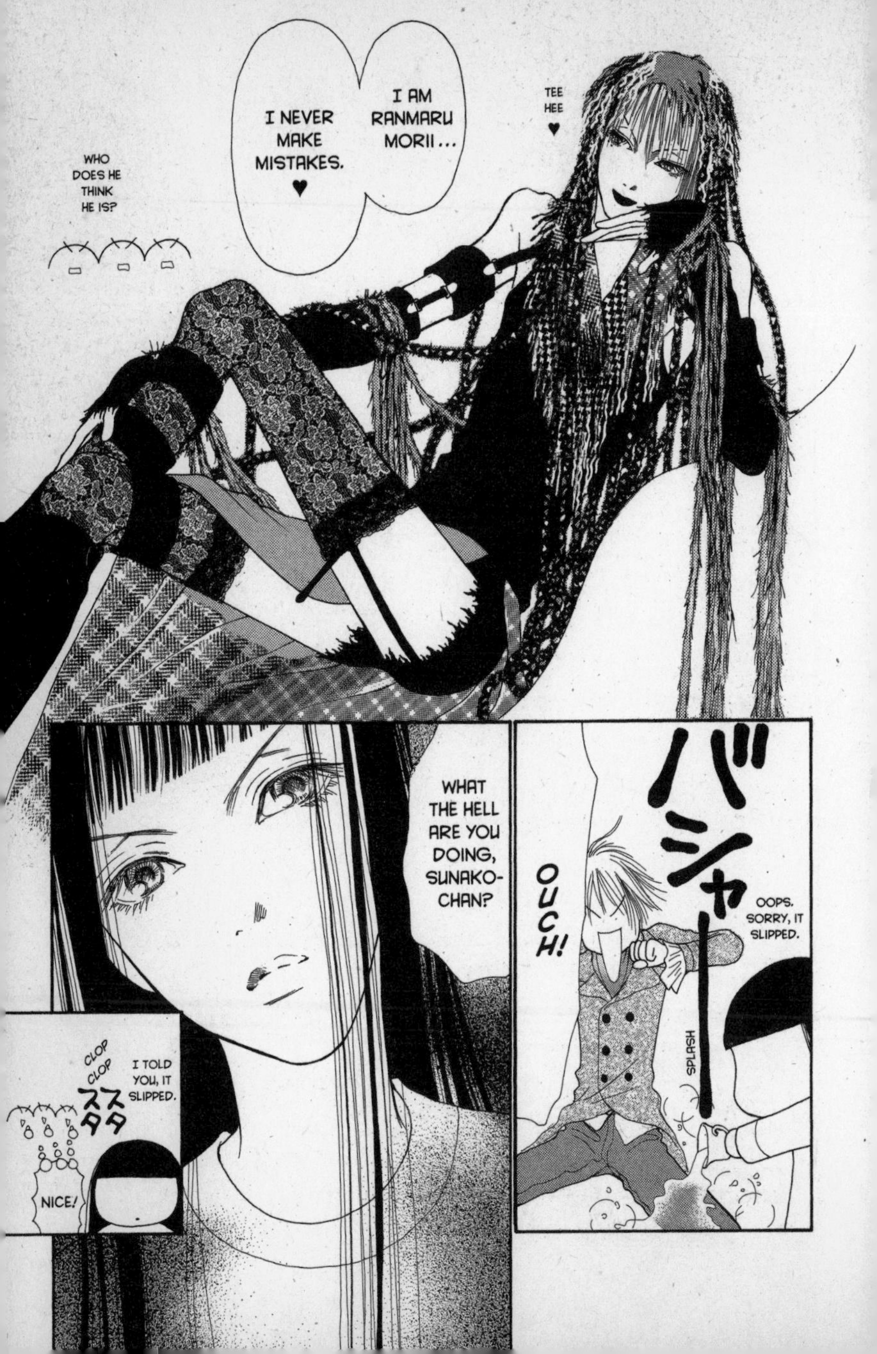
TEE HEE ♥
I AM RANMARU MORII... I NEVER MAKE MISTAKES. ♥
WHO DOES HE THINK HE IS?
バシャー
OOPS. SORRY, IT SLIPPED.
OUCH!
SPLASH
WHAT THE HELL ARE YOU DOING, SUNAKO-CHAN?
I TOLD YOU, IT SLIPPED.
CLOP CLOP
スタスタ
NICE!

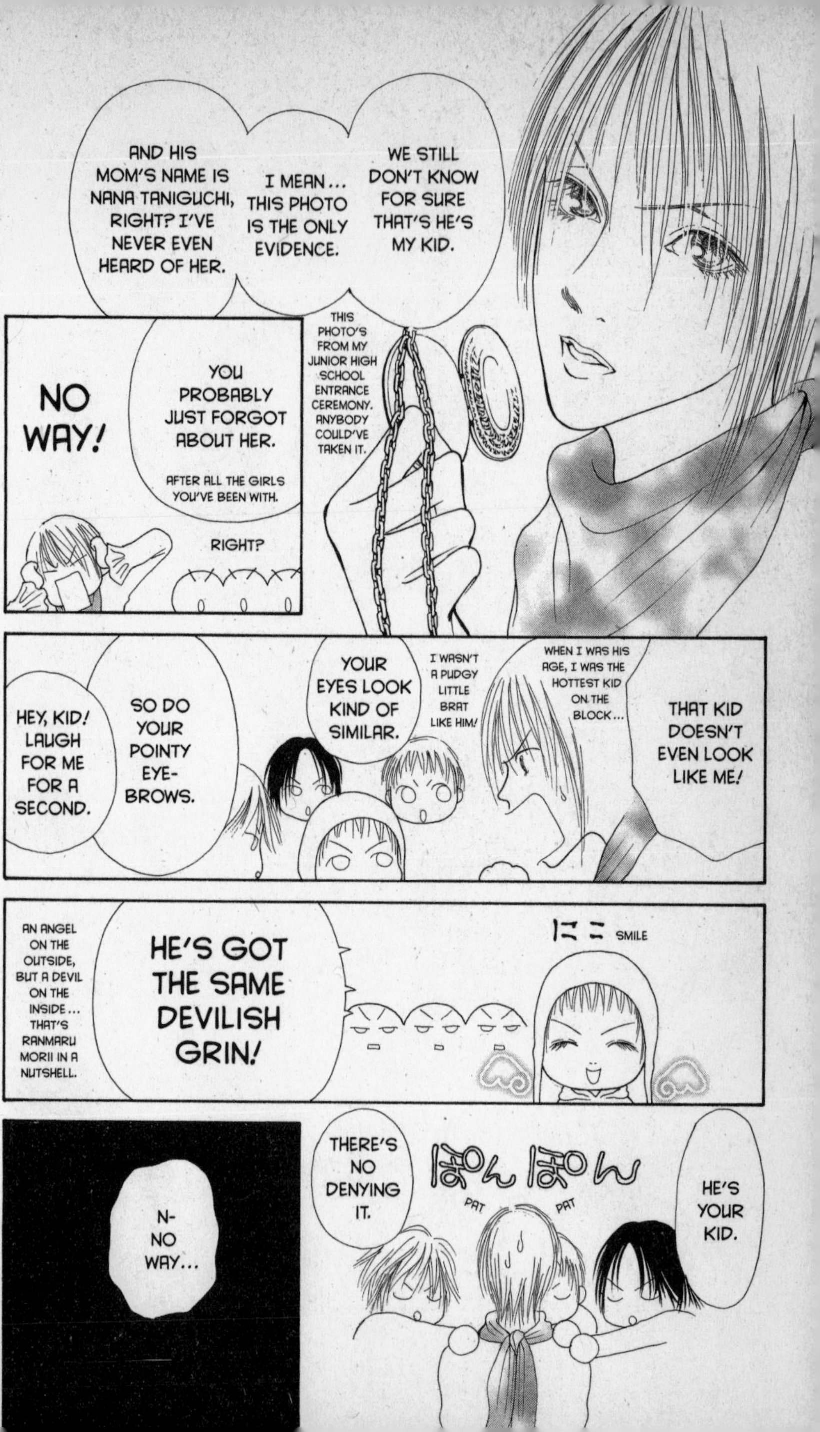
WE STILL DON'T KNOW FOR SURE THAT'S HE'S MY KID.
I MEAN... THIS PHOTO IS THE ONLY EVIDENCE.
AND HIS MOM'S NAME IS NANA TANIGUCHI, RIGHT? I'VE NEVER EVEN HEARD OF HER.
THIS PHOTO'S FROM MY JUNIOR HIGH SCHOOL ENTRANCE CEREMONY. ANYBODY COULD'VE TAKEN IT.
YOU PROBABLY JUST FORGOT ABOUT HER.
AFTER ALL THE GIRLS YOU'VE BEEN WITH.
RIGHT?
NO WAY!
THAT KID DOESN'T EVEN LOOK LIKE ME!
WHEN I WAS HIS AGE, I WAS THE HOTTEST KID ON THE BLOCK...
I WASN'T A PUDGY LITTLE BRAT LIKE HIM!
YOUR EYES LOOK KIND OF SIMILAR.
SO DO YOUR POINTY EYE-BROWS.
HEY, KID! LAUGH FOR ME FOR A SECOND.
にこ SMILE
HE'S GOT THE SAME DEVILISH GRIN!
AN ANGEL ON THE OUTSIDE, BUT A DEVIL ON THE INSIDE... THAT'S RANMARU MORII IN A NUTSHELL.
HE'S YOUR KID.
ぽんぽん
PAT PAT
THERE'S NO DENYING IT.
N- NO WAY...

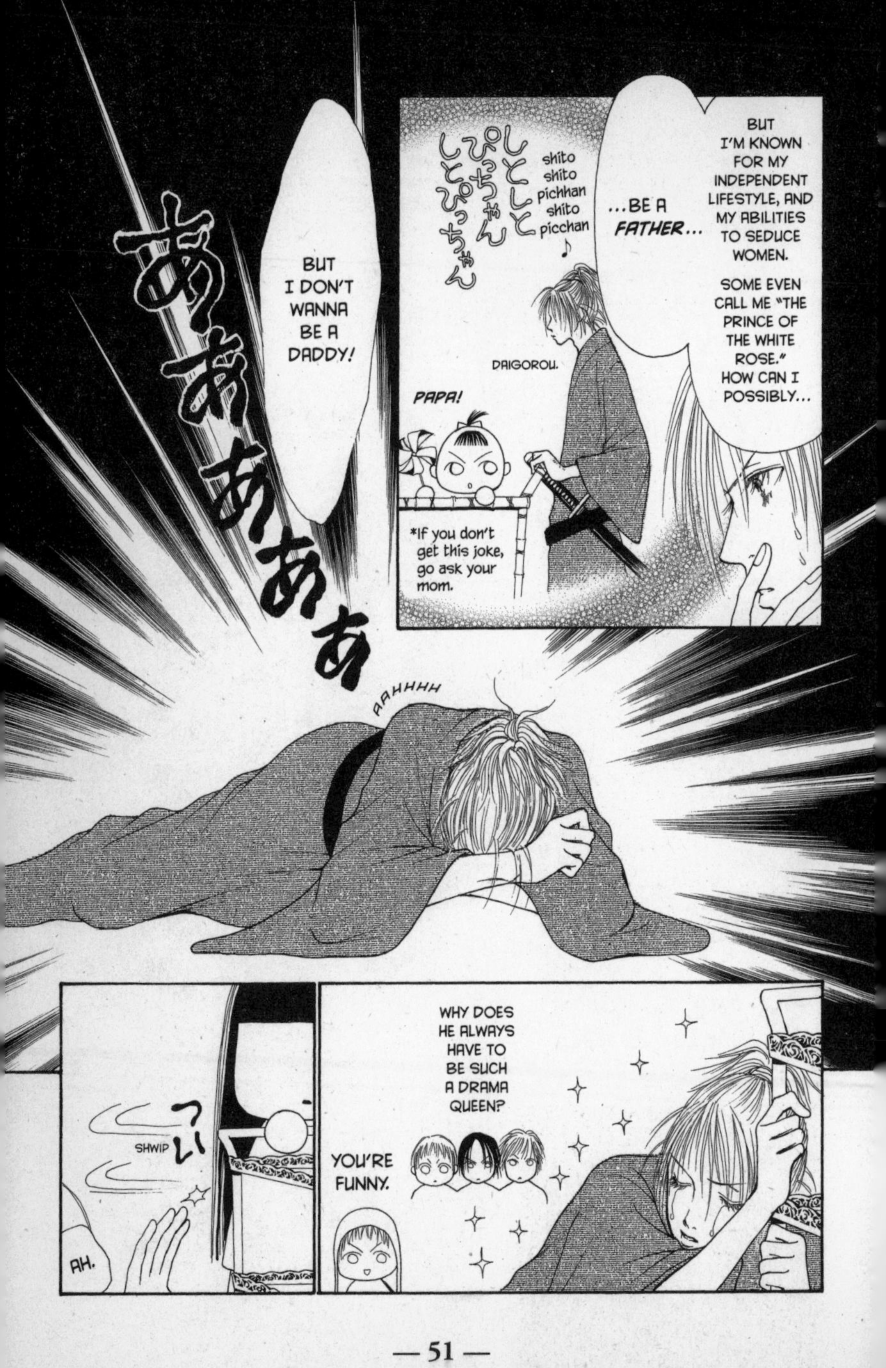

BUT I'M KNOWN FOR MY INDEPENDENT LIFESTYLE, AND MY ABILITIES TO SEDUCE WOMEN.
SOME EVEN CALL ME "THE PRINCE OF THE WHITE ROSE." HOW CAN I POSSIBLY...
...BE A FATHER...
しとしとぴっちゃんしとぴっちゃん
shito shito pichhan shito picchan ♪
DAIGOROU.
PAPA!
*If you don't get this joke, go ask your mom.
BUT I DON'T WANNA BE A DADDY!
あああああ
AAHHHH
WHY DOES HE ALWAYS HAVE TO BE SUCH A DRAMA QUEEN?
YOU'RE FUNNY.
つい
SHWIP
AH.

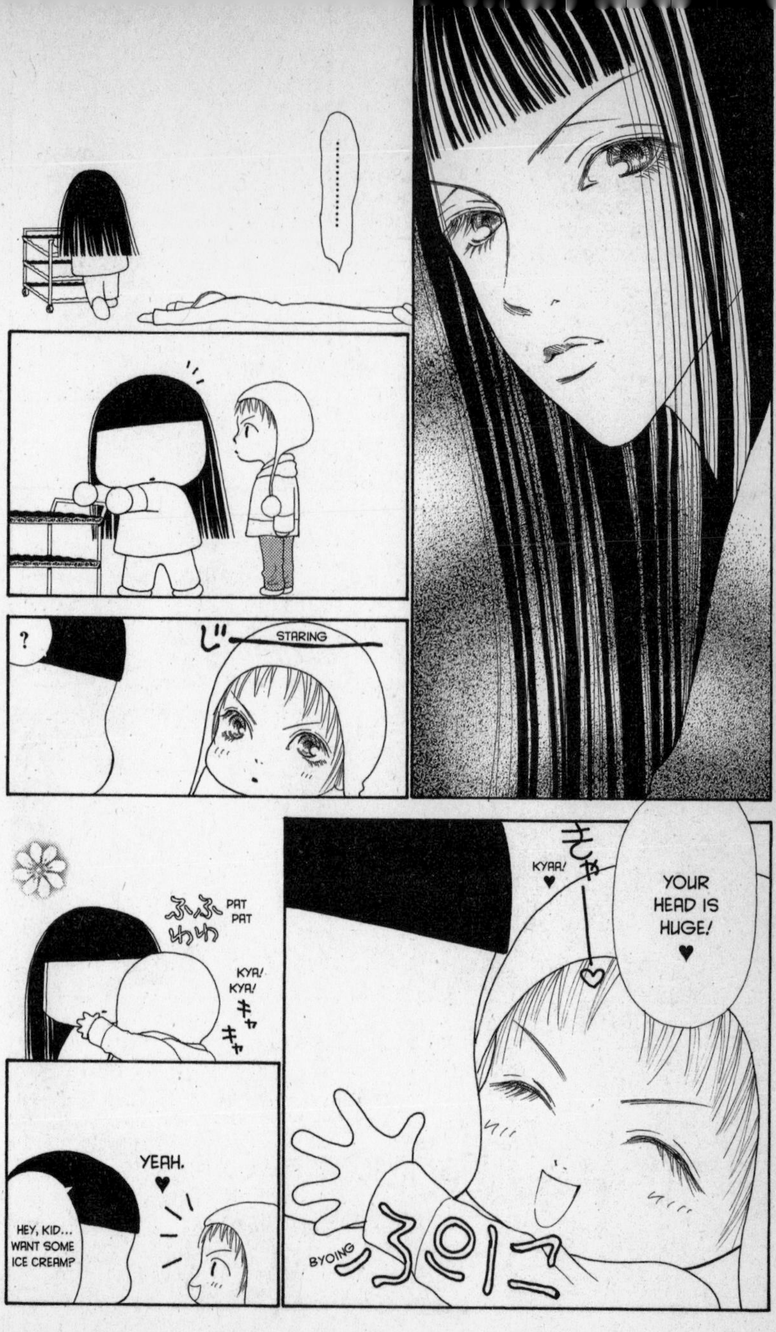
……
?
じ
STARING
KYAA! ♥
YOUR HEAD IS HUGE! ♥
BYOING
PAT PAT
KYA! KYA!
キャキャ
HEY, KID... WANT SOME ICE CREAM?
YEAH. ♥

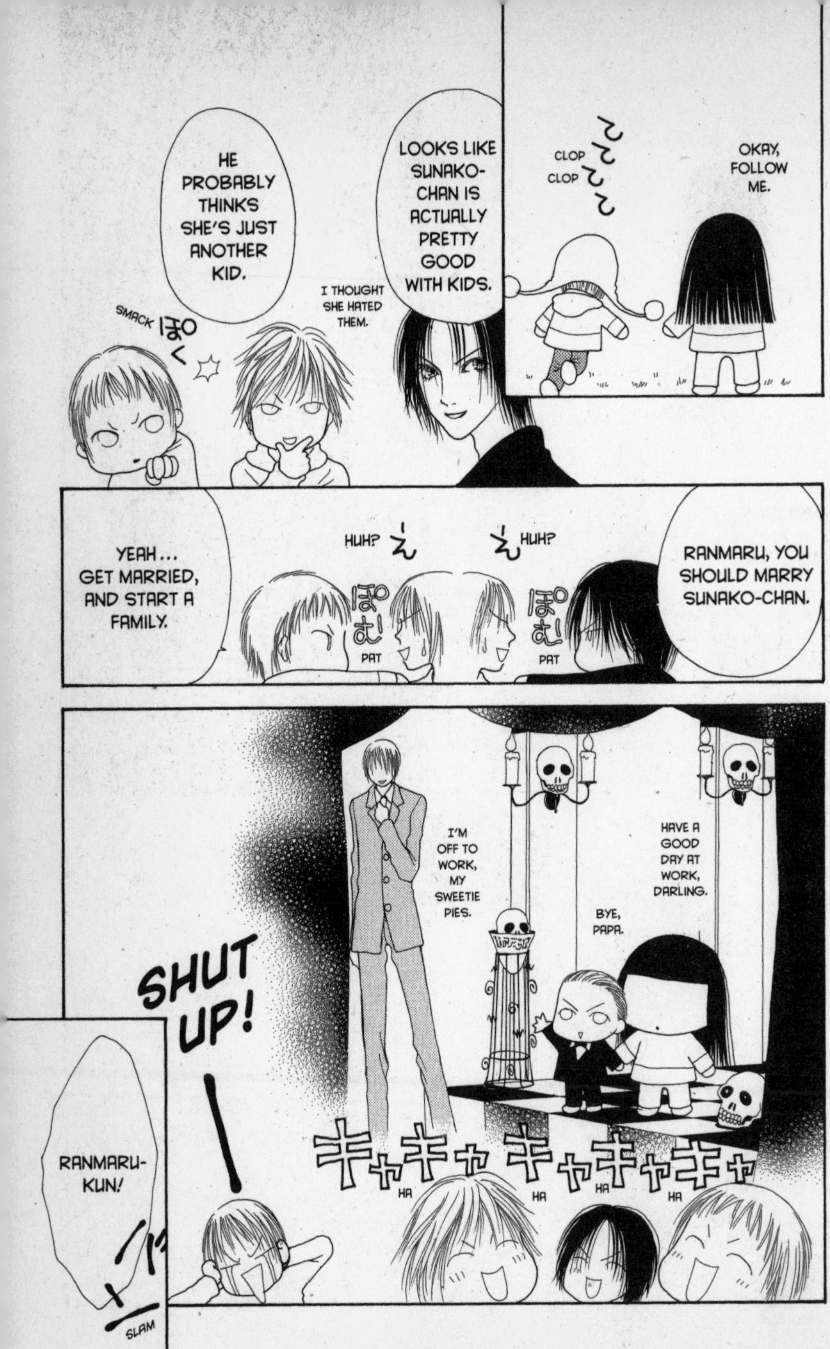
OKAY, FOLLOW ME.
CLOP CLOP
てててて
LOOKS LIKE SUNAKO-CHAN IS ACTUALLY PRETTY GOOD WITH KIDS.
I THOUGHT SHE HATED THEM.
HE PROBABLY THINKS SHE'S JUST ANOTHER KID.
SMACK ぽく
RANMARU, YOU SHOULD MARRY SUNAKO-CHAN.
HUH? え
え HUH?
ぽむ PAT
ぽむ PAT
YEAH... GET MARRIED, AND START A FAMILY.
HAVE A GOOD DAY AT WORK, DARLING.
BYE, PAPA.
I'M OFF TO WORK, MY SWEETIE PIES.
キャキャ キャキャキャ
HA HA HA HA
SHUT UP!
RANMARU-KUN!
SLAM

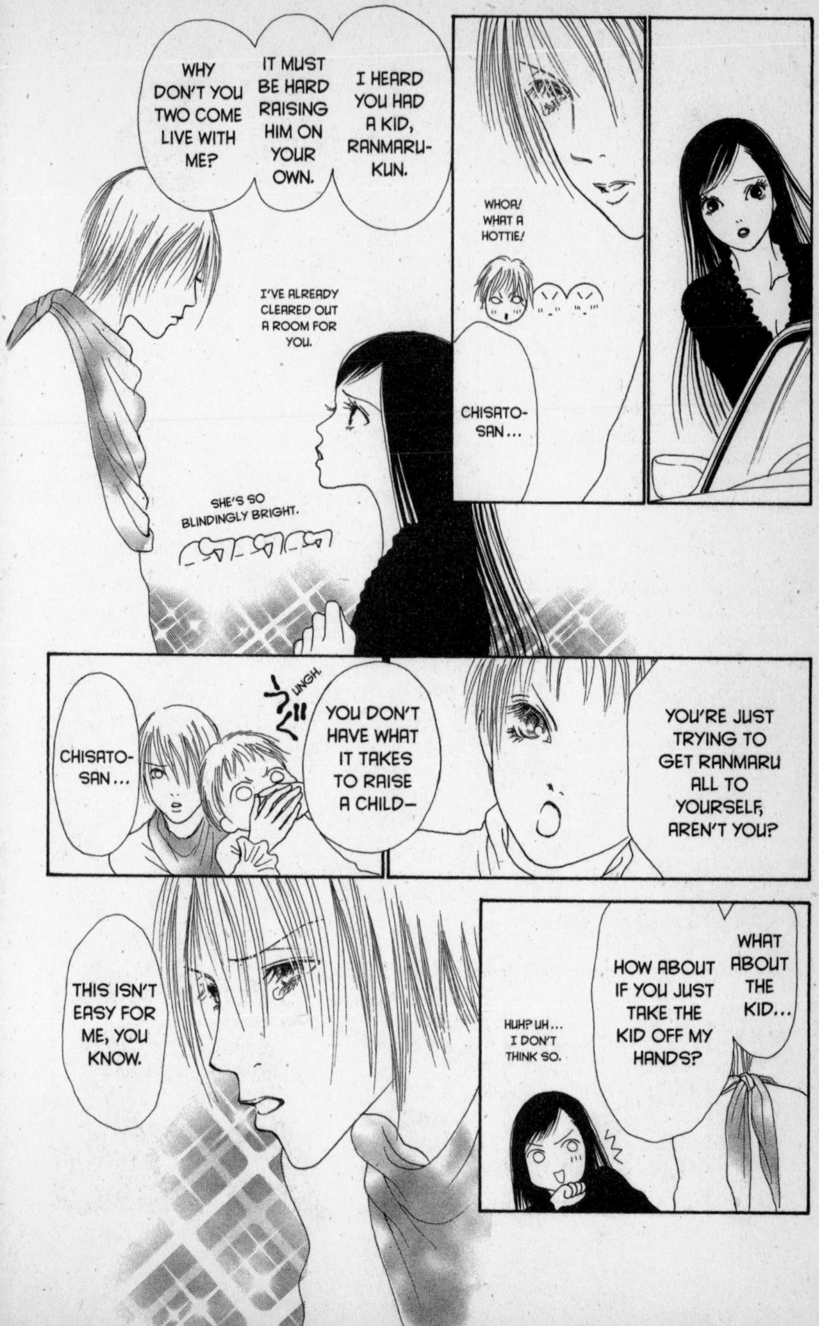
WHOA! WHAT A HOTTIE!
CHISATO-SAN...
I HEARD YOU HAD A KID, RANMARU-KUN.
IT MUST BE HARD RAISING HIM ON YOUR OWN.
WHY DON'T YOU TWO COME LIVE WITH ME?
I'VE ALREADY CLEARED OUT A ROOM FOR YOU.
SHE'S SO BLINDINGLY BRIGHT.
YOU'RE JUST TRYING TO GET RANMARU ALL TO YOURSELF, AREN'T YOU?
UNGH.
YOU DON'T HAVE WHAT IT TAKES TO RAISE A CHILD—
CHISATO-SAN...
WHAT ABOUT THE KID...
HOW ABOUT IF YOU JUST TAKE THE KID OFF MY HANDS?
HUH? UH... I DON'T THINK SO.
THIS ISN'T EASY FOR ME, YOU KNOW.

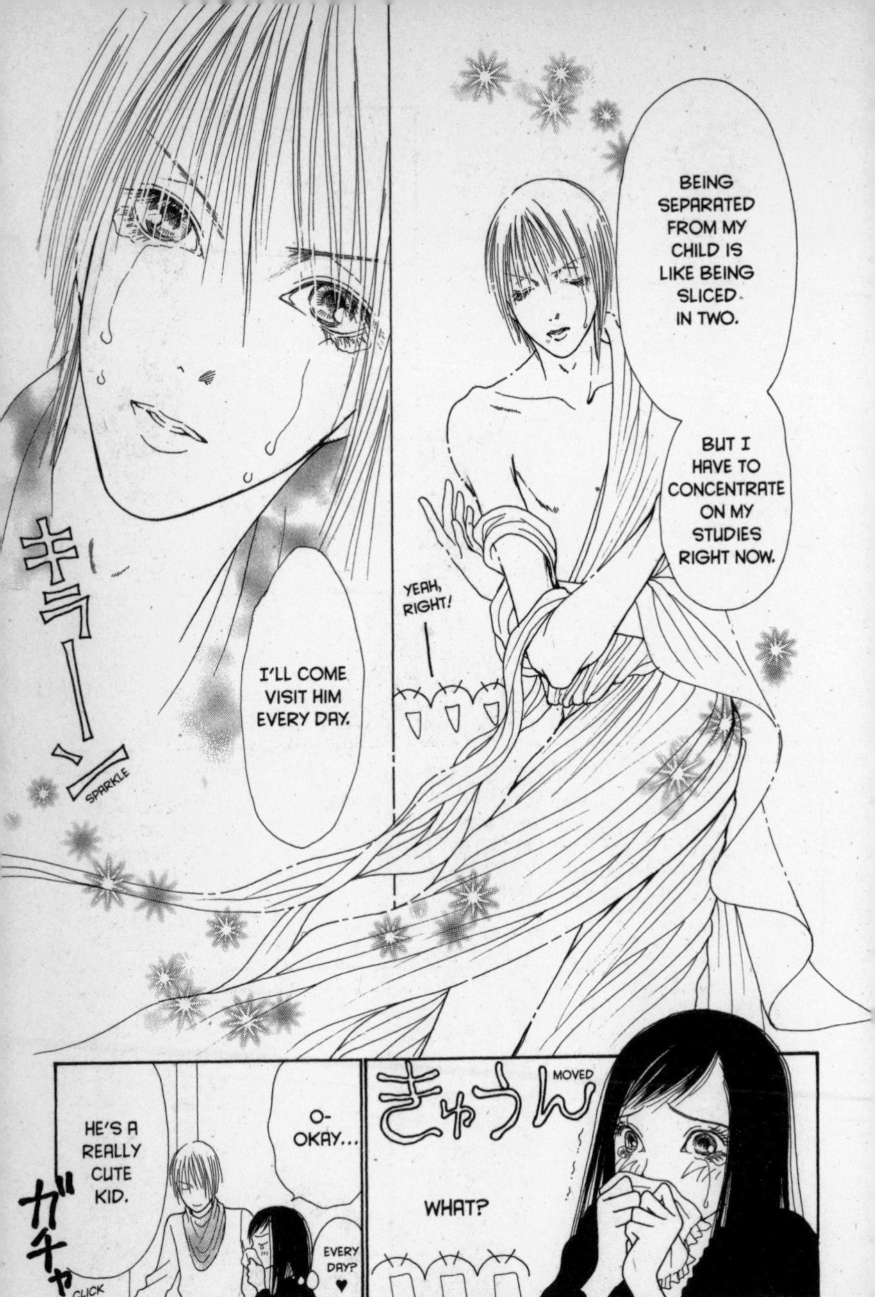
BEING SEPARATED FROM MY CHILD IS LIKE BEING SLICED IN TWO.
BUT I HAVE TO CONCENTRATE ON MY STUDIES RIGHT NOW.
YEAH, RIGHT!
I'LL COME VISIT HIM EVERY DAY.
キラーン
SPARKLE
きゅうん
MOVED
WHAT?
O-OKAY...
EVERY DAY? ♥
HE'S A REALLY CUTE KID.
ガチャ
CLICK

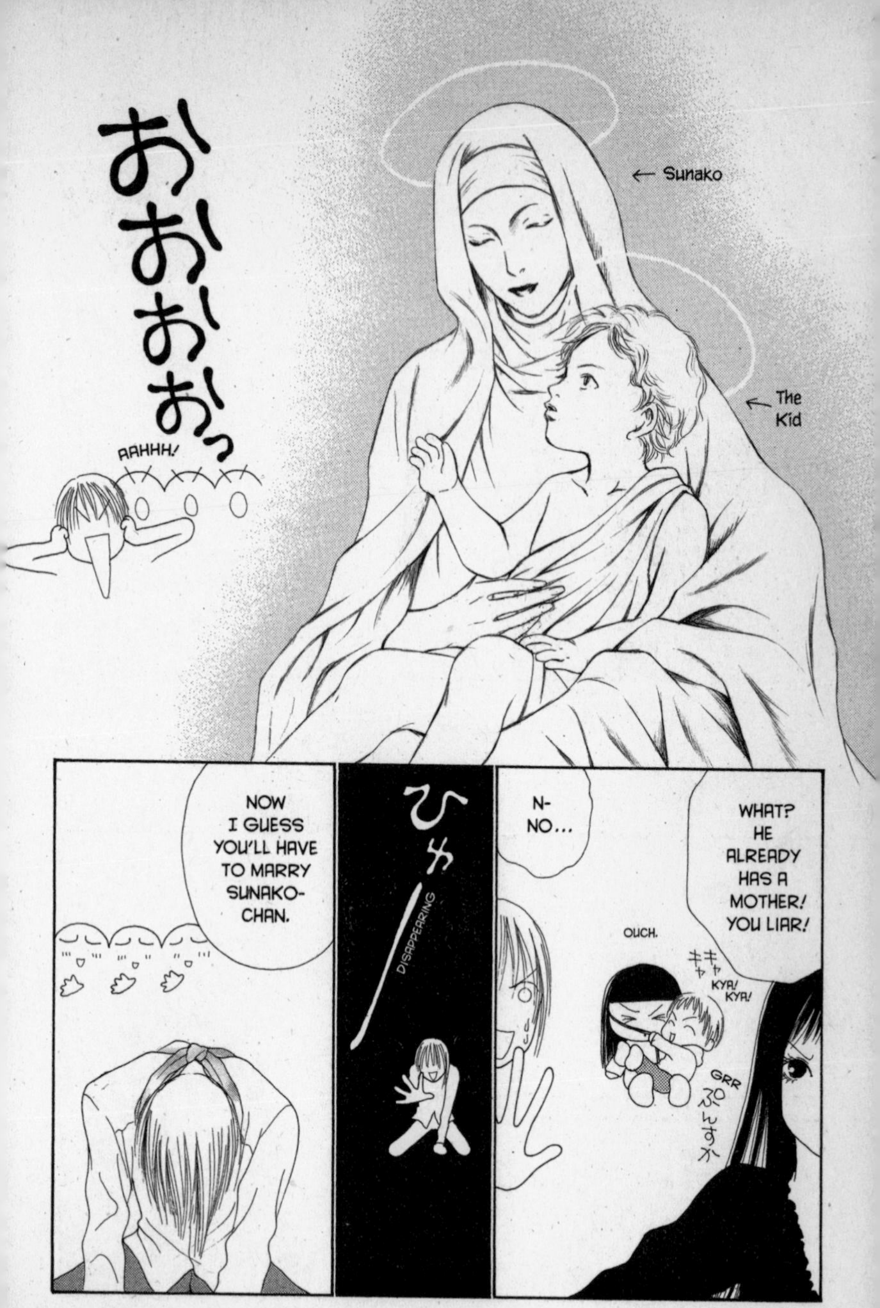
おおおおっ
AAHHH!
← Sunako
← The Kid
WHAT? HE ALREADY HAS A MOTHER! YOU LIAR!
N- NO...
OUCH.
キャ キャ
KYA! KYA!
GRR
ぷんすか
ひゅ
DISAPPEARING
NOW I GUESS YOU'LL HAVE TO MARRY SUNAKO-CHAN.

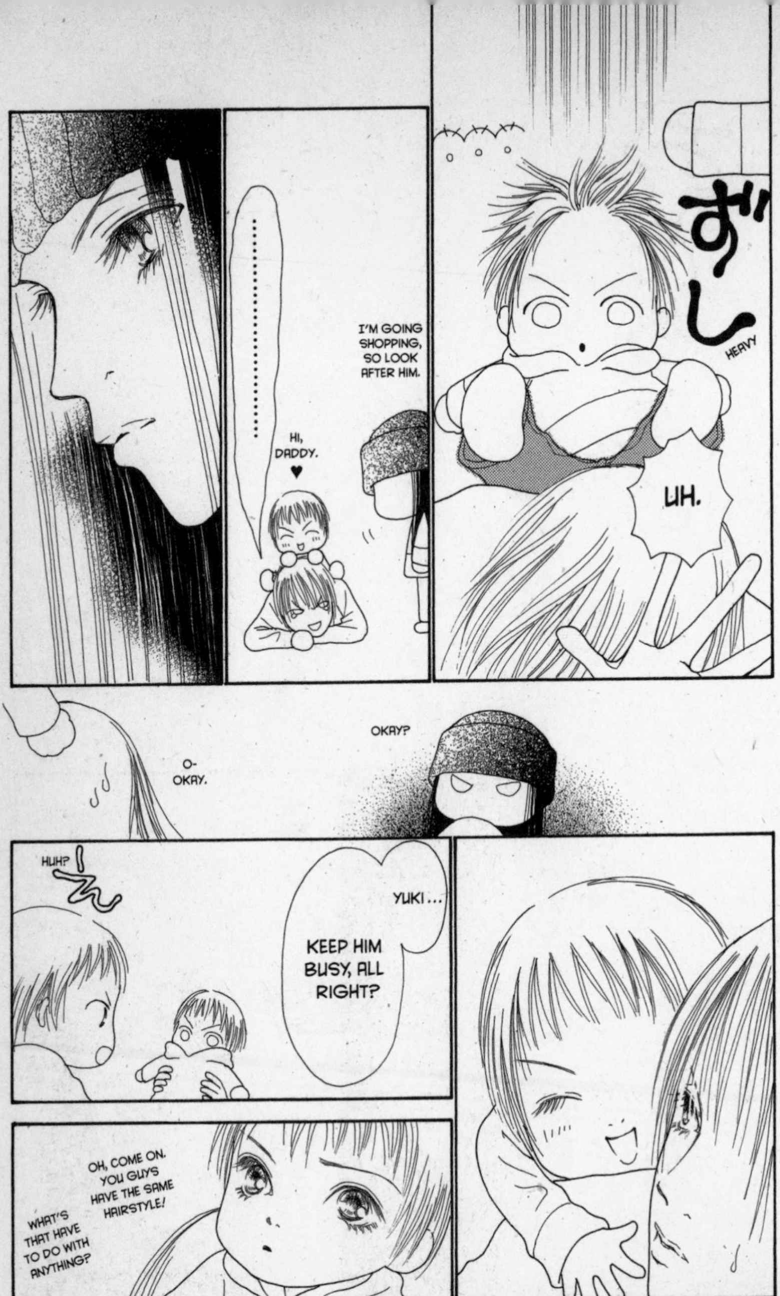
ずし
HEAVY
UH.
I'M GOING SHOPPING, SO LOOK AFTER HIM.
HI, DADDY. ♥
....
OKAY?
O- OKAY.
YUKI...
KEEP HIM BUSY, ALL RIGHT?
え
HUH?
OH, COME ON. YOU GUYS HAVE THE SAME HAIRSTYLE!
WHAT'S THAT HAVE TO DO WITH ANYTHING?

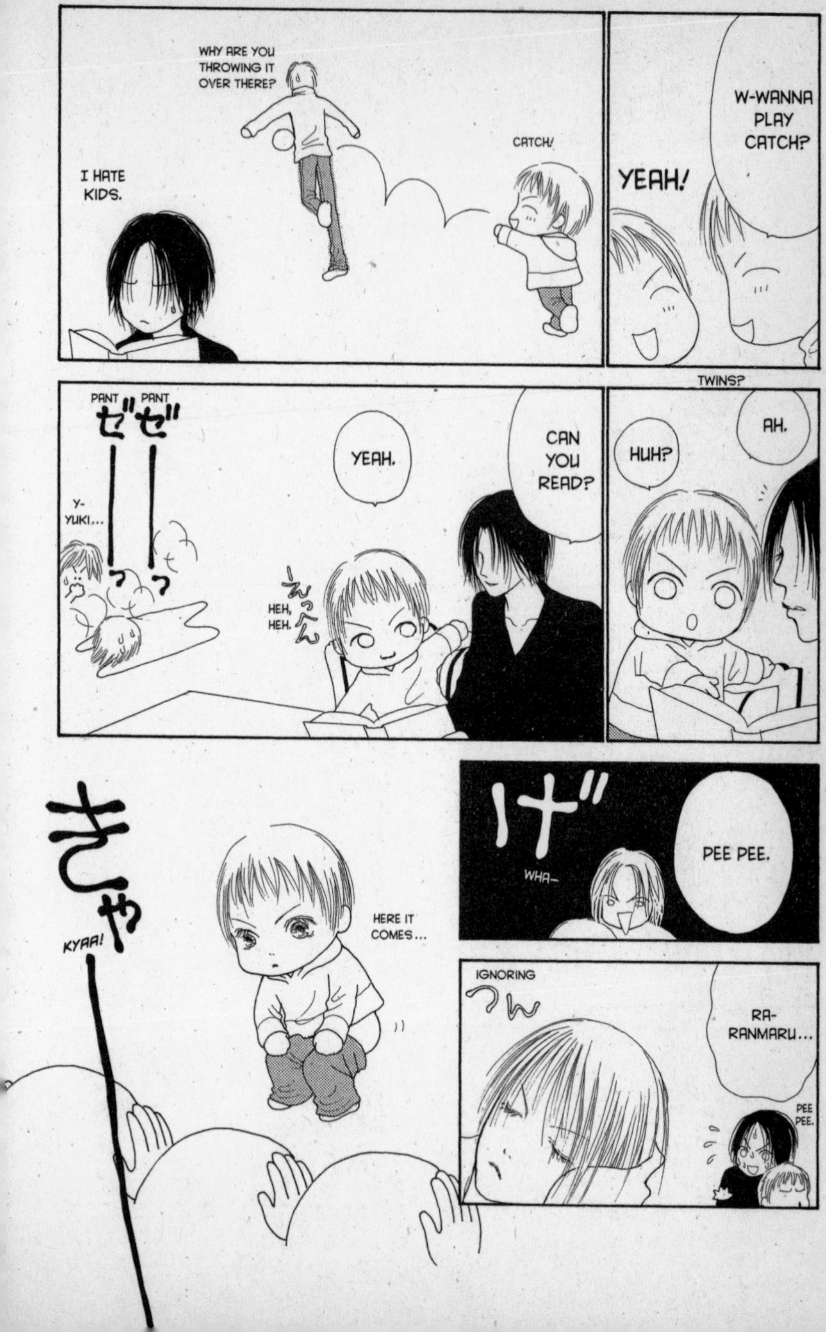
W-WANNA PLAY CATCH?
YEAH!
CATCH!
WHY ARE YOU THROWING IT OVER THERE?
I HATE KIDS.
TWINS?
AH.
HUH?
CAN YOU READ?
YEAH.
えっへん
HEH, HEH.
ゼー ゼー
PANT PANT
Y-YUKI...
PEE PEE.
ゲ
WHA-
RA-RANMARU...
つん
IGNORING
PEE PEE.
HERE IT COMES...
きゃー
KYAA!

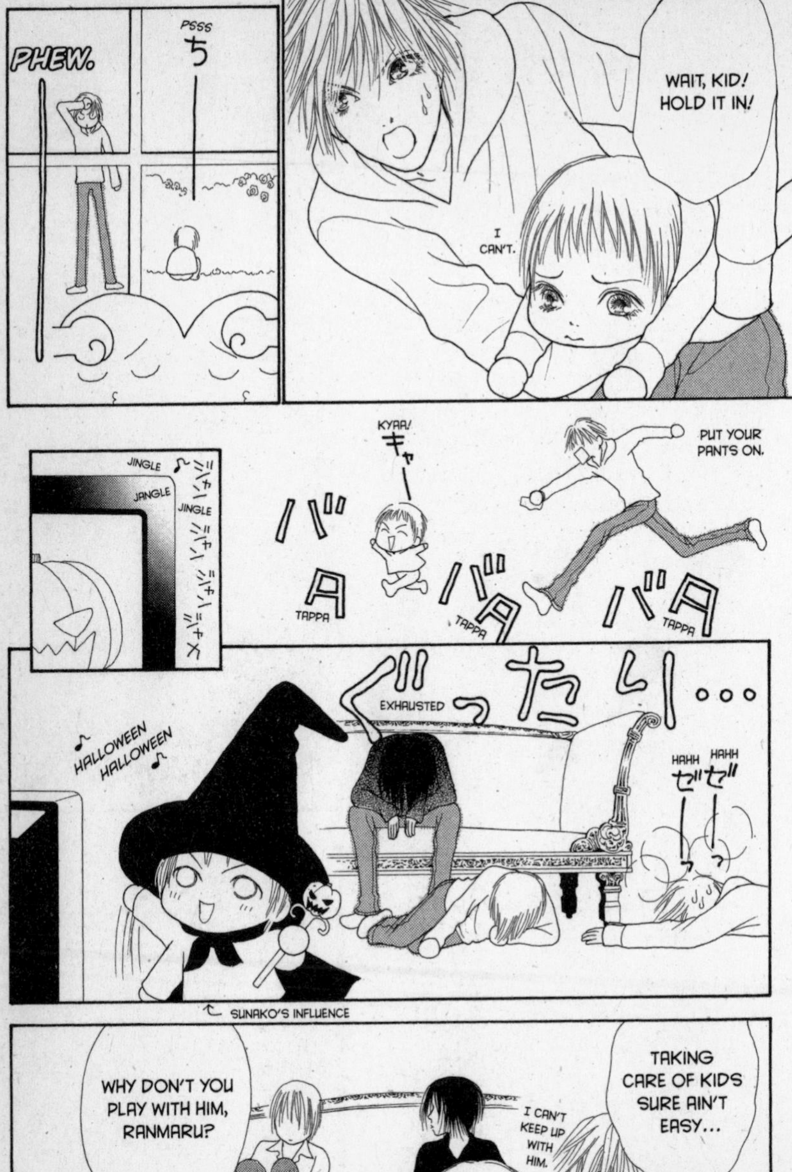
WAIT, KID! HOLD IT IN!
I CAN'T.
PSSS
ち
PHEW.
KYAA!
キャー
PUT YOUR PANTS ON.
バタ
TAPPA
バタ
TAPPA
バタ
TAPPA
JINGLE
JANGLE
JINGLE
ぐったり…
EXHAUSTED
HAHH HAHH
ぜぜ
HALLOWEEN HALLOWEEN
SUNAKO'S INFLUENCE
TAKING CARE OF KIDS SURE AIN'T EASY…
I CAN'T KEEP UP WITH HIM.
WHY DON'T YOU PLAY WITH HIM, RANMARU?

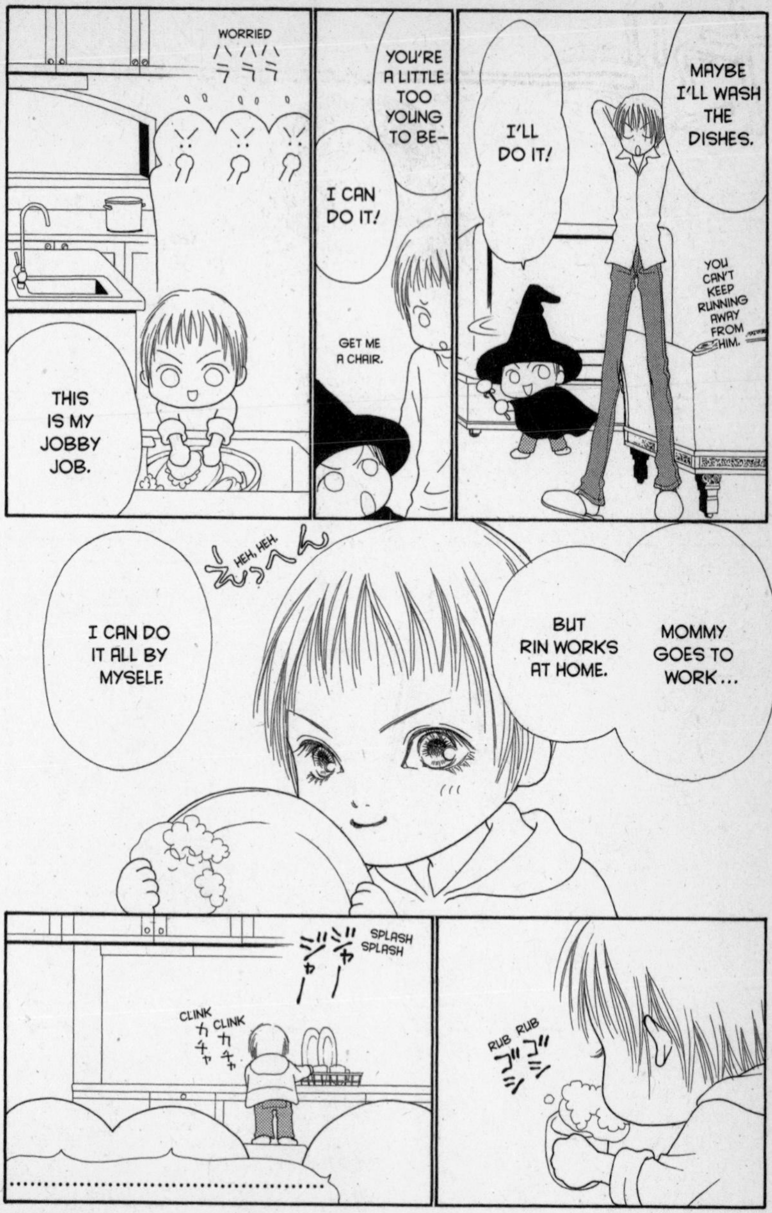
MAYBE I'LL WASH THE DISHES.
I'LL DO IT!
YOU CAN'T KEEP RUNNING AWAY FROM HIM.
YOU'RE A LITTLE TOO YOUNG TO BE—
I CAN DO IT!
GET ME A CHAIR.
WORRIED
ハラハラハラ
THIS IS MY JOBBY JOB.
MOMMY GOES TO WORK...
BUT RIN WORKS AT HOME.
HEH, HEH.
えっへん
I CAN DO IT ALL BY MYSELF.
RUB RUB
ゴシゴシ
SPLASH SPLASH
ジャージャー
CLINK CLINK
カチャカチャ
....

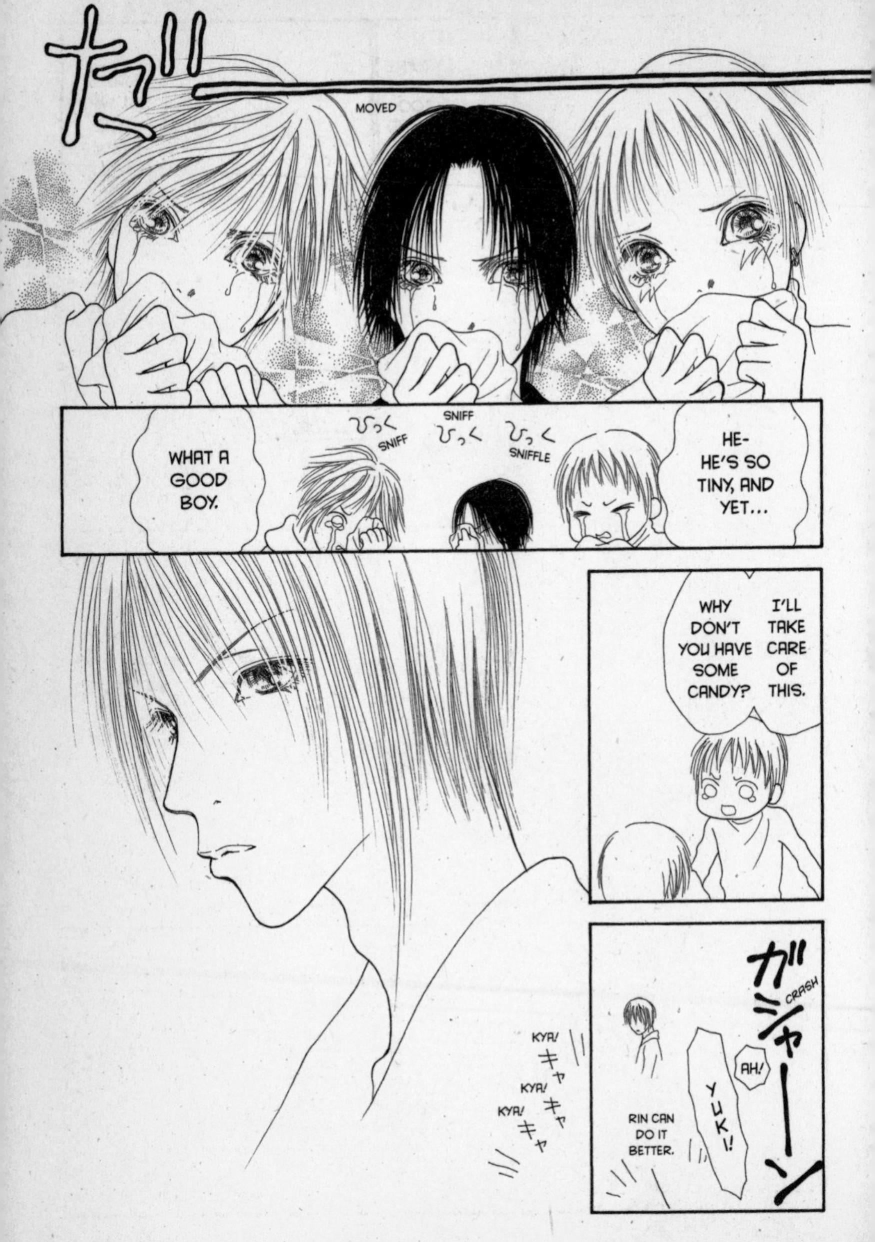

MOVED
HE- HE'S SO TINY, AND YET…
ひっく SNIFFLE
ひっく SNIFF
ひっく SNIFF
WHAT A GOOD BOY.
I'LL TAKE CARE OF THIS.
WHY DON'T YOU HAVE SOME CANDY?
ガシャーン CRASH
AH!
YUKI!
RIN CAN DO IT BETTER.
KYA! キャ
KYA! キャ
KYA! キャ

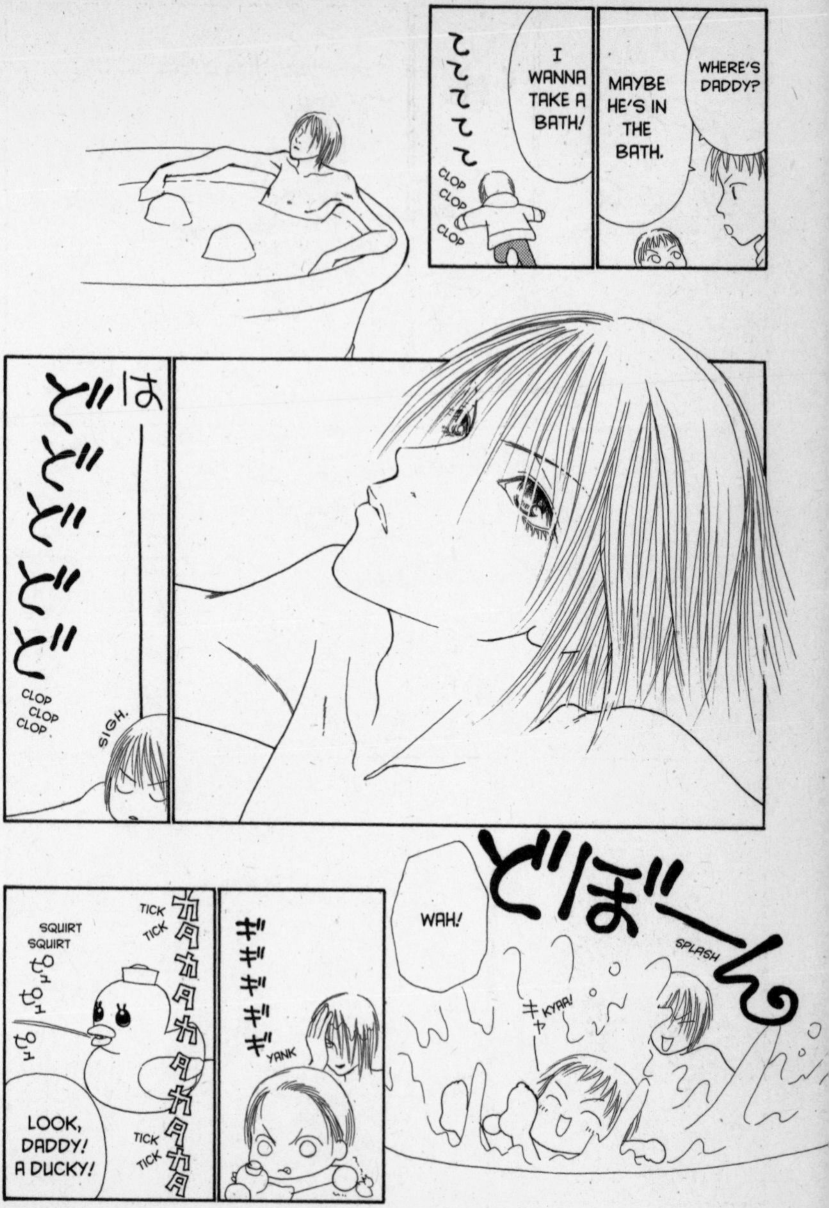
WHERE'S DADDY?
MAYBE HE'S IN THE BATH.
I WANNA TAKE A BATH!
てててててて
CLOP CLOP CLOP
はー
SIGH.
どどどどど
CLOP CLOP CLOP
どぼーん
SPLASH
WAH!
キャ
KYAA!
ギギギギギ
YANK
カタカタカタカタ
TICK TICK
TICK TICK
ピュピュピュ
SQUIRT SQUIRT
LOOK, DADDY! A DUCKY!

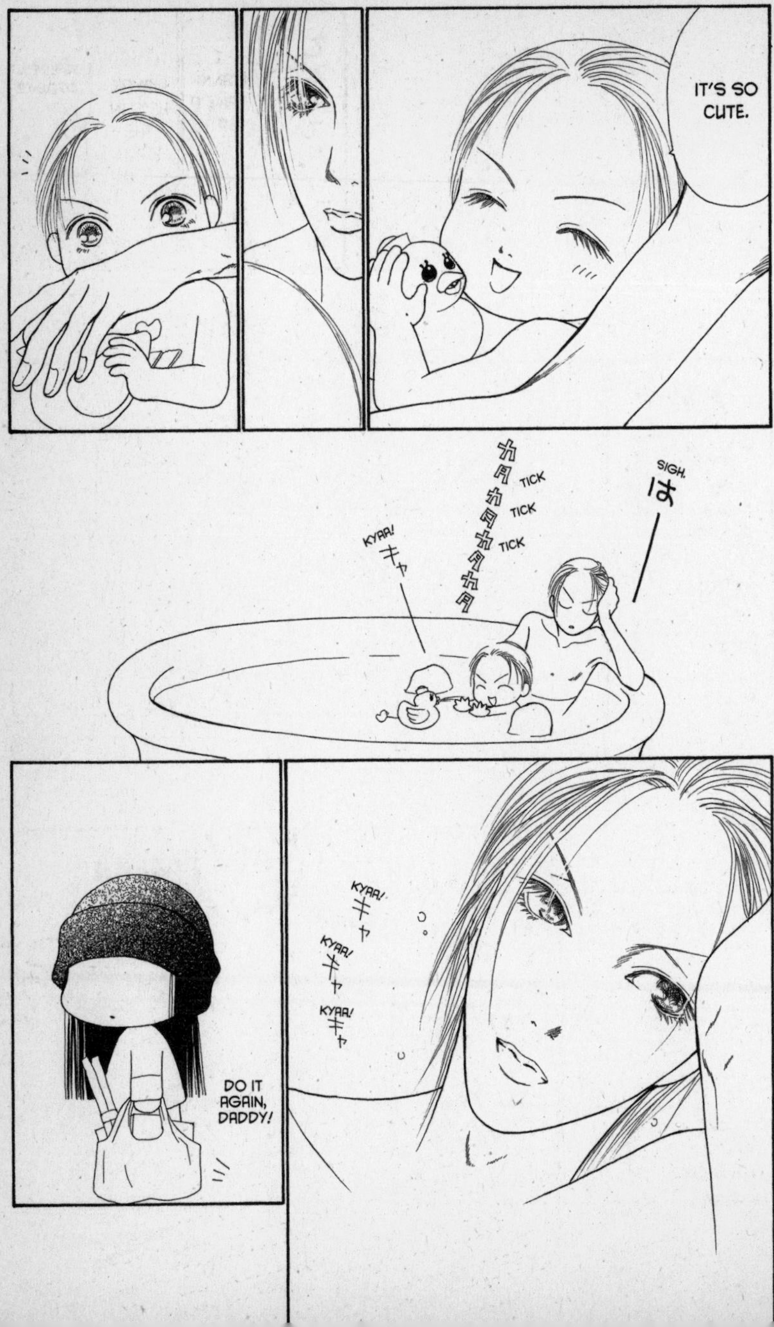
IT'S SO CUTE.
SIGH.
はー
カタカタカタカタカタ
TICK
TICK
TICK
KYAA!
キャー
KYAA!
キャ
KYAA!
キャ
KYAA!
キャ
DO IT AGAIN, DADDY!

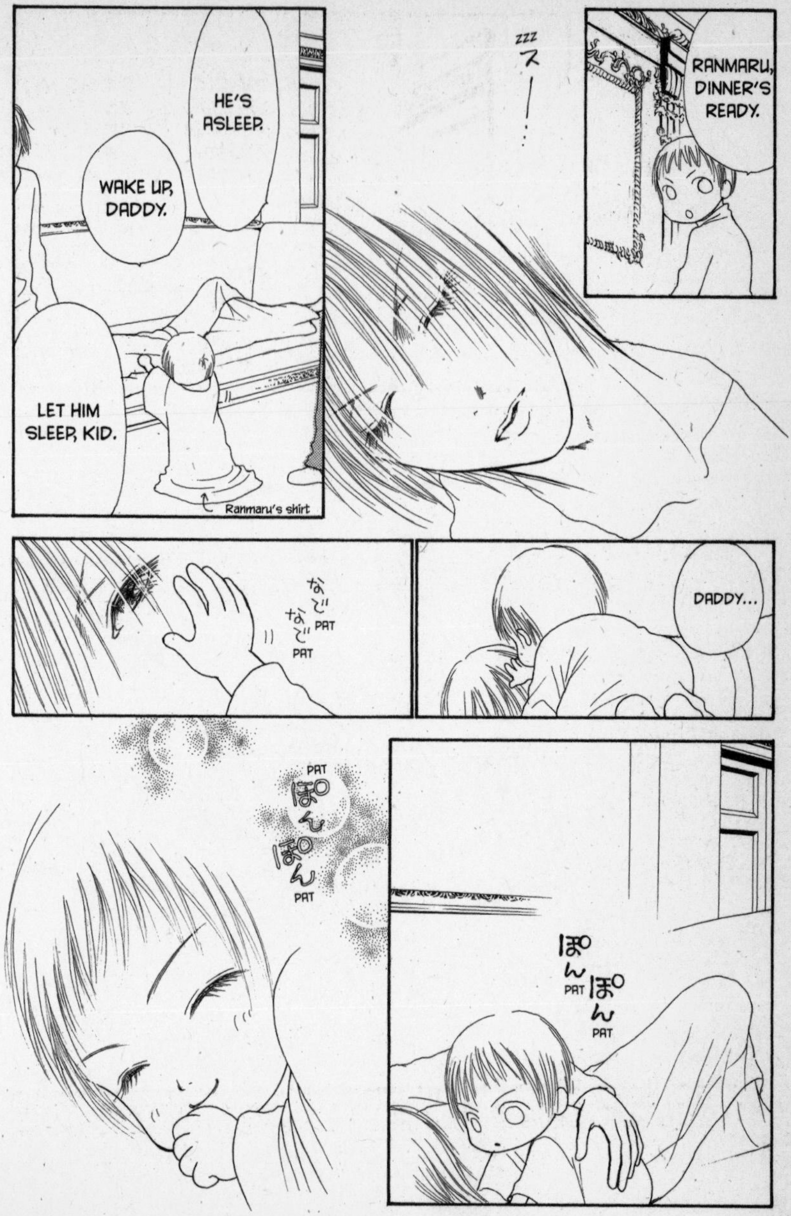
RANMARU, DINNER'S READY.
zzz
スー…
HE'S ASLEEP.
WAKE UP, DADDY.
LET HIM SLEEP, KID.
Ranmaru's shirt
DADDY...
なでなで PAT PAT
ぽんぽん PAT PAT
PAT ぽんぽん PAT

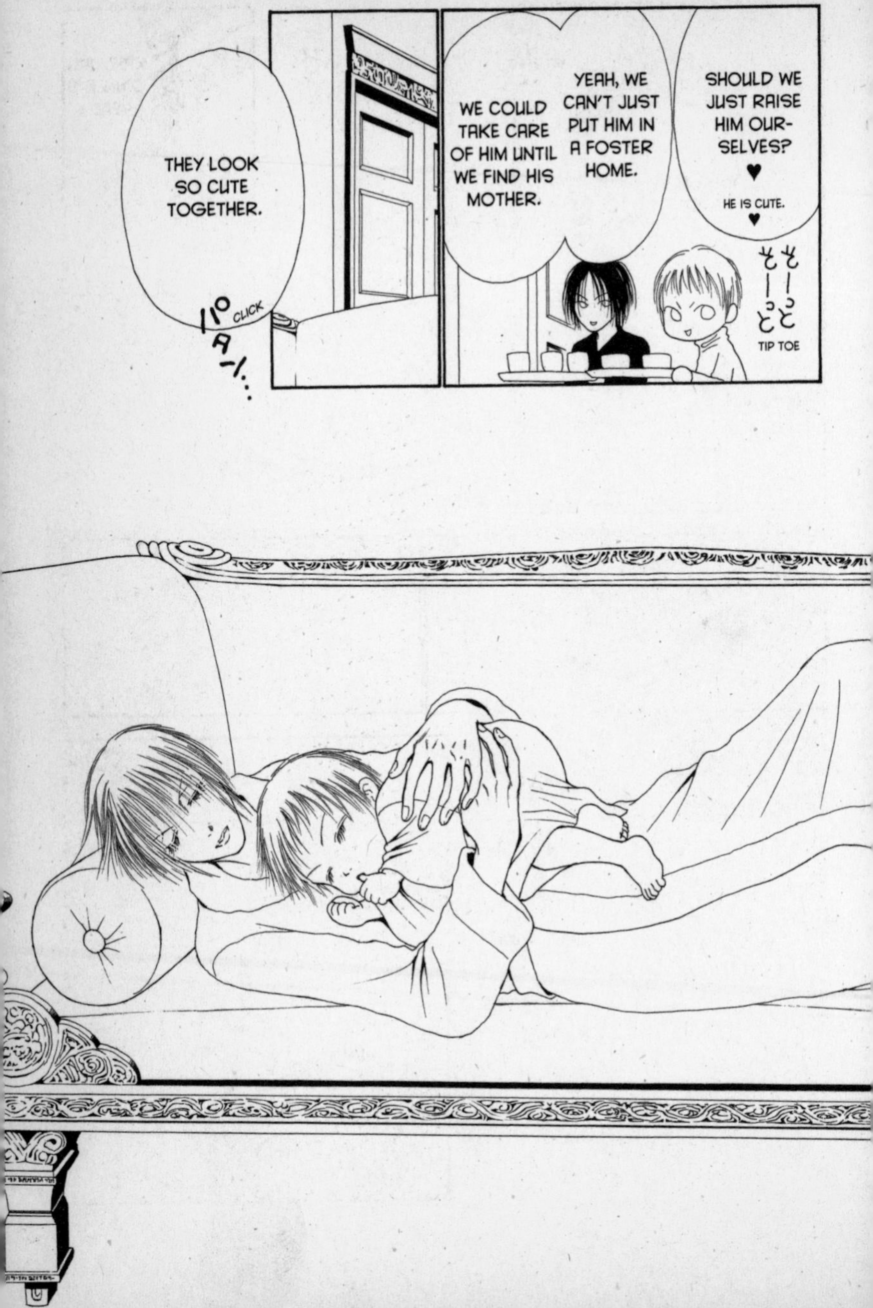
SHOULD WE JUST RAISE HIM OUR-SELVES? ♥
HE IS CUTE. ♥
YEAH, WE CAN'T JUST PUT HIM IN A FOSTER HOME.
WE COULD TAKE CARE OF HIM UNTIL WE FIND HIS MOTHER.
そーっと そーっと
TIP TOE
THEY LOOK SO CUTE TOGETHER.
パターン…
CLICK

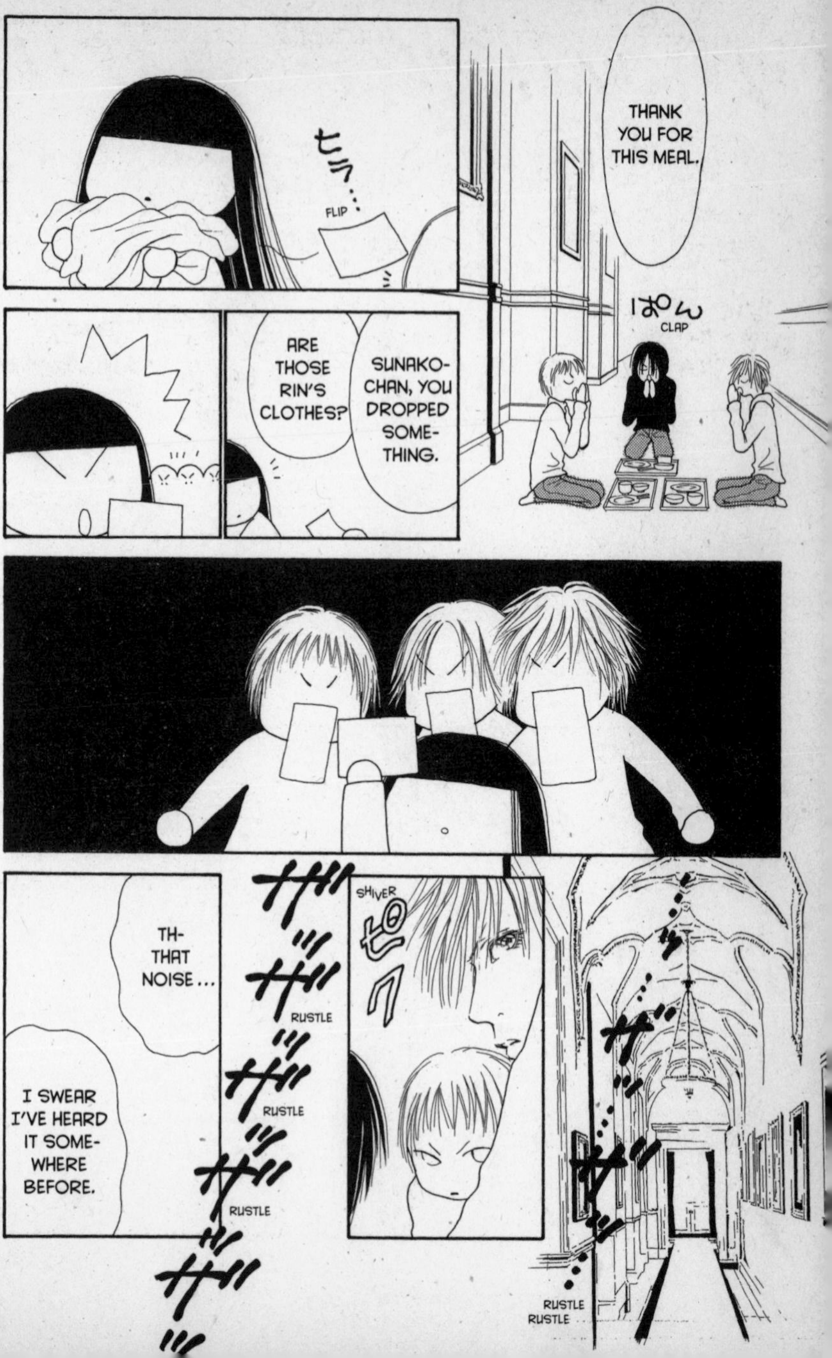
THANK YOU FOR THIS MEAL.
CLAP
FLIP
SUNAKO-CHAN, YOU DROPPED SOMETHING.
ARE THOSE RIN'S CLOTHES?
RUSTLE
RUSTLE
SHIVER
RUSTLE
RUSTLE
RUSTLE
TH-THAT NOISE...
I SWEAR I'VE HEARD IT SOMEWHERE BEFORE.

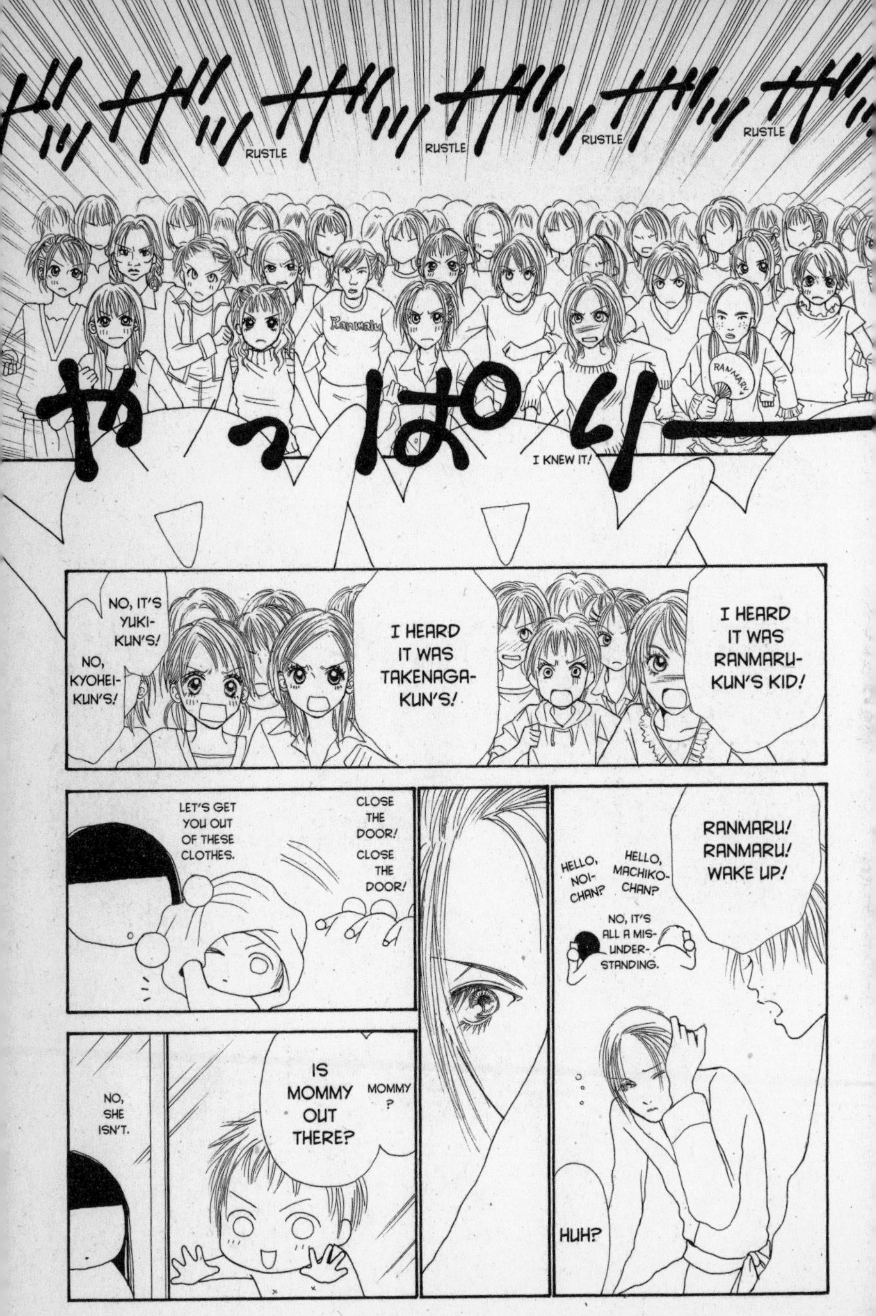
RUSTLE
RUSTLE
RUSTLE
RUSTLE
I KNEW IT!
I HEARD IT WAS RANMARU-KUN'S KID!
I HEARD IT WAS TAKENAGA-KUN'S!
NO, IT'S YUKI-KUN'S!
NO, KYOHEI-KUN'S!
RANMARU! RANMARU! WAKE UP!
HELLO, MACHIKO-CHAN?
HELLO, NOI-CHAN?
NO, IT'S ALL A MIS-UNDER-STANDING.
HUH?
CLOSE THE DOOR! CLOSE THE DOOR!
LET'S GET YOU OUT OF THESE CLOTHES.
MOMMY?
IS MOMMY OUT THERE?
NO, SHE ISN'T.

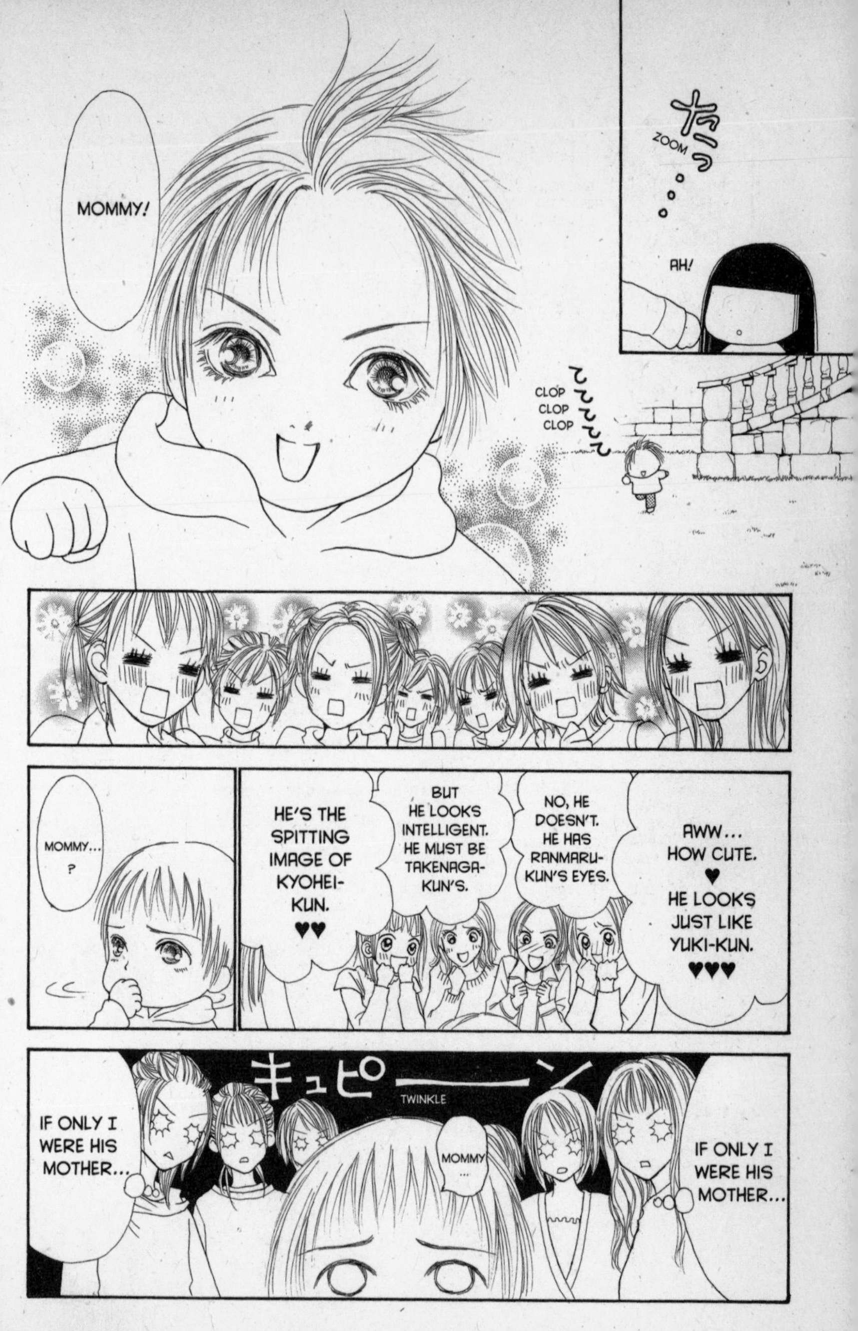

タタッ
ZOOM
AH!
てててて
CLOP
CLOP
CLOP
MOMMY!
AWW... HOW CUTE. ♥ HE LOOKS JUST LIKE YUKI-KUN. ♥♥♥
NO, HE DOESN'T. HE HAS RANMARU-KUN'S EYES.
BUT HE LOOKS INTELLIGENT. HE MUST BE TAKENAGA-KUN'S.
HE'S THE SPITTING IMAGE OF KYOHEI-KUN. ♥♥
MOMMY...?
IF ONLY I WERE HIS MOTHER...
キュピーーン
TWINKLE
MOMMY...
IF ONLY I WERE HIS MOTHER...

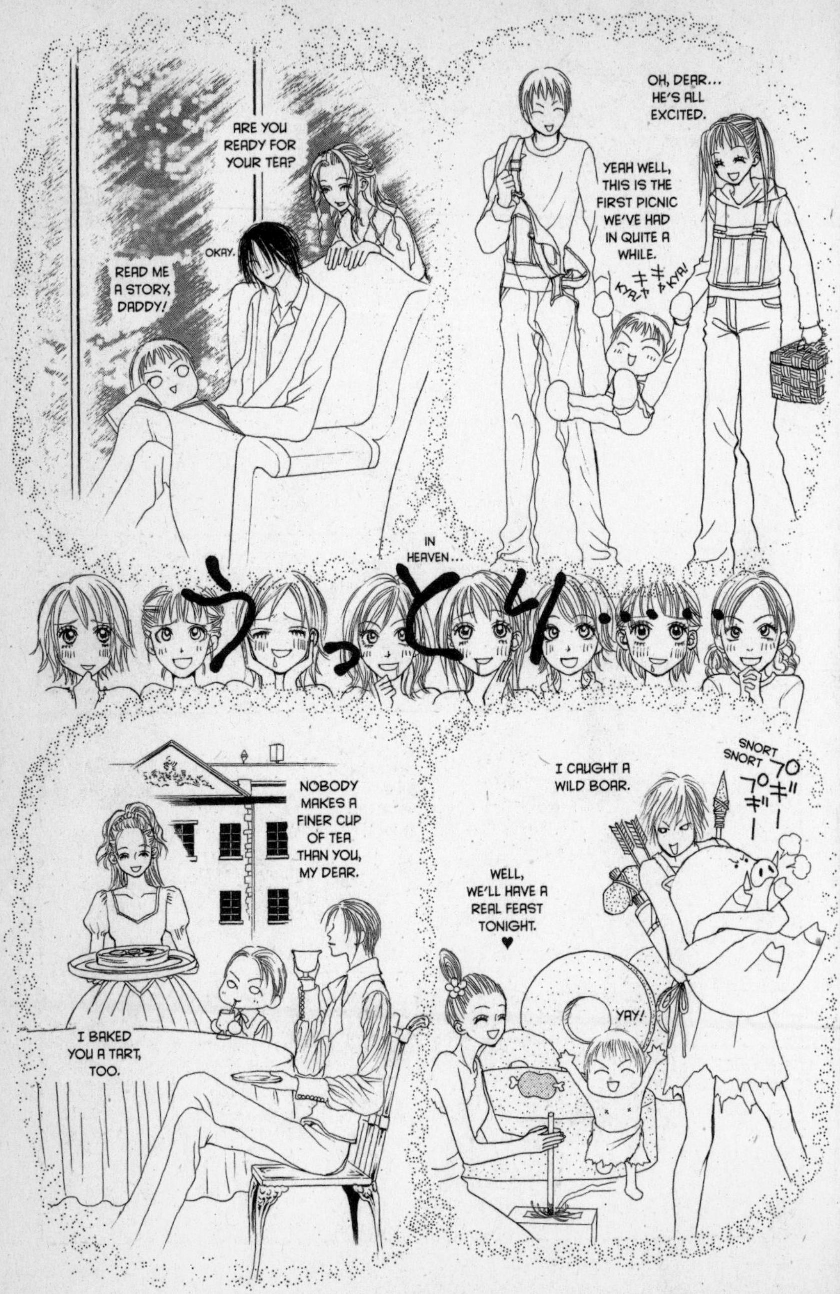
OH, DEAR... HE'S ALL EXCITED.
YEAH WELL, THIS IS THE FIRST PICNIC WE'VE HAD IN QUITE A WHILE.
KYA! KYA!
ARE YOU READY FOR YOUR TEA?
OKAY.
READ ME A STORY, DADDY!
IN HEAVEN...
うっとり…
SNORT SNORT
I CAUGHT A WILD BOAR.
WELL, WE'LL HAVE A REAL FEAST TONIGHT. ♥
YAY!
NOBODY MAKES A FINER CUP OF TEA THAN YOU, MY DEAR.
I BAKED YOU A TART, TOO.

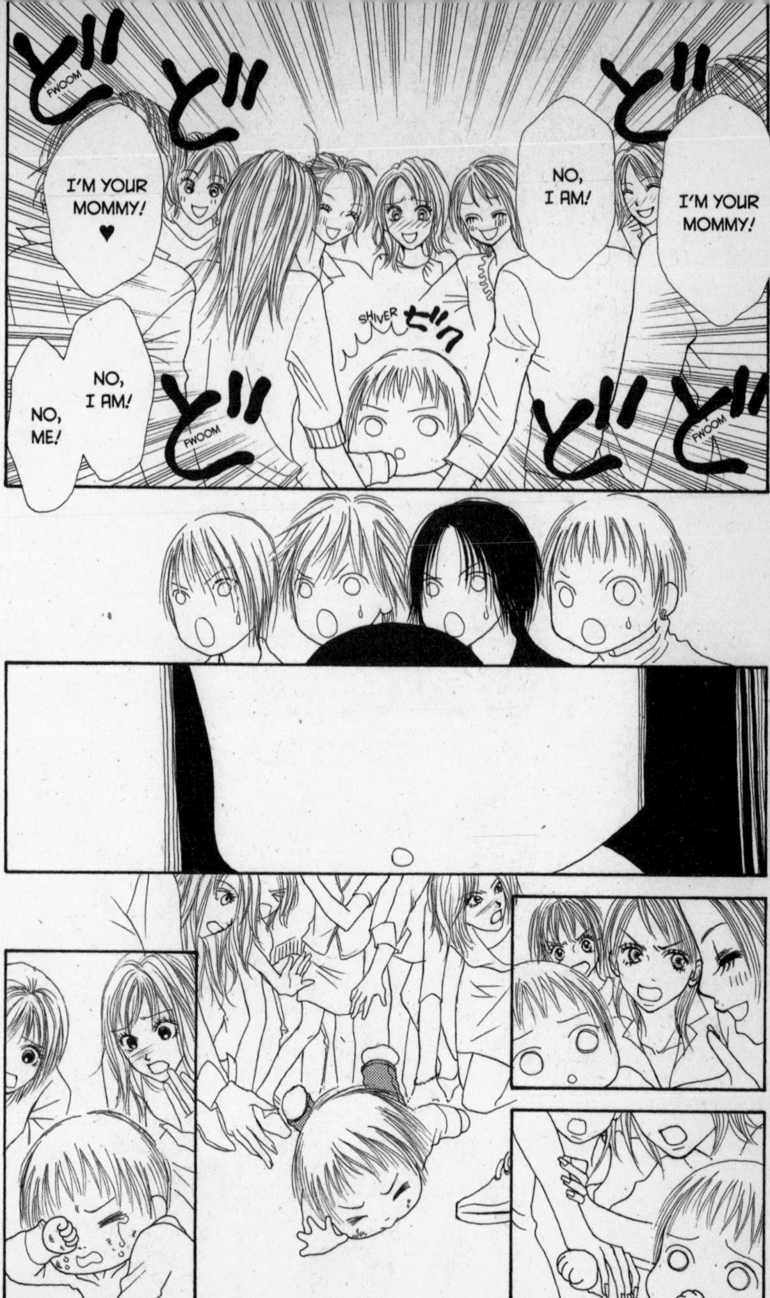
I'M YOUR MOMMY!
NO, I AM!
FWOOM
I'M YOUR MOMMY! ♥
FWOOM
SHIVER
FWOOM
FWOOM
NO, I AM!
NO, ME!

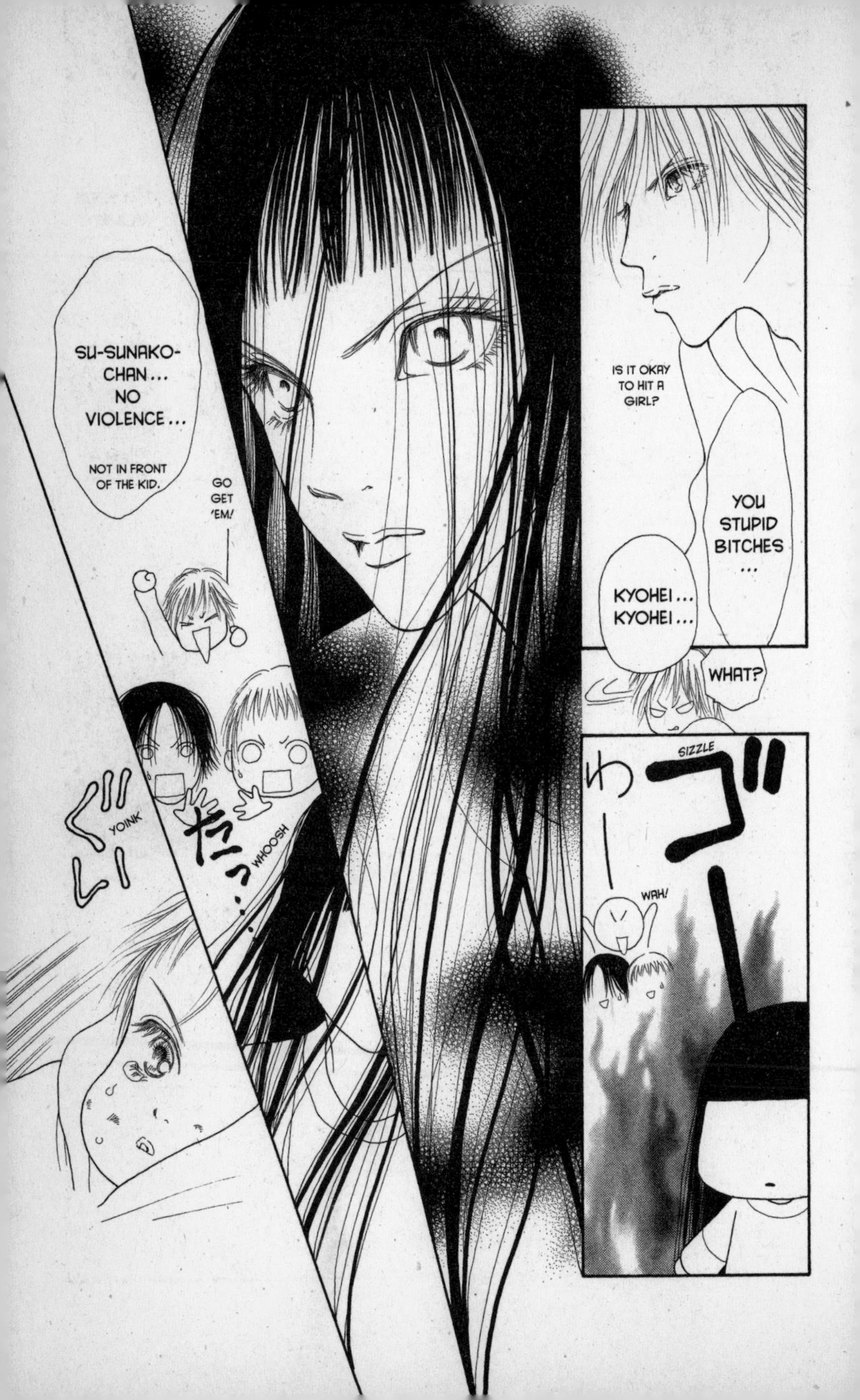

IS IT OKAY TO HIT A GIRL?
YOU STUPID BITCHES ...
KYOHEI... KYOHEI...
WHAT?
ゴ
SIZZLE
わー
WAH!
SU-SUNAKO-CHAN... NO VIOLENCE...
NOT IN FRONT OF THE KID.
GO GET 'EM!
たっ…
WHOOSH
ぐいー
YOINK

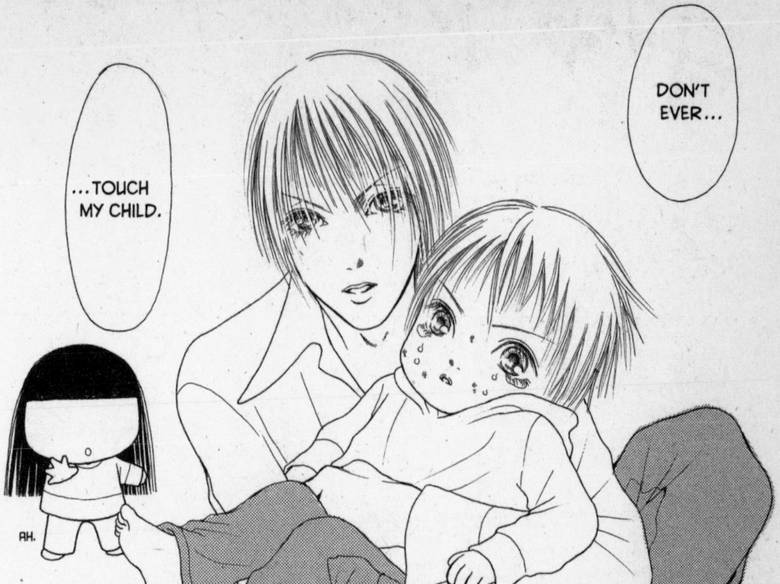
DON'T EVER...
...TOUCH MY CHILD.
AH.

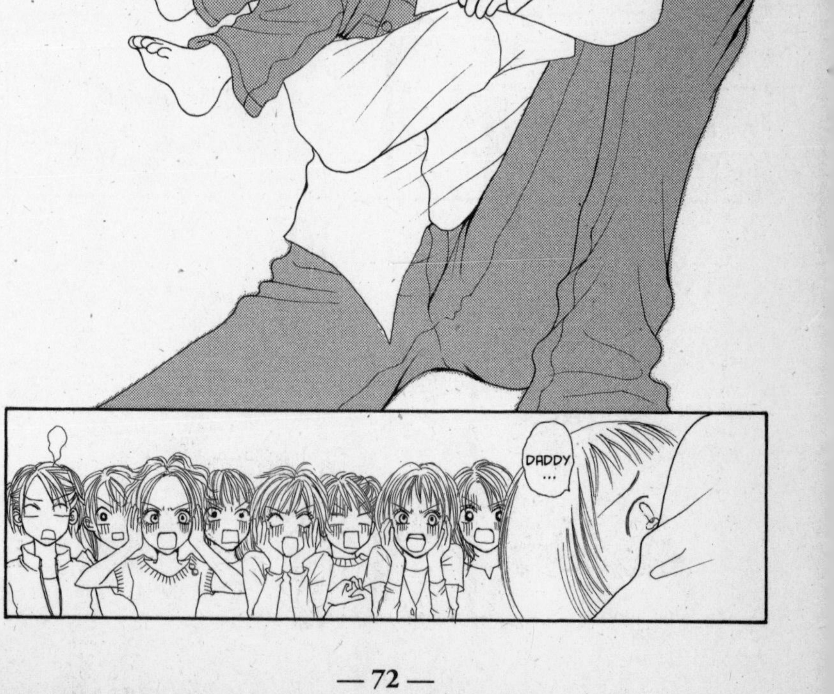
DADDY ...

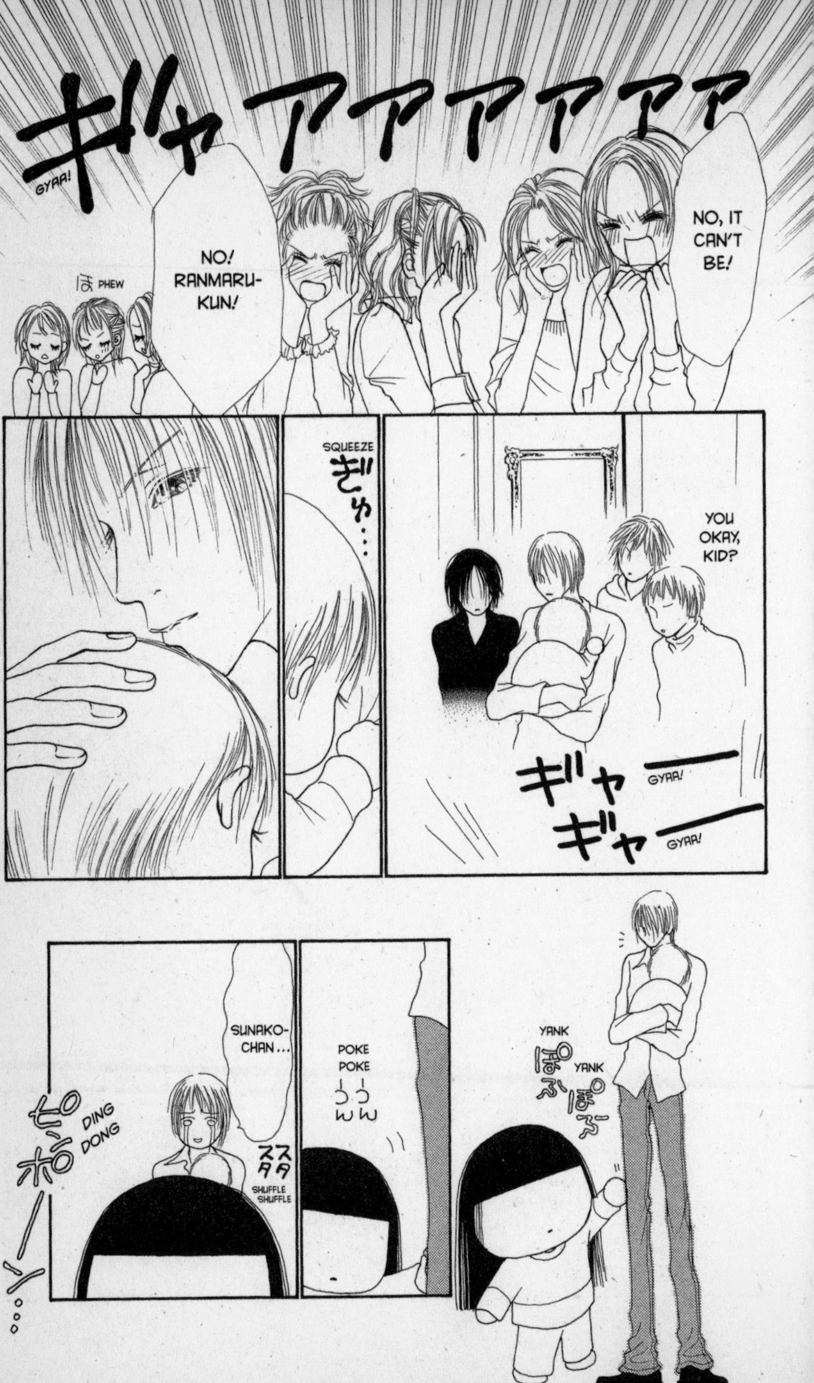
ギャアアアアアア
GYAA!
NO, IT CAN'T BE!
NO! RANMARU-KUN!
ほ PHEW
YOU OKAY, KID?
ギャー
GYAA!
ギャー
GYAA!
SQUEEZE
ぎゅ…
YANK
ぽふぽふ
YANK
POKE POKE
つんつん
SUNAKO-CHAN…
スタスタ
SHUFFLE SHUFFLE
ピンポーン…
DING DONG

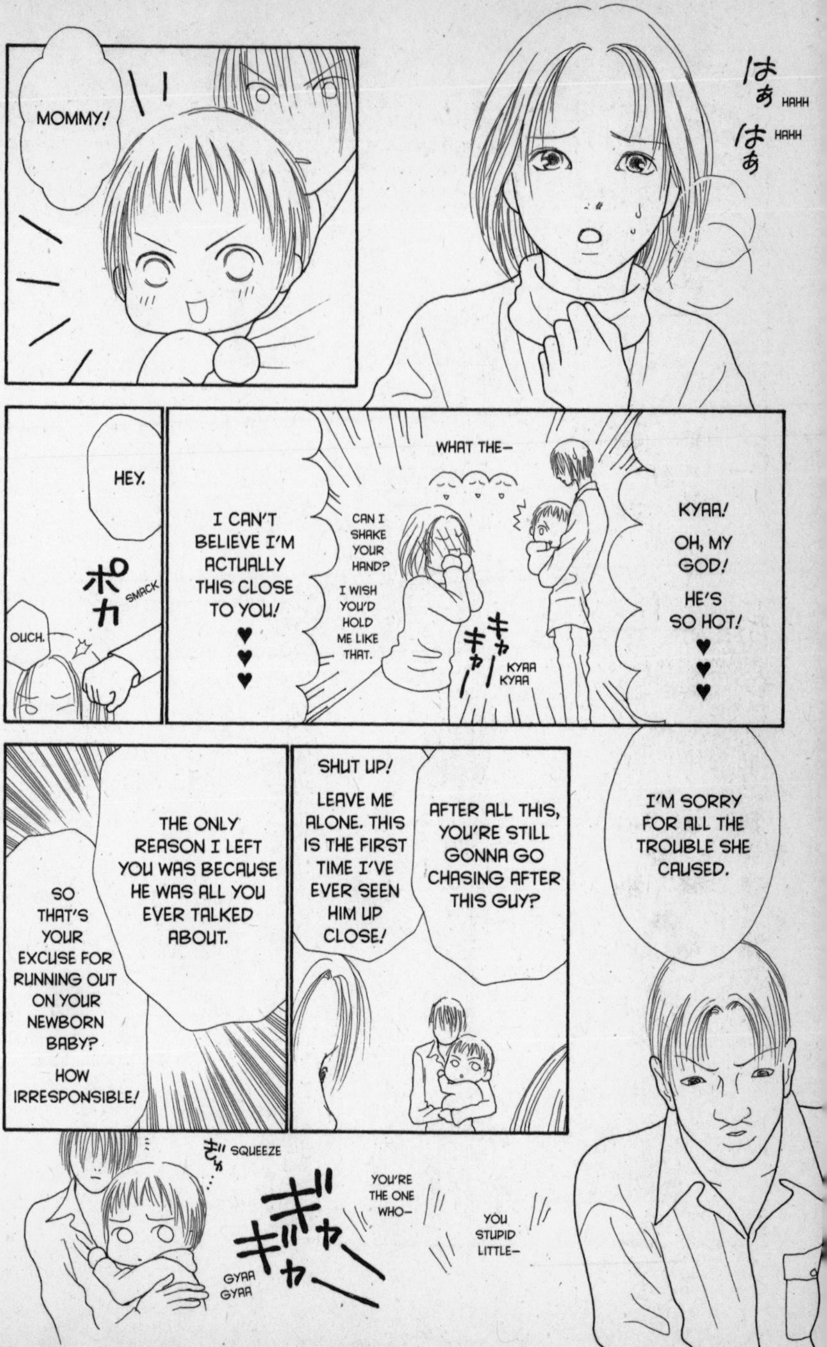
はぁ HAHH
はぁ HAHH
MOMMY!
KYAA!
OH, MY GOD!
HE'S SO HOT! ♥ ♥ ♥
WHAT THE—
キャ キャー KYAA KYAA
CAN I SHAKE YOUR HAND?
I WISH YOU'D HOLD ME LIKE THAT.
I CAN'T BELIEVE I'M ACTUALLY THIS CLOSE TO YOU! ♥ ♥ ♥
HEY.
ポカ SMACK
OUCH.
I'M SORRY FOR ALL THE TROUBLE SHE CAUSED.
AFTER ALL THIS, YOU'RE STILL GONNA GO CHASING AFTER THIS GUY?
SHUT UP!
LEAVE ME ALONE. THIS IS THE FIRST TIME I'VE EVER SEEN HIM UP CLOSE!
THE ONLY REASON I LEFT YOU WAS BECAUSE HE WAS ALL YOU EVER TALKED ABOUT.
SO THAT'S YOUR EXCUSE FOR RUNNING OUT ON YOUR NEWBORN BABY?
HOW IRRESPONSIBLE!
YOU STUPID LITTLE—
YOU'RE THE ONE WHO—
ギャーギャー GYAA GYAA
ぎゅ… SQUEEZE

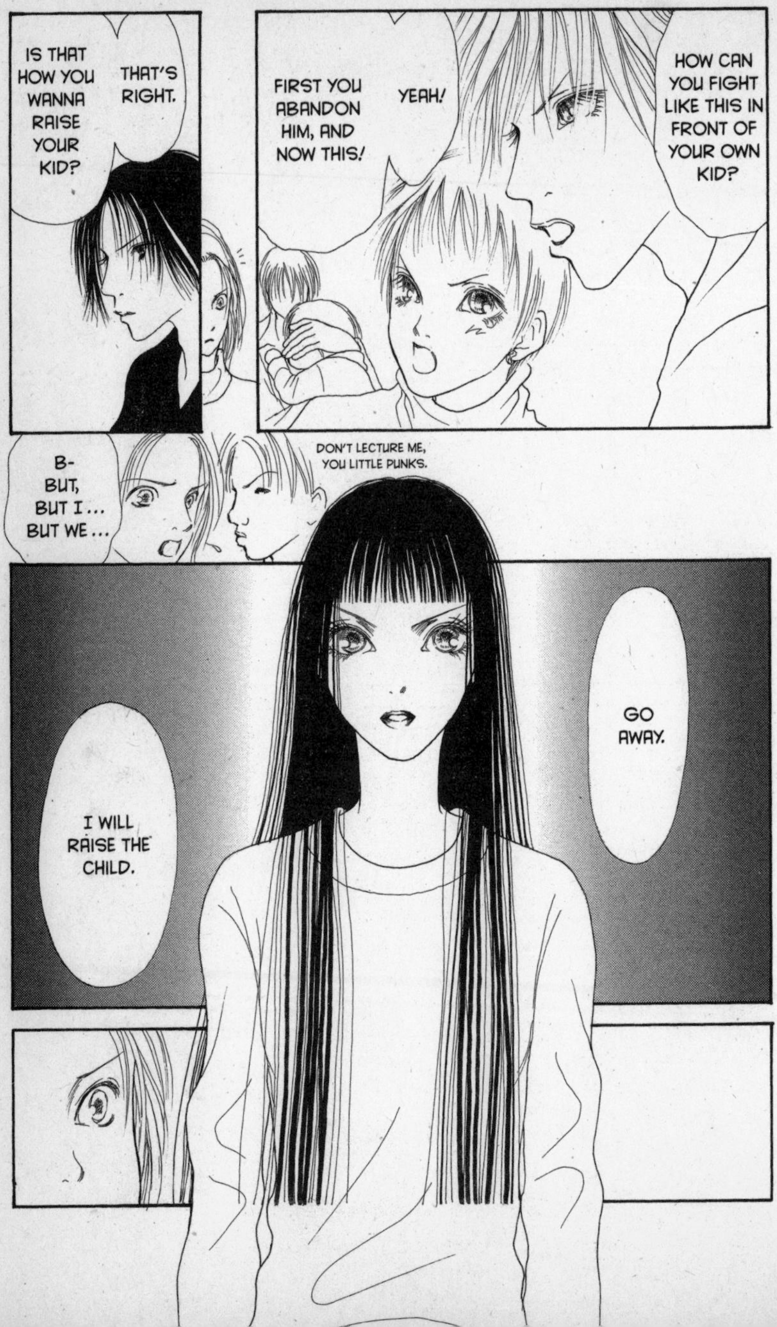
HOW CAN YOU FIGHT LIKE THIS IN FRONT OF YOUR OWN KID?
YEAH!
FIRST YOU ABANDON HIM, AND NOW THIS!
THAT'S RIGHT.
IS THAT HOW YOU WANNA RAISE YOUR KID?
DON'T LECTURE ME, YOU LITTLE PUNKS.
B-BUT, BUT I... BUT WE...
GO AWAY.
I WILL RAISE THE CHILD.

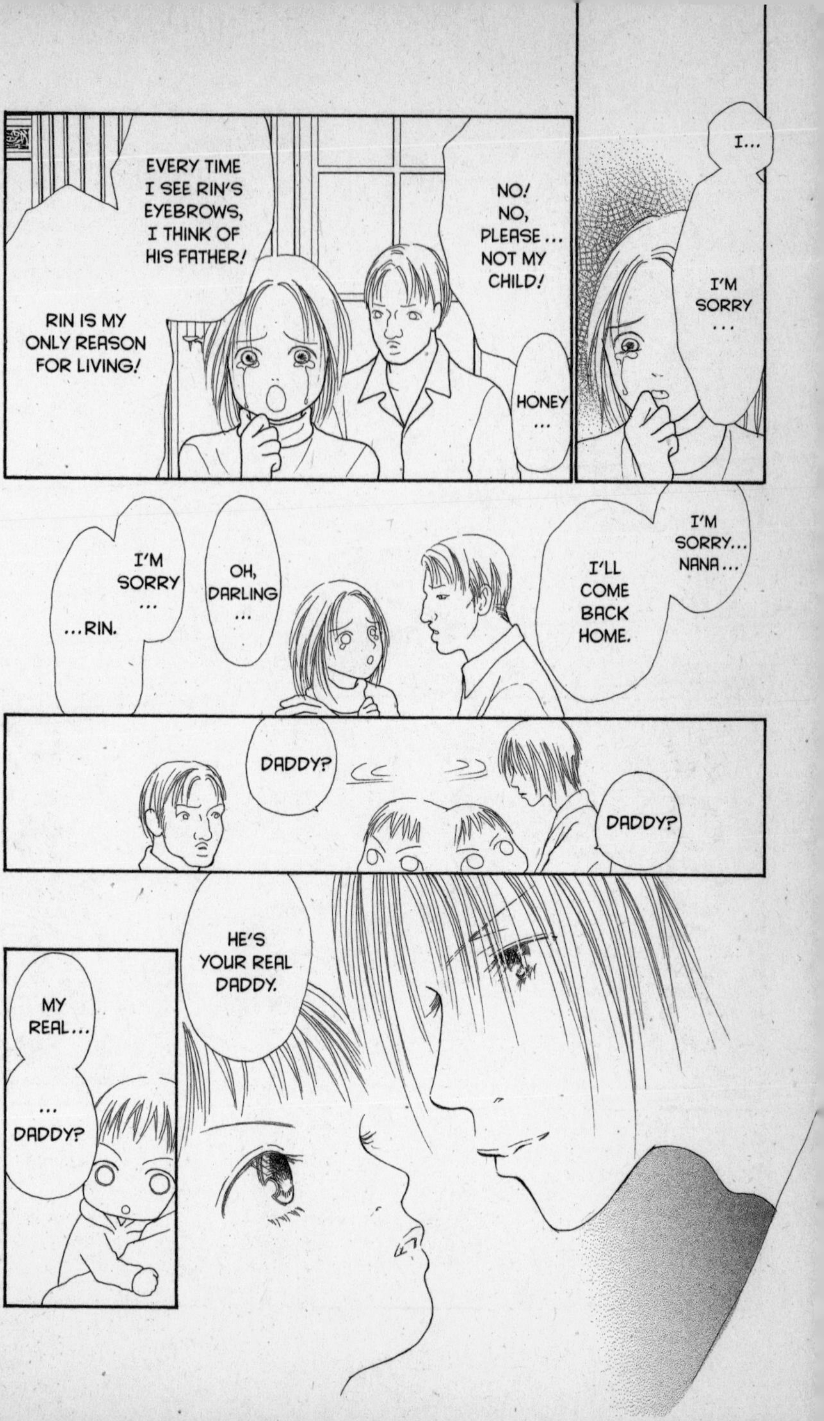
I...
I'M SORRY...
NO! NO, PLEASE... NOT MY CHILD!
HONEY...
EVERY TIME I SEE RIN'S EYEBROWS, I THINK OF HIS FATHER!
RIN IS MY ONLY REASON FOR LIVING!
I'M SORRY... NANA...
I'LL COME BACK HOME.
OH, DARLING...
I'M SORRY...
...RIN.
DADDY?
DADDY?
HE'S YOUR REAL DADDY.
MY REAL...
...DADDY?

RIN...

NOOOO!

JUST LET HIM GO.

I'M SORRY, RIN. HE'S TOO GORGEOUS FOR US.

I KNOW HOW HE FEELS. ♥

SHOCK

WAH! WAH!

SQUEEZE

I WANNA STAY WITH HIM!

I WANT A COOL DADDY!

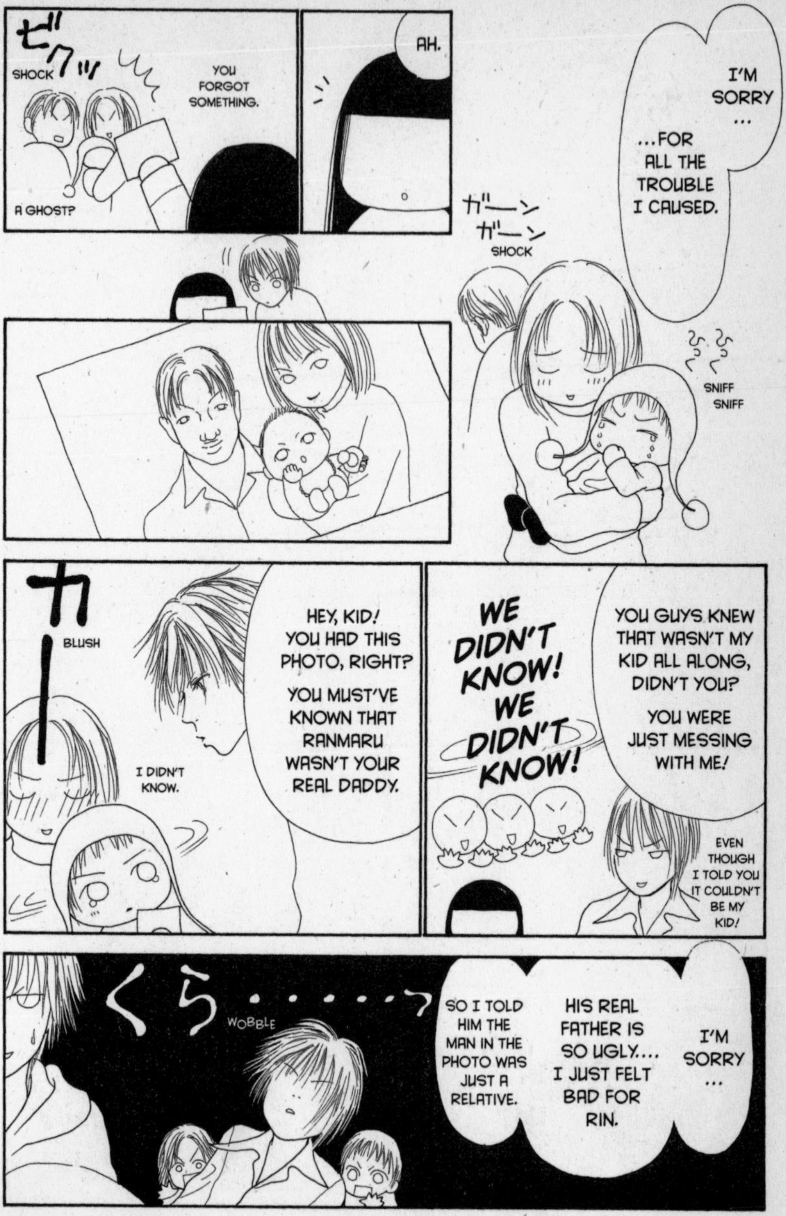
I'M SORRY ...
...FOR ALL THE TROUBLE I CAUSED.
ガーン ガーン
SHOCK
SNIFF SNIFF
AH.
ビクッ
SHOCK
YOU FORGOT SOMETHING.
A GHOST?
YOU GUYS KNEW THAT WASN'T MY KID ALL ALONG, DIDN'T YOU?
YOU WERE JUST MESSING WITH ME!
WE DIDN'T KNOW! WE DIDN'T KNOW!
EVEN THOUGH I TOLD YOU IT COULDN'T BE MY KID!
HEY, KID! YOU HAD THIS PHOTO, RIGHT?
YOU MUST'VE KNOWN THAT RANMARU WASN'T YOUR REAL DADDY.
カー
BLUSH
I DIDN'T KNOW.
I'M SORRY ...
HIS REAL FATHER IS SO UGLY.... I JUST FELT BAD FOR RIN.
SO I TOLD HIM THE MAN IN THE PHOTO WAS JUST A RELATIVE.
くら.....
WOBBLE

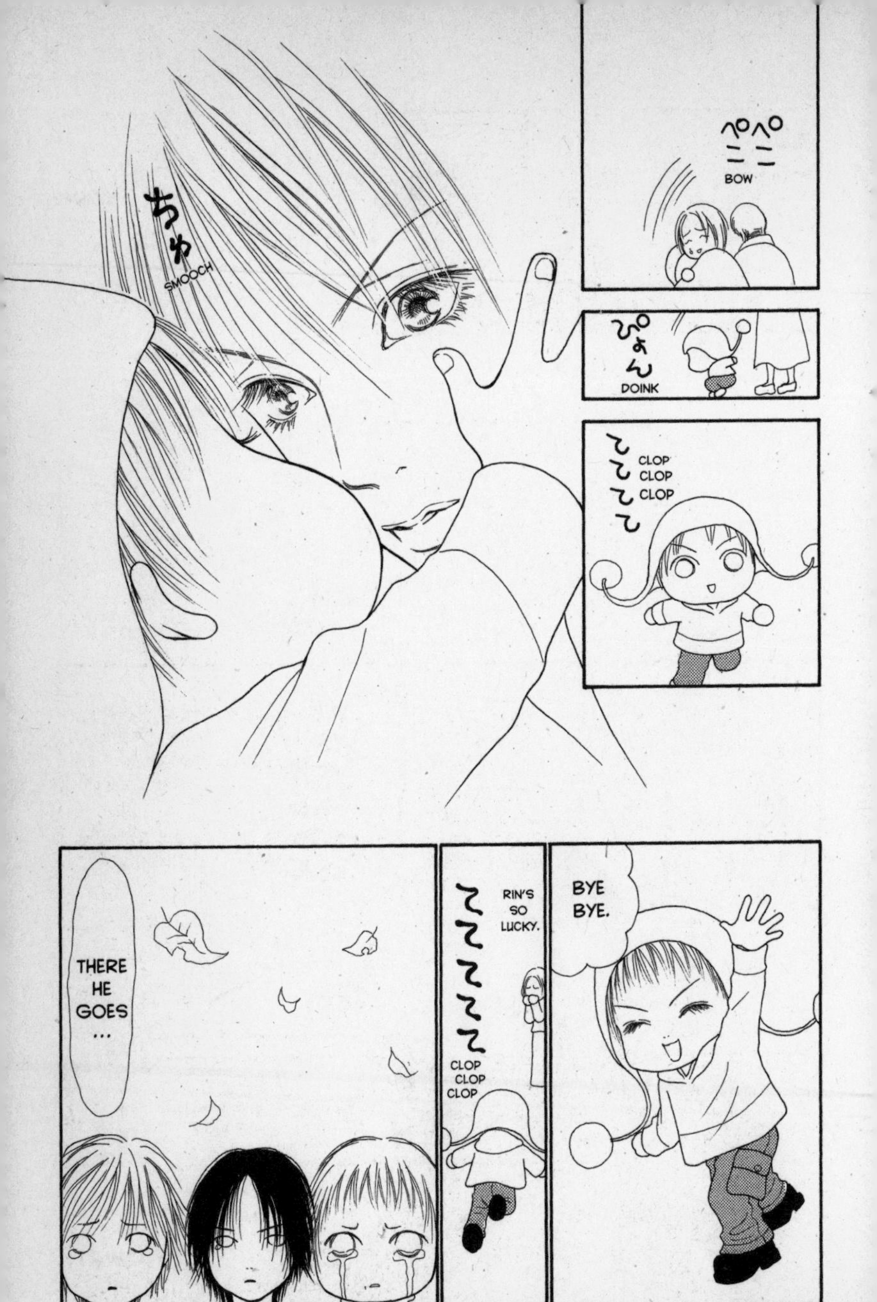
ぺこぺこ
BOW
ぴょん
DOINK
てててて
CLOP
CLOP
CLOP
ちゅ
SMOOCH
BYE BYE.
RIN'S SO LUCKY.
ててててて
CLOP
CLOP
CLOP
THERE HE GOES...

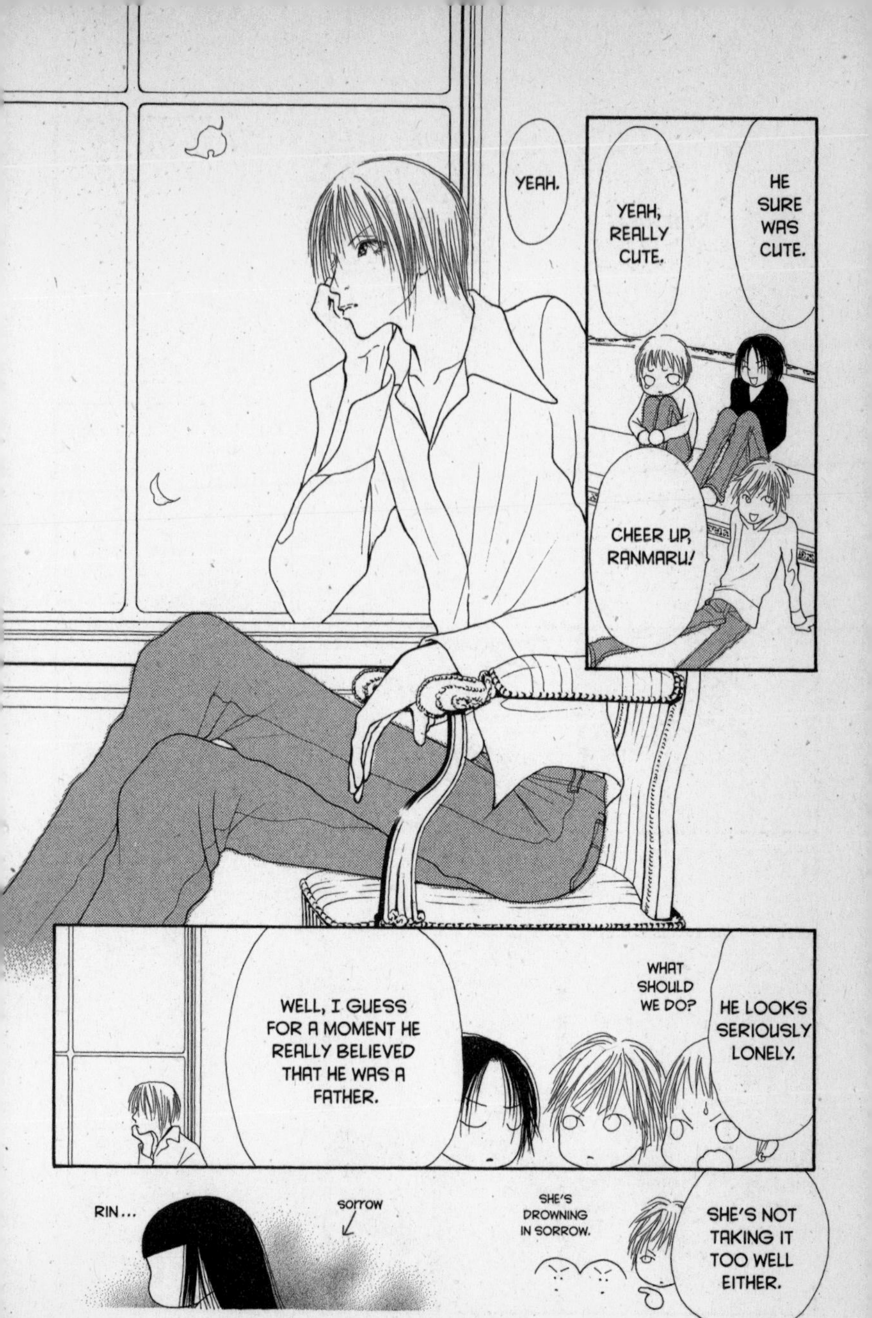
HE SURE WAS CUTE.
YEAH, REALLY CUTE.
CHEER UP, RANMARU!
YEAH.
HE LOOKS SERIOUSLY LONELY.
WHAT SHOULD WE DO?
WELL, I GUESS FOR A MOMENT HE REALLY BELIEVED THAT HE WAS A FATHER.
SHE'S NOT TAKING IT TOO WELL EITHER.
SHE'S DROWNING IN SORROW.
sorrow
RIN...

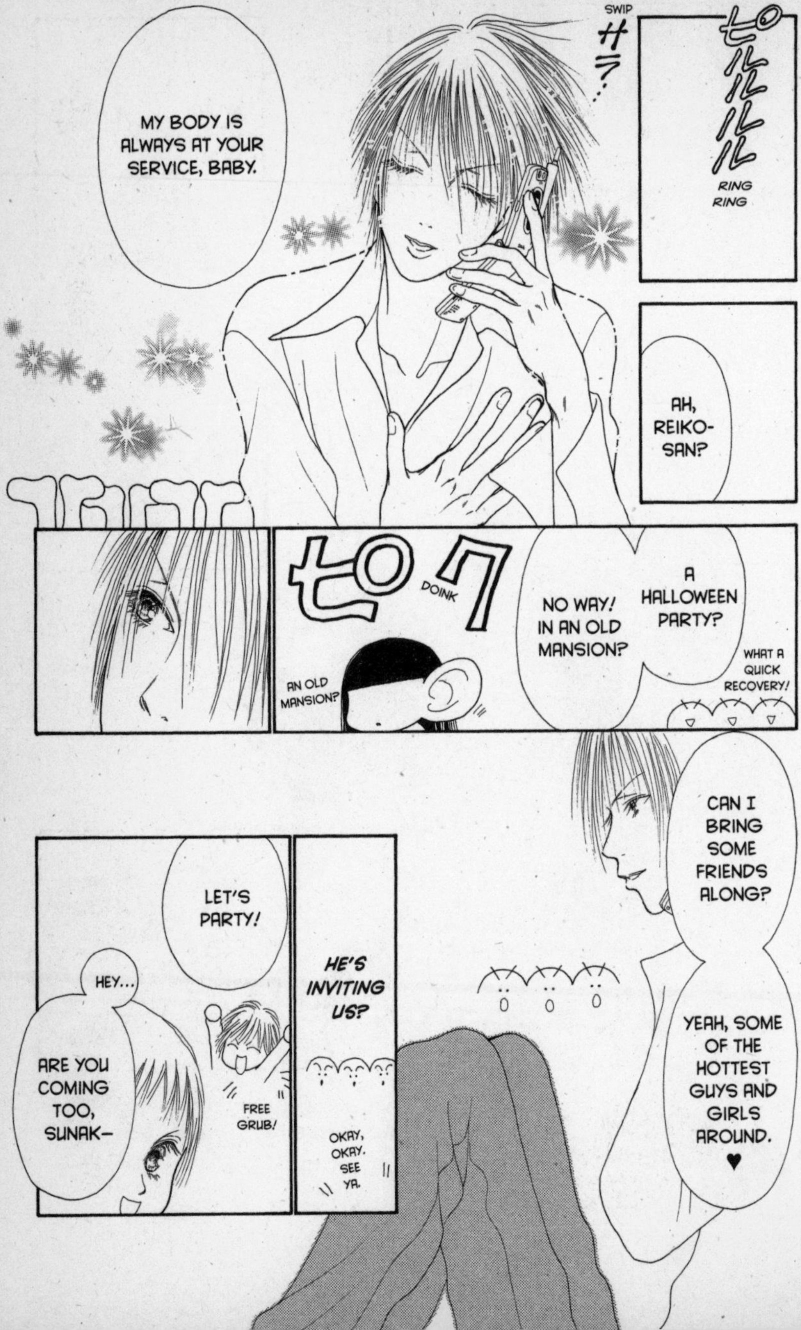
ピルルルル
RING RING
AH, REIKO-SAN?
SWIP
サラ…
MY BODY IS ALWAYS AT YOUR SERVICE, BABY.
A HALLOWEEN PARTY?
NO WAY! IN AN OLD MANSION?
WHAT A QUICK RECOVERY!
ピク
DOINK
AN OLD MANSION?
CAN I BRING SOME FRIENDS ALONG?
YEAH, SOME OF THE HOTTEST GUYS AND GIRLS AROUND. ♥
HE'S INVITING US?
OKAY, OKAY. SEE YA.
LET'S PARTY!
FREE GRUB!
HEY...
ARE YOU COMING TOO, SUNAK–

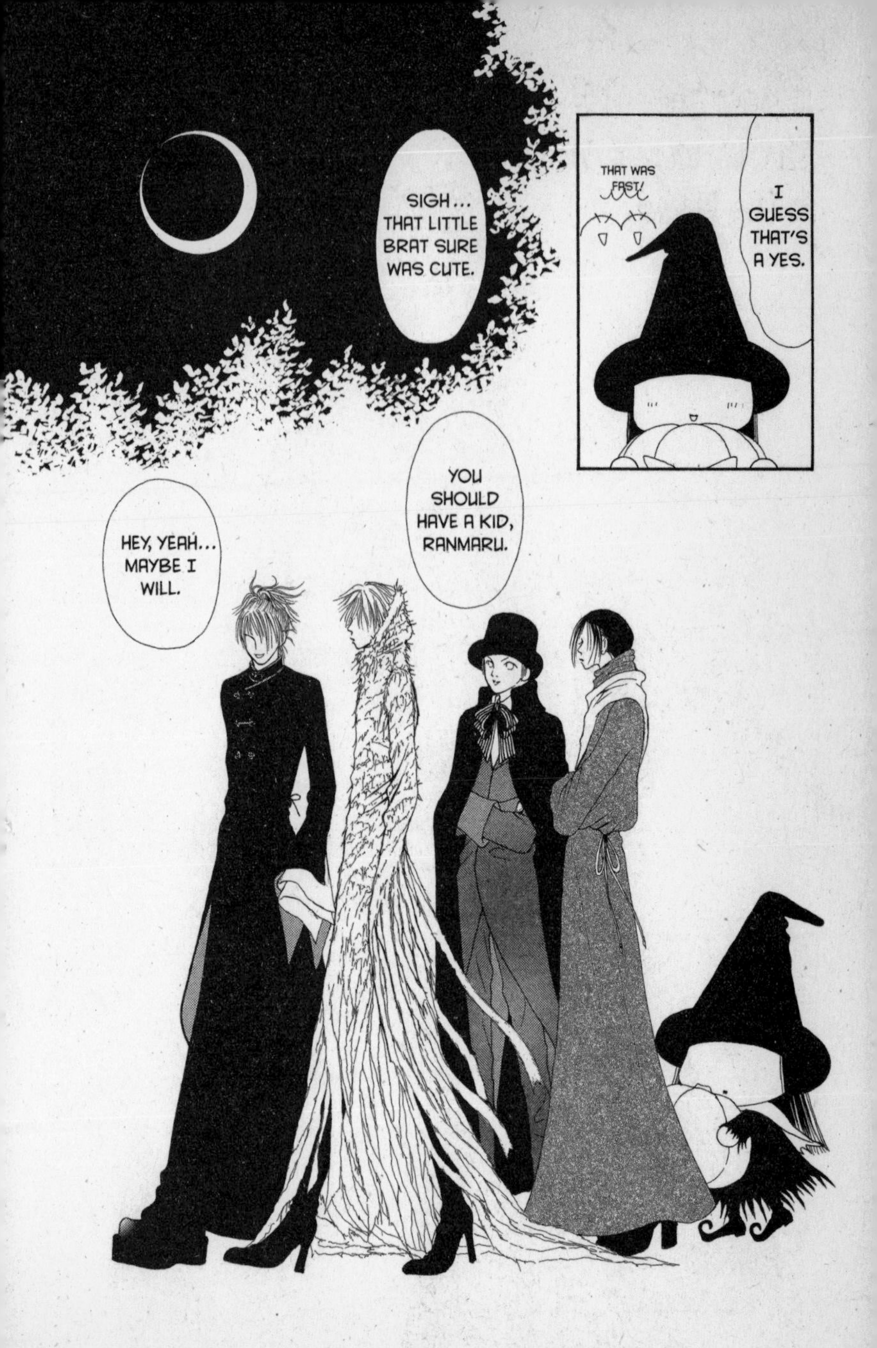
I GUESS THAT'S A YES.
THAT WAS FAST!
SIGH... THAT LITTLE BRAT SURE WAS CUTE.
YOU SHOULD HAVE A KID, RANMARU.
HEY, YEAH... MAYBE I WILL.

Chapter 29
The Strongest Women in the World

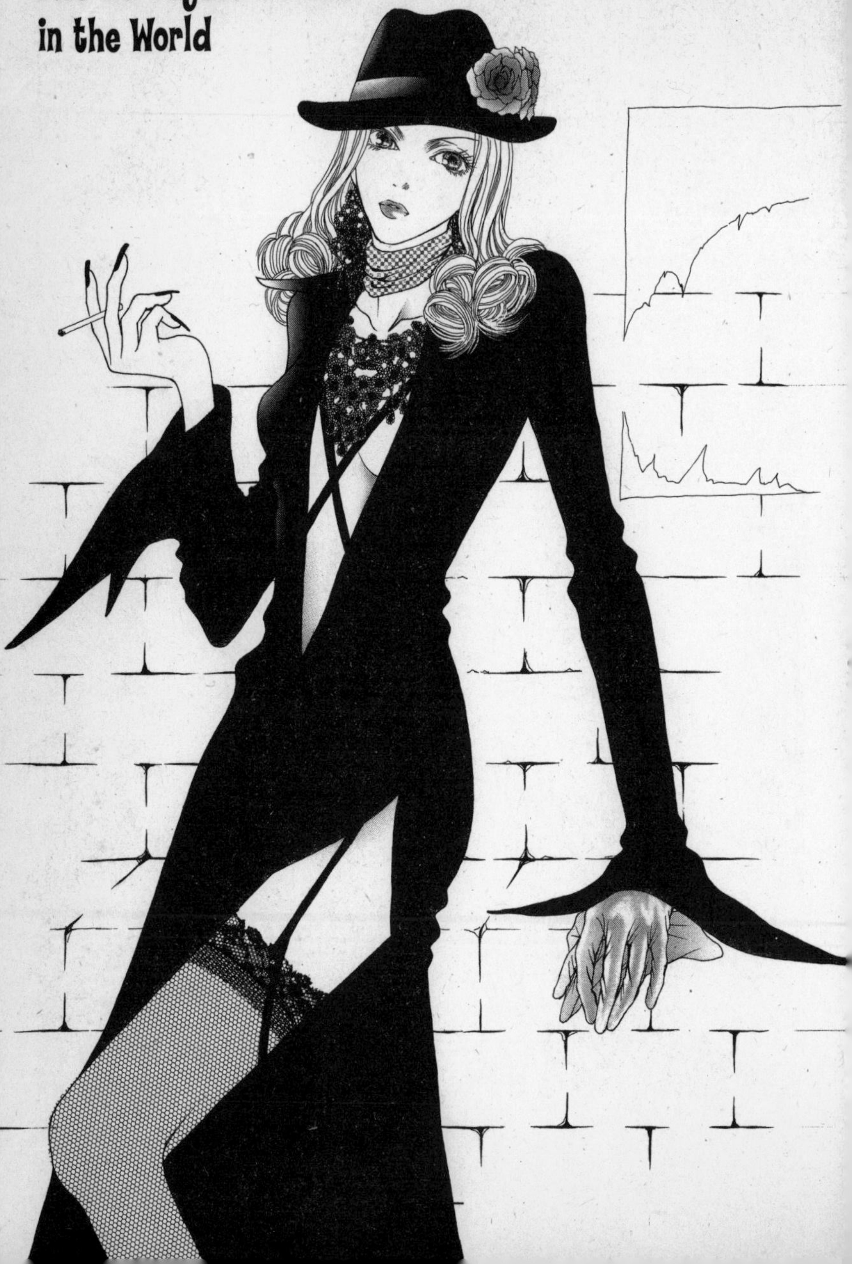

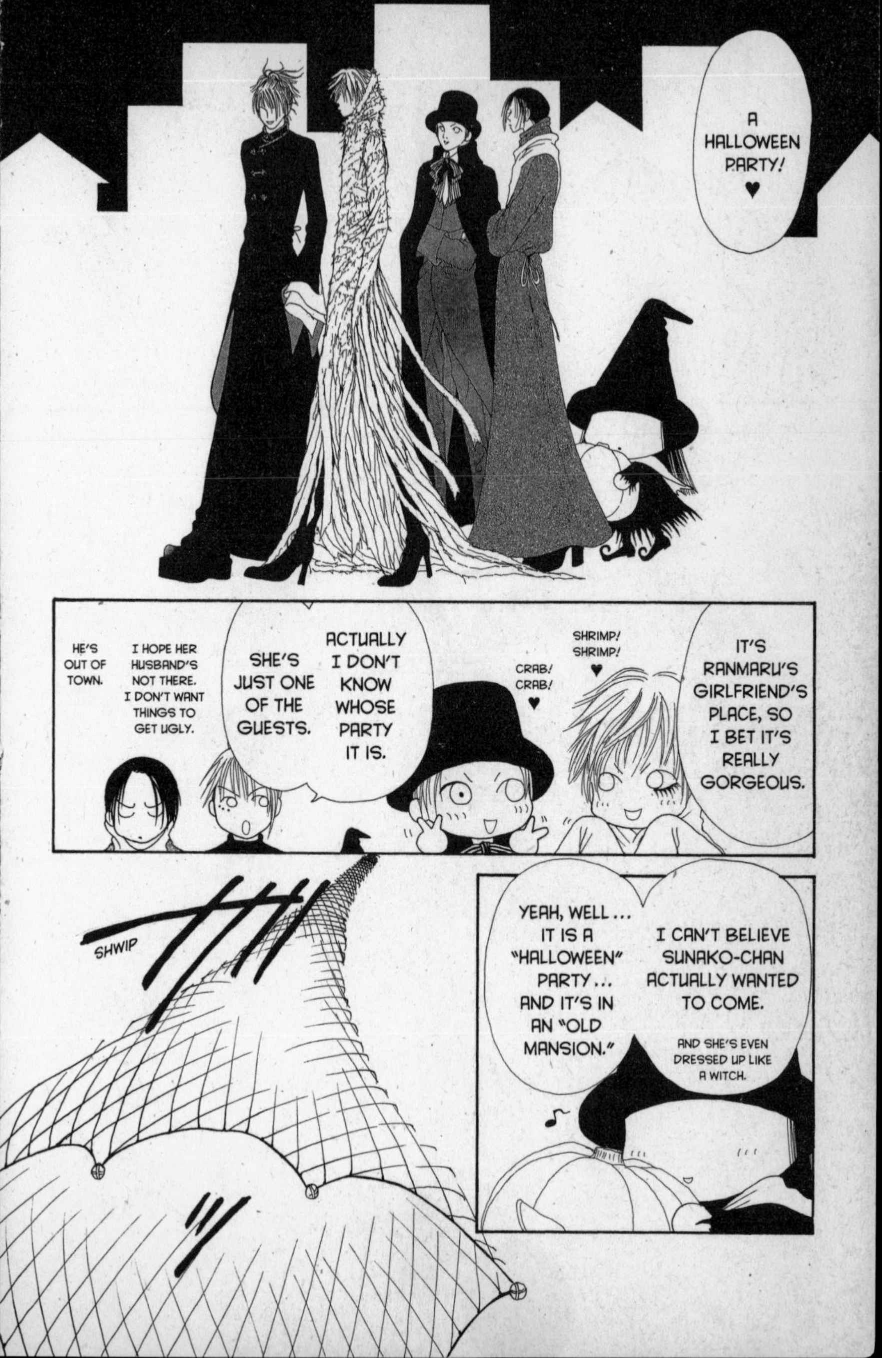
A HALLOWEEN PARTY! ♥
IT'S RANMARU'S GIRLFRIEND'S PLACE, SO I BET IT'S REALLY GORGEOUS.
SHRIMP! SHRIMP! ♥
CRAB! CRAB! ♥
ACTUALLY I DON'T KNOW WHOSE PARTY IT IS.
SHE'S JUST ONE OF THE GUESTS.
I HOPE HER HUSBAND'S NOT THERE. I DON'T WANT THINGS TO GET UGLY.
HE'S OUT OF TOWN.
I CAN'T BELIEVE SUNAKO-CHAN ACTUALLY WANTED TO COME.
YEAH, WELL ... IT IS A "HALLOWEEN" PARTY ... AND IT'S IN AN "OLD MANSION."
AND SHE'S EVEN DRESSED UP LIKE A WITCH.
SHWIP

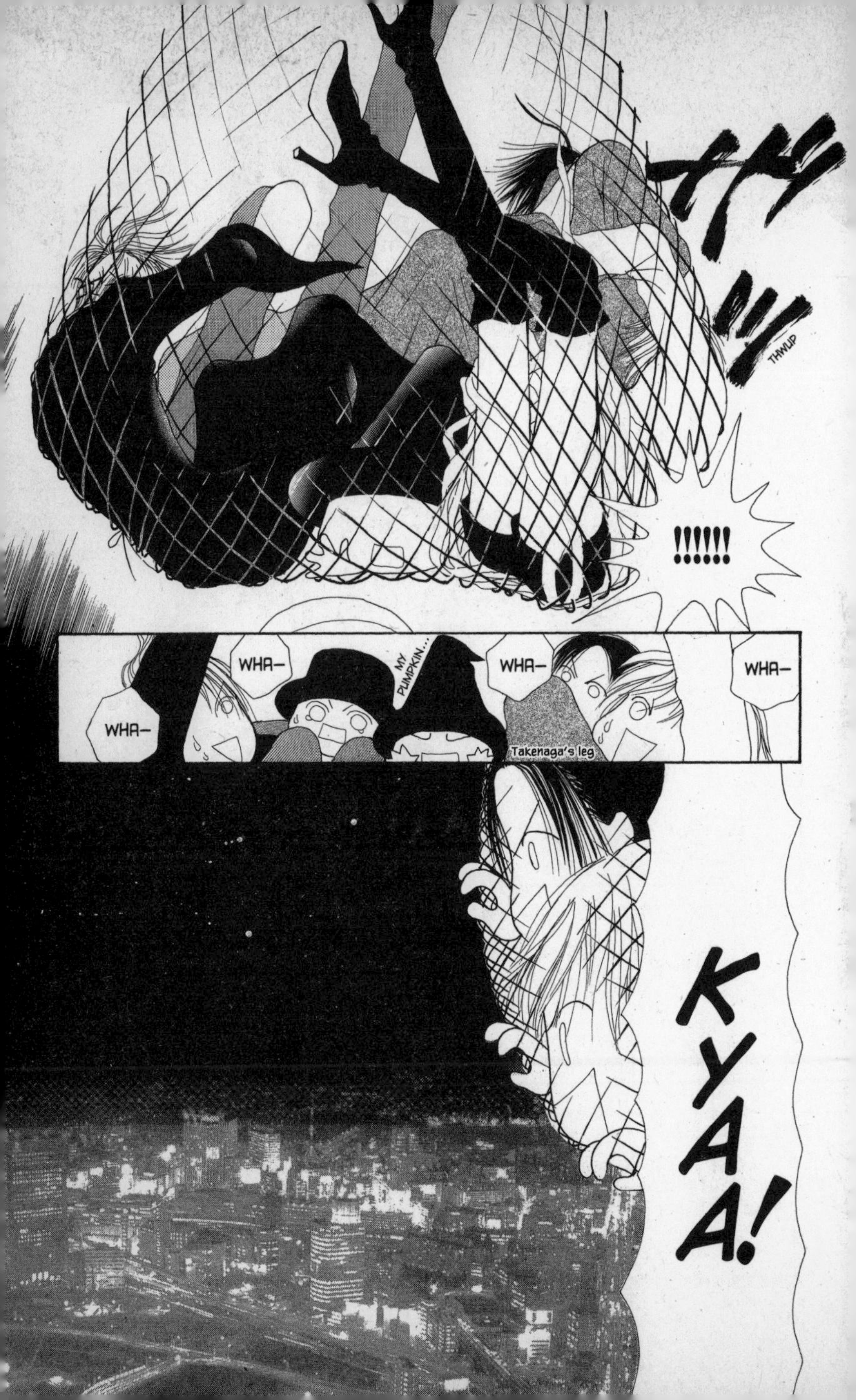
THWUP
!!!!!!
WHA–
WHA–
Takenaga's leg
MY PUMPKIN...
WHA–
WHA–
KYAA!

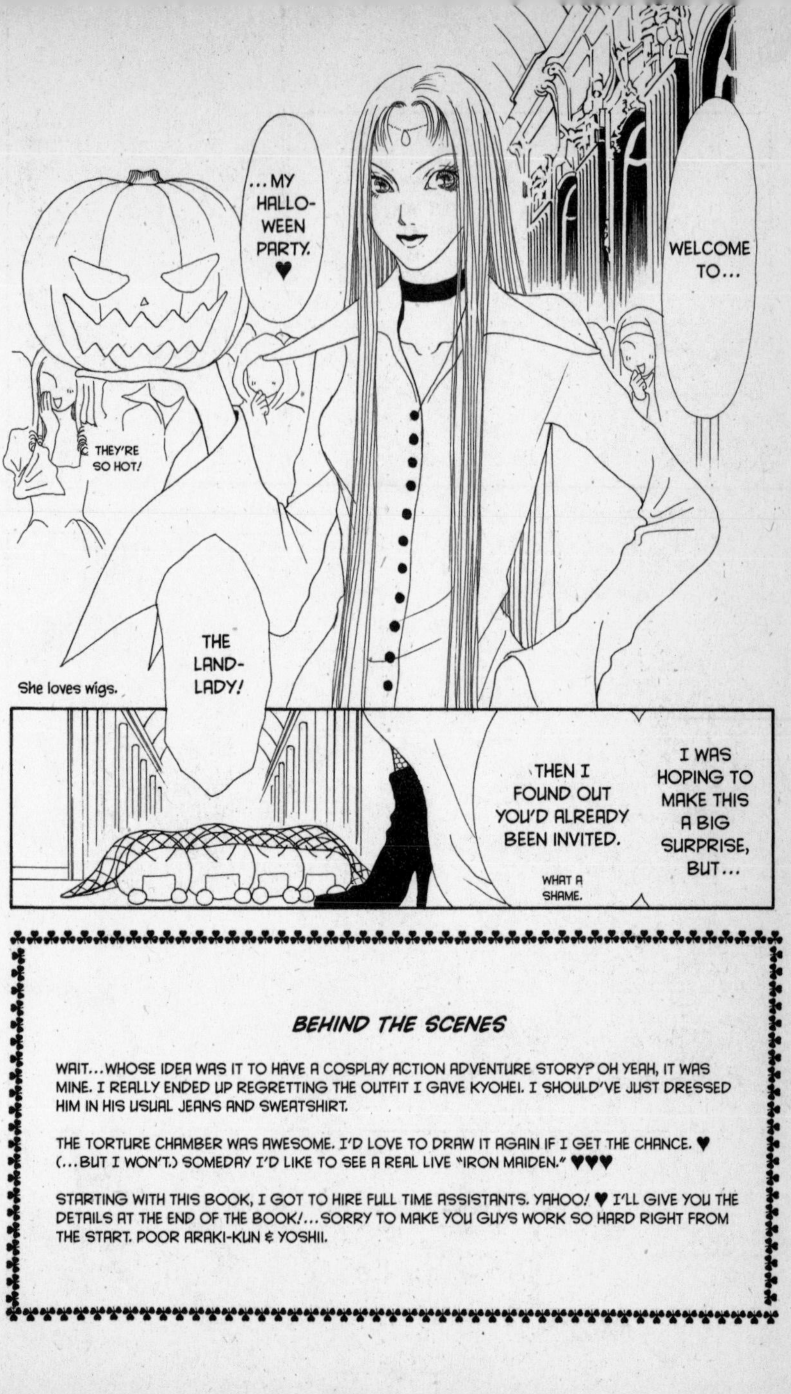
WELCOME TO...
...MY HALLOWEEN PARTY. ♥
THEY'RE SO HOT!
THE LANDLADY!
She loves wigs.
I WAS HOPING TO MAKE THIS A BIG SURPRISE, BUT...
THEN I FOUND OUT YOU'D ALREADY BEEN INVITED.
WHAT A SHAME.

BEHIND THE SCENES

WAIT...WHOSE IDEA WAS IT TO HAVE A COSPLAY ACTION ADVENTURE STORY? OH YEAH, IT WAS MINE. I REALLY ENDED UP REGRETTING THE OUTFIT I GAVE KYOHEI. I SHOULD'VE JUST DRESSED HIM IN HIS USUAL JEANS AND SWEATSHIRT.

THE TORTURE CHAMBER WAS AWESOME. I'D LOVE TO DRAW IT AGAIN IF I GET THE CHANCE. ♥ (...BUT I WON'T.) SOMEDAY I'D LIKE TO SEE A REAL LIVE "IRON MAIDEN." ♥♥♥

STARTING WITH THIS BOOK, I GOT TO HIRE FULL TIME ASSISTANTS. YAHOO! ♥ I'LL GIVE YOU THE DETAILS AT THE END OF THE BOOK!...SORRY TO MAKE YOU GUYS WORK SO HARD RIGHT FROM THE START. POOR ARAKI-KUN & YOSHII.

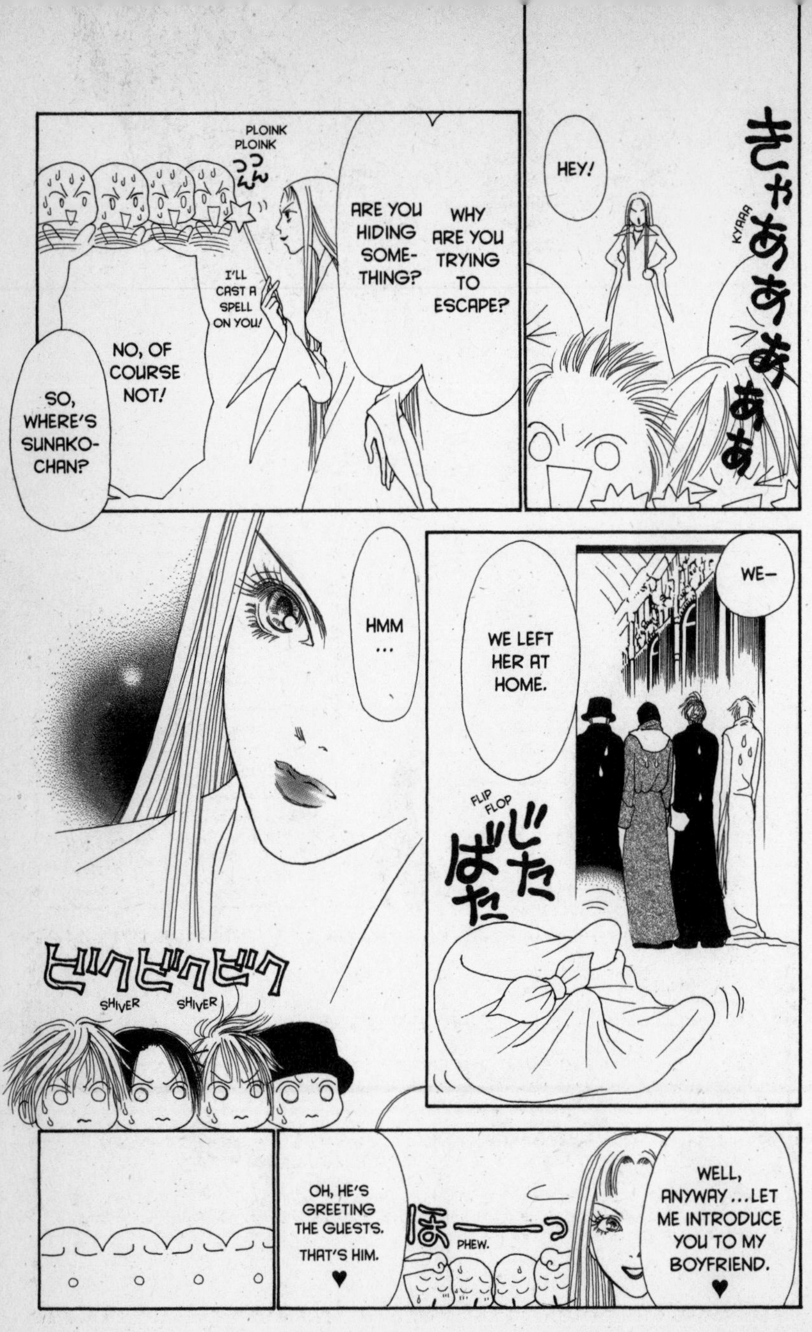

きゃあああああ
KYAAA
HEY!
WHY ARE YOU TRYING TO ESCAPE?
ARE YOU HIDING SOMETHING?
PLOINK PLOINK
つつん
I'LL CAST A SPELL ON YOU!
NO, OF COURSE NOT!
SO, WHERE'S SUNAKO-CHAN?
WE—
WE LEFT HER AT HOME.
じたばた
FLIP FLOP
HMM...
ビクビクビク
SHIVER SHIVER
WELL, ANYWAY...LET ME INTRODUCE YOU TO MY BOYFRIEND. ♥
ほーっ
PHEW.
OH, HE'S GREETING THE GUESTS. THAT'S HIM. ♥

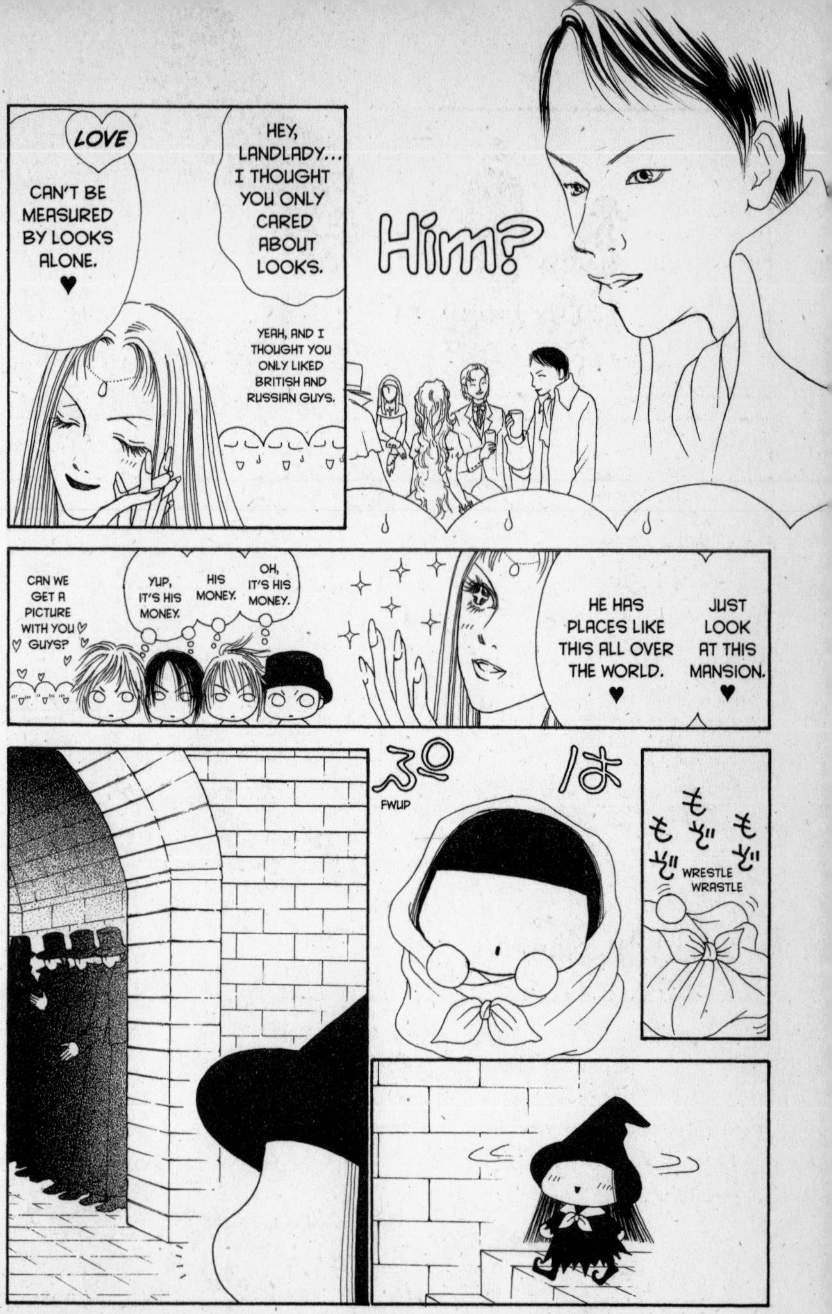
Him?
HEY, LANDLADY... I THOUGHT YOU ONLY CARED ABOUT LOOKS.
LOVE
CAN'T BE MEASURED BY LOOKS ALONE. ♥
YEAH, AND I THOUGHT YOU ONLY LIKED BRITISH AND RUSSIAN GUYS.
JUST LOOK AT THIS MANSION. ♥
HE HAS PLACES LIKE THIS ALL OVER THE WORLD. ♥
OH, IT'S HIS MONEY.
HIS MONEY.
YUP, IT'S HIS MONEY.
CAN WE GET A PICTURE WITH YOU GUYS?
もぞもぞ
WRESTLE WRASTLE
ぷは
FWUP

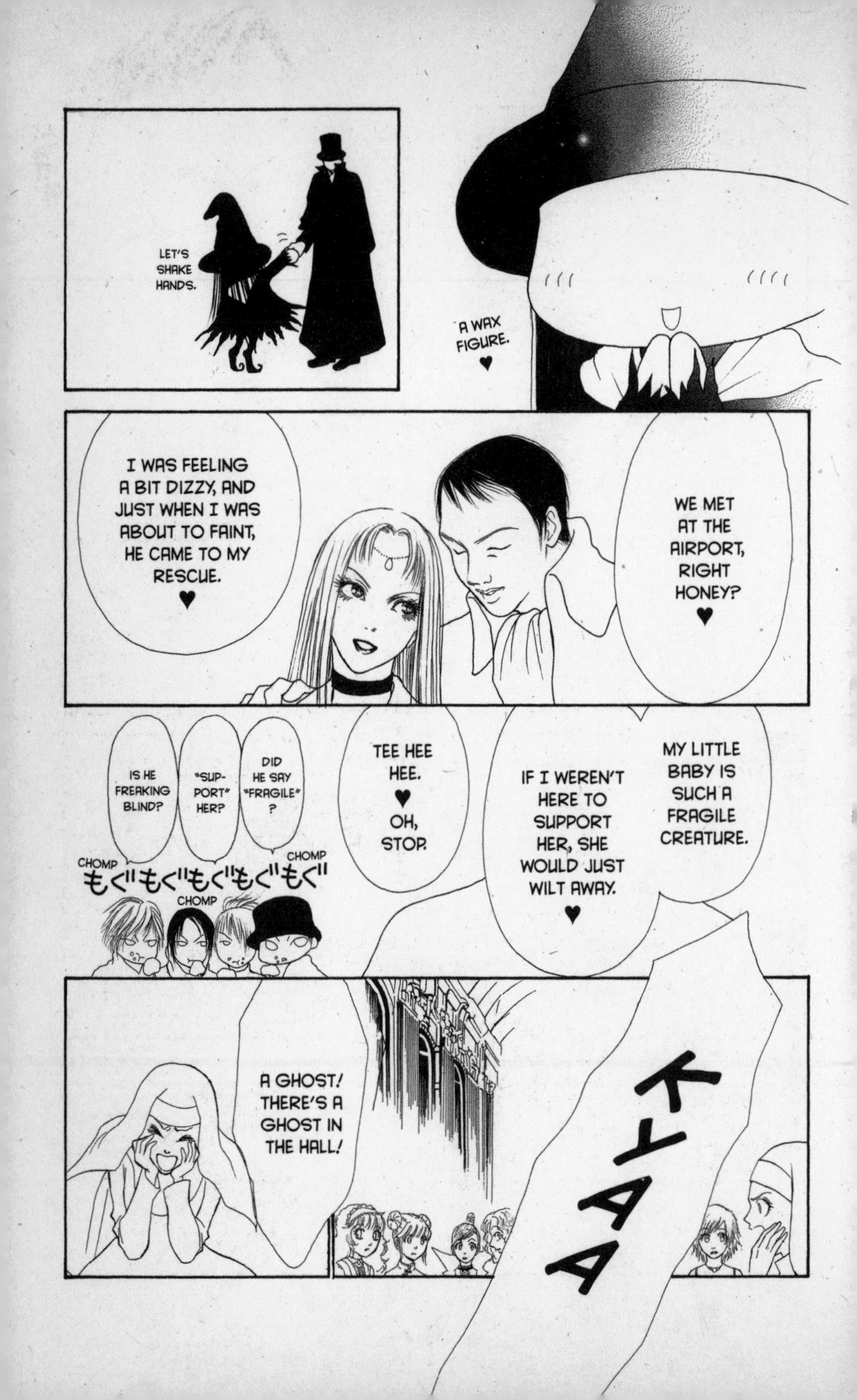
A WAX FIGURE. ♥
LET'S SHAKE HANDS.
WE MET AT THE AIRPORT, RIGHT HONEY? ♥
I WAS FEELING A BIT DIZZY, AND JUST WHEN I WAS ABOUT TO FAINT, HE CAME TO MY RESCUE. ♥
MY LITTLE BABY IS SUCH A FRAGILE CREATURE.
IF I WEREN'T HERE TO SUPPORT HER, SHE WOULD JUST WILT AWAY. ♥
TEE HEE HEE. ♥ OH, STOP.
DID HE SAY "FRAGILE"?
"SUP-PORT" HER?
IS HE FREAKING BLIND?
CHOMP
もぐもぐもぐもぐもぐ
CHOMP
CHOMP
KYAAA
A GHOST! THERE'S A GHOST IN THE HALL!

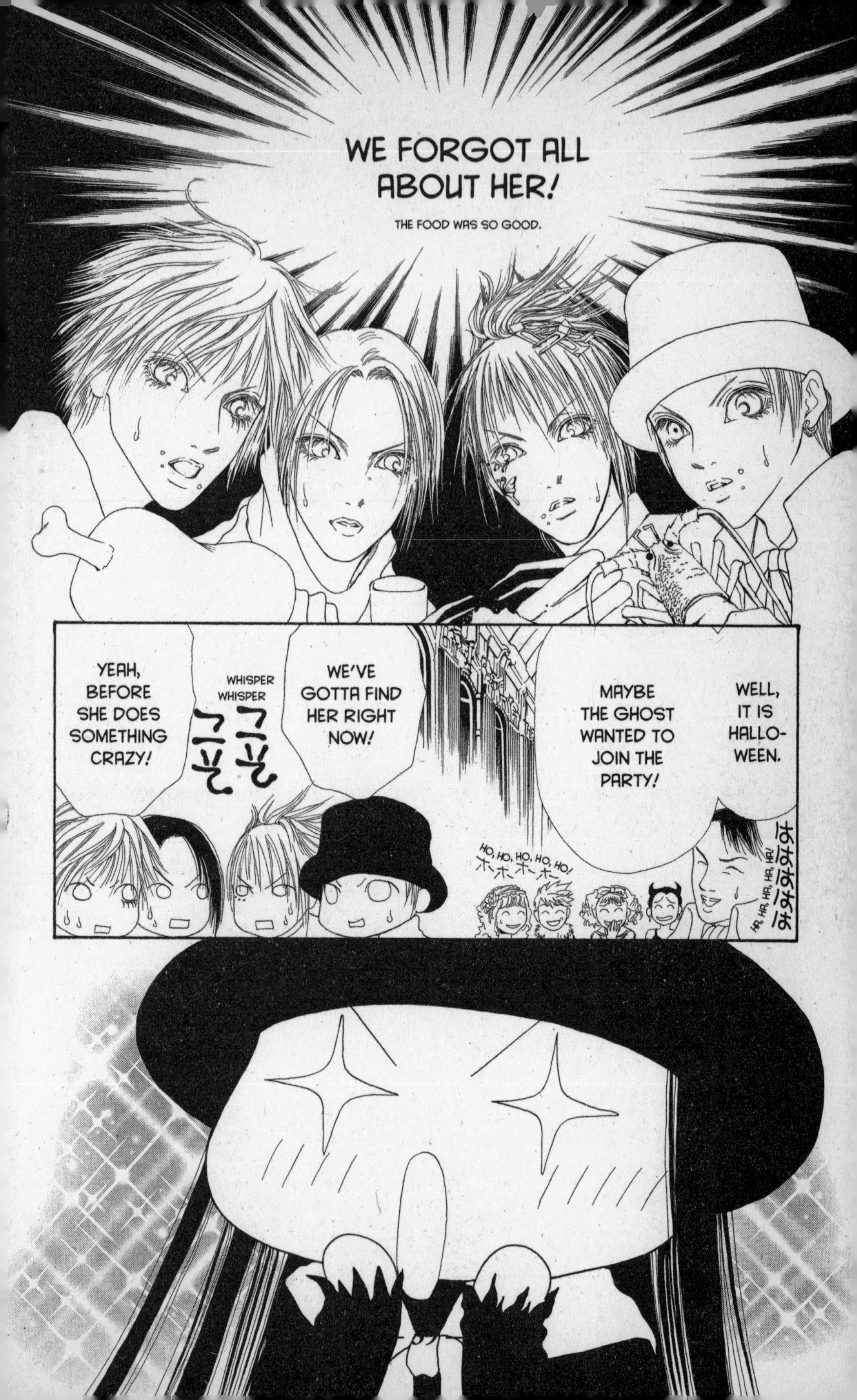
WE FORGOT ALL ABOUT HER!
THE FOOD WAS SO GOOD.
WELL, IT IS HALLO-WEEN.
HA, HA, HA, HA!
MAYBE THE GHOST WANTED TO JOIN THE PARTY!
HO, HO, HO, HO, HO!
WE'VE GOTTA FIND HER RIGHT NOW!
WHISPER WHISPER
YEAH, BEFORE SHE DOES SOMETHING CRAZY!

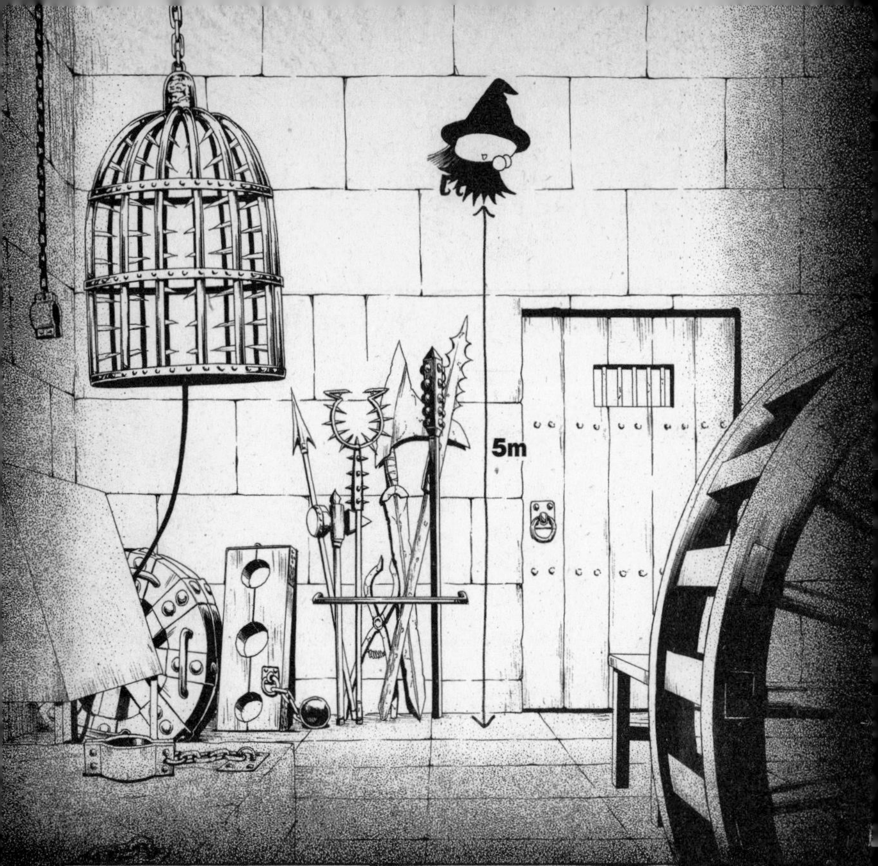
5m

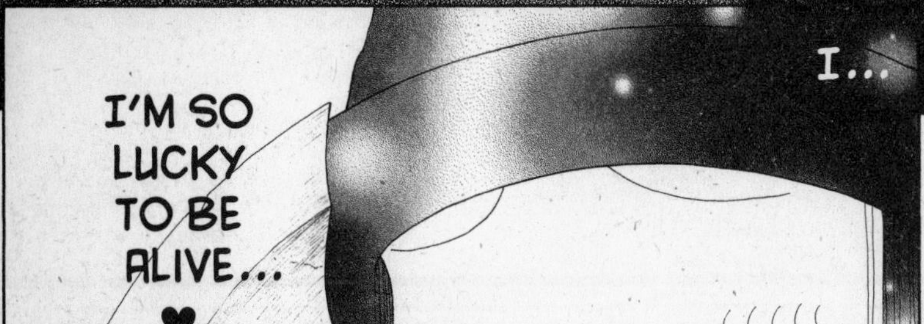
I...
I'M SO LUCKY TO BE ALIVE...

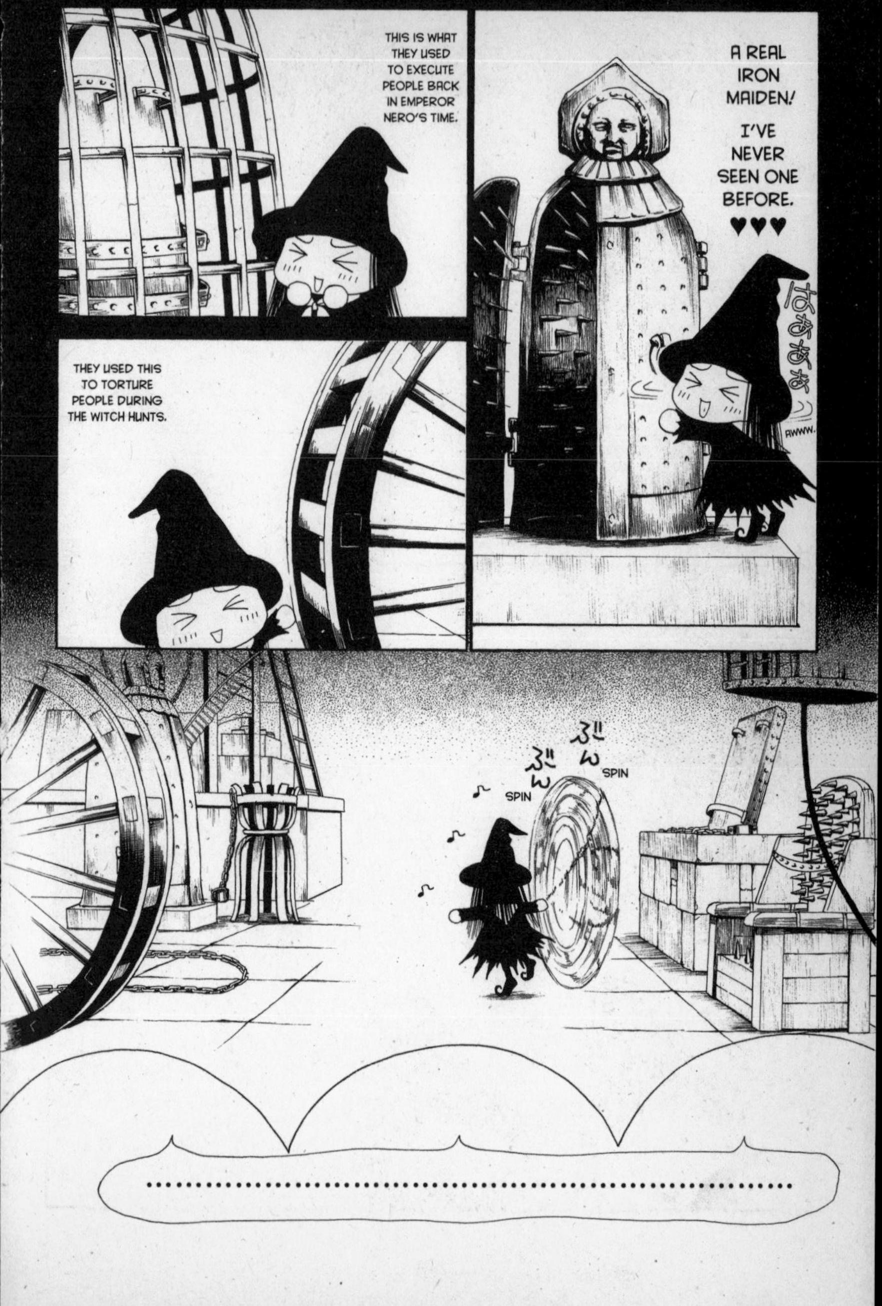
A REAL IRON MAIDEN!
I'VE NEVER SEEN ONE BEFORE. ♥♥♥
はあああ
AWWW.
THIS IS WHAT THEY USED TO EXECUTE PEOPLE BACK IN EMPEROR NERO'S TIME.
THEY USED THIS TO TORTURE PEOPLE DURING THE WITCH HUNTS.
ぶん
SPIN
ぶん
SPIN
………………………………

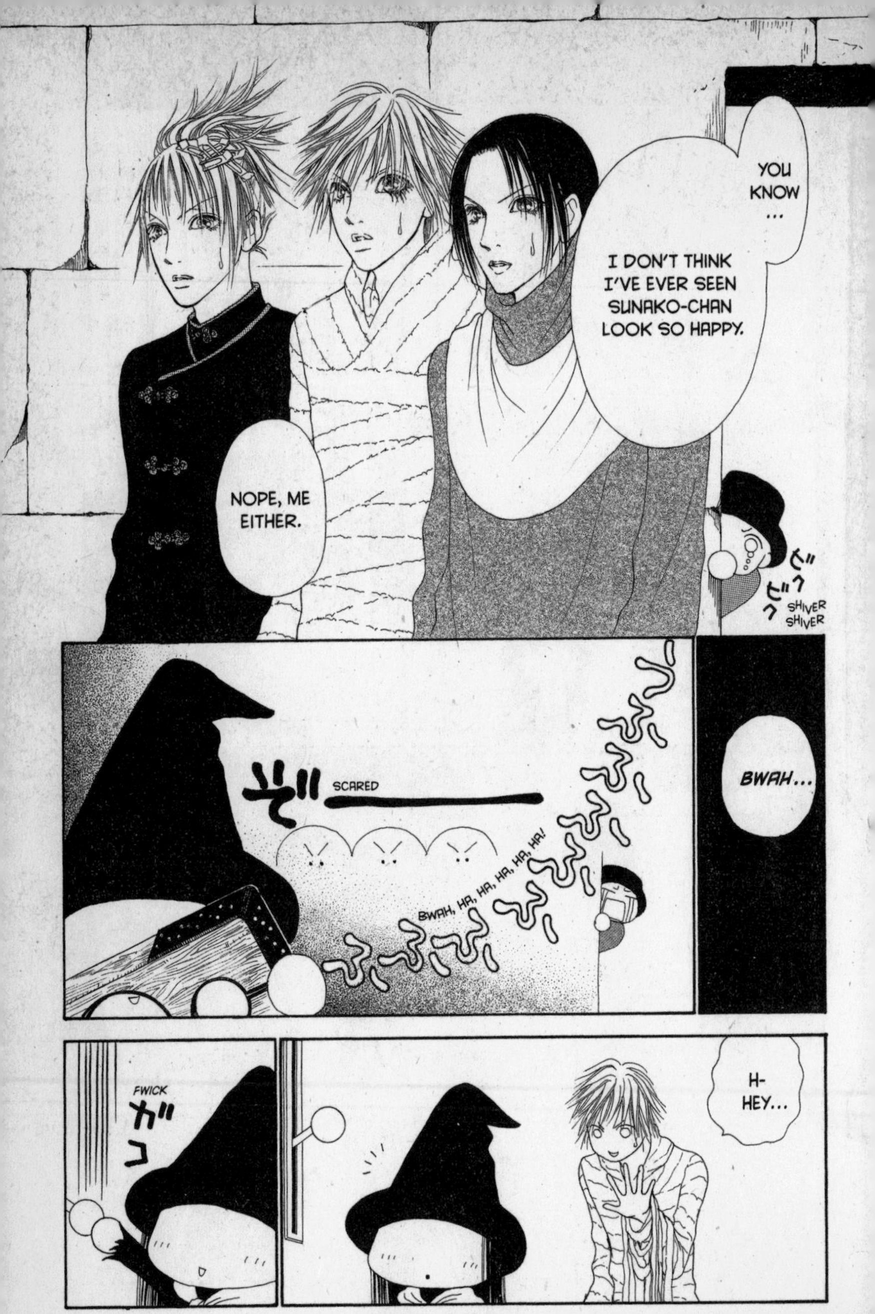
YOU KNOW …
I DON'T THINK I'VE EVER SEEN SUNAKO-CHAN LOOK SO HAPPY.
NOPE, ME EITHER.
SHIVER SHIVER
BWAH…
BWAH, HA, HA, HA, HA, HA!
SCARED
H- HEY…
FWICK

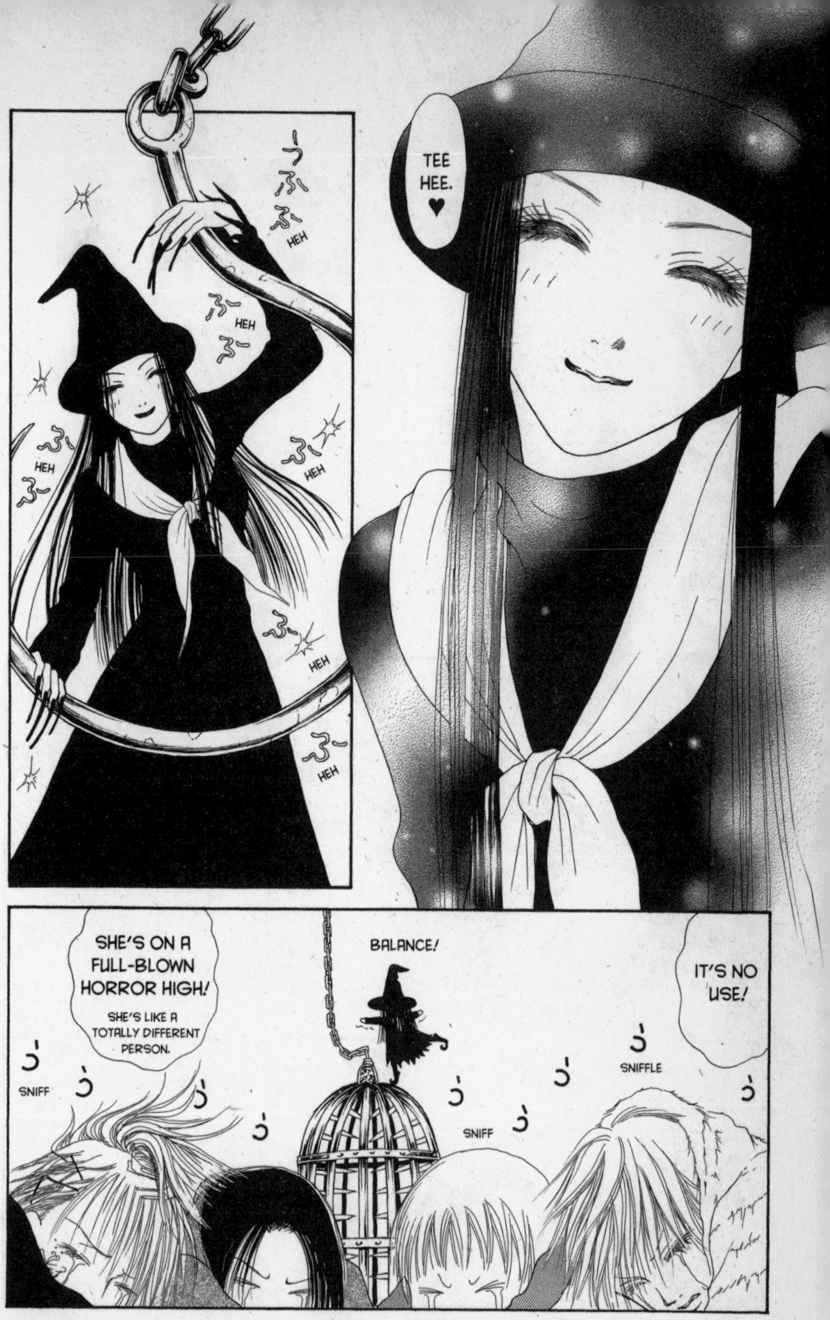
TEE HEE. ♥
うふふ
HEH
ふー
HEH
ふー
ふー
HEH
ふー
HEH
ふー
HEH
ふー
HEH
IT'S NO USE!
SNIFFLE
BALANCE!
SNIFF
SHE'S ON A FULL-BLOWN HORROR HIGH!
SHE'S LIKE A TOTALLY DIFFERENT PERSON.
SNIFF

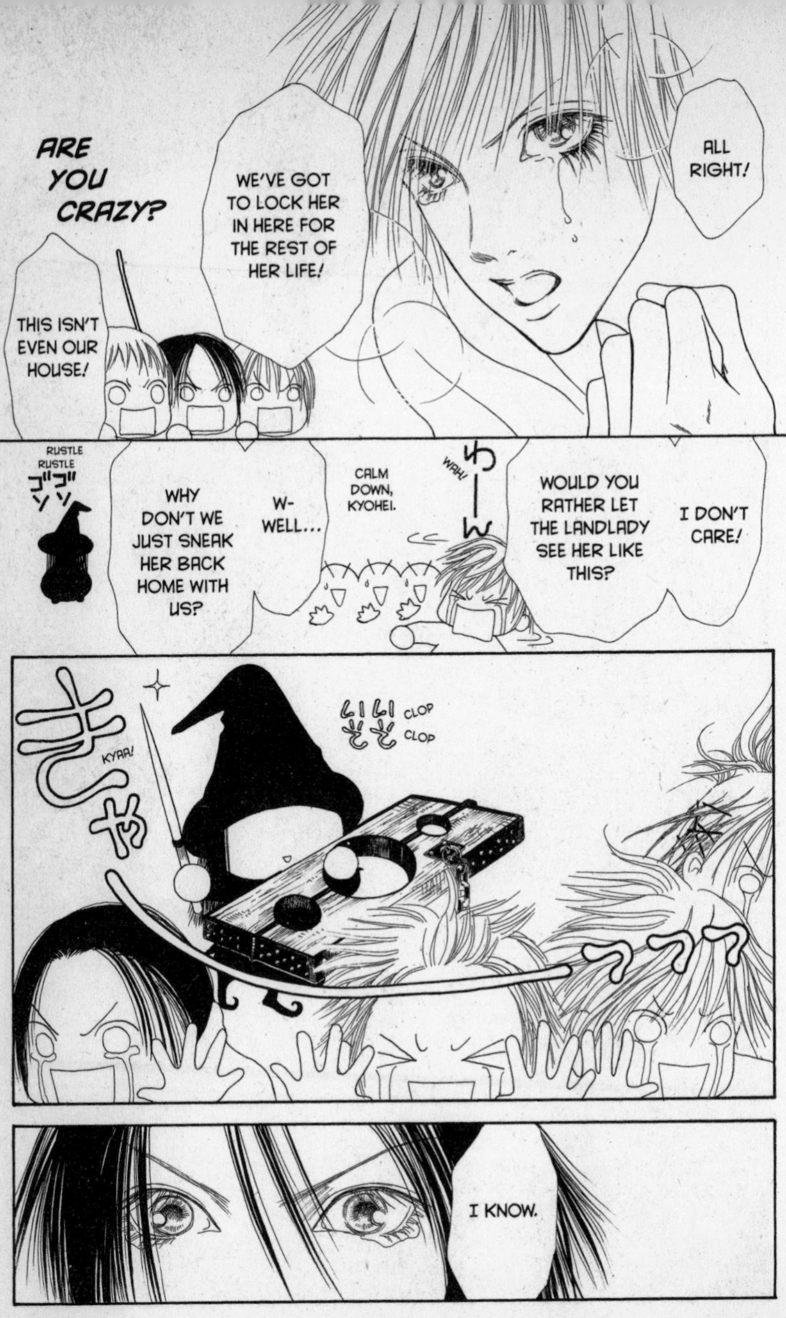
ALL RIGHT!
WE'VE GOT TO LOCK HER IN HERE FOR THE REST OF HER LIFE!
ARE YOU CRAZY?
THIS ISN'T EVEN OUR HOUSE!
I DON'T CARE!
WOULD YOU RATHER LET THE LANDLADY SEE HER LIKE THIS?
わーん WAH!
CALM DOWN, KYOHEI.
W- WELL...
WHY DON'T WE JUST SNEAK HER BACK HOME WITH US?
ゴソゴソ RUSTLE RUSTLE
???
CLOP CLOP
きゃ KYAA!
I KNOW.

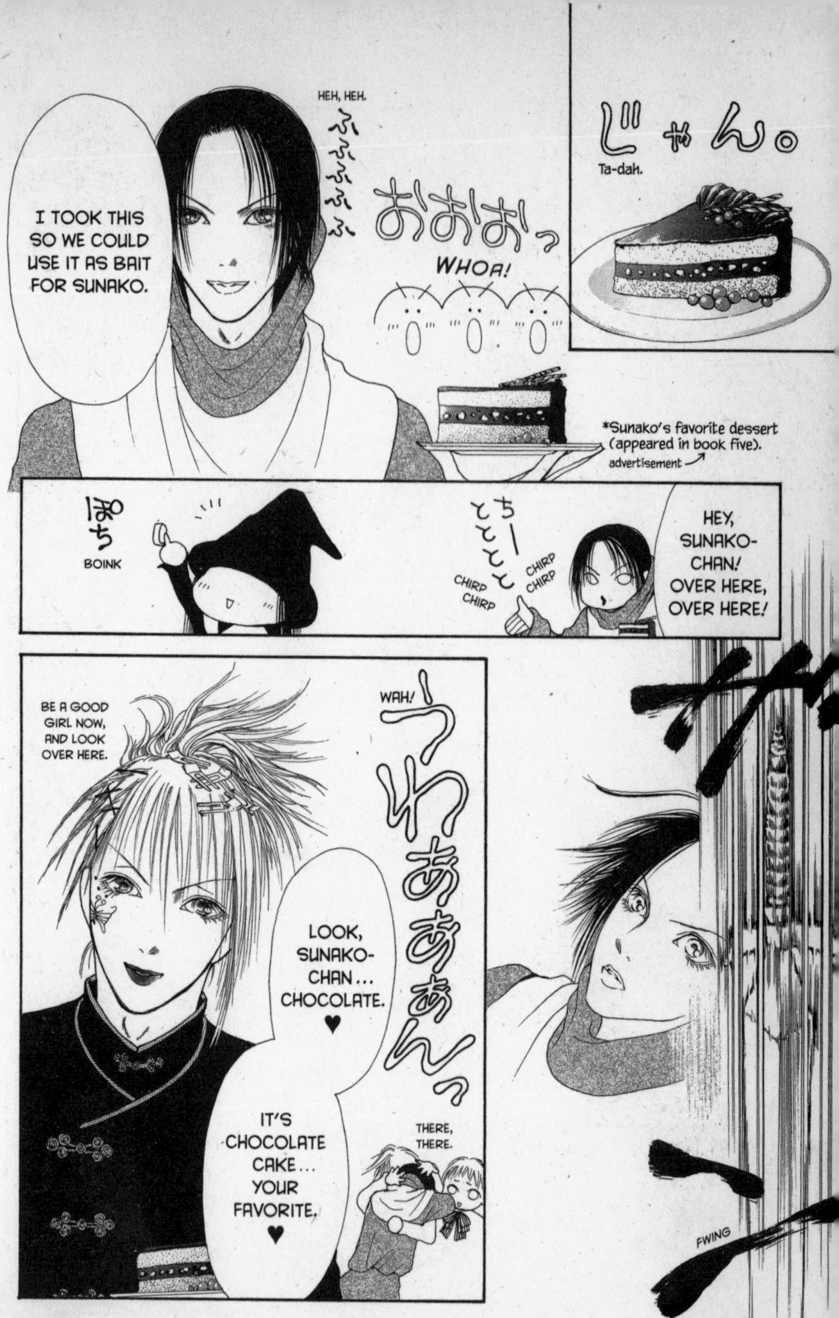
じゃん。
Ta-dah.
おおおっ
WHOA!
ふふふふふ
HEH, HEH.
I TOOK THIS SO WE COULD USE IT AS BAIT FOR SUNAKO.
*Sunako's favorite dessert (appeared in book five).
advertisement
HEY, SUNAKO-CHAN! OVER HERE, OVER HERE!
ちーとととと
CHIRP CHIRP
CHIRP CHIRP
ぽち
BOINK
FWING
うわああぁんっ
WAH!
LOOK, SUNAKO-CHAN... CHOCOLATE. ♥
IT'S CHOCOLATE CAKE... YOUR FAVORITE. ♥
THERE, THERE.
BE A GOOD GIRL NOW, AND LOOK OVER HERE.

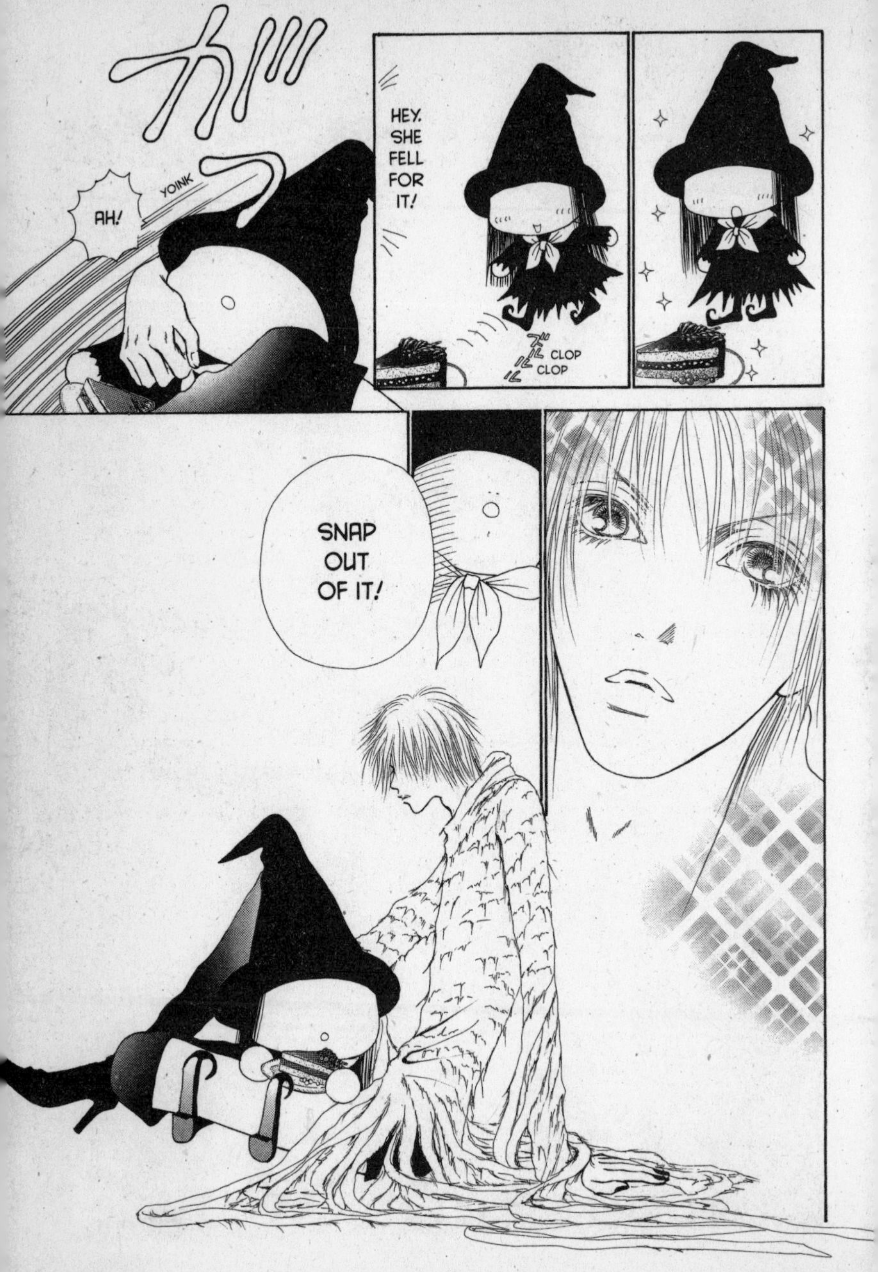
HEY. SHE FELL FOR IT!
CLOP CLOP
AH!
YOINK
SNAP OUT OF IT!

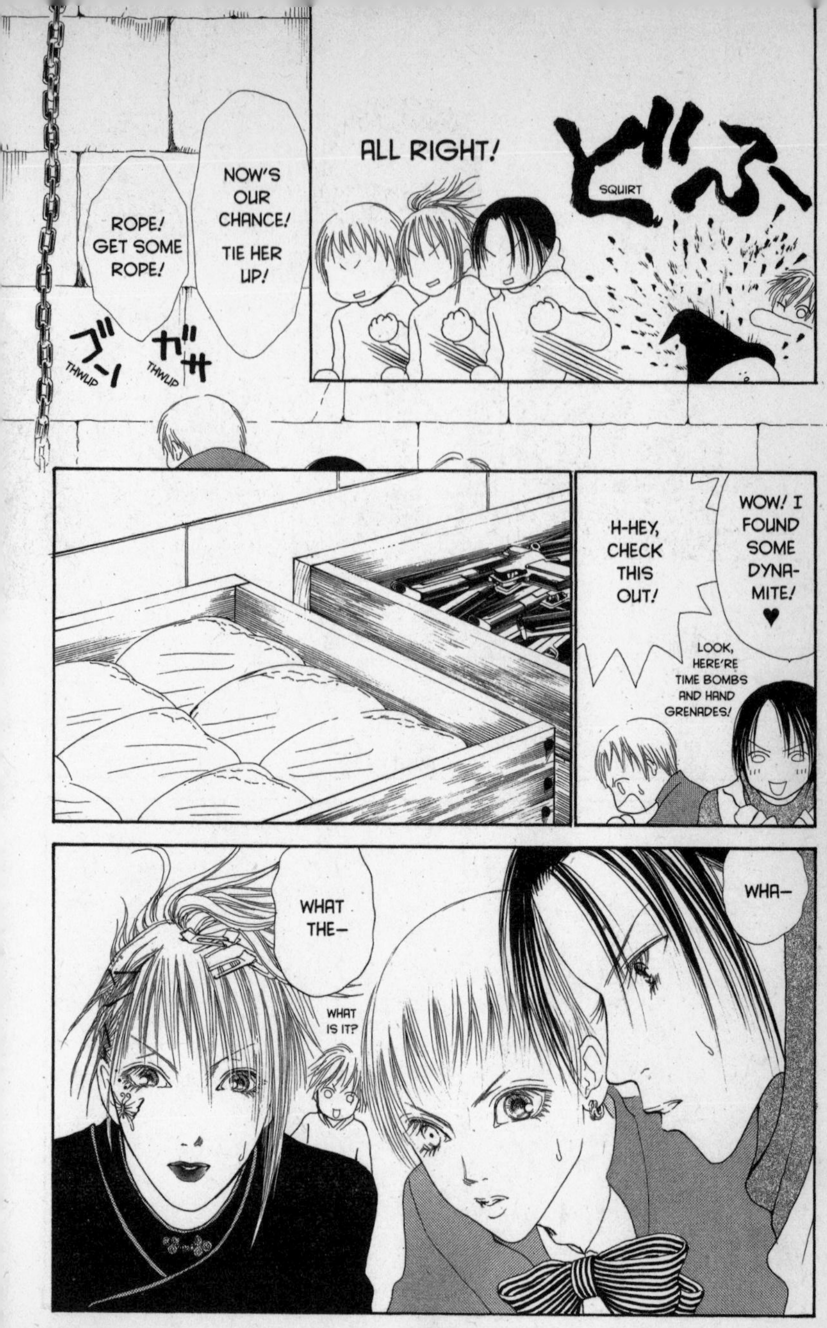
SQUIRT
ALL RIGHT!
NOW'S OUR CHANCE!
TIE HER UP!
ROPE! GET SOME ROPE!
THWUP
THWUP
WOW! I FOUND SOME DYNA-MITE! ♥
H-HEY, CHECK THIS OUT!
LOOK, HERE'RE TIME BOMBS AND HAND GRENADES!
WHA-
WHAT THE-
WHAT IS IT?

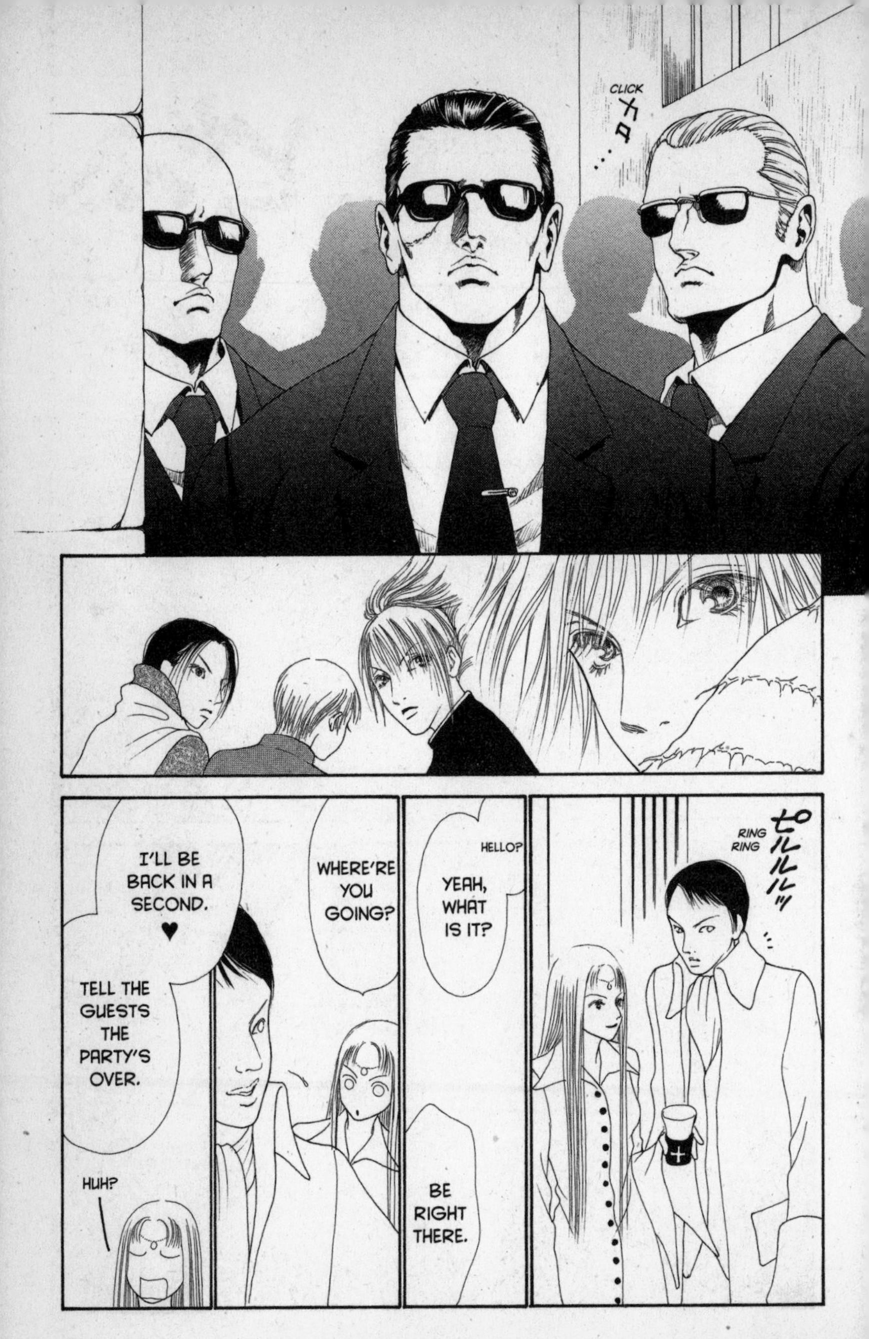

CLICK
カタ…
RING RING
ピルルルッ
HELLO?
YEAH, WHAT IS IT?
BE RIGHT THERE.
WHERE'RE YOU GOING?
I'LL BE BACK IN A SECOND. ♥
TELL THE GUESTS THE PARTY'S OVER.
HUH?

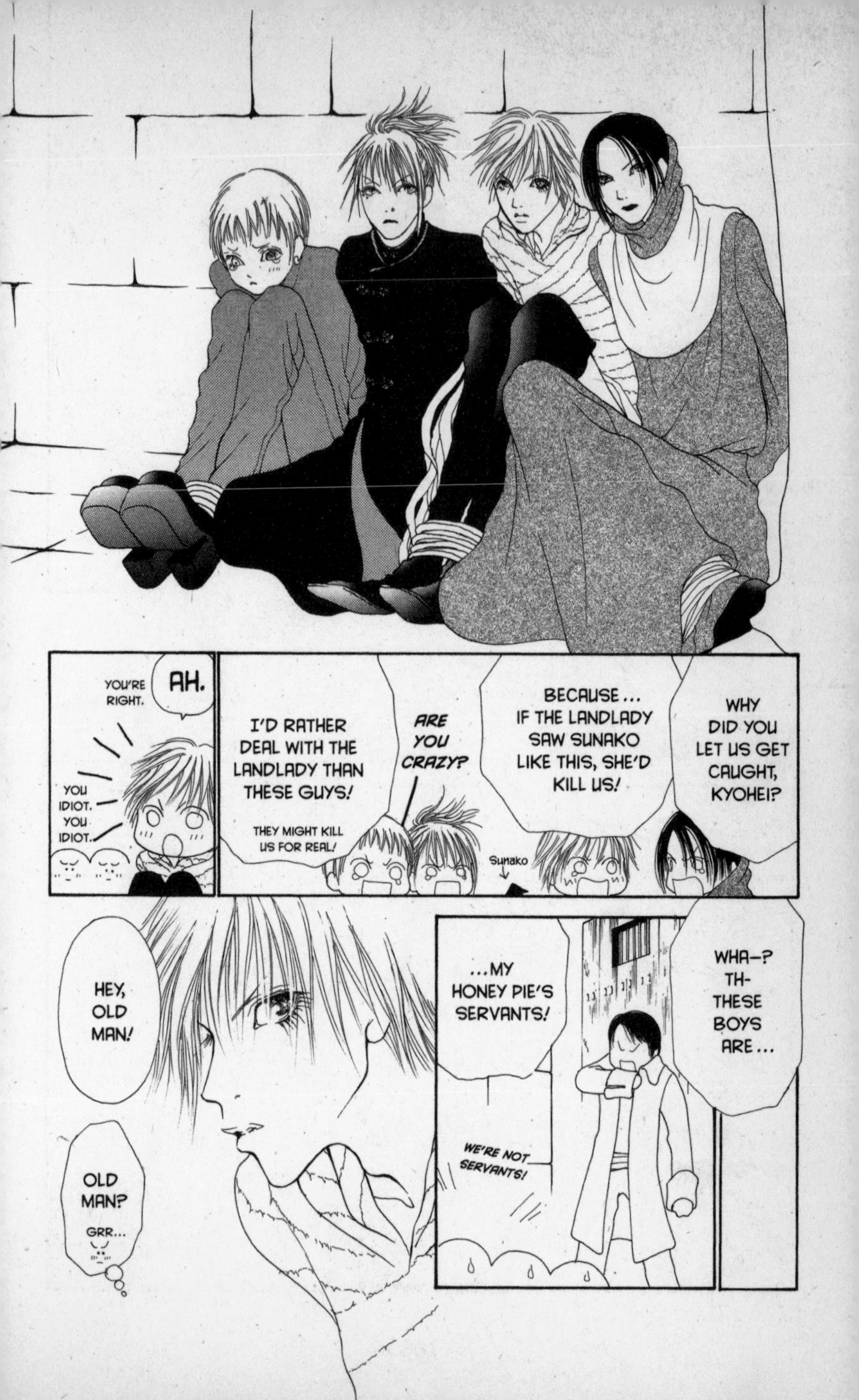
WHY DID YOU LET US GET CAUGHT, KYOHEI?
BECAUSE... IF THE LANDLADY SAW SUNAKO LIKE THIS, SHE'D KILL US!
Sunako
ARE YOU CRAZY?
I'D RATHER DEAL WITH THE LANDLADY THAN THESE GUYS!
THEY MIGHT KILL US FOR REAL!
AH.
YOU'RE RIGHT.
YOU IDIOT. YOU IDIOT.
WHA-? TH- THESE BOYS ARE...
...MY HONEY PIE'S SERVANTS!
WE'RE NOT SERVANTS!
HEY, OLD MAN!
OLD MAN?
GRR...

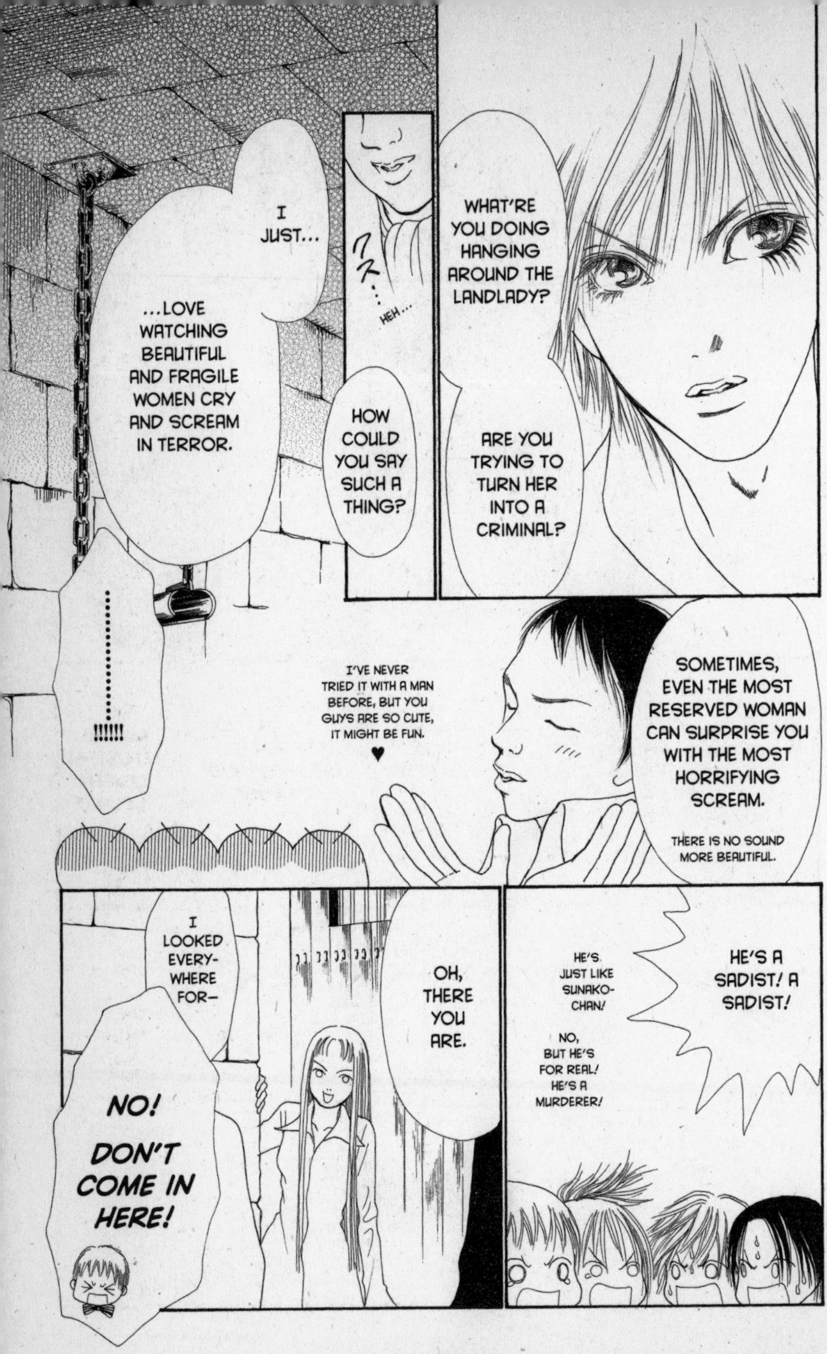
WHAT'RE YOU DOING HANGING AROUND THE LANDLADY?
ARE YOU TRYING TO TURN HER INTO A CRIMINAL?
HEH...
HOW COULD YOU SAY SUCH A THING?
I JUST...
...LOVE WATCHING BEAUTIFUL AND FRAGILE WOMEN CRY AND SCREAM IN TERROR.
......!!!!!!
SOMETIMES, EVEN THE MOST RESERVED WOMAN CAN SURPRISE YOU WITH THE MOST HORRIFYING SCREAM.
THERE IS NO SOUND MORE BEAUTIFUL.
I'VE NEVER TRIED IT WITH A MAN BEFORE, BUT YOU GUYS ARE SO CUTE, IT MIGHT BE FUN. ♥
HE'S A SADIST! A SADIST!
HE'S. JUST LIKE SUNAKO-CHAN!
NO, BUT HE'S FOR REAL! HE'S A MURDERER!
OH, THERE YOU ARE.
I LOOKED EVERY-WHERE FOR—
NO! DON'T COME IN HERE!

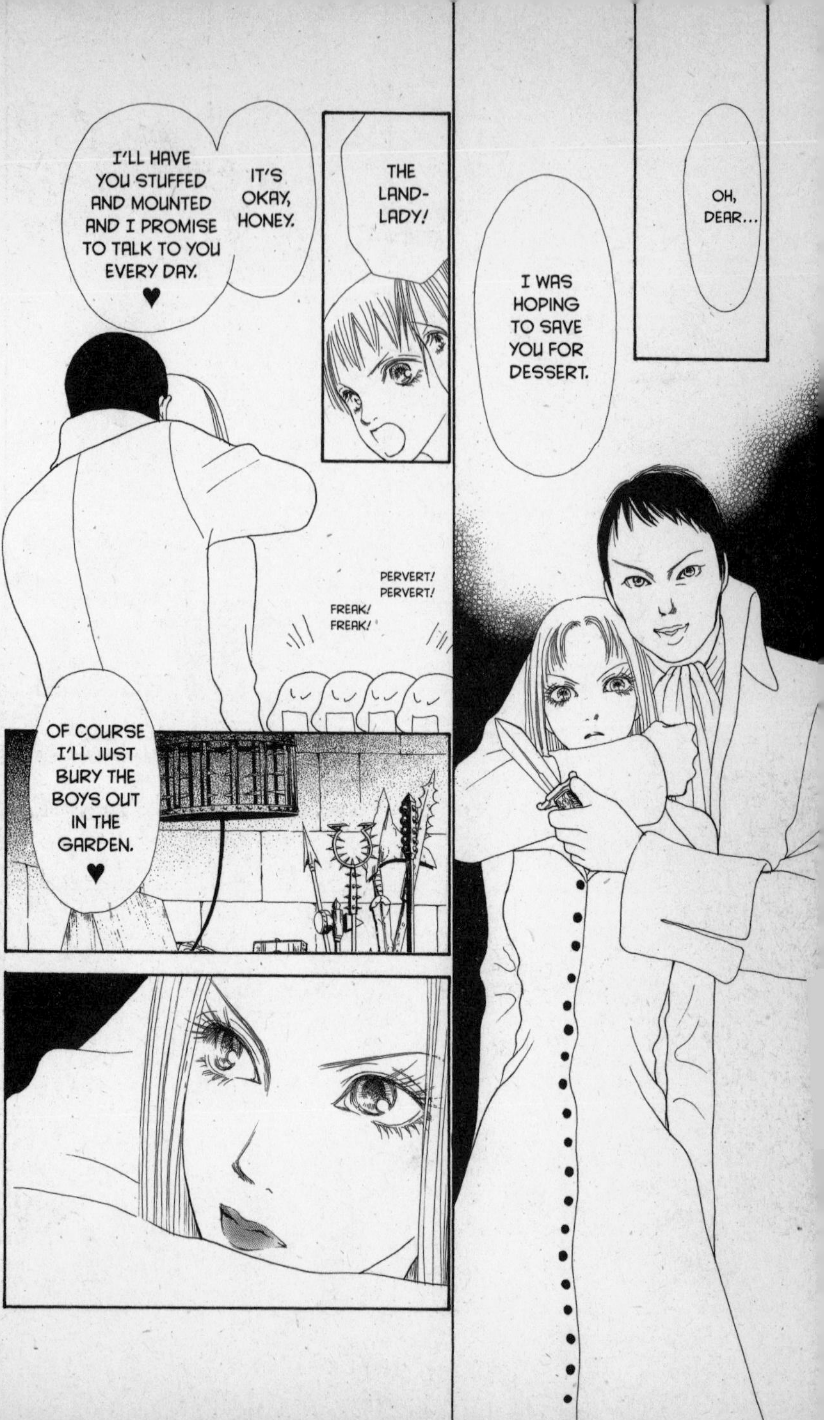
OH, DEAR...
I WAS HOPING TO SAVE YOU FOR DESSERT.
THE LAND-LADY!
IT'S OKAY, HONEY.
I'LL HAVE YOU STUFFED AND MOUNTED AND I PROMISE TO TALK TO YOU EVERY DAY. ♥
PERVERT! PERVERT!
FREAK! FREAK!
OF COURSE I'LL JUST BURY THE BOYS OUT IN THE GARDEN. ♥

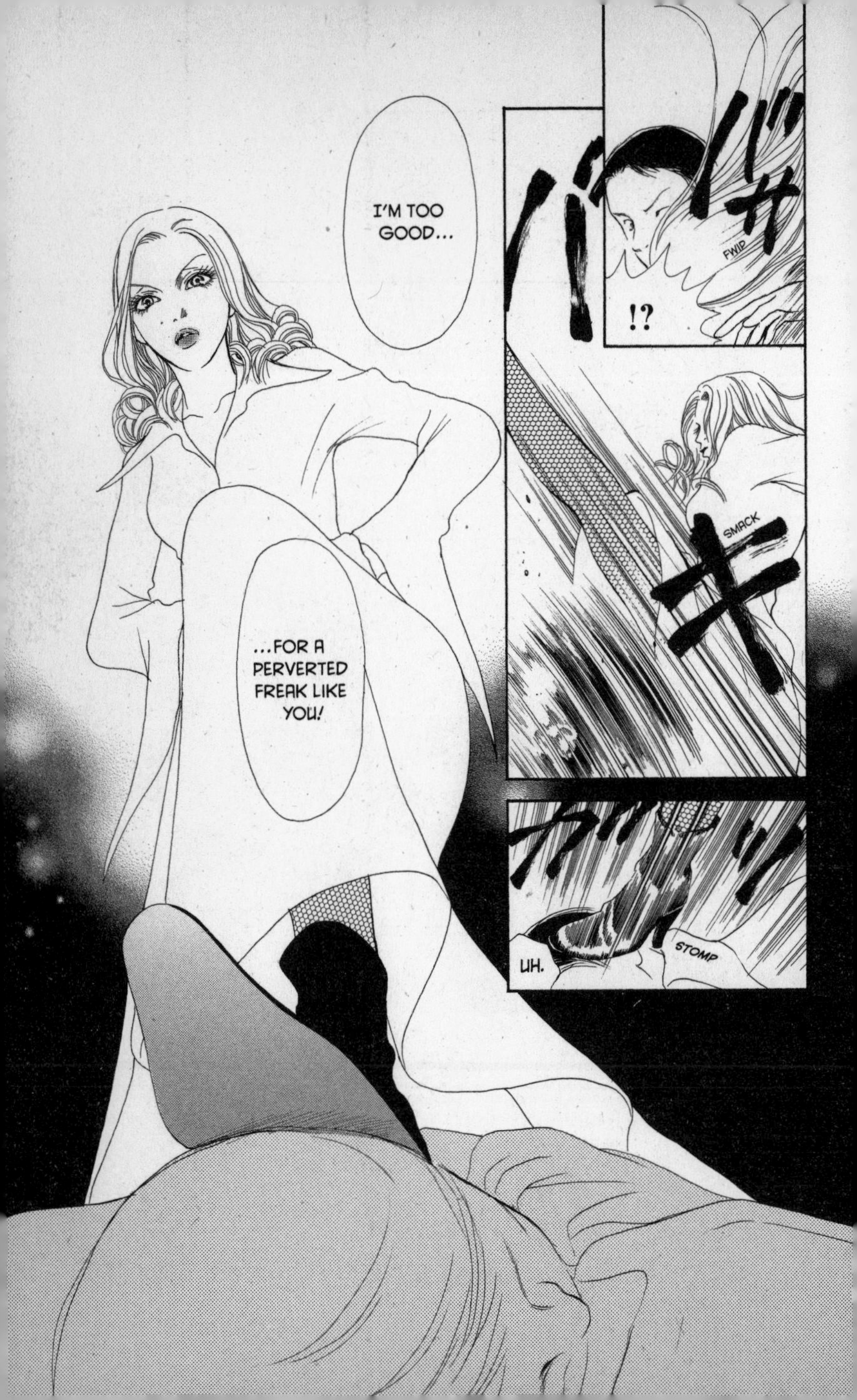
FWIP
!?
SMACK
STOMP
UH.
I'M TOO GOOD...
...FOR A PERVERTED FREAK LIKE YOU!

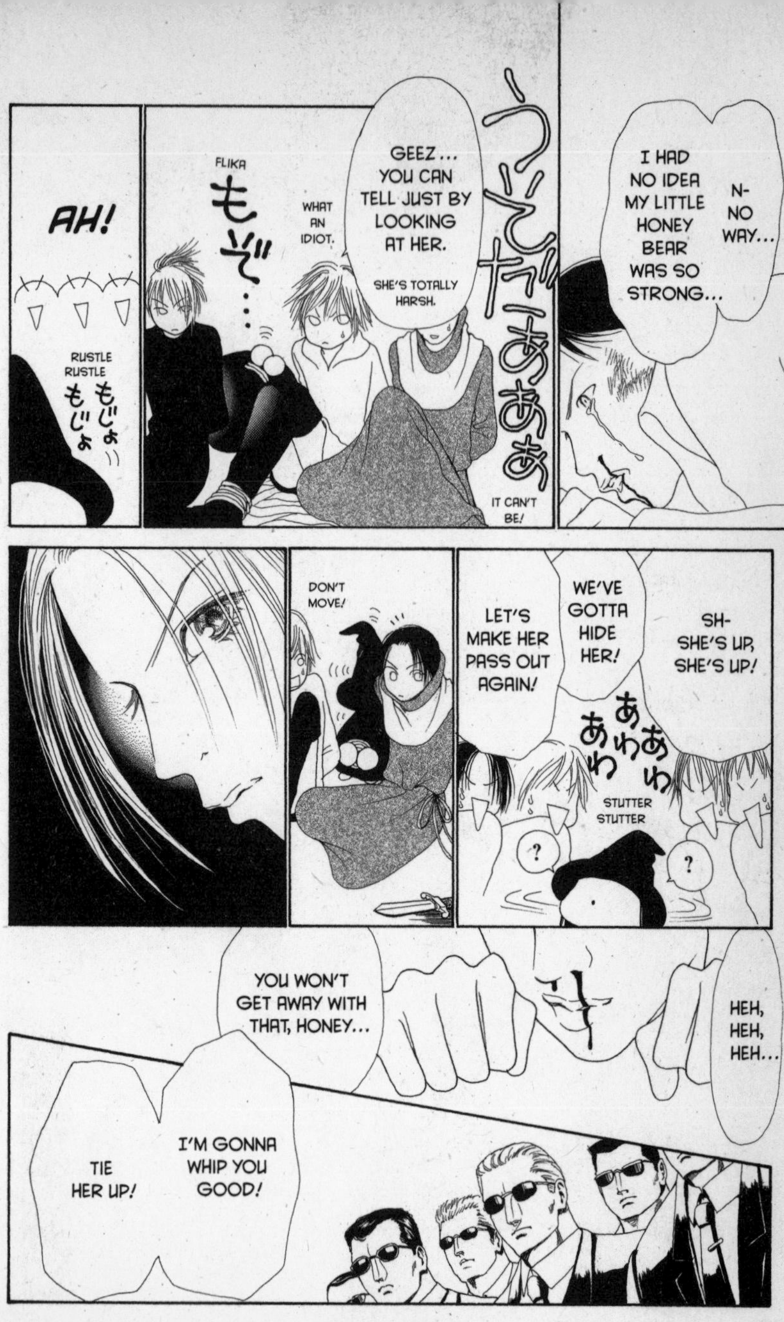
N-
NO
WAY...
I HAD
NO IDEA
MY LITTLE
HONEY
BEAR
WAS SO
STRONG...
うそだぁあぁ
IT CAN'T
BE!
GEEZ...
YOU CAN
TELL JUST BY
LOOKING
AT HER.
SHE'S TOTALLY
HARSH.
WHAT
AN
IDIOT.
もぞ...
FLIKA
AH!
もじょもじょ
RUSTLE
RUSTLE
SH-
SHE'S UP,
SHE'S UP!
WE'VE
GOTTA
HIDE
HER!
LET'S
MAKE HER
PASS OUT
AGAIN!
あわあわあわ
STUTTER
STUTTER
?
?
DON'T
MOVE!
HEH,
HEH,
HEH...
YOU WON'T
GET AWAY WITH
THAT, HONEY...
I'M GONNA
WHIP YOU
GOOD!
TIE
HER UP!

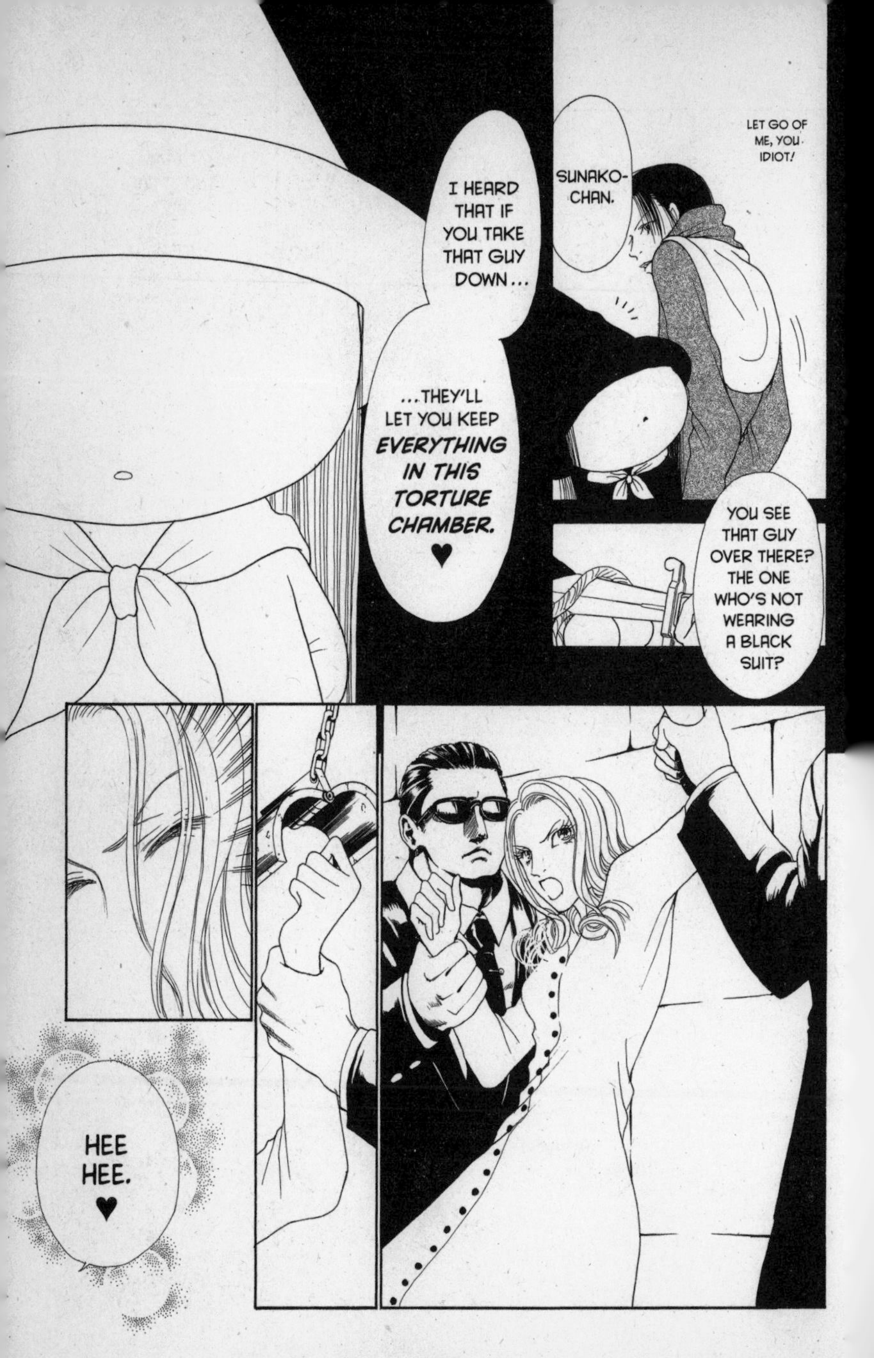
LET GO OF ME, YOU IDIOT!
SUNAKO-CHAN.
YOU SEE THAT GUY OVER THERE? THE ONE WHO'S NOT WEARING A BLACK SUIT?
I HEARD THAT IF YOU TAKE THAT GUY DOWN...
...THEY'LL LET YOU KEEP *EVERYTHING IN THIS TORTURE CHAMBER.* ♥
HEE HEE. ♥

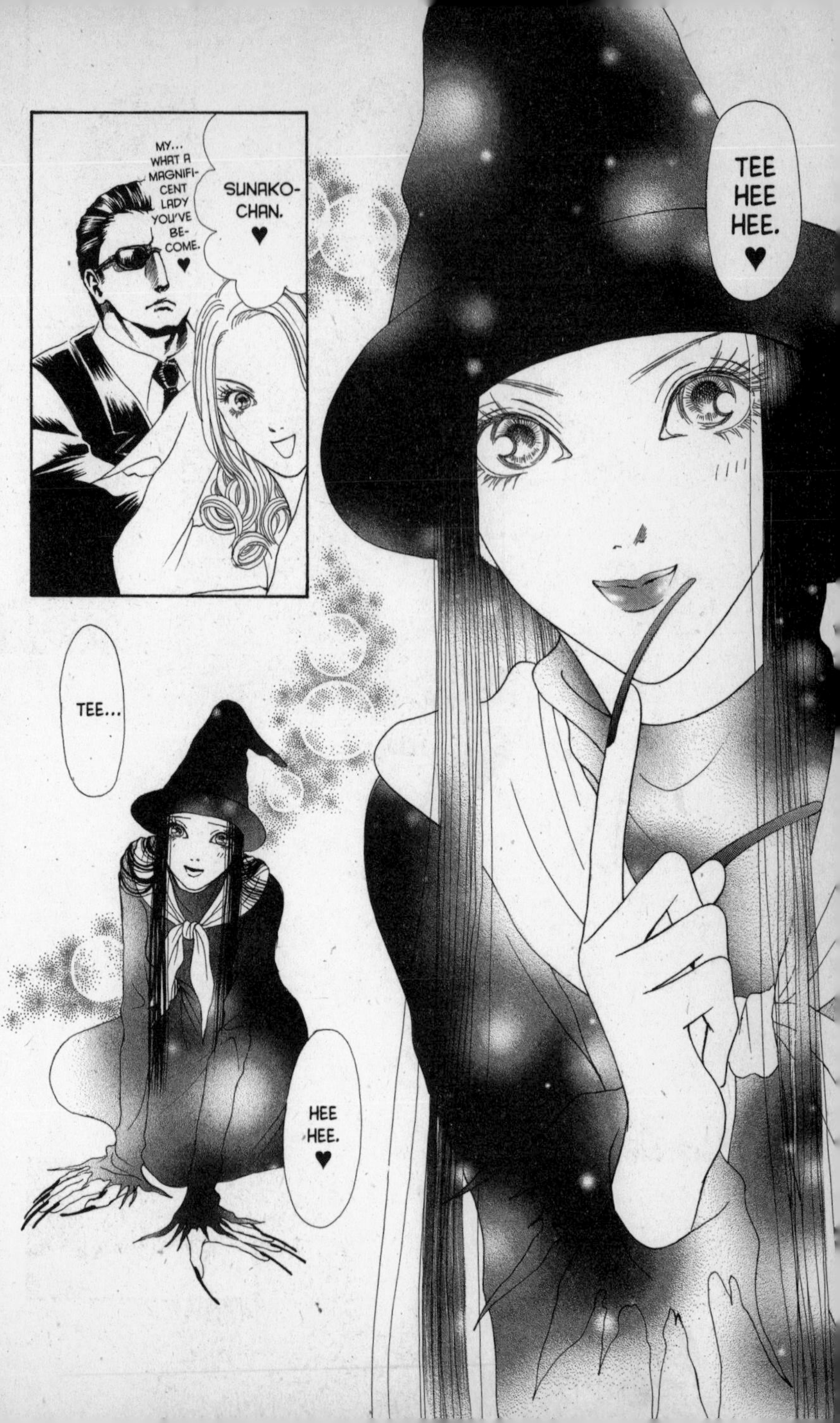
TEE HEE HEE. ♥
SUNAKO-CHAN. ♥
MY... WHAT A MAGNIFICENT LADY YOU'VE BECOME. ♥
TEE...
HEE HEE. ♥

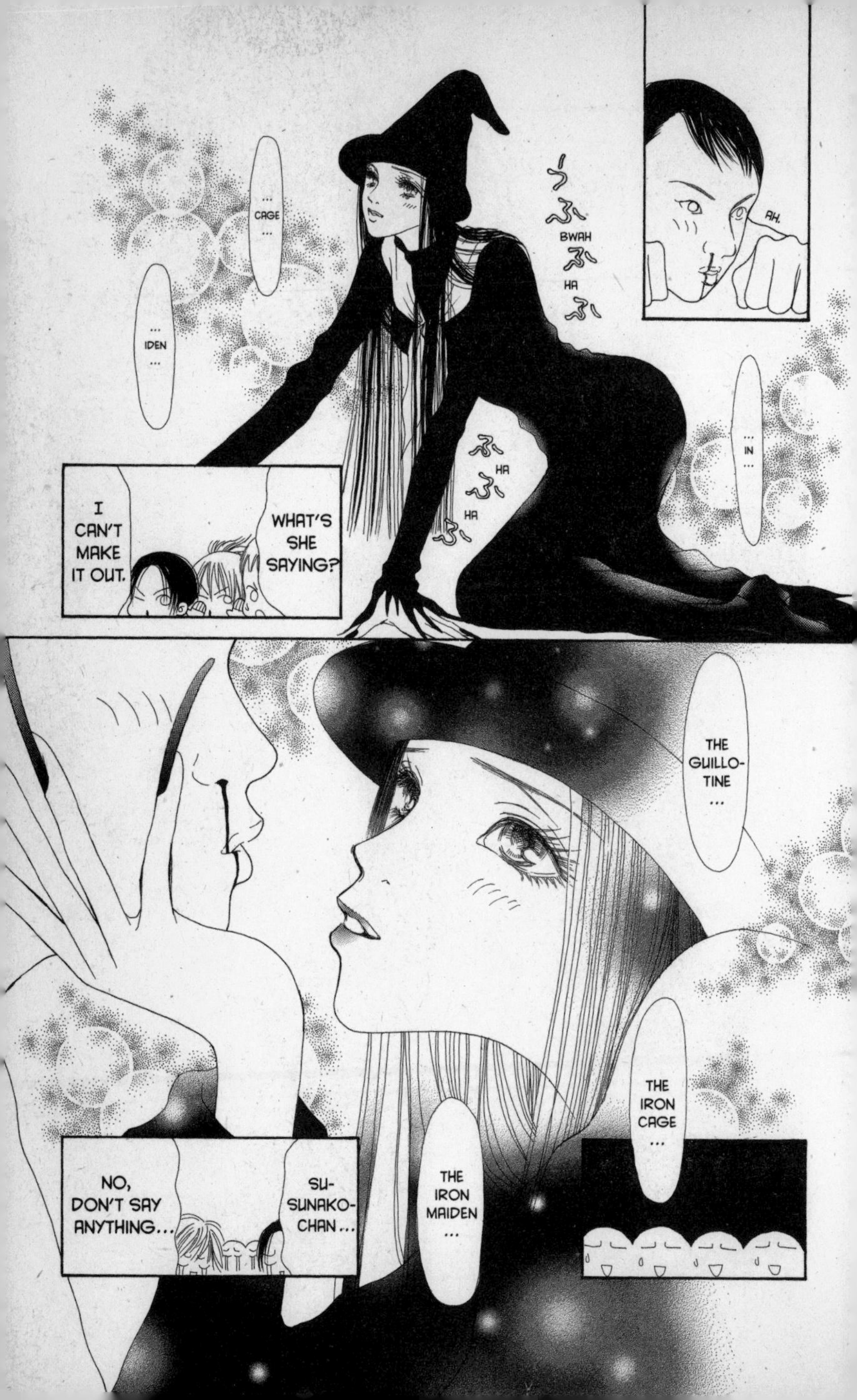
AH.
うふ
BWAH
ふ
HA
ふ
...IN...
...CAGE...
...IDEN...
ふ
HA
ふ
HA
ふ
WHAT'S SHE SAYING?
I CAN'T MAKE IT OUT.
THE GUILLO-TINE...
THE IRON CAGE...
THE IRON MAIDEN...
SU-SUNAKO-CHAN...
NO, DON'T SAY ANYTHING...

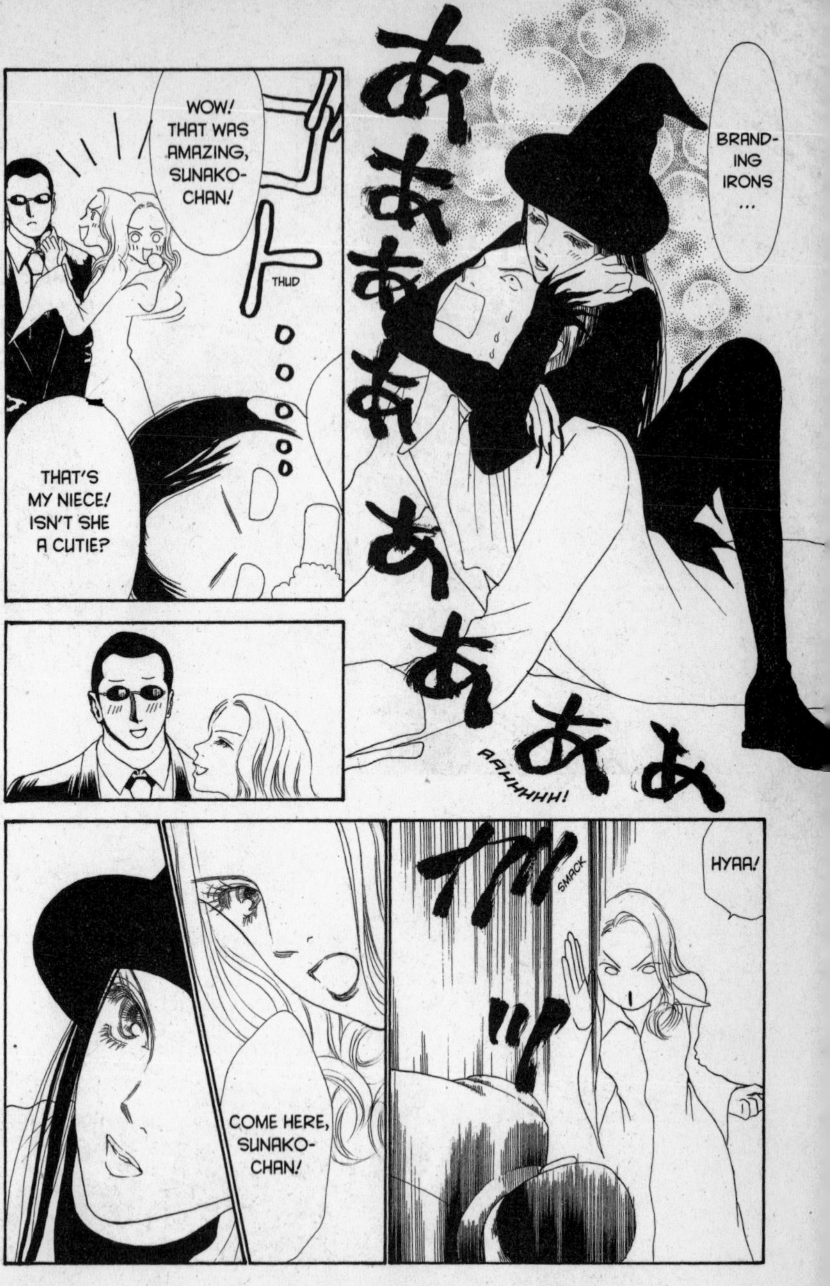
BRANDING IRONS ...
AAHHHHH!
WOW! THAT WAS AMAZING, SUNAKO-CHAN!
THUD
THAT'S MY NIECE! ISN'T SHE A CUTIE?
HYAA!
SMACK
COME HERE, SUNAKO-CHAN!

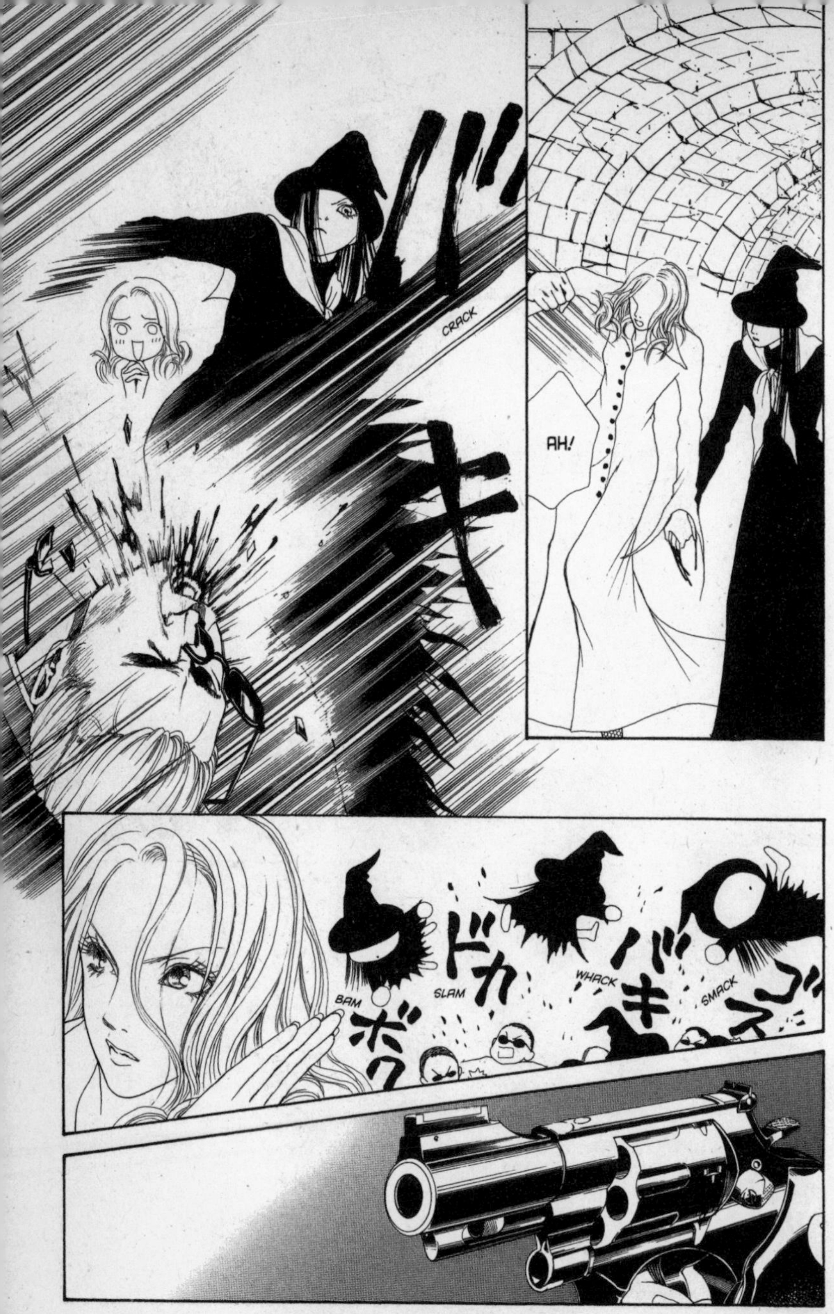
AH!
CRACK
キ
SMACK
ゴス
WHACK
バキ
SLAM
ドカ
BAM
ボグ

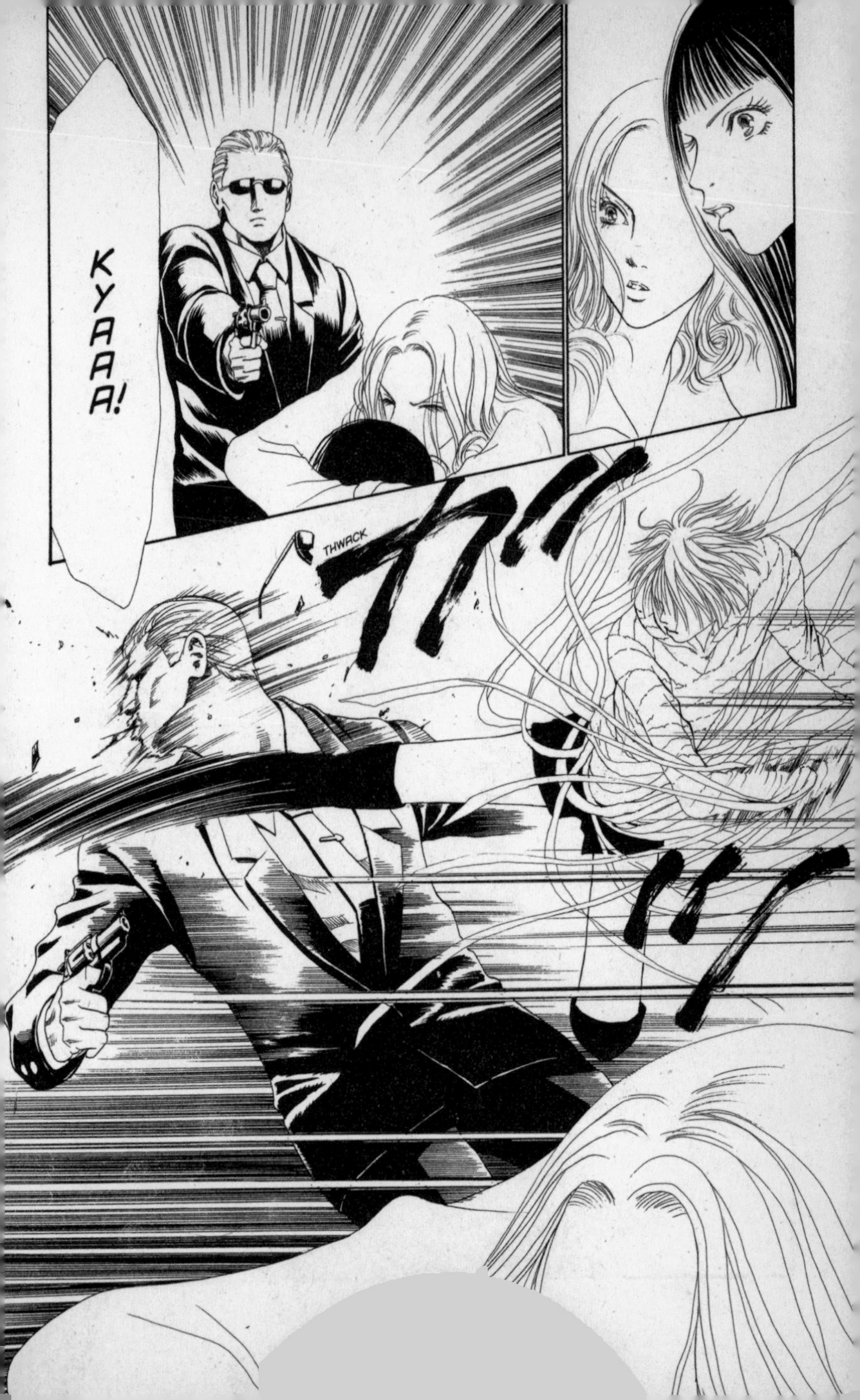
KYAAAA!
THWACK

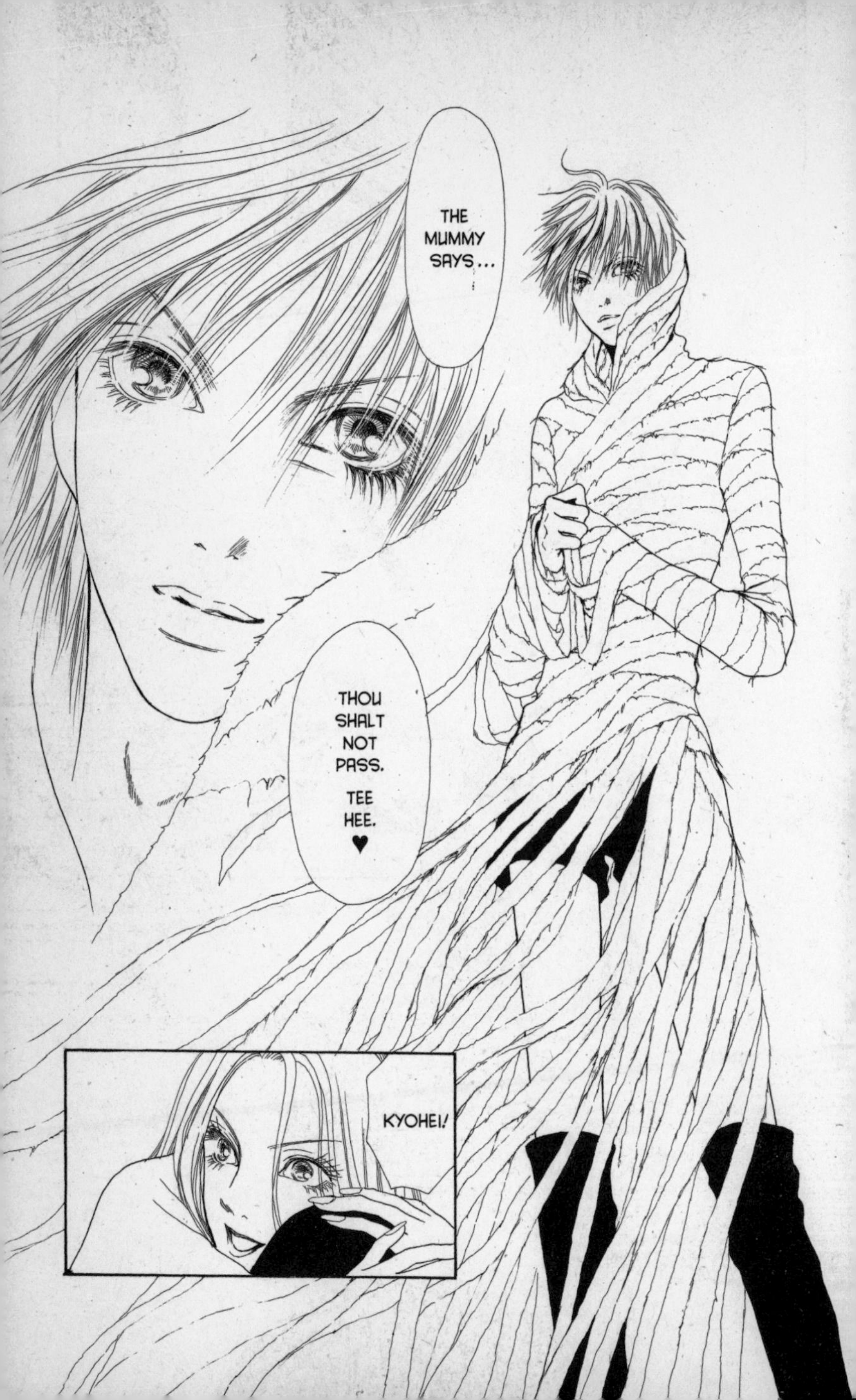
THE MUMMY SAYS...
THOU SHALT NOT PASS. TEE HEE. ♥
KYOHEI!

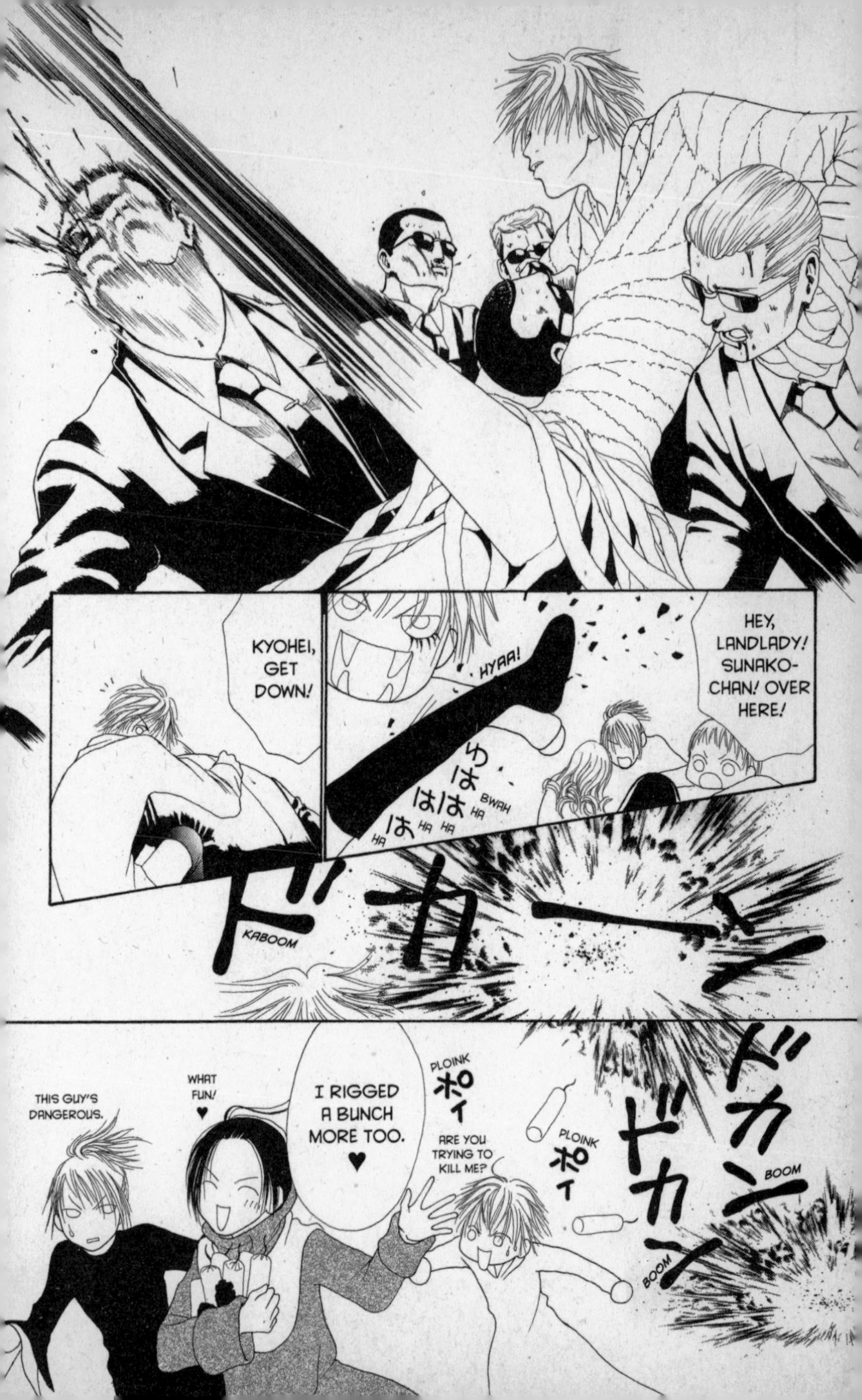
HEY, LANDLADY! SUNAKO-CHAN! OVER HERE!
HYAA!
ゆははははは
BWAH HA HA HA HA
KYOHEI, GET DOWN!
ドカーン
KABOOM
ドカン
BOOM
ドカン
BOOM
PLOINK
ポイ
ARE YOU TRYING TO KILL ME?
PLOINK
ポイ
I RIGGED A BUNCH MORE TOO. ♥
WHAT FUN! ♥
THIS GUY'S DANGEROUS.

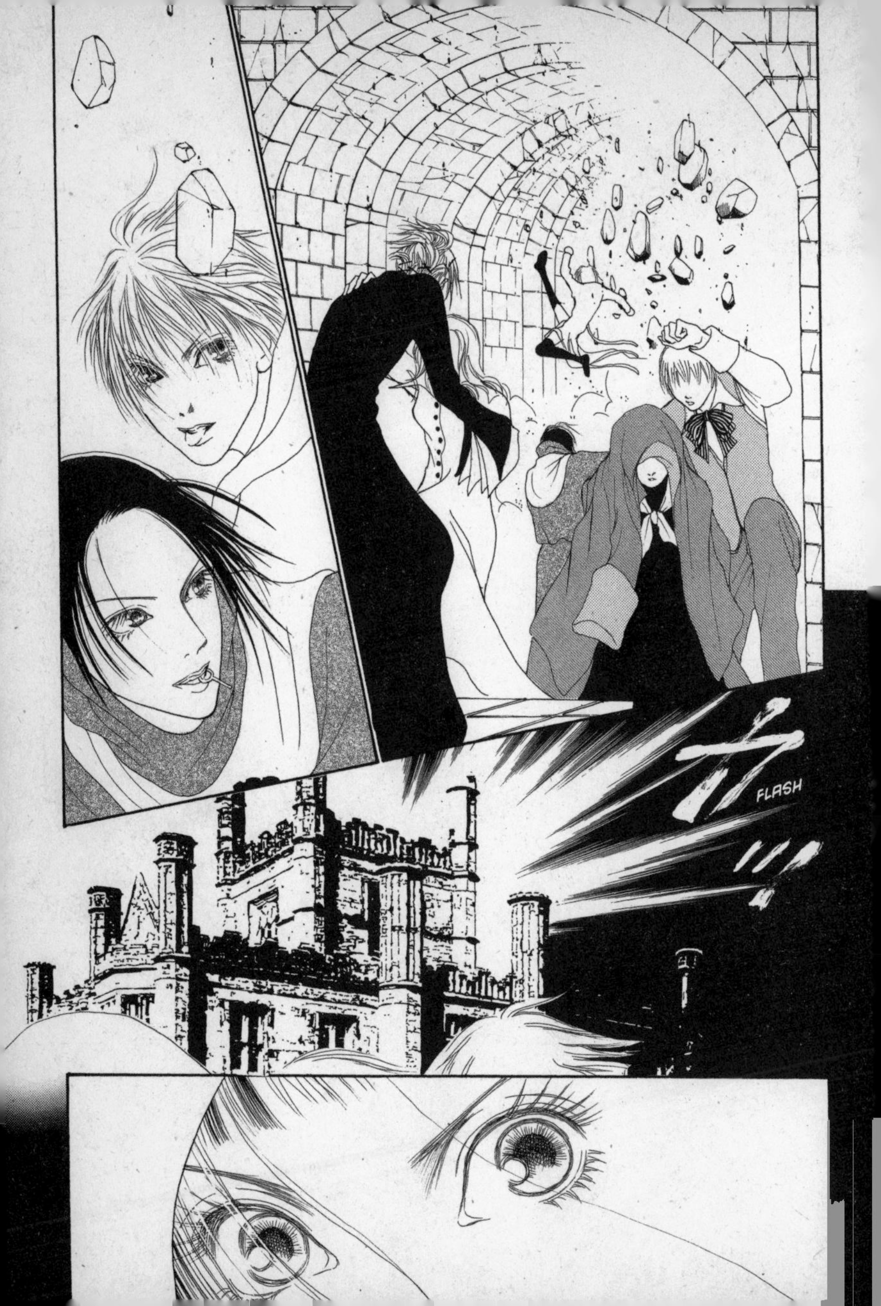
FLASH

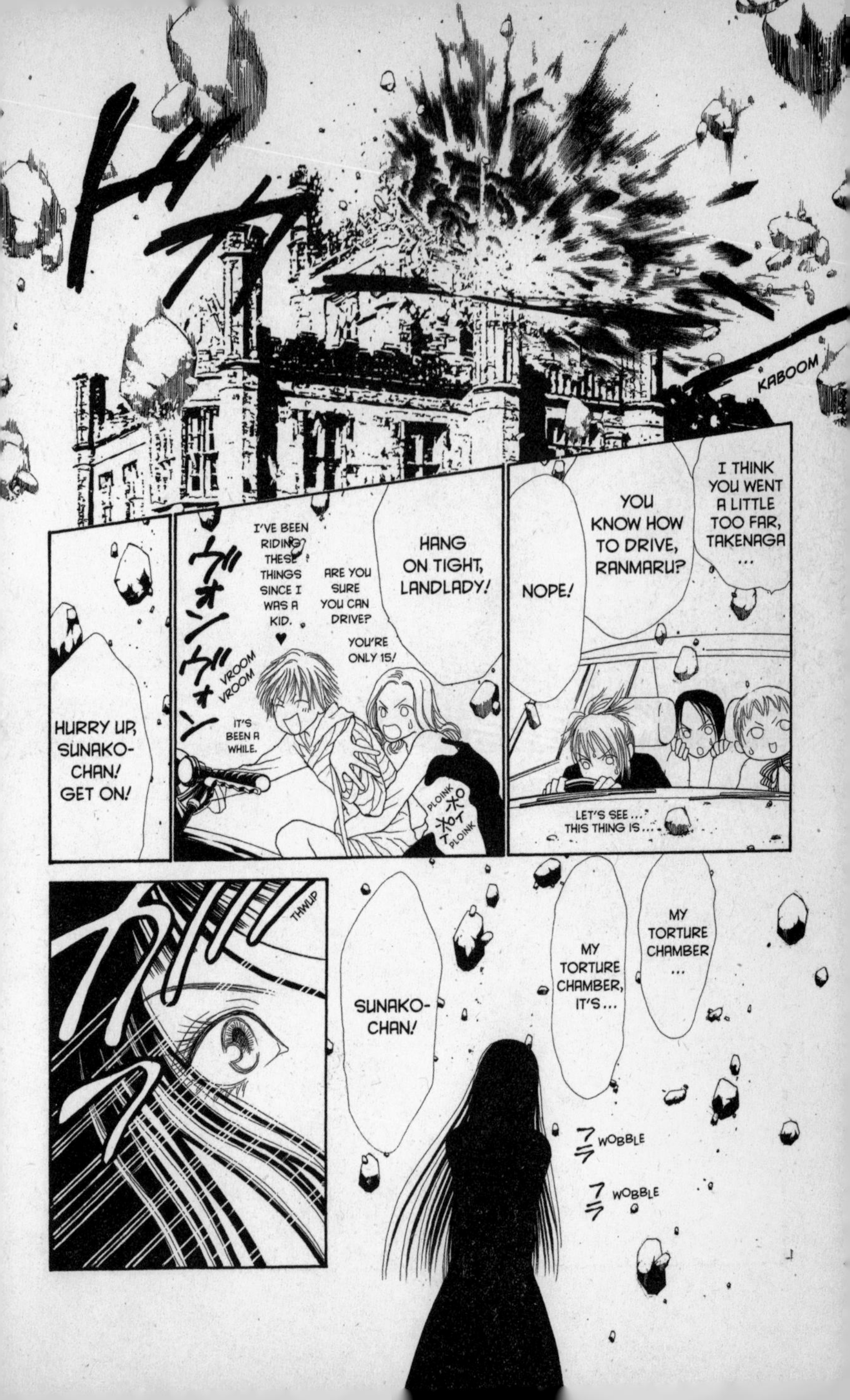
KABOOM
I THINK YOU WENT A LITTLE TOO FAR, TAKENAGA ...
YOU KNOW HOW TO DRIVE, RANMARU?
NOPE!
LET'S SEE... THIS THING IS...
HANG ON TIGHT, LANDLADY!
ARE YOU SURE YOU CAN DRIVE?
YOU'RE ONLY 15!
I'VE BEEN RIDING THESE THINGS SINCE I WAS A KID. ♥
ヴォンヴォン
VROOM VROOM
IT'S BEEN A WHILE.
PLOINK PLOINK
HURRY UP, SUNAKO-CHAN! GET ON!
MY TORTURE CHAMBER ...
MY TORTURE CHAMBER, IT'S...
SUNAKO-CHAN!
WOBBLE
WOBBLE
THWUP

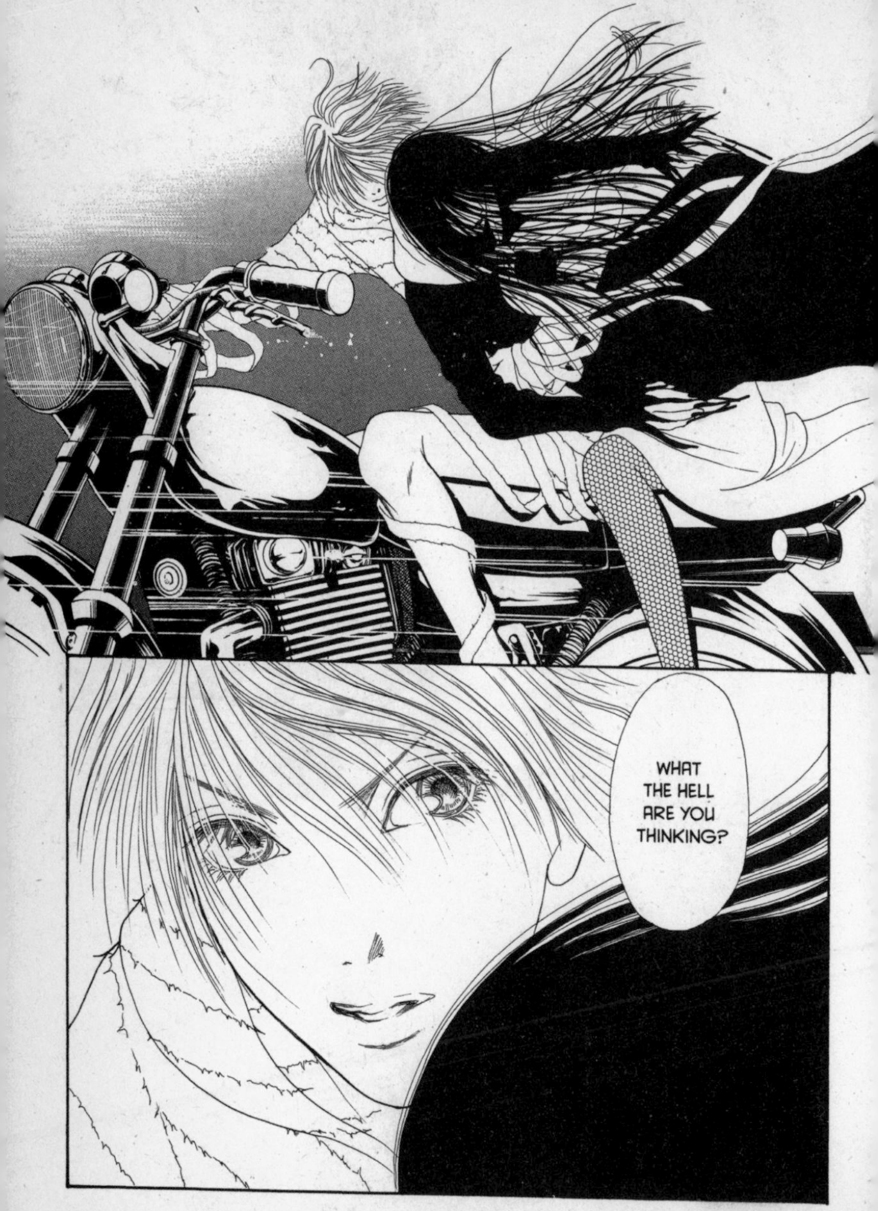
WHAT THE HELL ARE YOU THINKING?

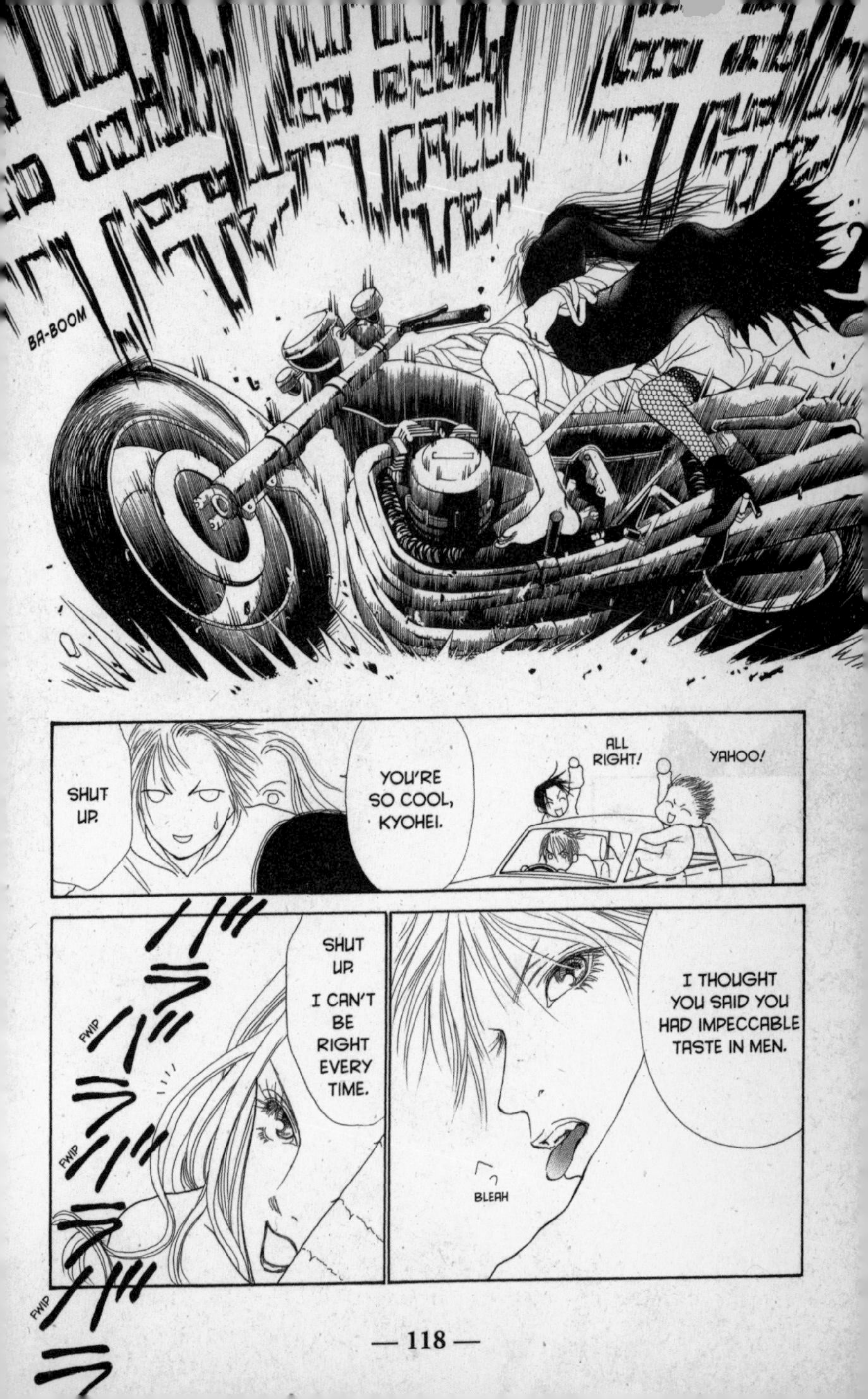
BA-BOOM
YAHOO!
ALL RIGHT!
YOU'RE SO COOL, KYOHEI.
SHUT UP.
I THOUGHT YOU SAID YOU HAD IMPECCABLE TASTE IN MEN.
BLEAH
SHUT UP.
I CAN'T BE RIGHT EVERY TIME.
FWIP
FWIP
FWIP

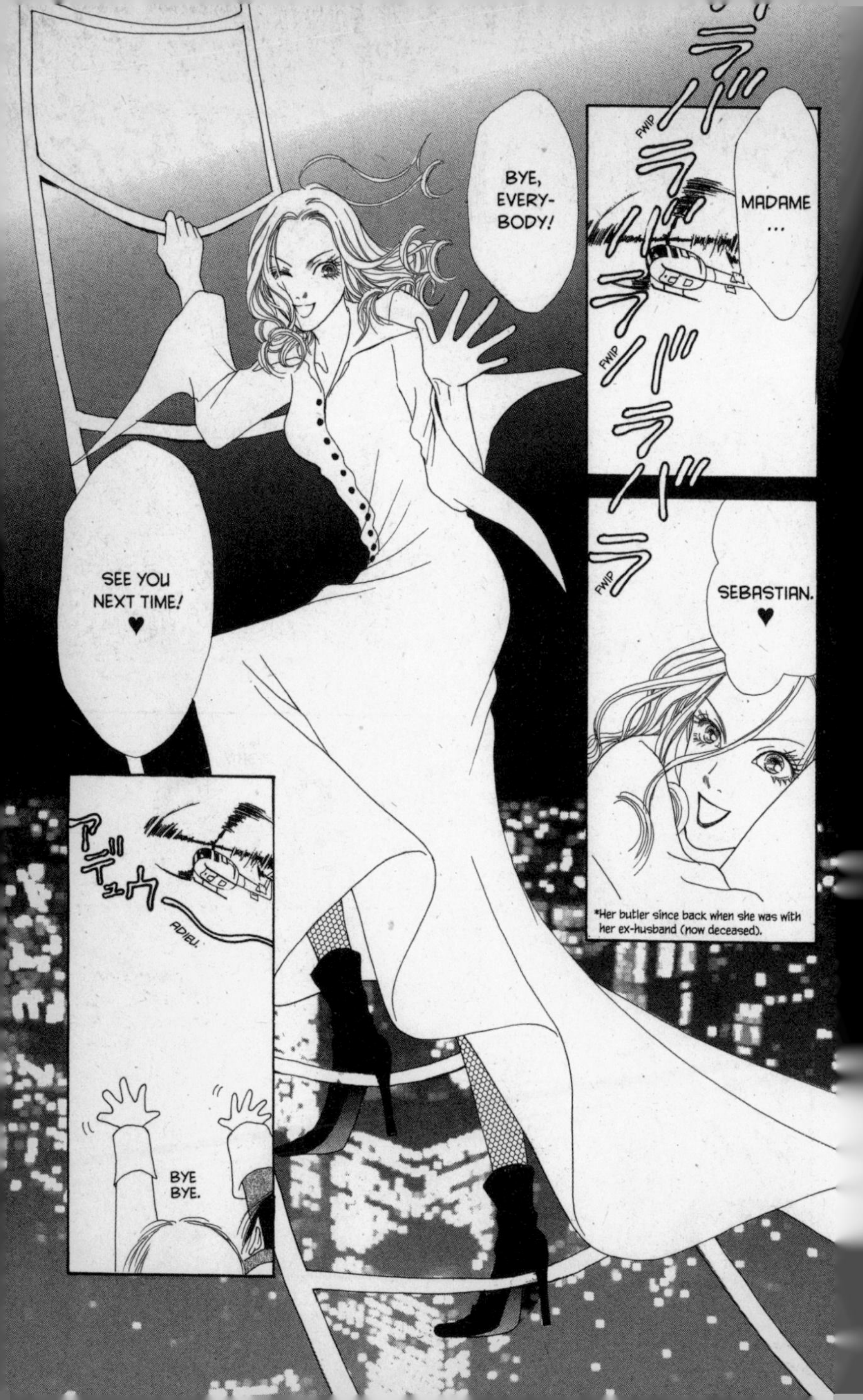
FWIP
MADAME ...
FWIP
FWIP
SEBASTIAN. ♥
*Her butler since back when she was with her ex-husband (now deceased).
BYE, EVERY-BODY!
SEE YOU NEXT TIME! ♥
アデュウ
ADIEU.
BYE BYE.

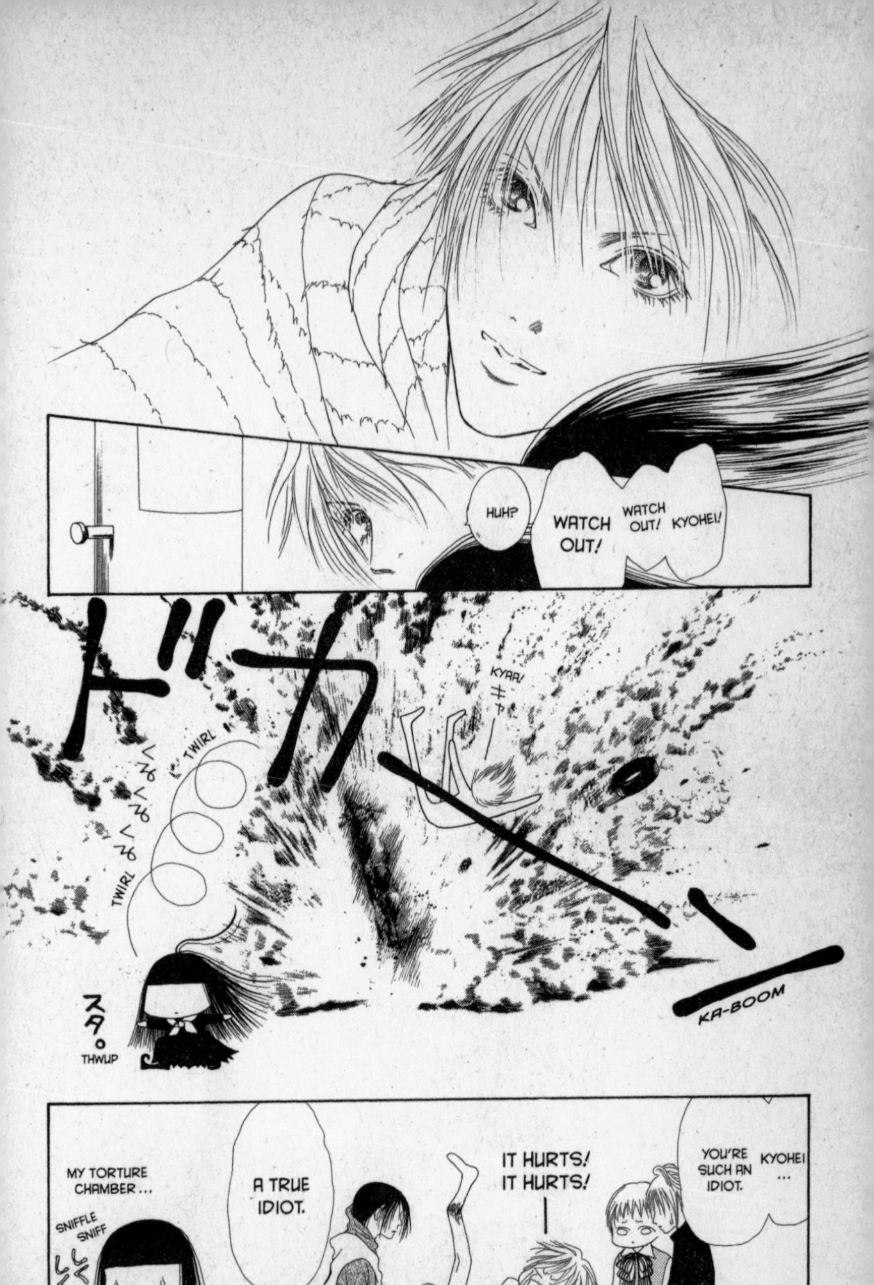
WATCH OUT! KYOHEI!
WATCH OUT!
HUH?
ドカーン
KA-BOOM
キャ
KYAA!
くるくるくる
TWIRL TWIRL
スタ。
THWUP
KYOHEI ...
YOU'RE SUCH AN IDIOT.
IT HURTS! IT HURTS!
A TRUE IDIOT.
MY TORTURE CHAMBER...
しくしく
SNIFFLE SNIFF

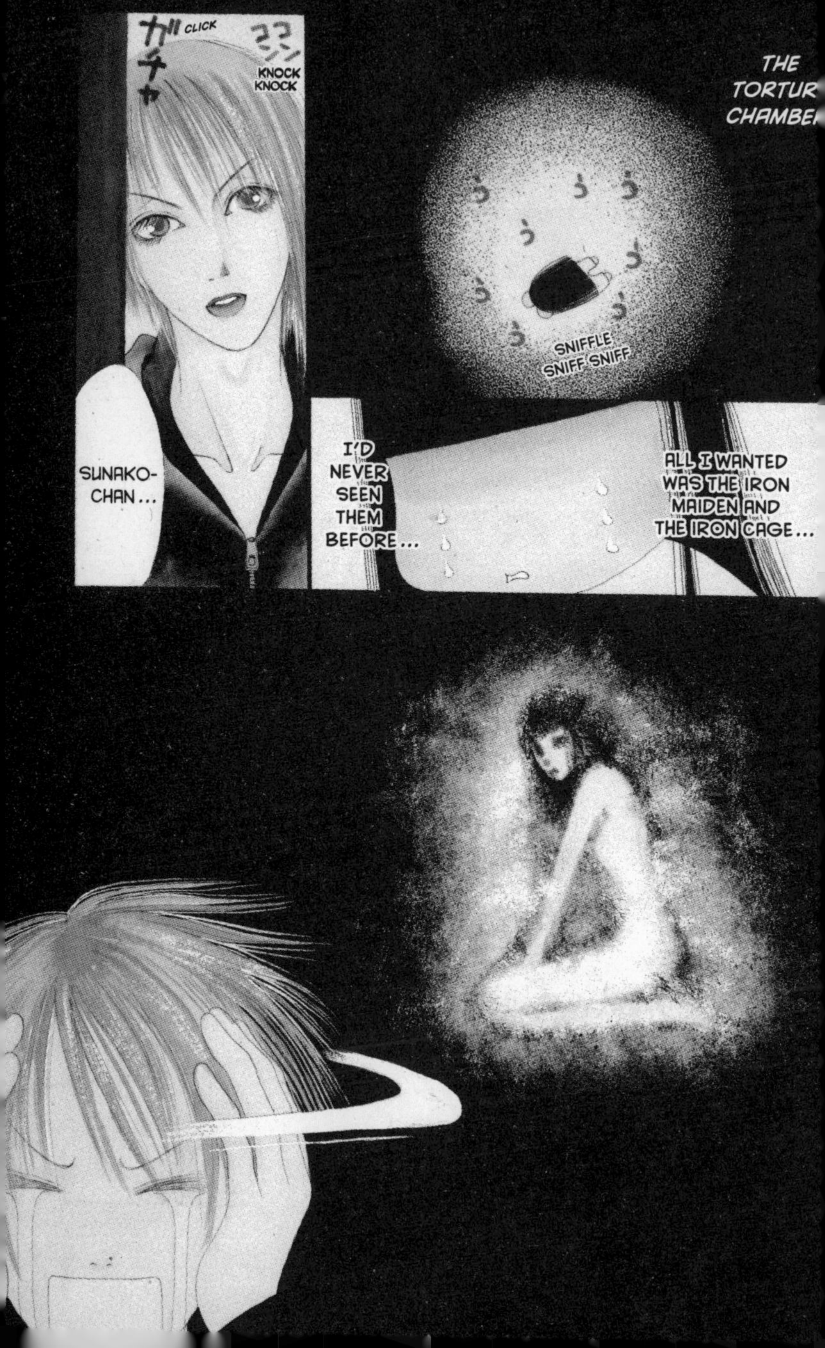
THE TORTUR CHAMBE
SNIFFLE SNIFF SNIFF
ALL I WANTED WAS THE IRON MAIDEN AND THE IRON CAGE...
I'D NEVER SEEN THEM BEFORE...
KNOCK KNOCK
ガチャ CLICK
SUNAKO-CHAN...

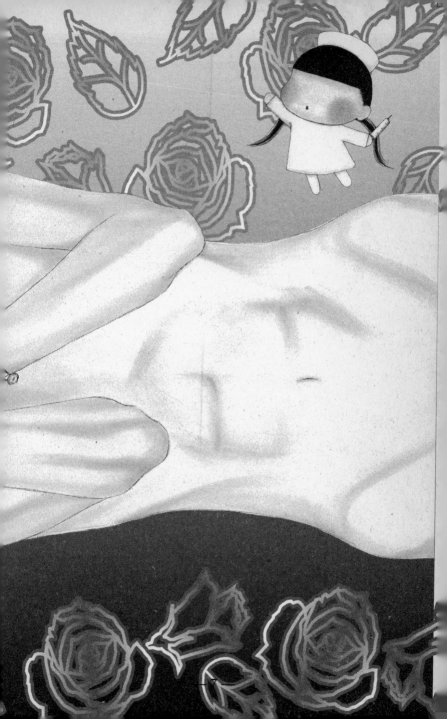

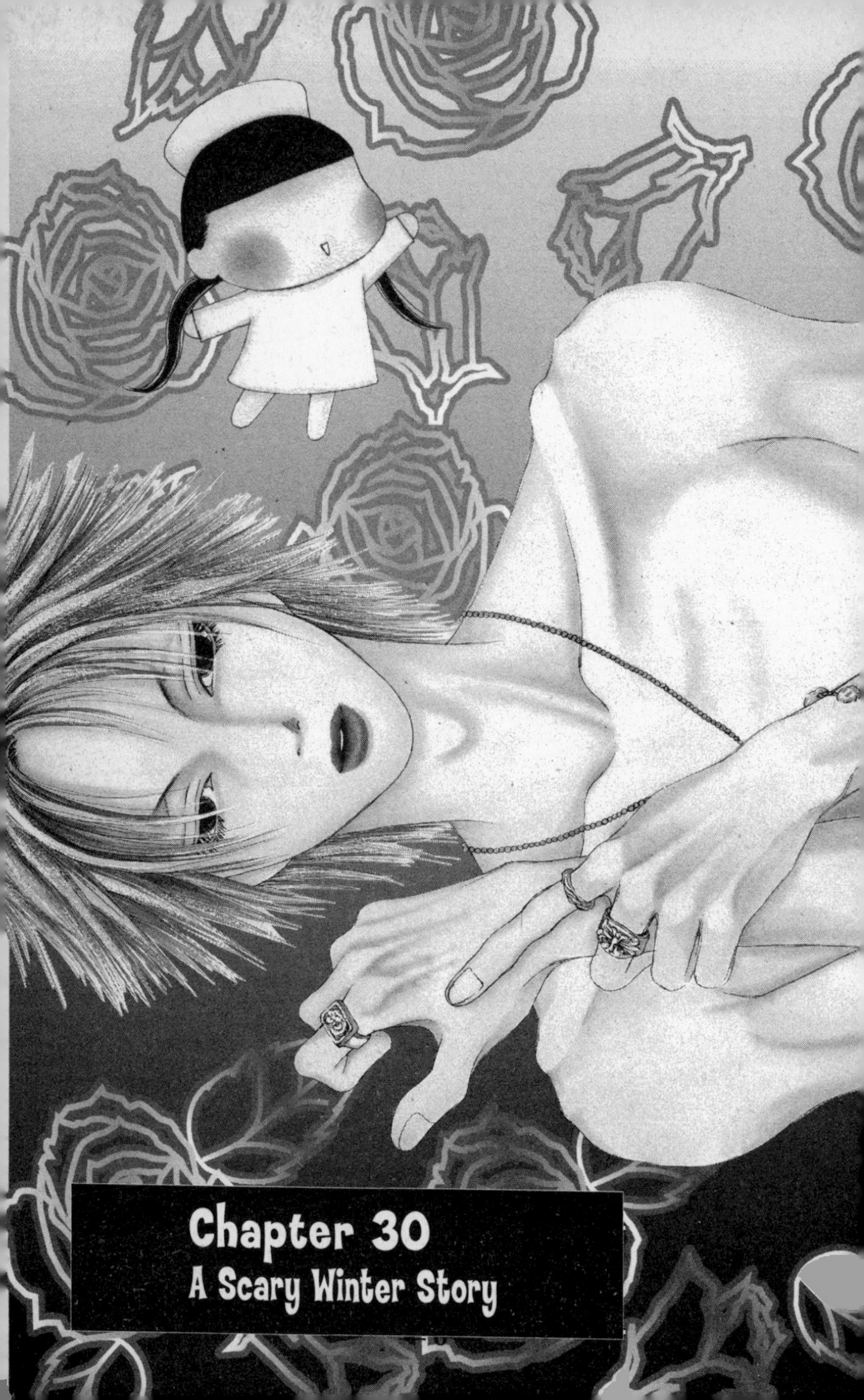

Chapter 30
A Scary Winter Story

WEIRD PEOPLE I FOUND IN THE CITY

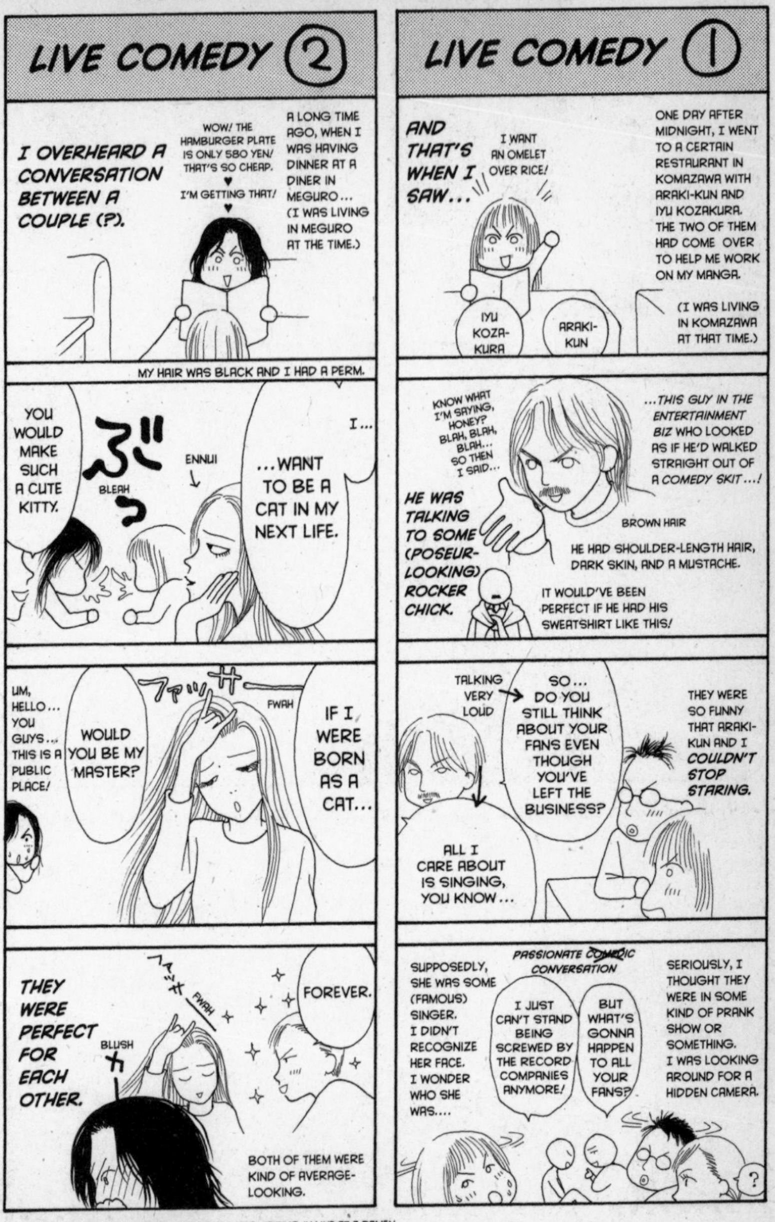
LIVE COMEDY ①
ONE DAY AFTER MIDNIGHT, I WENT TO A CERTAIN RESTAURANT IN KOMAZAWA WITH ARAKI-KUN AND IYU KOZAKURA. THE TWO OF THEM HAD COME OVER TO HELP ME WORK ON MY MANGA.
(I WAS LIVING IN KOMAZAWA AT THAT TIME.)
I WANT AN OMELET OVER RICE!
AND THAT'S WHEN I SAW...
ARAKI-KUN
IYU KOZA-KURA
...THIS GUY IN THE ENTERTAINMENT BIZ WHO LOOKED AS IF HE'D WALKED STRAIGHT OUT OF A COMEDY SKIT...!
KNOW WHAT I'M SAYING, HONEY? BLAH, BLAH, BLAH... SO THEN I SAID...
BROWN HAIR
HE HAD SHOULDER-LENGTH HAIR, DARK SKIN, AND A MUSTACHE.
HE WAS TALKING TO SOME (POSEUR-LOOKING) ROCKER CHICK.
IT WOULD'VE BEEN PERFECT IF HE HAD HIS SWEATSHIRT LIKE THIS!
THEY WERE SO FUNNY THAT ARAKI-KUN AND I COULDN'T STOP STARING.
SO... DO YOU STILL THINK ABOUT YOUR FANS EVEN THOUGH YOU'VE LEFT THE BUSINESS?
TALKING VERY LOUD
ALL I CARE ABOUT IS SINGING, YOU KNOW...
SERIOUSLY, I THOUGHT THEY WERE IN SOME KIND OF PRANK SHOW OR SOMETHING. I WAS LOOKING AROUND FOR A HIDDEN CAMERA.
PASSIONATE COMEDIC CONVERSATION
BUT WHAT'S GONNA HAPPEN TO ALL YOUR FANS?
I JUST CAN'T STAND BEING SCREWED BY THE RECORD COMPANIES ANYMORE!
SUPPOSEDLY, SHE WAS SOME (FAMOUS) SINGER. I DIDN'T RECOGNIZE HER FACE. I WONDER WHO SHE WAS....
?
LIVE COMEDY ②
A LONG TIME AGO, WHEN I WAS HAVING DINNER AT A DINER IN MEGURO... (I WAS LIVING IN MEGURO AT THE TIME.)
WOW! THE HAMBURGER PLATE IS ONLY 580 YEN! THAT'S SO CHEAP. ♥ I'M GETTING THAT! ♥
I OVERHEARD A CONVERSATION BETWEEN A COUPLE (?).
MY HAIR WAS BLACK AND I HAD A PERM.
I...
...WANT TO BE A CAT IN MY NEXT LIFE.
ENNUI
BLEAH
YOU WOULD MAKE SUCH A CUTE KITTY.
IF I WERE BORN AS A CAT...
FWAH
WOULD YOU BE MY MASTER?
UM, HELLO... YOU GUYS... THIS IS A PUBLIC PLACE!
FOREVER.
FWAH
BLUSH
THEY WERE PERFECT FOR EACH OTHER.
BOTH OF THEM WERE KIND OF AVERAGE-LOOKING.

ONE TIME, I SAW A GIRL SINGING OUT LOUD WHILE WAITING IN LINE AT A RAMEN RESTAURANT IN SETAGAYA. MAYBE IT WAS THE SAME GIRL... (SHE WAS WITH A GUY TOO.) ↖ THE SONG SHE WAS SINGING WAS ♪ *MEOW, MEOW, MEOW* ♪

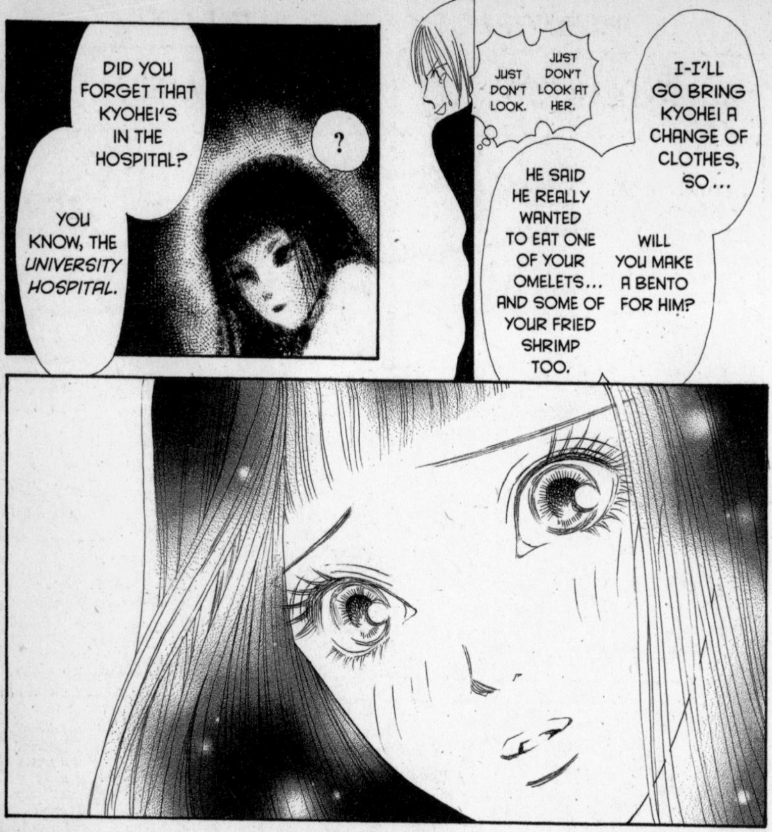
JUST DON'T LOOK AT HER.
JUST DON'T LOOK.
I-I'LL GO BRING KYOHEI A CHANGE OF CLOTHES, SO...
WILL YOU MAKE A BENTO FOR HIM?
HE SAID HE REALLY WANTED TO EAT ONE OF YOUR OMELETS... AND SOME OF YOUR FRIED SHRIMP TOO.
DID YOU FORGET THAT KYOHEI'S IN THE HOSPITAL?
?
YOU KNOW, THE *UNIVERSITY HOSPITAL.*

BEHIND THE SCENES

FOR A LONG TIME, I'VE WANTED TO DRAW A STORY ABOUT A "FRAGILE BISHONEN BOY," SINCE THE FOUR MAIN CHARACTERS ARE SO TOUGH. IT WAS REALLY HARD TO COME UP WITH A GOOD HAIRSTYLE FOR HIM. HEH, HEH.

WHEN I WAS DRAWING THE NAKED PICTURE OF KYOHEI FOR THE SPLASH PAGE, I NEEDED A MODEL, SO I MADE A FRIEND OF MINE, WHO JUST HAPPENED TO BE VISITING, STRIP DOWN... THEN I TOOK A PHOTO. MY POOR FRIEND.... I'M SORRY.... YOU WERE JUST IN THE WRONG PLACE AT THE WRONG TIME.

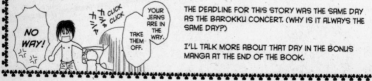

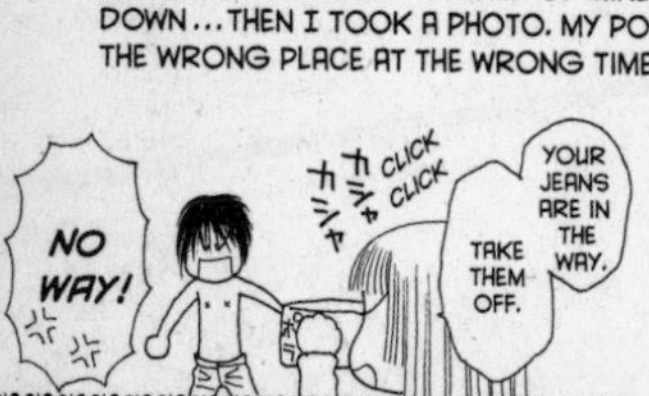
YOUR JEANS ARE IN THE WAY.
TAKE THEM OFF.
CLICK CLICK
NO WAY!

THE DEADLINE FOR THIS STORY WAS THE SAME DAY AS THE BAROKKU CONCERT. (WHY IS IT ALWAYS THE SAME DAY?)

I'LL TALK MORE ABOUT THAT DAY IN THE BONUS MANGA AT THE END OF THE BOOK.

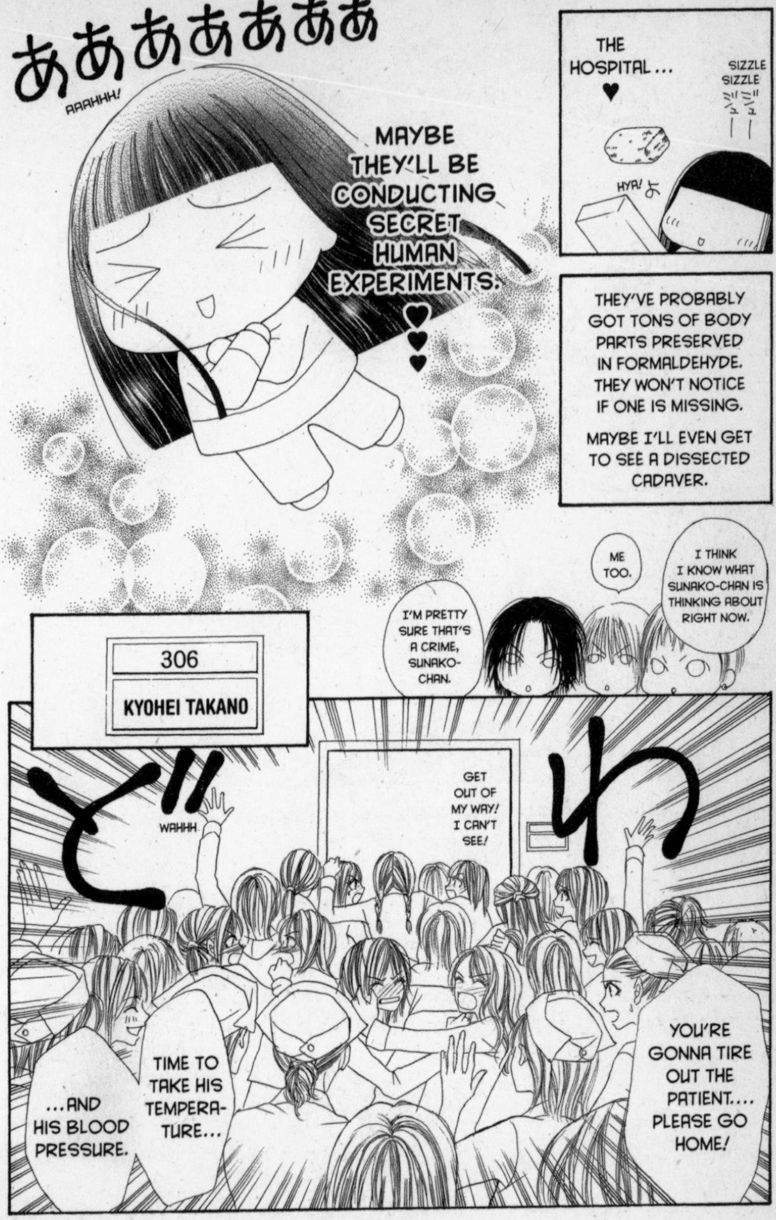
THE HOSPITAL... ♥
SIZZLE SIZZLE
HYA!
THEY'VE PROBABLY GOT TONS OF BODY PARTS PRESERVED IN FORMALDEHYDE. THEY WON'T NOTICE IF ONE IS MISSING.
MAYBE I'LL EVEN GET TO SEE A DISSECTED CADAVER.
ああああああ
AAAHHH!
MAYBE THEY'LL BE CONDUCTING SECRET HUMAN EXPERIMENTS. ♥♥♥
I THINK I KNOW WHAT SUNAKO-CHAN IS THINKING ABOUT RIGHT NOW.
ME TOO.
I'M PRETTY SURE THAT'S A CRIME, SUNAKO-CHAN.
306
KYOHEI TAKANO
ど
わ
GET OUT OF MY WAY! I CAN'T SEE!
WAHHH
YOU'RE GONNA TIRE OUT THE PATIENT.... PLEASE GO HOME!
TIME TO TAKE HIS TEMPERA-TURE...
...AND HIS BLOOD PRESSURE.

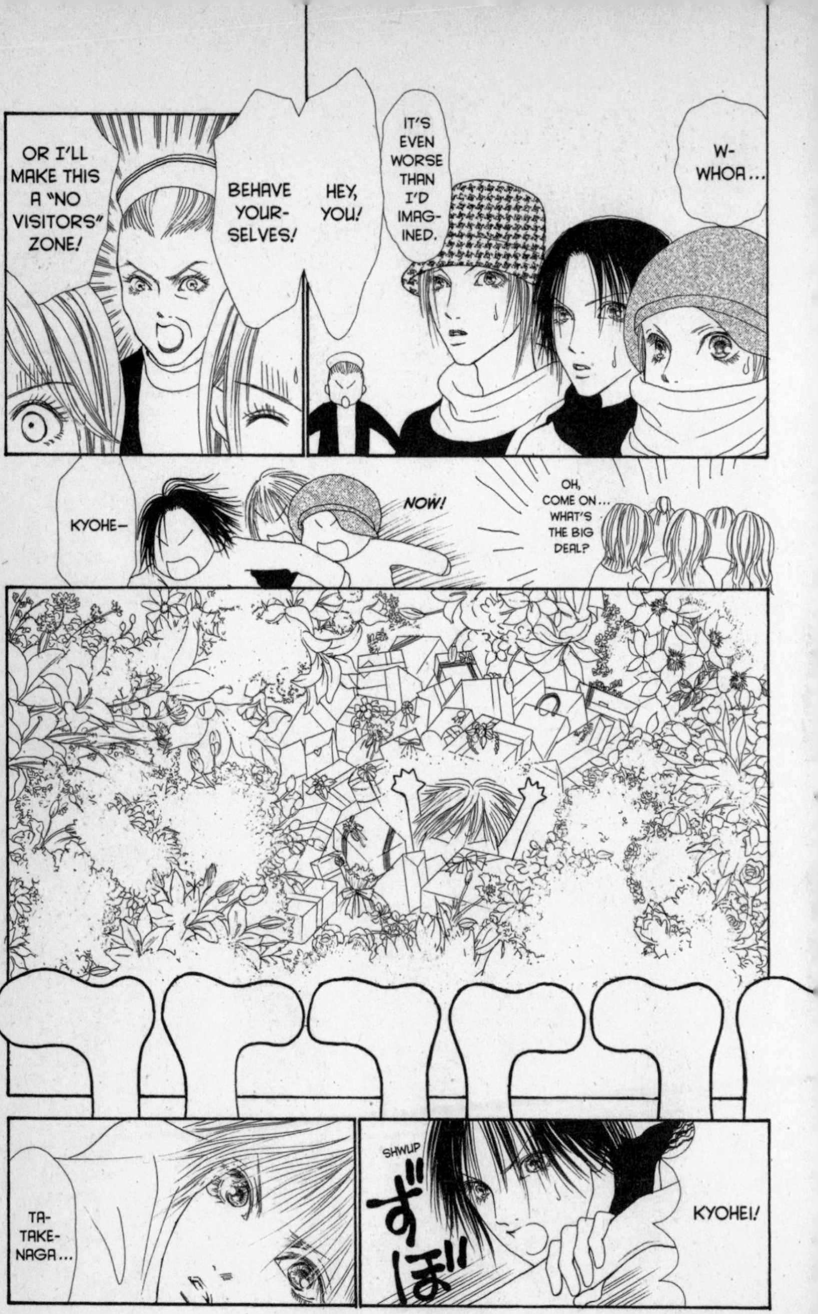
W-WHOA...
IT'S EVEN WORSE THAN I'D IMAG-INED.
HEY, YOU!
BEHAVE YOUR-SELVES!
OR I'LL MAKE THIS A "NO VISITORS" ZONE!
OH, COME ON... WHAT'S THE BIG DEAL?
NOW!
KYOHE—
KYOHEI!
SHWUP
ずぼ
TA-TAKE-NAGA...

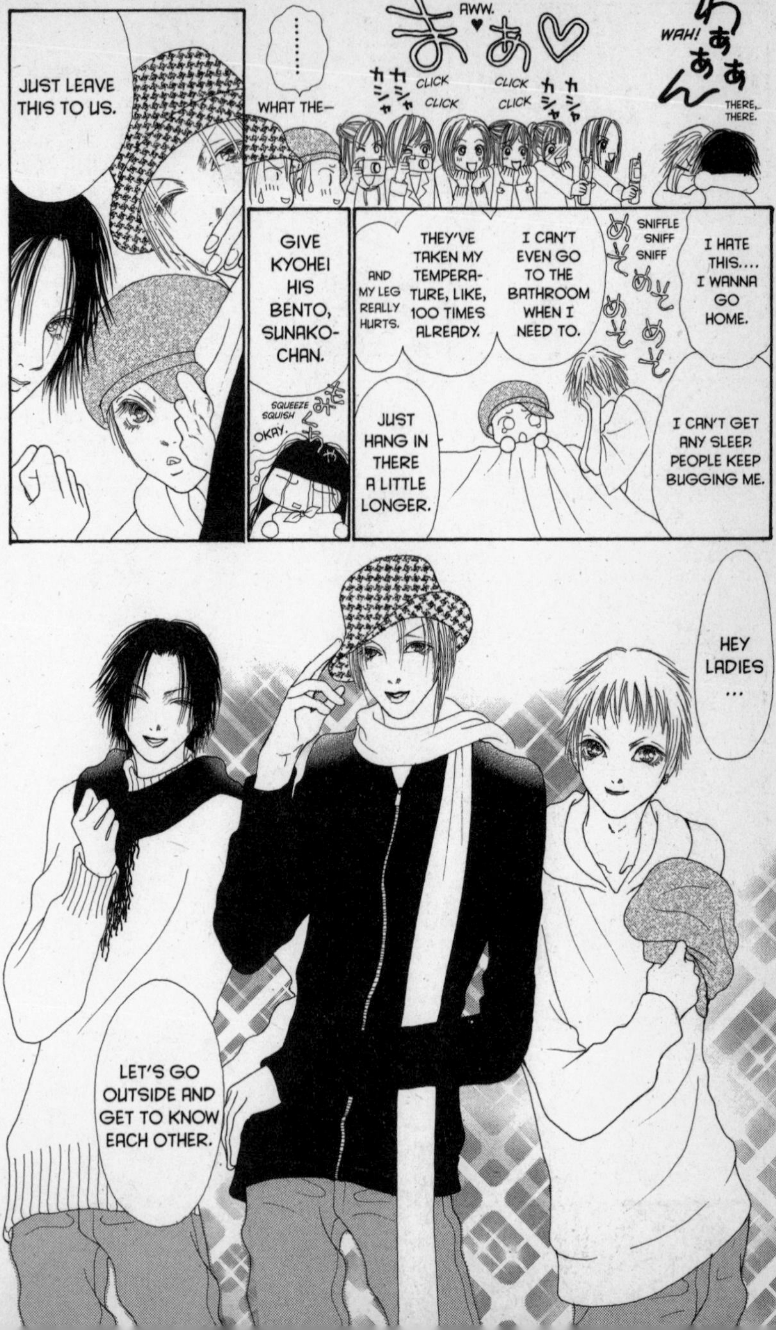
わああああん
WAH!
THERE, THERE.
まあ♡
AWW. ♥
カシャカシャ
CLICK CLICK
カシャカシャ
CLICK CLICK
WHAT THE—
……
I HATE THIS.... I WANNA GO HOME.
めそめそめそめそ
SNIFFLE SNIFF SNIFF
I CAN'T EVEN GO TO THE BATHROOM WHEN I NEED TO.
THEY'VE TAKEN MY TEMPERATURE, LIKE, 100 TIMES ALREADY.
AND MY LEG REALLY HURTS.
I CAN'T GET ANY SLEEP. PEOPLE KEEP BUGGING ME.
JUST HANG IN THERE A LITTLE LONGER.
GIVE KYOHEI HIS BENTO, SUNAKO-CHAN.
みそくちゃ
SQUEEZE SQUISH
OKAY.
JUST LEAVE THIS TO US.
HEY LADIES ...
LET'S GO OUTSIDE AND GET TO KNOW EACH OTHER.

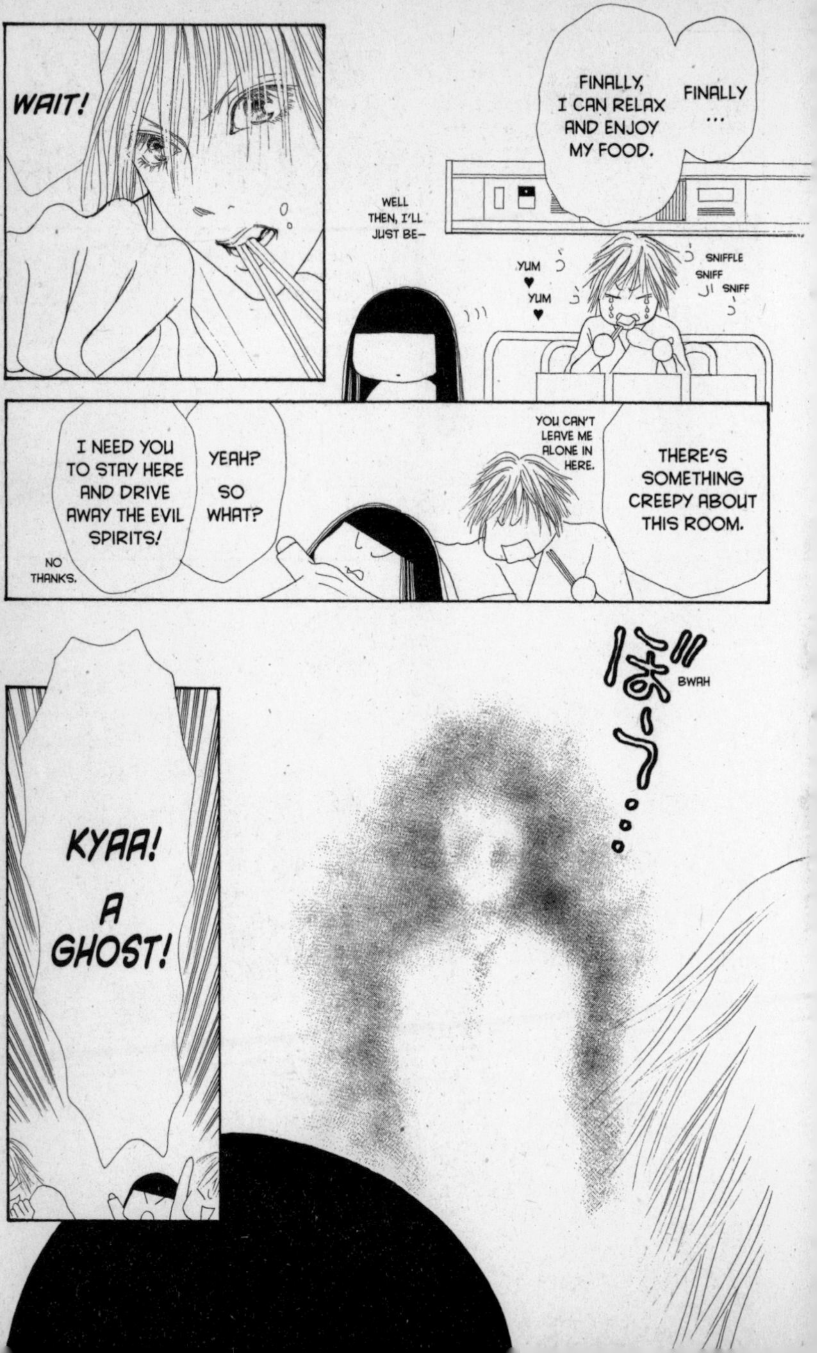
FINALLY...
FINALLY, I CAN RELAX AND ENJOY MY FOOD.
SNIFFLE
SNIFF
SNIFF
YUM
YUM
WELL THEN, I'LL JUST BE—
WAIT!
THERE'S SOMETHING CREEPY ABOUT THIS ROOM.
YOU CAN'T LEAVE ME ALONE IN HERE.
YEAH? SO WHAT?
I NEED YOU TO STAY HERE AND DRIVE AWAY THE EVIL SPIRITS!
NO THANKS.
ぼ〜っ。。。
BWAH
KYAA! A GHOST!

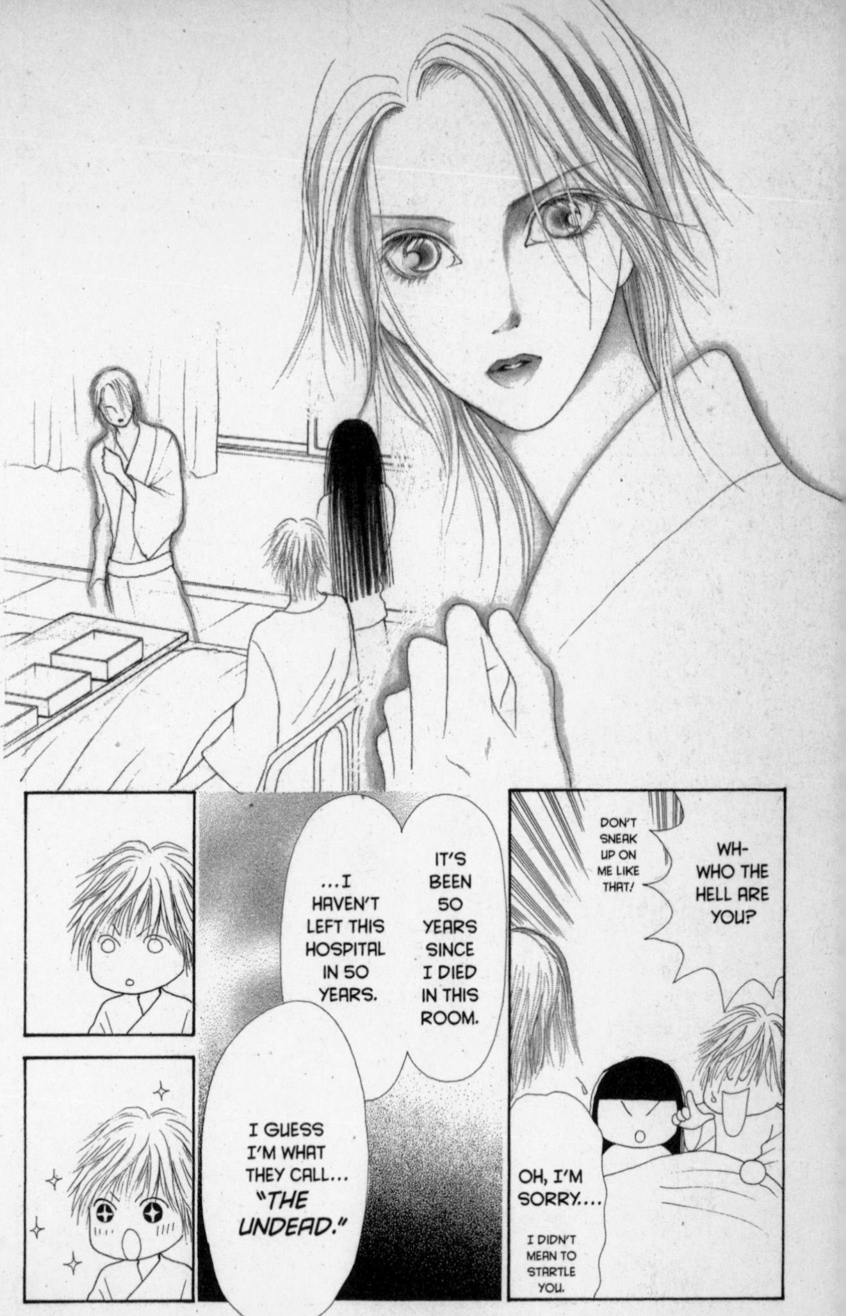
WH- WHO THE HELL ARE YOU?
DON'T SNEAK UP ON ME LIKE THAT!
OH, I'M SORRY....
I DIDN'T MEAN TO STARTLE YOU.
IT'S BEEN 50 YEARS SINCE I DIED IN THIS ROOM.
...I HAVEN'T LEFT THIS HOSPITAL IN 50 YEARS.
I GUESS I'M WHAT THEY CALL... "THE UNDEAD."

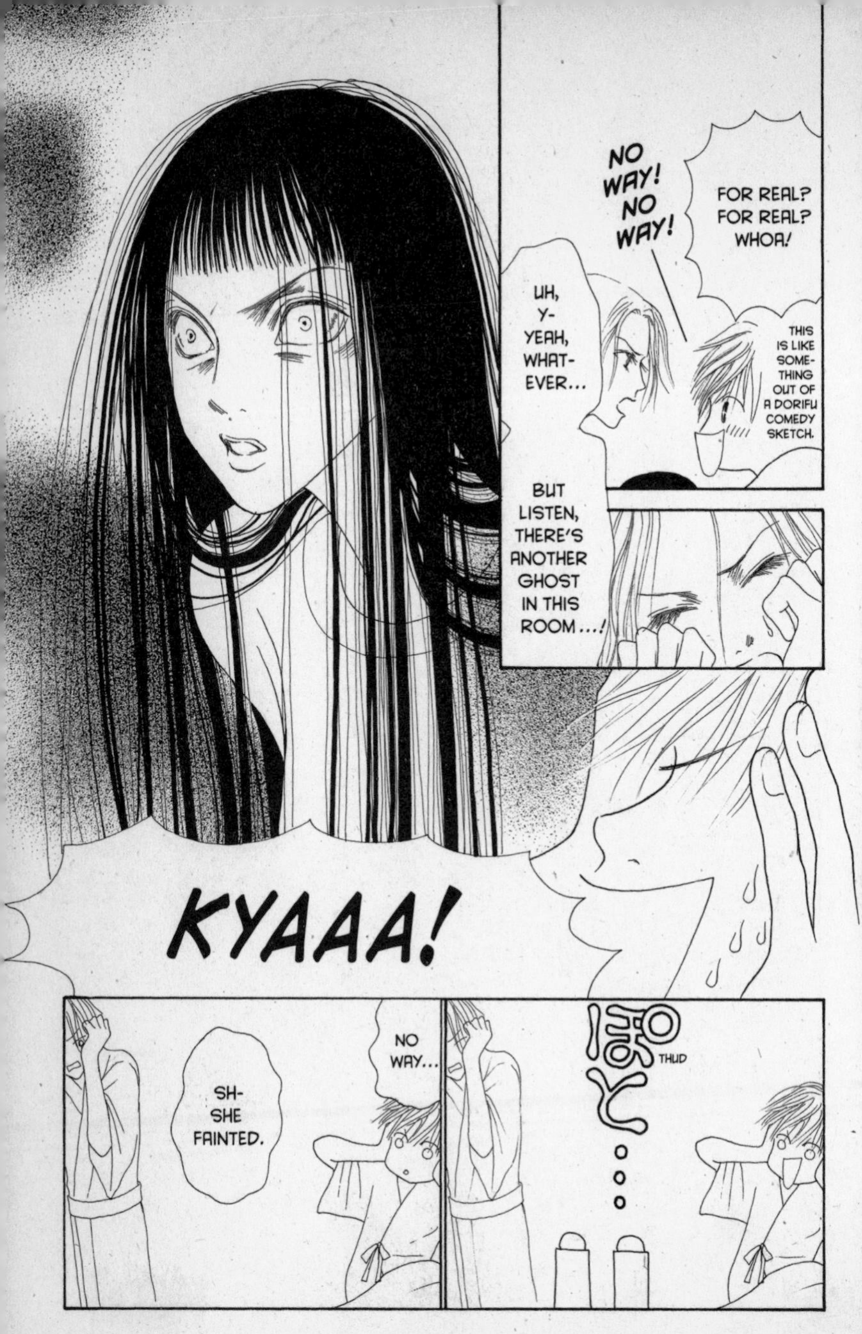
FOR REAL? FOR REAL? WHOA!
NO WAY! NO WAY!
THIS IS LIKE SOMETHING OUT OF A DORIFU COMEDY SKETCH.
UH, Y-YEAH, WHATEVER...
BUT LISTEN, THERE'S ANOTHER GHOST IN THIS ROOM...!
KYAAA!
ぽと…
THUD
NO WAY...
SH-SHE FAINTED.

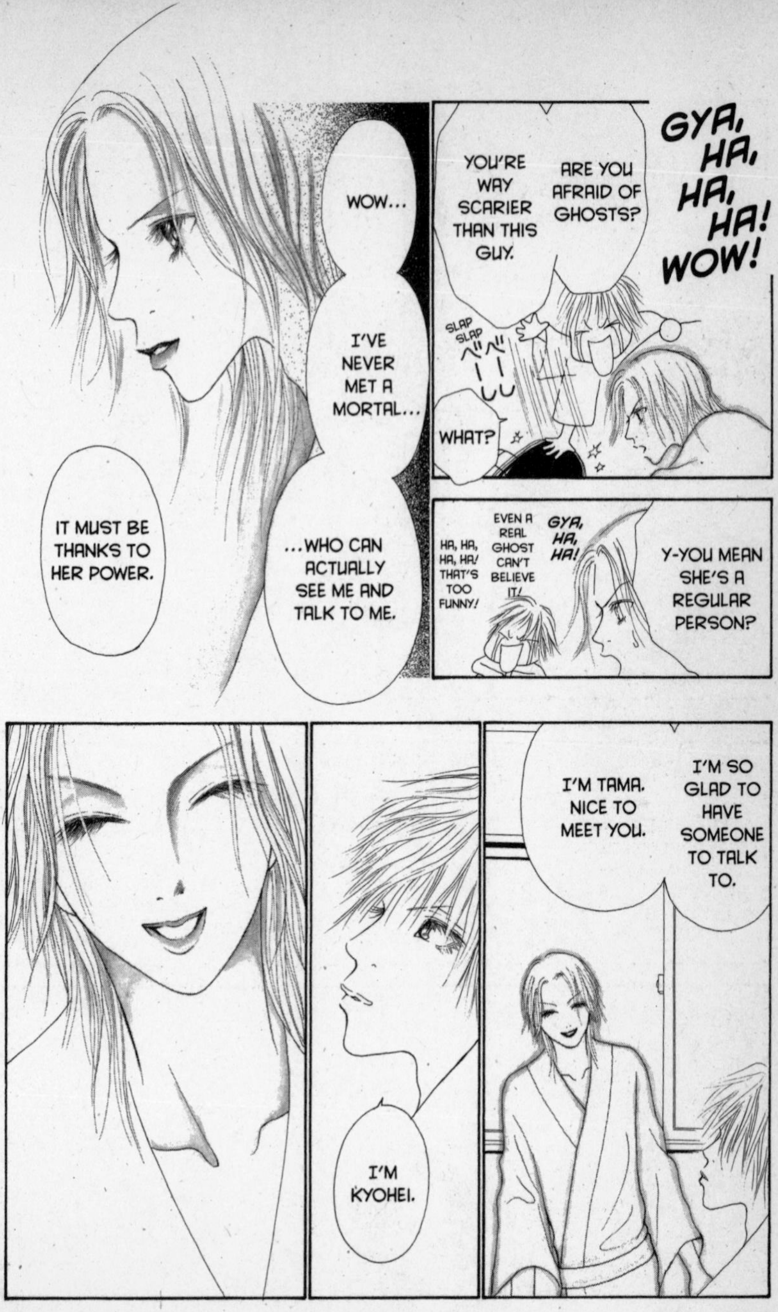
GYA, HA, HA, HA! WOW!
ARE YOU AFRAID OF GHOSTS?
YOU'RE WAY SCARIER THAN THIS GUY.
SLAP SLAP
WHAT?
Y-YOU MEAN SHE'S A REGULAR PERSON?
GYA, HA, HA!
EVEN A REAL GHOST CAN'T BELIEVE IT!
HA, HA, HA, HA! THAT'S TOO FUNNY!
WOW...
I'VE NEVER MET A MORTAL...
...WHO CAN ACTUALLY SEE ME AND TALK TO ME.
IT MUST BE THANKS TO HER POWER.
I'M SO GLAD TO HAVE SOMEONE TO TALK TO.
I'M TAMA. NICE TO MEET YOU.
I'M KYOHEI.

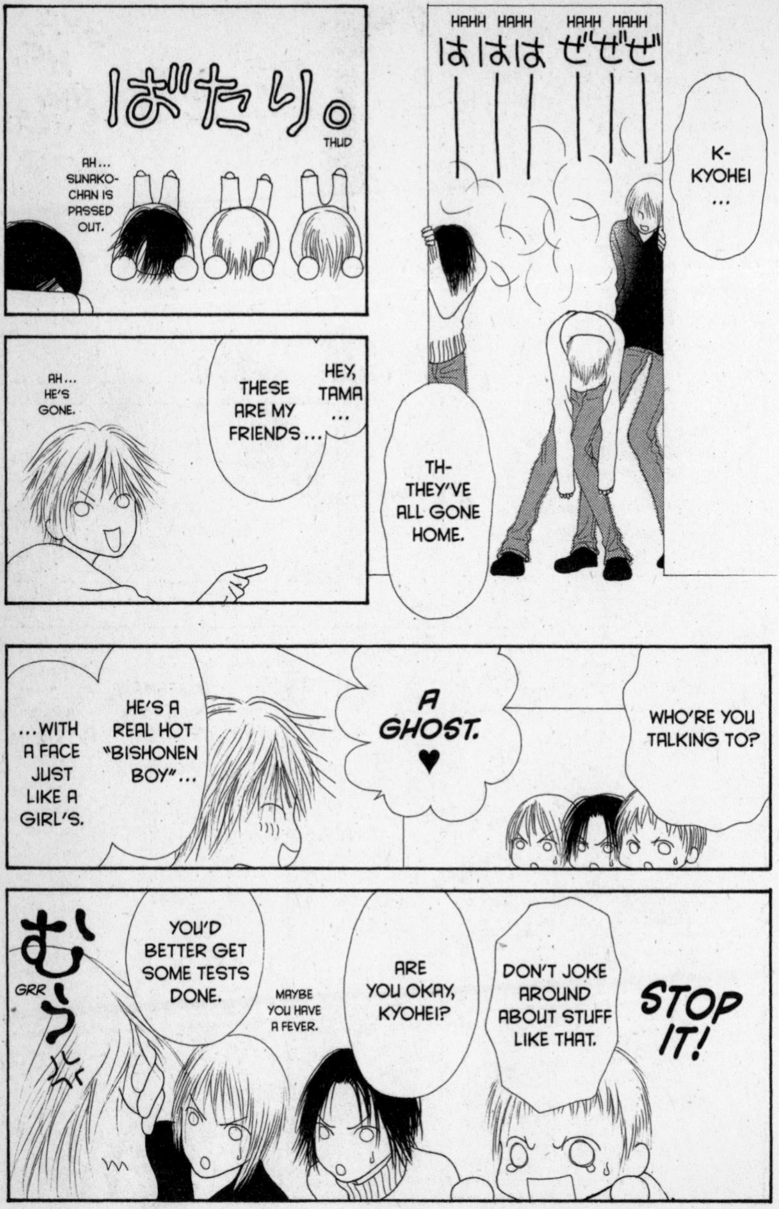

ははは ぜぜぜ
HAHH HAHH HAHH HAHH
K-KYOHEI...
TH-THEY'VE ALL GONE HOME.
ぱたり。
THUD
AH... SUNAKO-CHAN IS PASSED OUT.
HEY, TAMA...
THESE ARE MY FRIENDS...
AH... HE'S GONE.
WHO'RE YOU TALKING TO?
A GHOST. ♥
HE'S A REAL HOT "BISHONEN BOY"...
...WITH A FACE JUST LIKE A GIRL'S.
STOP IT!
DON'T JOKE AROUND ABOUT STUFF LIKE THAT.
ARE YOU OKAY, KYOHEI?
MAYBE YOU HAVE A FEVER.
YOU'D BETTER GET SOME TESTS DONE.
むう
GRR

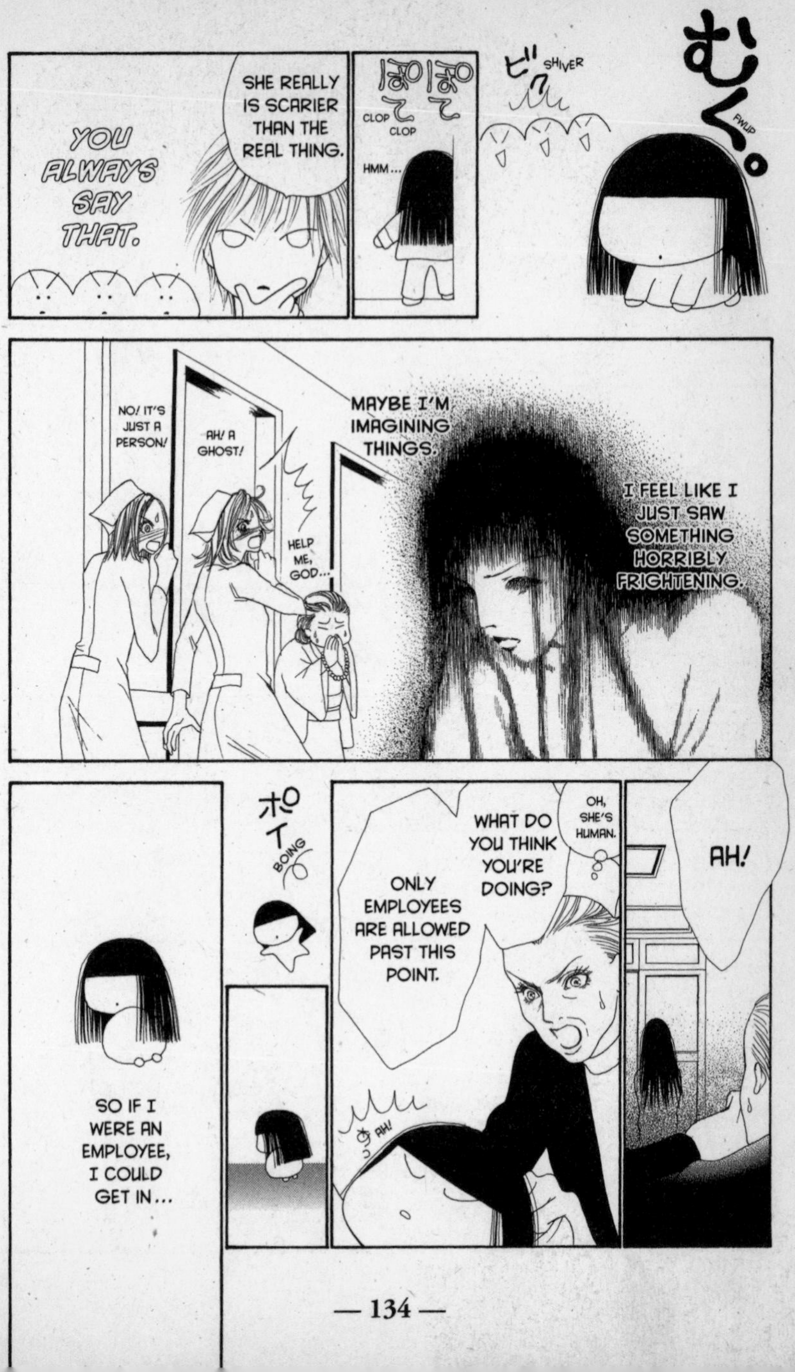

むく。
FWUP
ビク
SHIVER
ぽてぽて
CLOP CLOP
HMM...
SHE REALLY IS SCARIER THAN THE REAL THING.
YOU ALWAYS SAY THAT.
I FEEL LIKE I JUST SAW SOMETHING HORRIBLY FRIGHTENING.
MAYBE I'M IMAGINING THINGS.
HELP ME, GOD...
AH! A GHOST!
NO! IT'S JUST A PERSON!
AH!
OH, SHE'S HUMAN.
WHAT DO YOU THINK YOU'RE DOING?
ONLY EMPLOYEES ARE ALLOWED PAST THIS POINT.
AH!
ポイ
BOING
SO IF I WERE AN EMPLOYEE, I COULD GET IN...

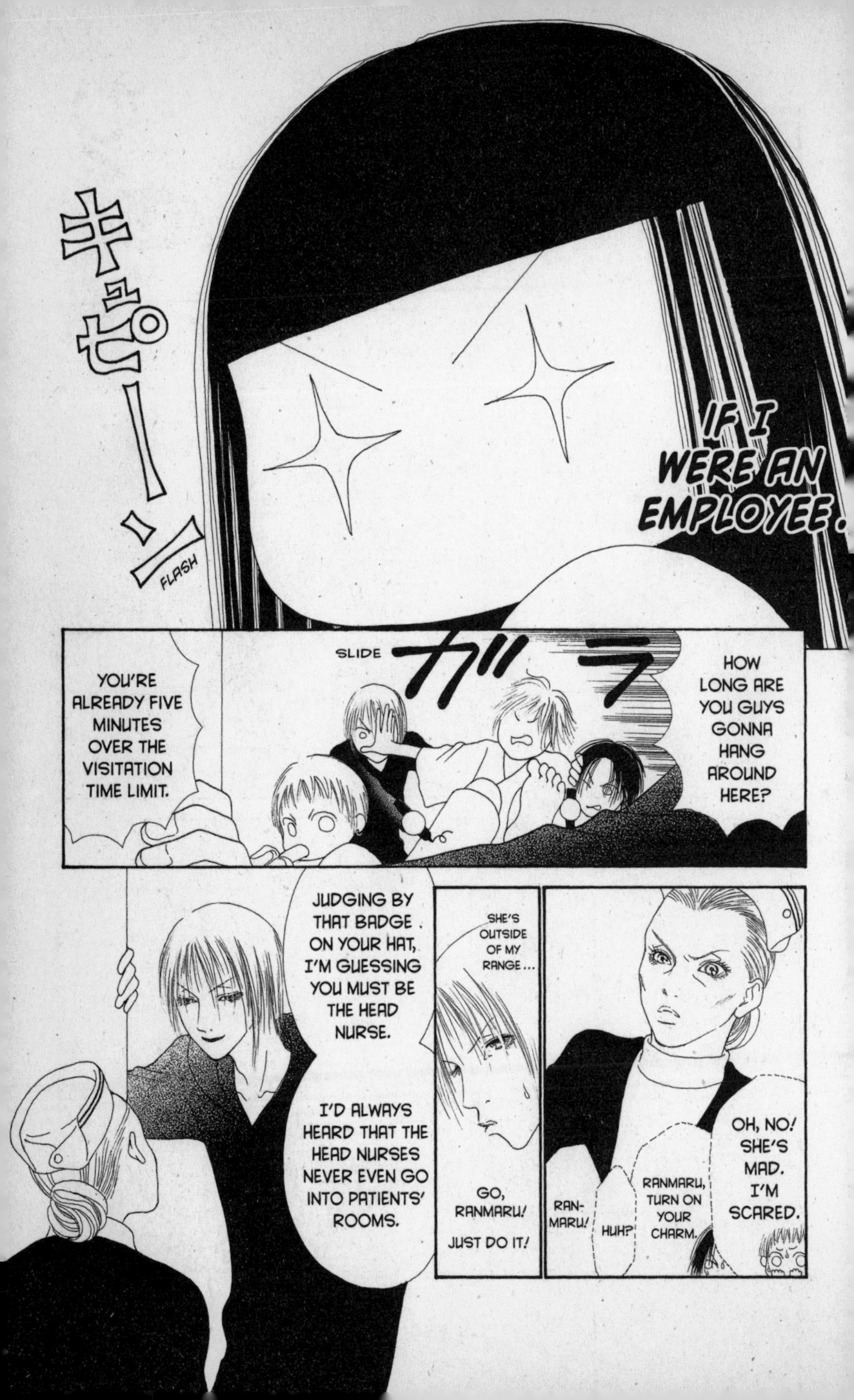
IF I WERE AN EMPLOYEE...
キュピーン
FLASH
HOW LONG ARE YOU GUYS GONNA HANG AROUND HERE?
ガラ
SLIDE
YOU'RE ALREADY FIVE MINUTES OVER THE VISITATION TIME LIMIT.
OH, NO! SHE'S MAD. I'M SCARED.
RANMARU, TURN ON YOUR CHARM.
HUH?
RAN-MARU!
SHE'S OUTSIDE OF MY RANGE...
GO, RANMARU!
JUST DO IT!
JUDGING BY THAT BADGE ON YOUR HAT, I'M GUESSING YOU MUST BE THE HEAD NURSE.
I'D ALWAYS HEARD THAT THE HEAD NURSES NEVER EVEN GO INTO PATIENTS' ROOMS.

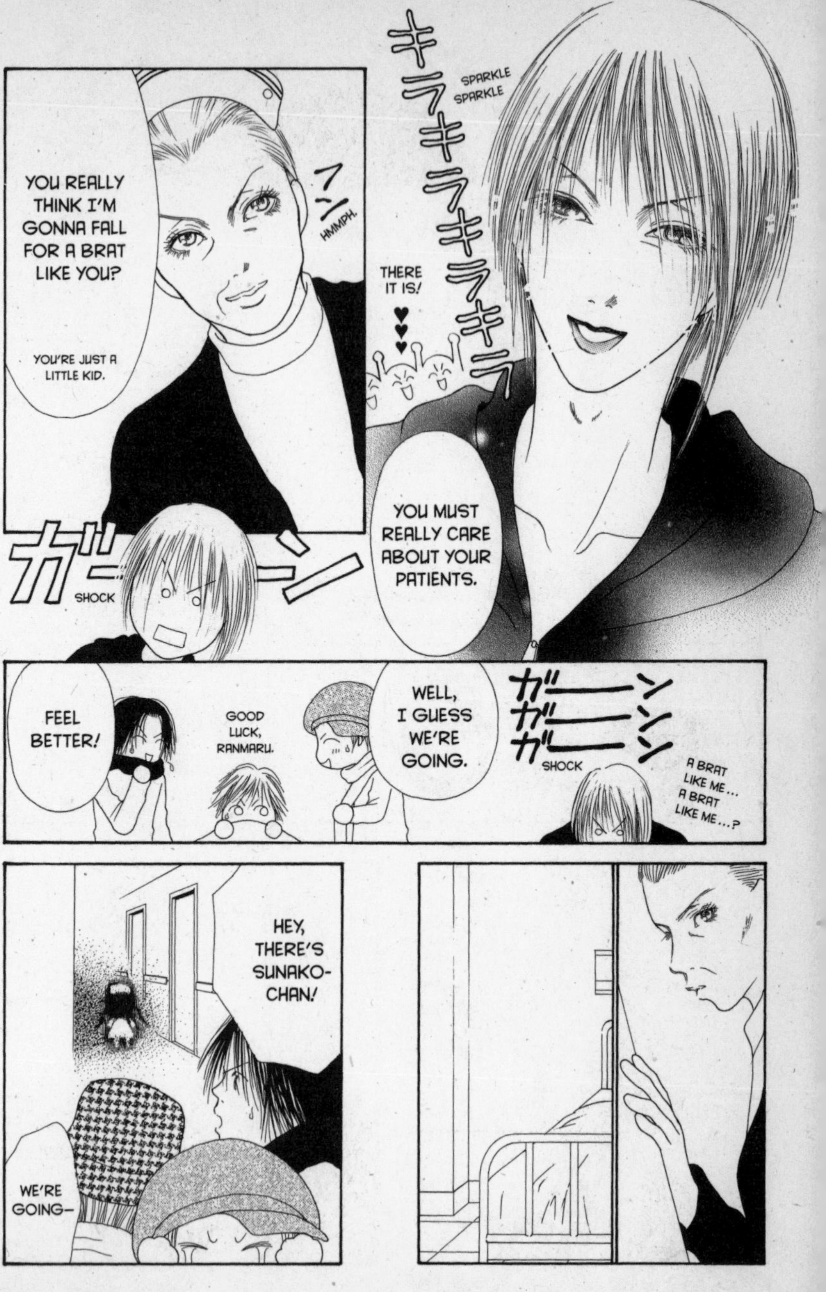
キラキラキラキラ
SPARKLE SPARKLE
THERE IT IS!
YOU MUST REALLY CARE ABOUT YOUR PATIENTS.
フン
HMMPH.
YOU REALLY THINK I'M GONNA FALL FOR A BRAT LIKE YOU?
YOU'RE JUST A LITTLE KID.
ガーン
SHOCK
ガーン ガーン ガーン
SHOCK
A BRAT LIKE ME... A BRAT LIKE ME...?
WELL, I GUESS WE'RE GOING.
GOOD LUCK, RANMARU.
FEEL BETTER!
HEY, THERE'S SUNAKO-CHAN!
WE'RE GOING—

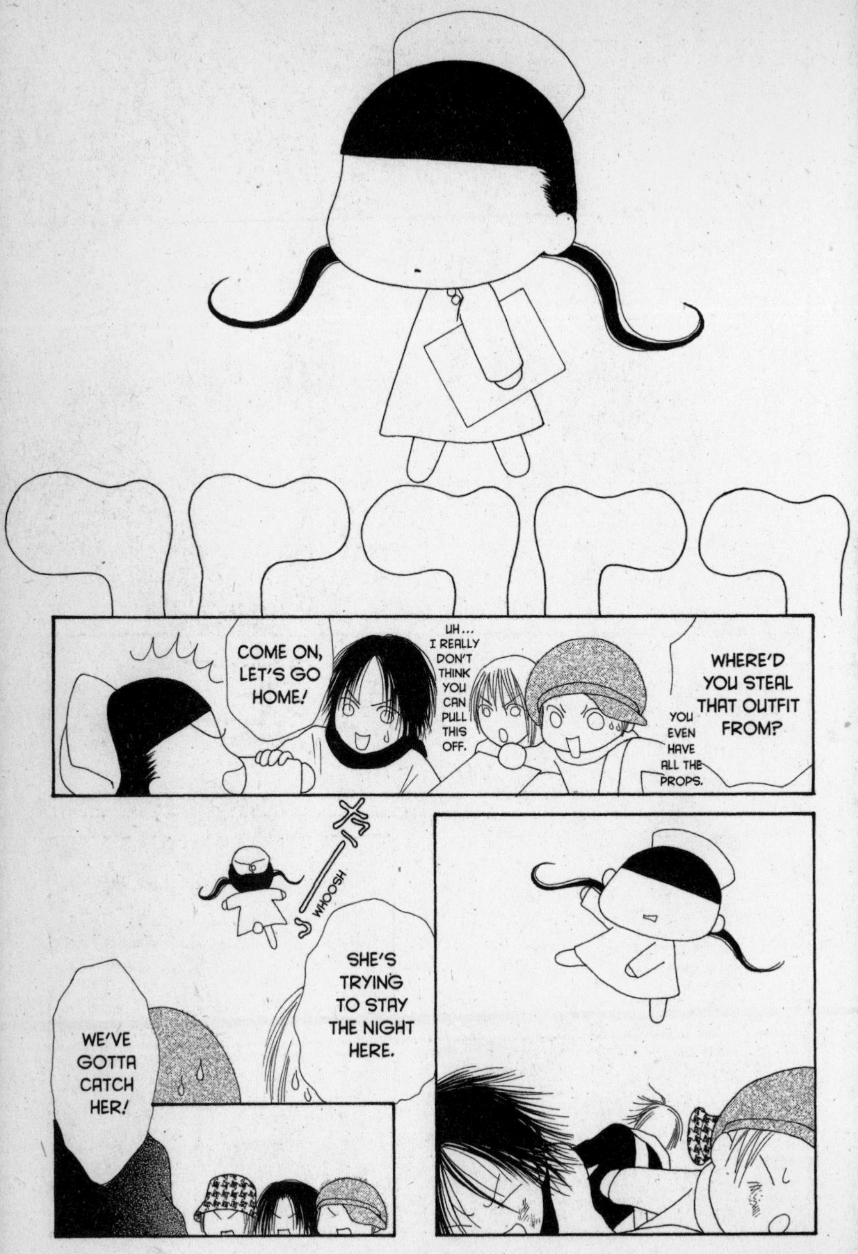
WHERE'D YOU STEAL THAT OUTFIT FROM?
YOU EVEN HAVE ALL THE PROPS.
UH... I REALLY DON'T THINK YOU CAN PULL THIS OFF.
COME ON, LET'S GO HOME!
WHOOSH
SHE'S TRYING TO STAY THE NIGHT HERE.
WE'VE GOTTA CATCH HER!

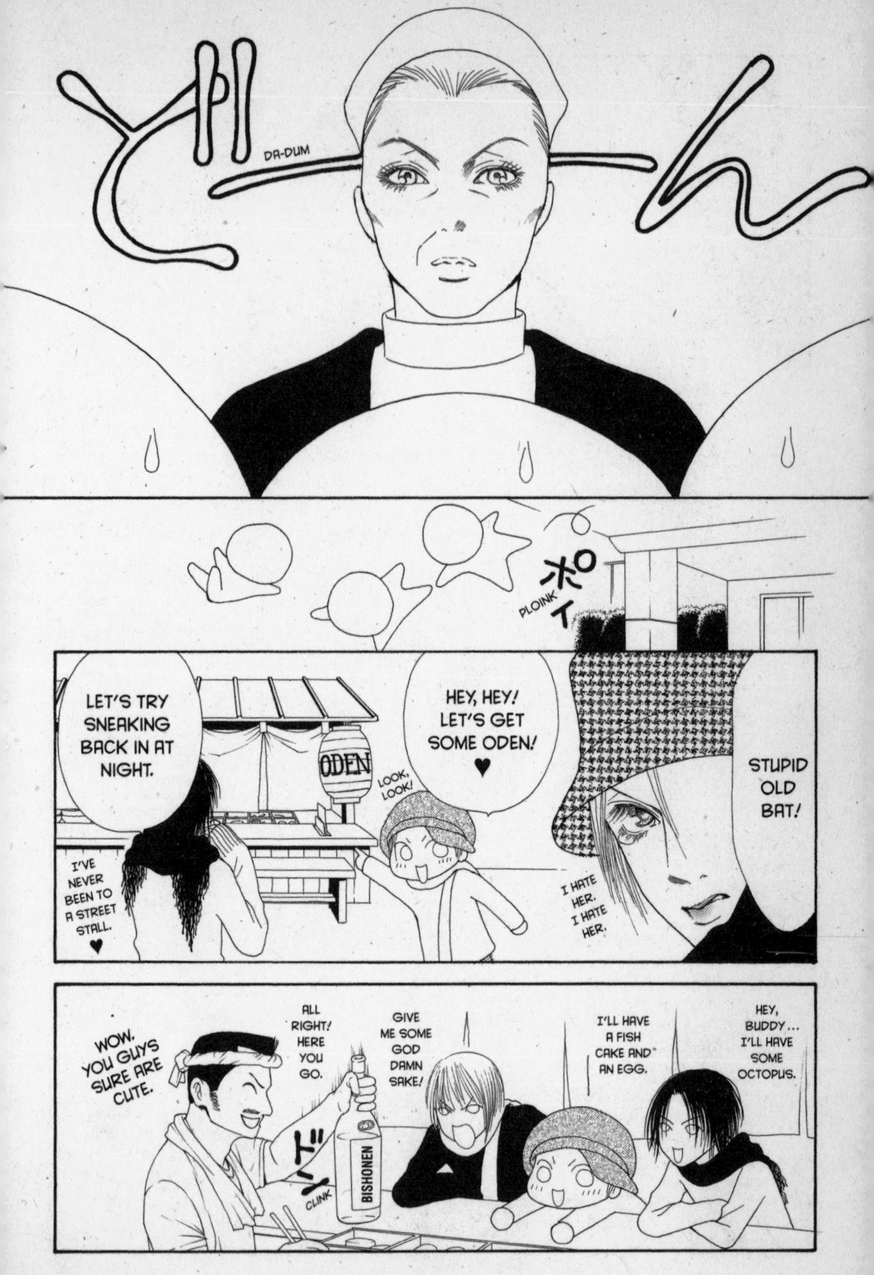
でーん
DA-DUM
ポイ
PLOINK
STUPID OLD BAT!
I HATE HER. I HATE HER.
HEY, HEY! LET'S GET SOME ODEN! ♥
LOOK, LOOK!
ODEN
LET'S TRY SNEAKING BACK IN AT NIGHT.
I'VE NEVER BEEN TO A STREET STALL. ♥
HEY, BUDDY... I'LL HAVE SOME OCTOPUS.
I'LL HAVE A FISH CAKE AND AN EGG.
GIVE ME SOME GOD DAMN SAKE!
ALL RIGHT! HERE YOU GO.
WOW. YOU GUYS SURE ARE CUTE.
BISHONEN
CLINK

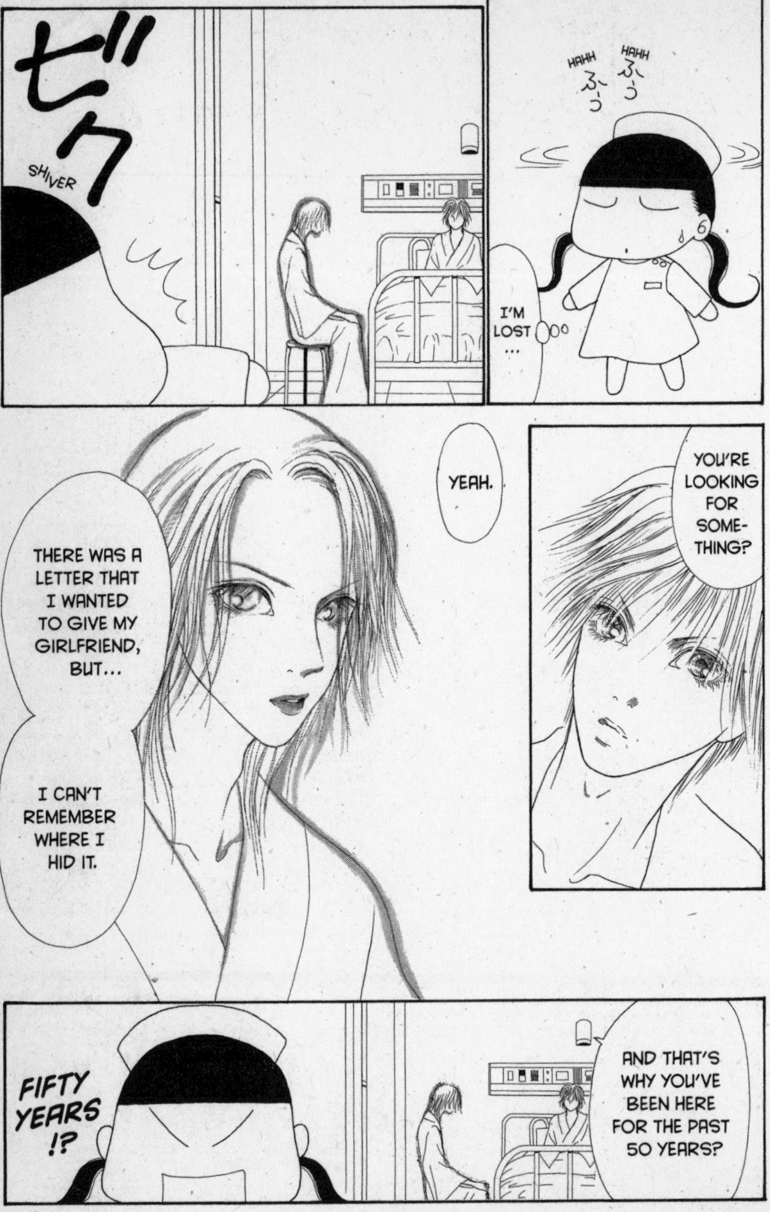
HAHH
ふぅ
HAHH
ふぅ
I'M LOST ...
ゾク
SHIVER
YOU'RE LOOKING FOR SOME-THING?
YEAH.
THERE WAS A LETTER THAT I WANTED TO GIVE MY GIRLFRIEND, BUT...
I CAN'T REMEMBER WHERE I HID IT.
AND THAT'S WHY YOU'VE BEEN HERE FOR THE PAST 50 YEARS?
FIFTY YEARS !?

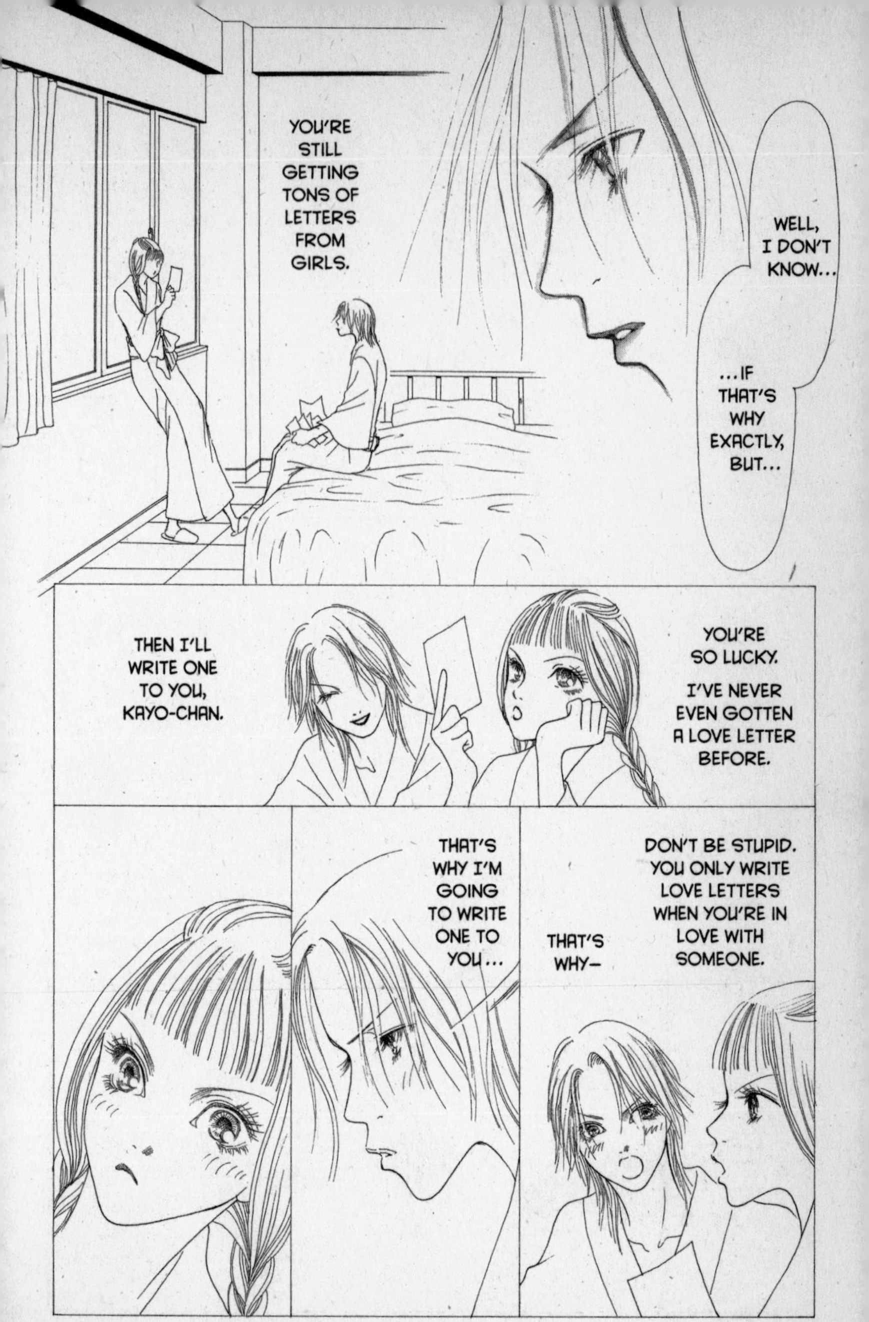
YOU'RE STILL GETTING TONS OF LETTERS FROM GIRLS.
WELL, I DON'T KNOW...
...IF THAT'S WHY EXACTLY, BUT...
YOU'RE SO LUCKY.
I'VE NEVER EVEN GOTTEN A LOVE LETTER BEFORE.
THEN I'LL WRITE ONE TO YOU, KAYO-CHAN.
DON'T BE STUPID. YOU ONLY WRITE LOVE LETTERS WHEN YOU'RE IN LOVE WITH SOMEONE.
THAT'S WHY—
THAT'S WHY I'M GOING TO WRITE ONE TO YOU...

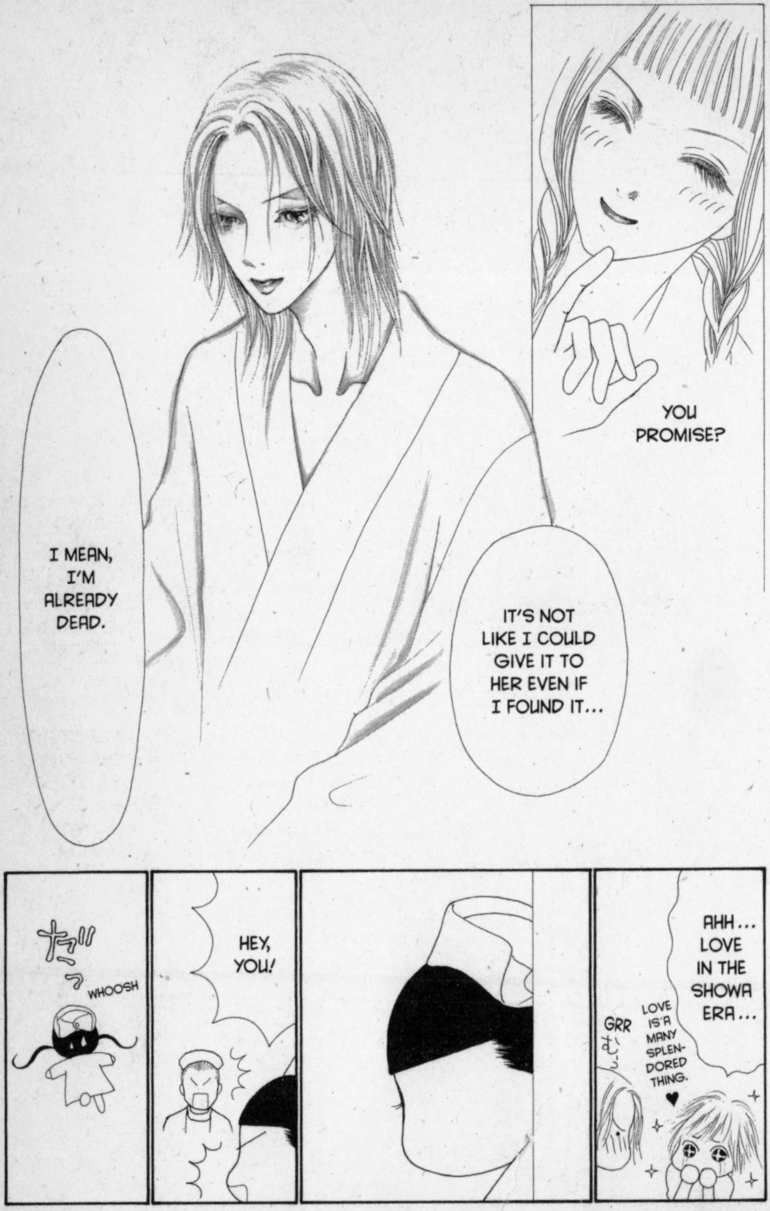
YOU PROMISE?
IT'S NOT LIKE I COULD GIVE IT TO HER EVEN IF I FOUND IT...
I MEAN, I'M ALREADY DEAD.
AHH... LOVE IN THE SHOWA ERA...
LOVE IS A MANY SPLENDORED THING.
GRR
HEY, YOU!
WHOOSH

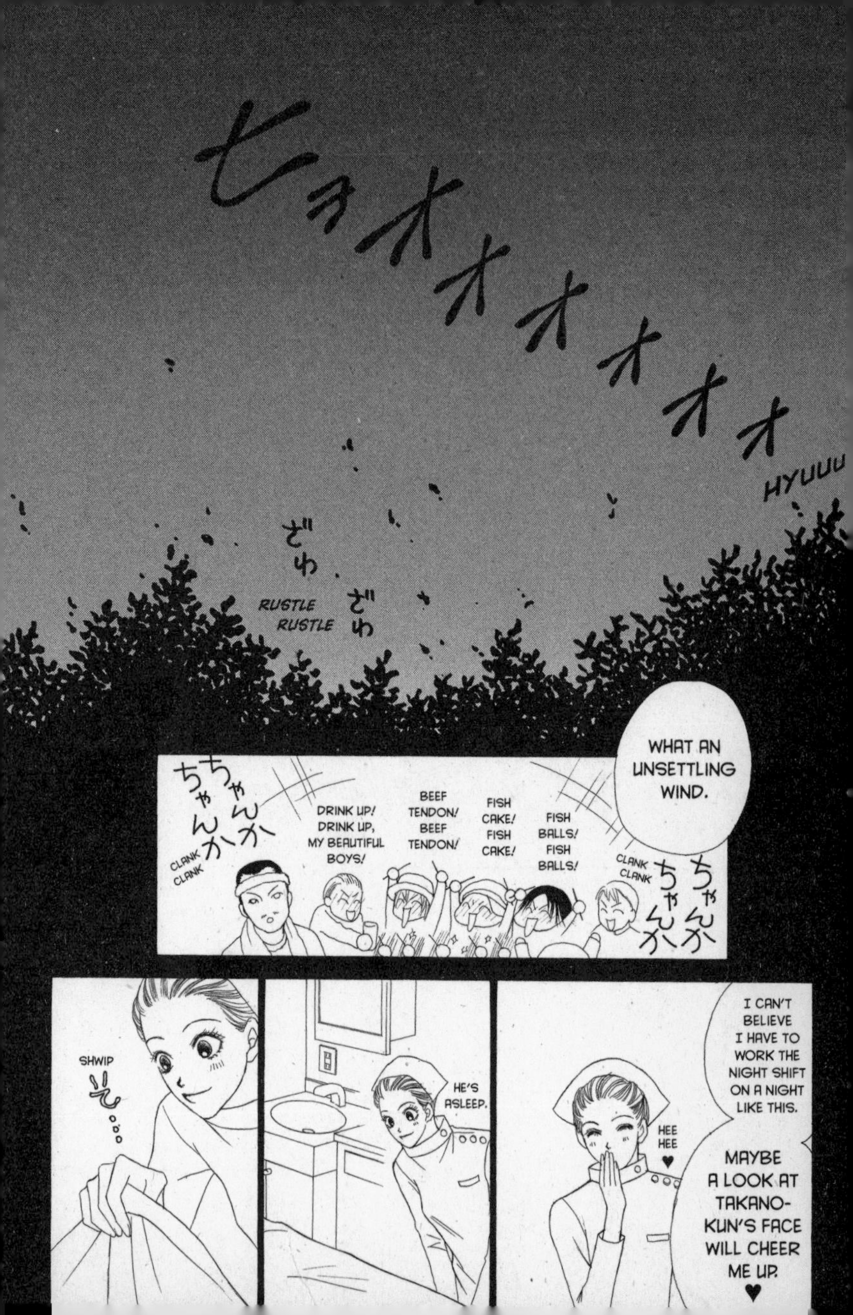
ヒョオオオオオオ
HYUUU
ざわ ざわ
RUSTLE RUSTLE
WHAT AN UNSETTLING WIND.
ちゃんかちゃんか
CLANK CLANK
FISH BALLS! FISH BALLS!
FISH CAKE! FISH CAKE!
BEEF TENDON! BEEF TENDON!
DRINK UP! DRINK UP, MY BEAUTIFUL BOYS!
ちゃんかちゃんか
CLANK CLANK
I CAN'T BELIEVE I HAVE TO WORK THE NIGHT SHIFT ON A NIGHT LIKE THIS.
HEE HEE ♥
MAYBE A LOOK AT TAKANO-KUN'S FACE WILL CHEER ME UP. ♥
HE'S ASLEEP.
SHWIP
そ

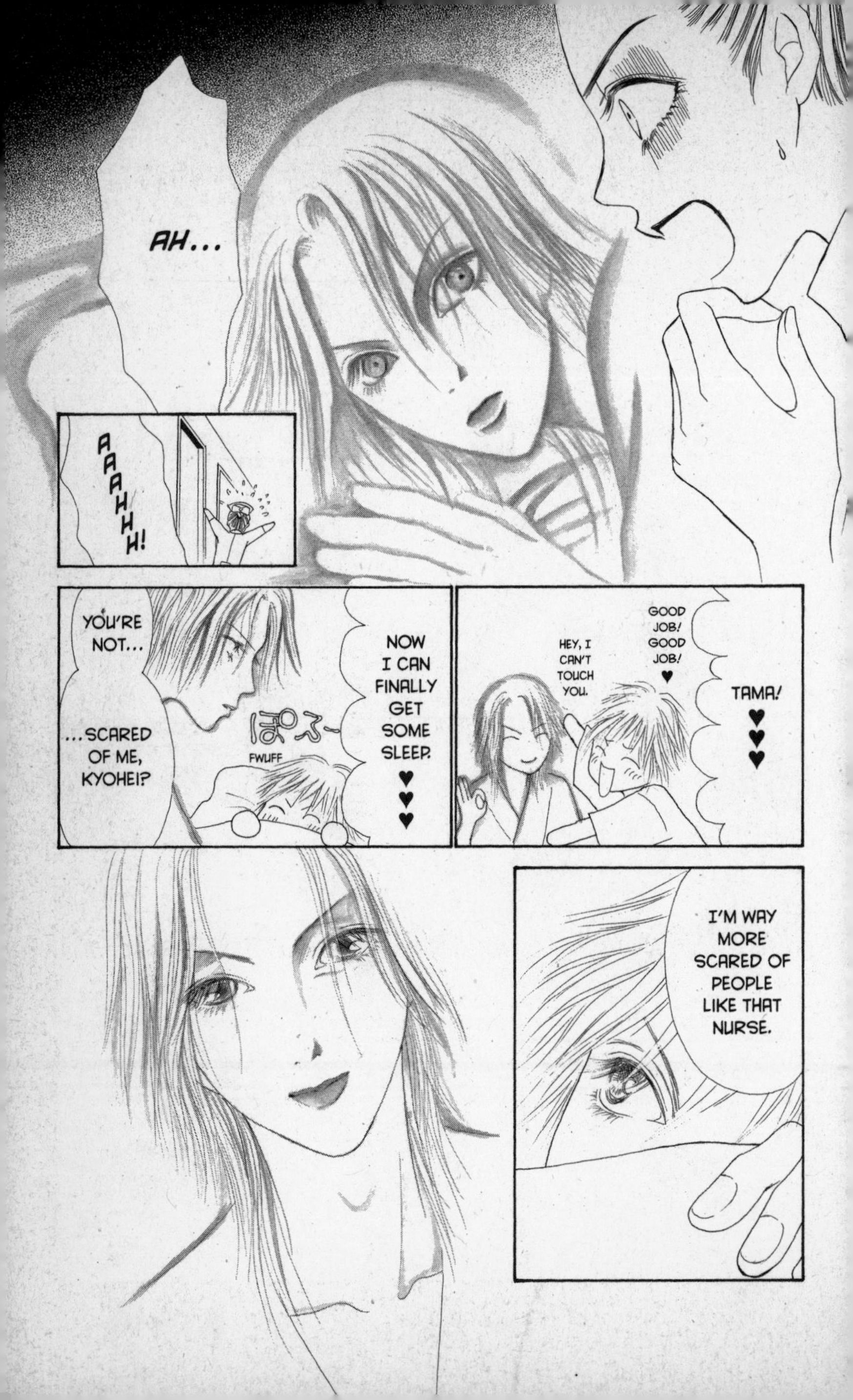
AH...
AAAHHH!
TAMA! ♥ ♥ ♥
GOOD JOB! GOOD JOB! ♥
HEY, I CAN'T TOUCH YOU.
NOW I CAN FINALLY GET SOME SLEEP. ♥ ♥ ♥
ぽふ~
FWUFF
YOU'RE NOT...
...SCARED OF ME, KYOHEI?
I'M WAY MORE SCARED OF PEOPLE LIKE THAT NURSE.

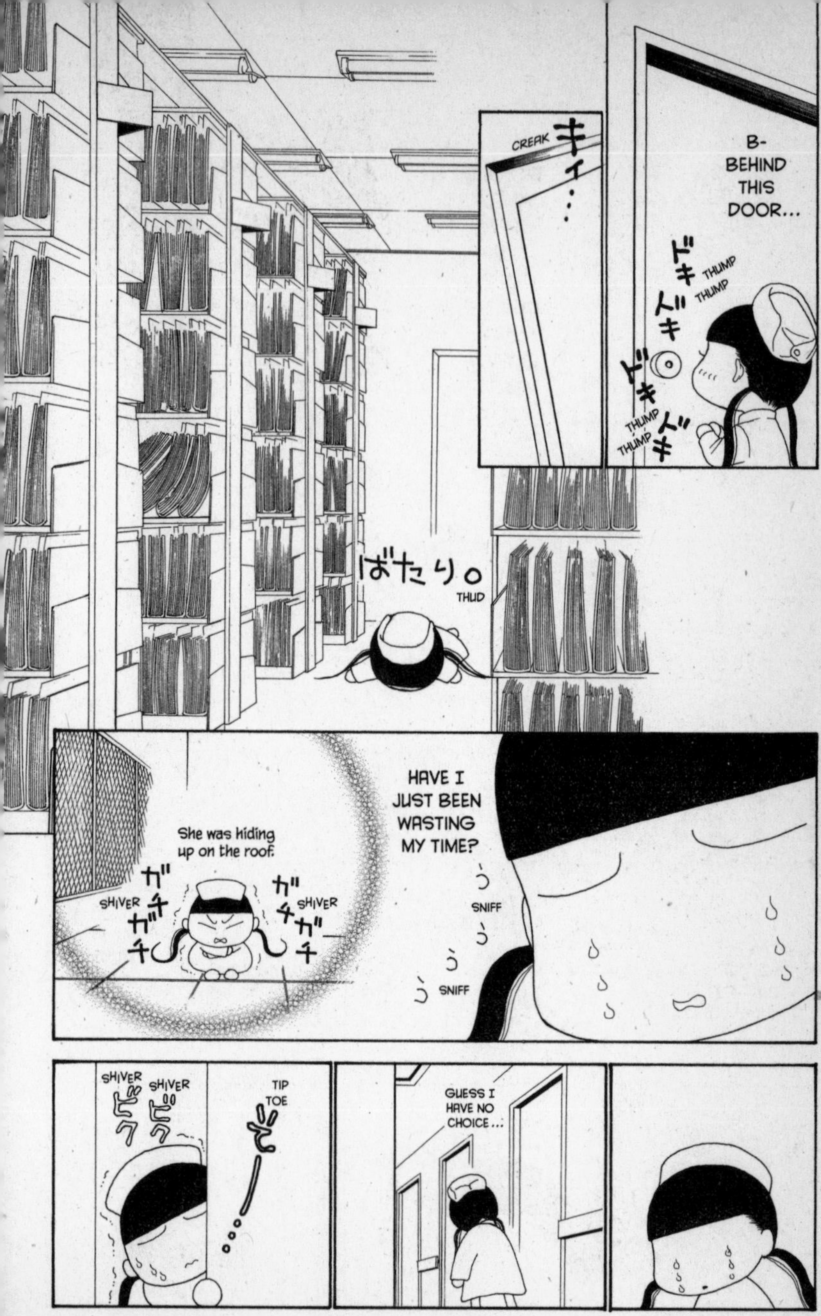
B-BEHIND THIS DOOR...
ドキドキ THUMP THUMP
ドキドキ THUMP THUMP
キィ… CREAK
ばたり。 THUD
HAVE I JUST BEEN WASTING MY TIME?
う SNIFF
う SNIFF
She was hiding up on the roof.
ガチガチ SHIVER
ガチガチ SHIVER
GUESS I HAVE NO CHOICE...
ビクビク SHIVER SHIVER
そーっ TIP TOE

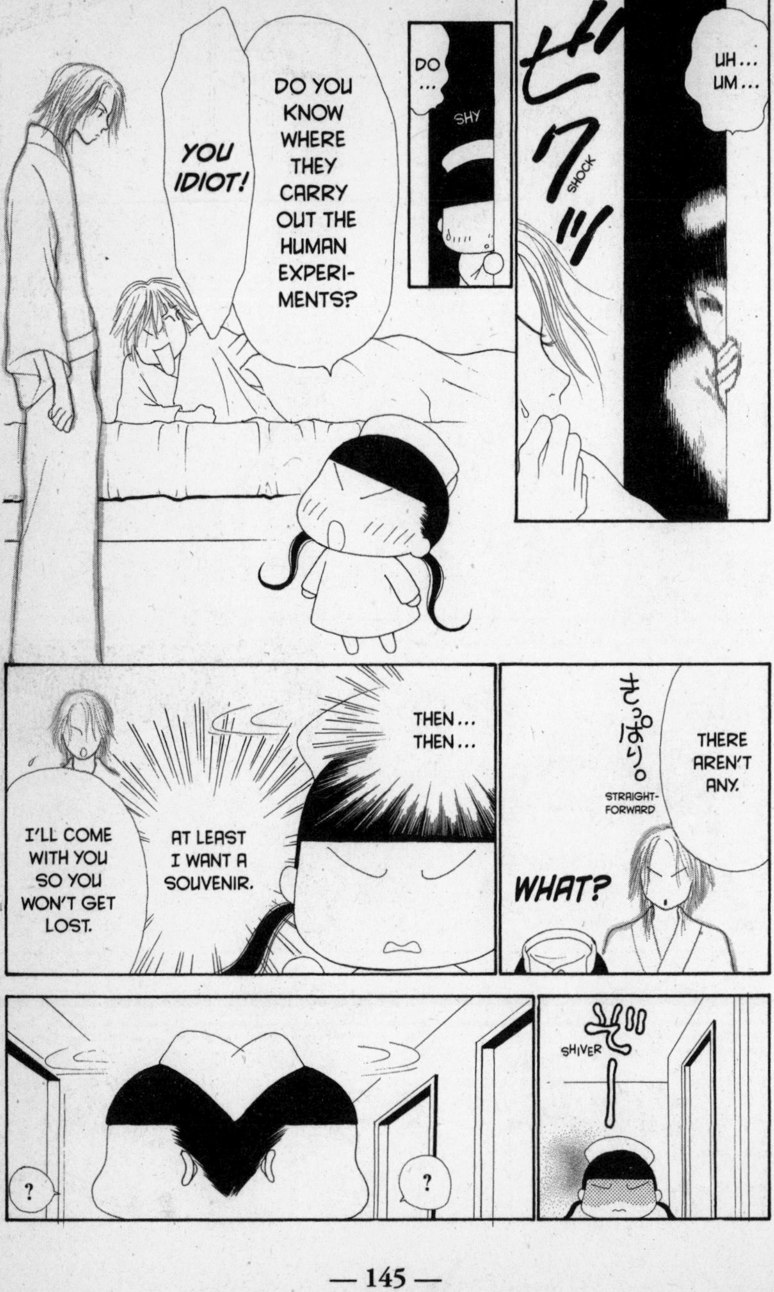
UH... UM...
SHOCK
DO...
SHY
DO YOU KNOW WHERE THEY CARRY OUT THE HUMAN EXPERIMENTS?
YOU IDIOT!
THERE AREN'T ANY.
きっぱり。
STRAIGHTFORWARD
WHAT?
THEN... THEN...
AT LEAST I WANT A SOUVENIR.
I'LL COME WITH YOU SO YOU WON'T GET LOST.
SHIVER
?
?

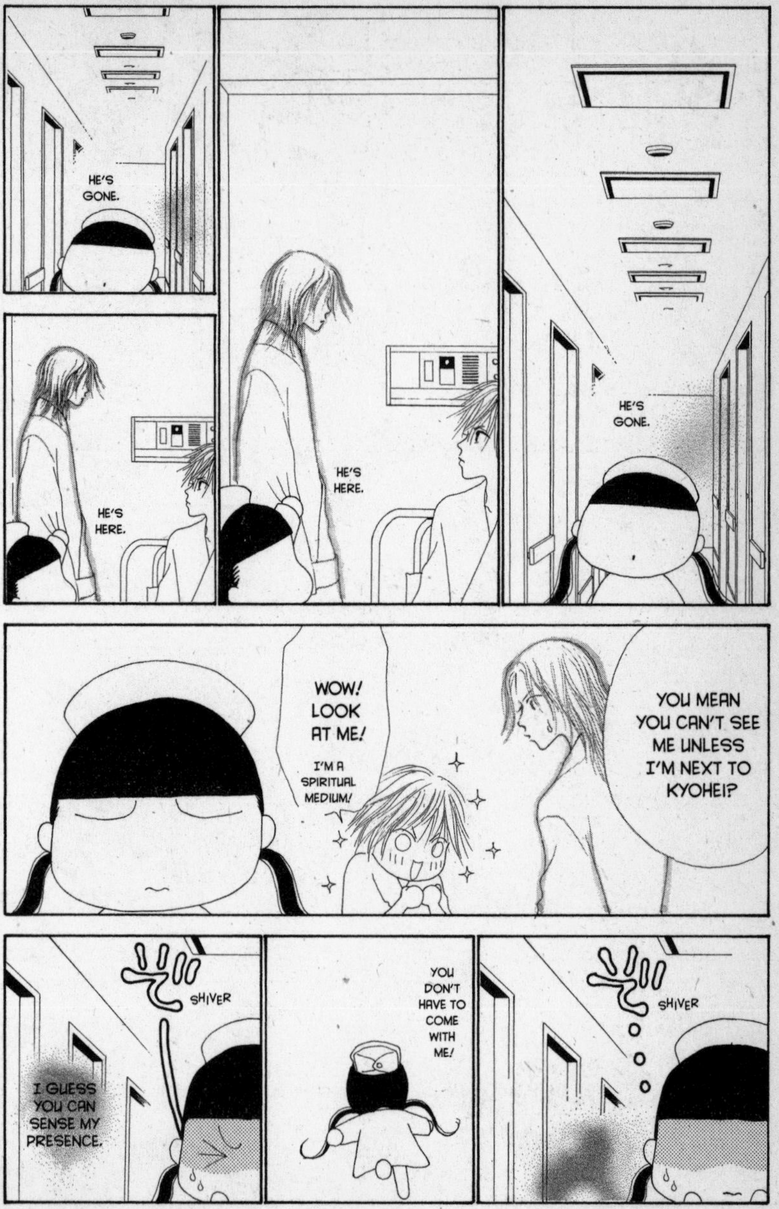
HE'S GONE.
HE'S HERE.
HE'S GONE.
HE'S HERE.
YOU MEAN YOU CAN'T SEE ME UNLESS I'M NEXT TO KYOHEI?
WOW! LOOK AT ME!
I'M A SPIRITUAL MEDIUM!
SHIVER
YOU DON'T HAVE TO COME WITH ME!
SHIVER
I GUESS YOU CAN SENSE MY PRESENCE.

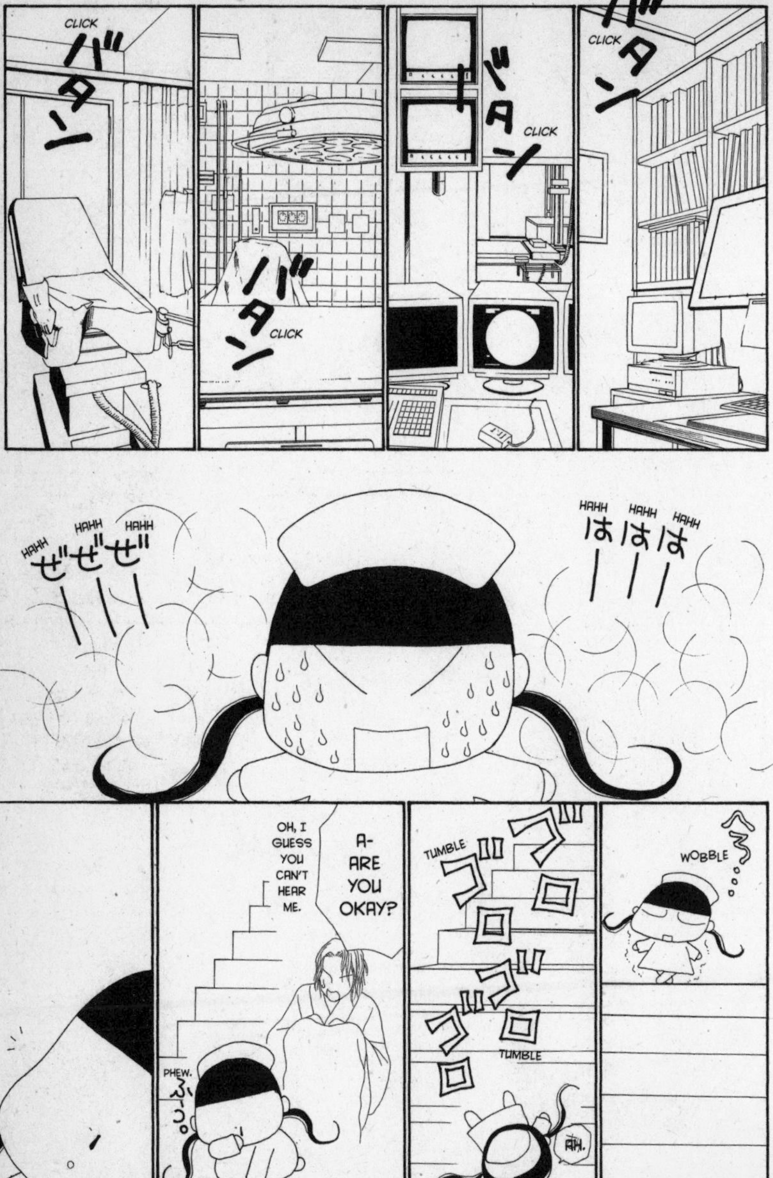
CLICK
バタン
CLICK
バタン
CLICK
バタン
CLICK
バタン
HAHH HAHH HAHH
はははー
HAHH HAHH HAHH
ぜぜぜー
WOBBLE
へろ
TUMBLE
ゴロゴロゴロゴロ
TUMBLE
AH.
A- ARE YOU OKAY?
OH, I GUESS YOU CAN'T HEAR ME.
PHEW.
ふぅっ。

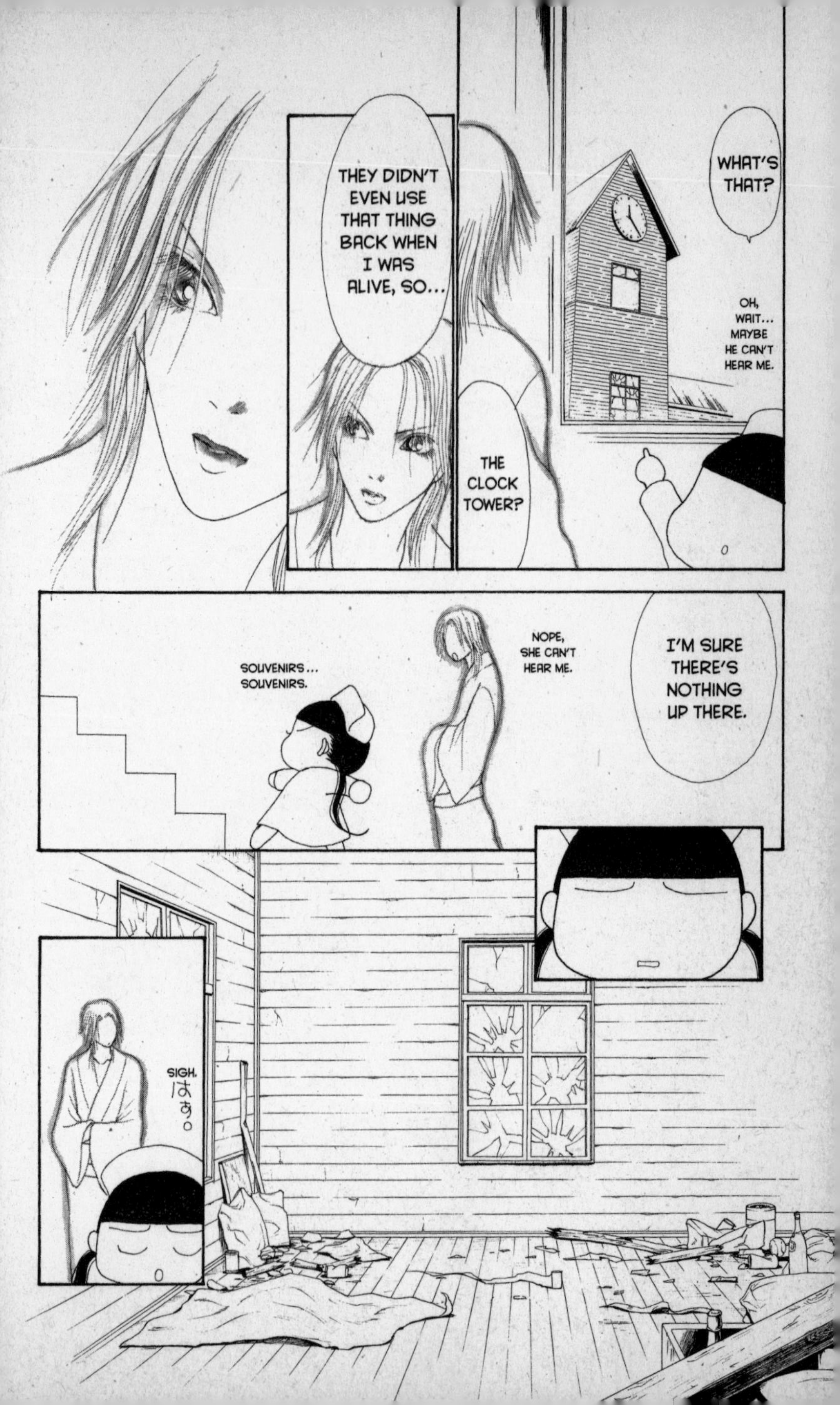
WHAT'S THAT?
OH, WAIT... MAYBE HE CAN'T HEAR ME.
THE CLOCK TOWER?
THEY DIDN'T EVEN USE THAT THING BACK WHEN I WAS ALIVE, SO...
I'M SURE THERE'S NOTHING UP THERE.
NOPE, SHE CAN'T HEAR ME.
SOUVENIRS... SOUVENIRS.
SIGH.
はぁ。

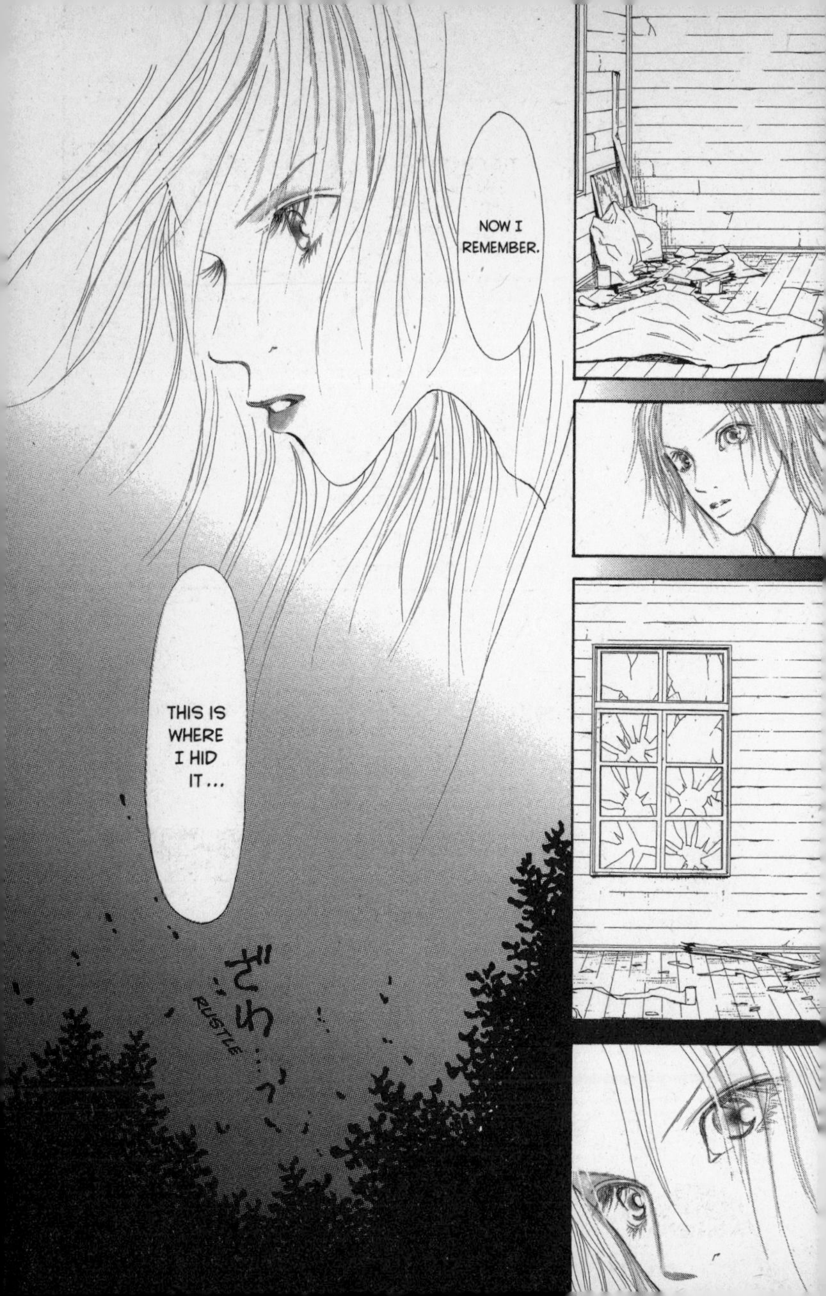
NOW I REMEMBER.
THIS IS WHERE I HID IT...
ざわ…
RUSTLE

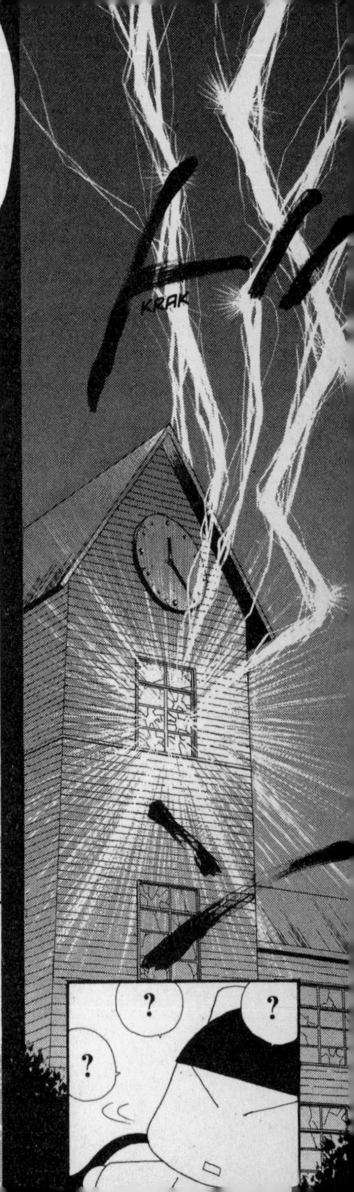
KRAK
?
?
?

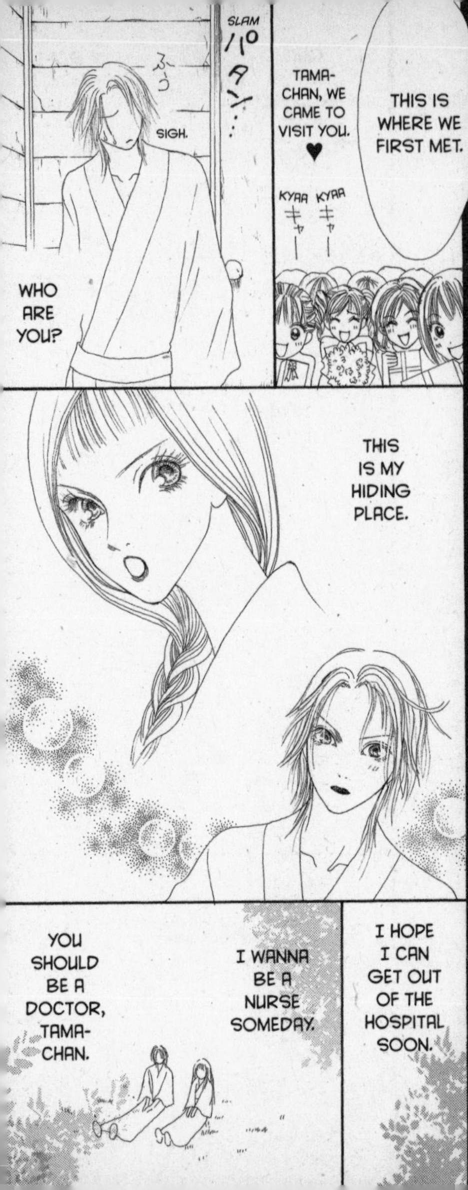
THIS IS WHERE WE FIRST MET.
TAMA-CHAN, WE CAME TO VISIT YOU. ♥
KYAA KYAA
キャー キャー
SLAM
バタン…
ふっ
SIGH.
WHO ARE YOU?
THIS IS MY HIDING PLACE.
I HOPE I CAN GET OUT OF THE HOSPITAL SOON.
I WANNA BE A NURSE SOMEDAY.
YOU SHOULD BE A DOCTOR, TAMA-CHAN.

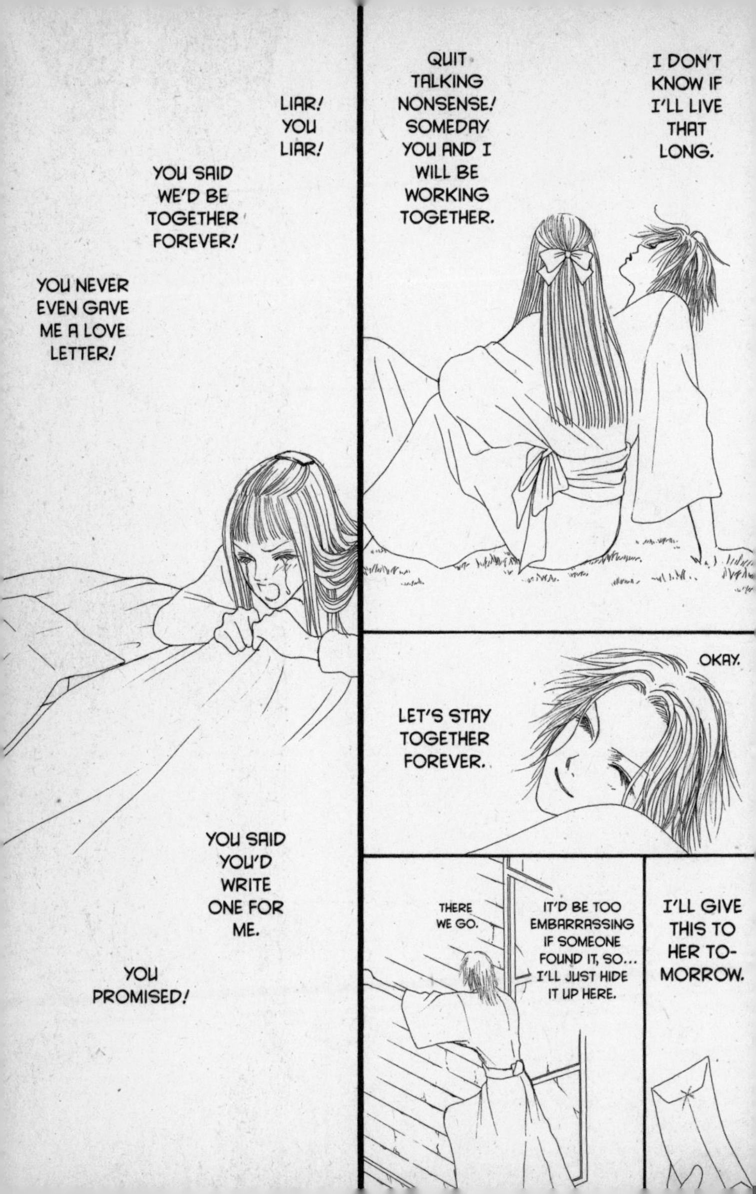
I DON'T KNOW IF I'LL LIVE THAT LONG.
QUIT TALKING NONSENSE! SOMEDAY YOU AND I WILL BE WORKING TOGETHER.
OKAY.
LET'S STAY TOGETHER FOREVER.
I'LL GIVE THIS TO HER TO-MORROW.
IT'D BE TOO EMBARRASSING IF SOMEONE FOUND IT, SO… I'LL JUST HIDE IT UP HERE.
THERE WE GO.
LIAR! YOU LIAR!
YOU SAID WE'D BE TOGETHER FOREVER!
YOU NEVER EVEN GAVE ME A LOVE LETTER!
YOU SAID YOU'D WRITE ONE FOR ME.
YOU PROMISED!

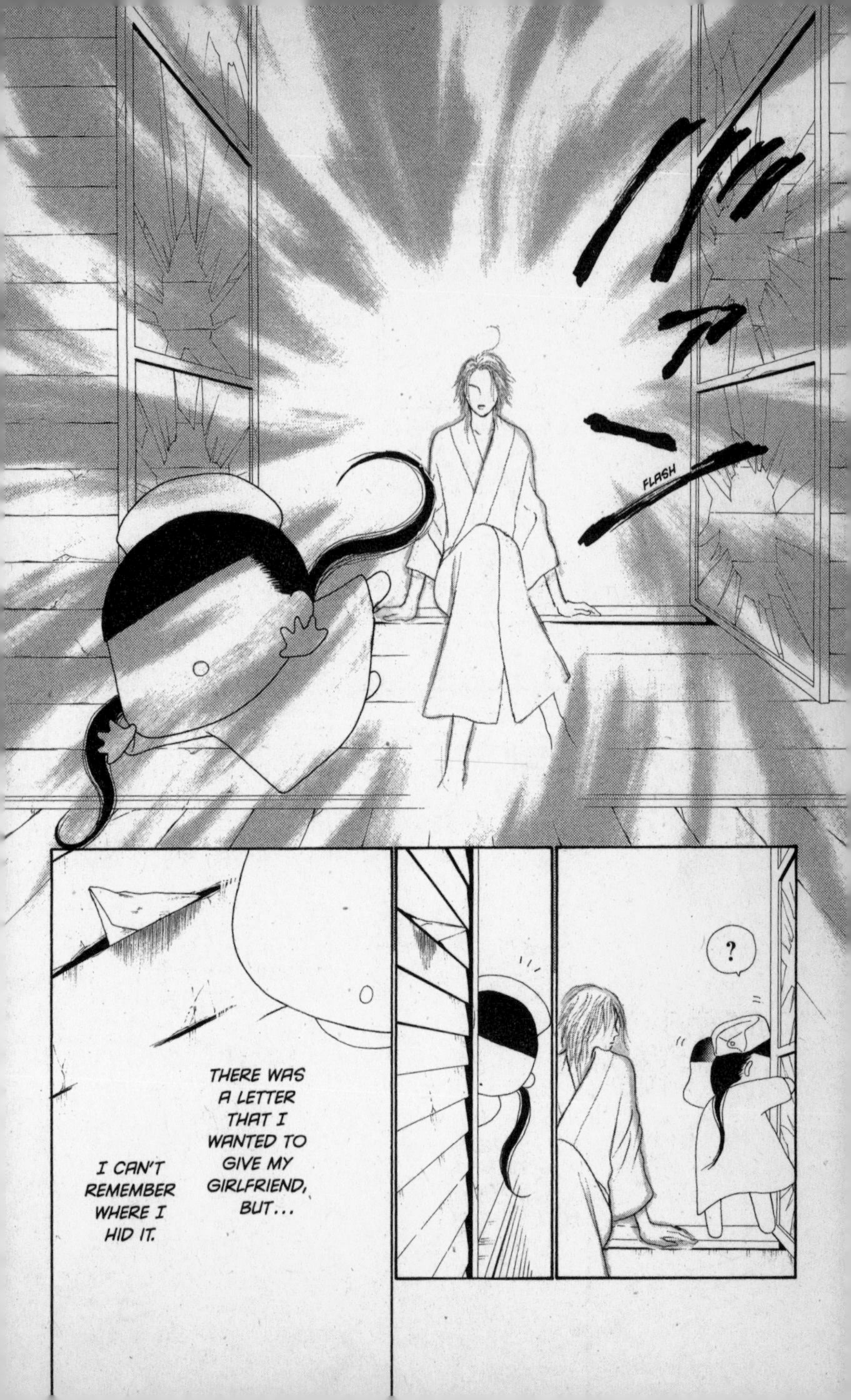
FLASH
?
THERE WAS A LETTER THAT I WANTED TO GIVE MY GIRLFRIEND, BUT...
I CAN'T REMEMBER WHERE I HID IT.

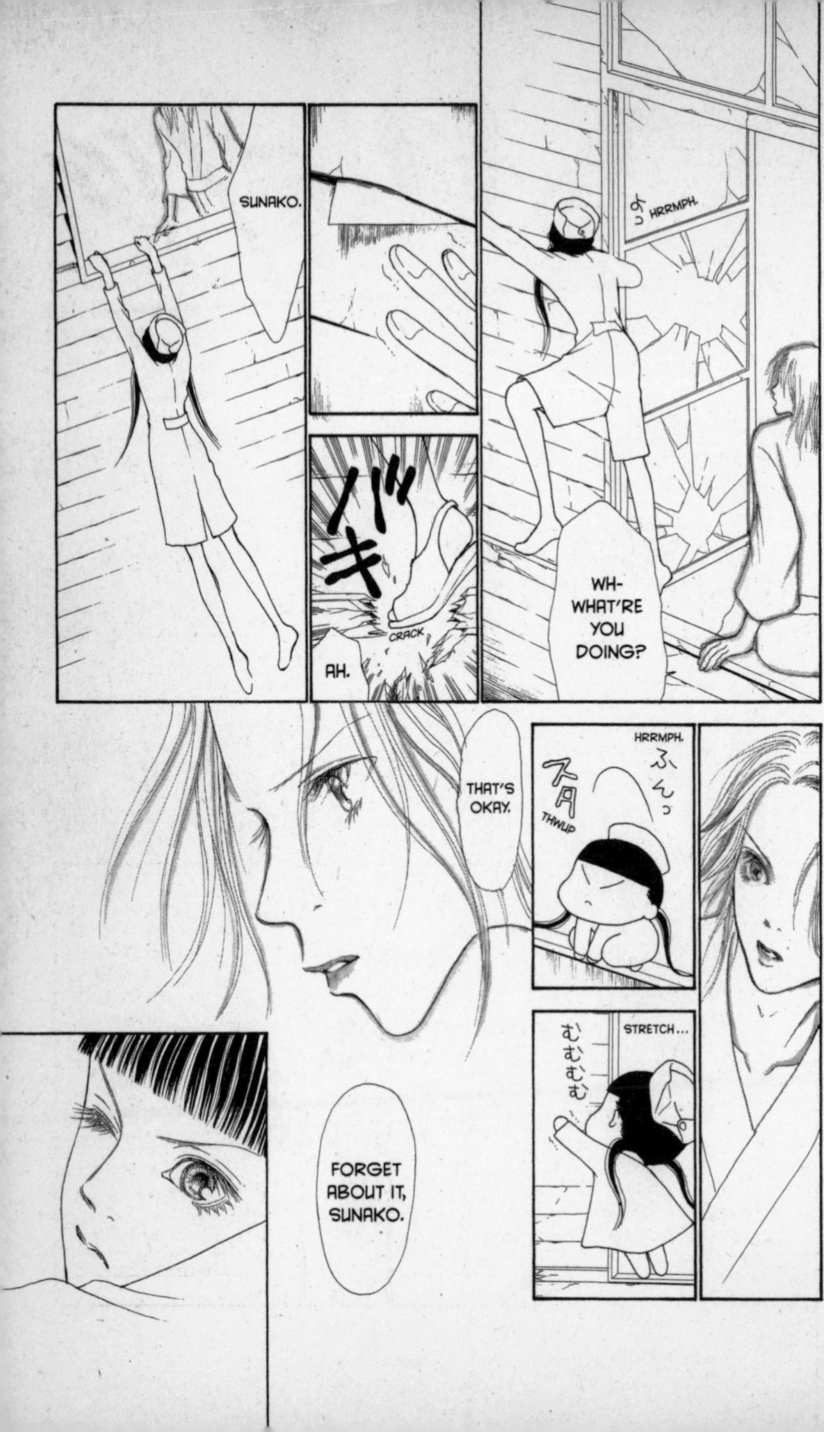
よっ HRRMPH.
WH-WHAT'RE YOU DOING?
バキ
CRACK
AH.
SUNAKO.
HRRMPH.
ふんっ
スタ
THWUP
STRETCH...
むむむむ
THAT'S OKAY.
FORGET ABOUT IT, SUNAKO.

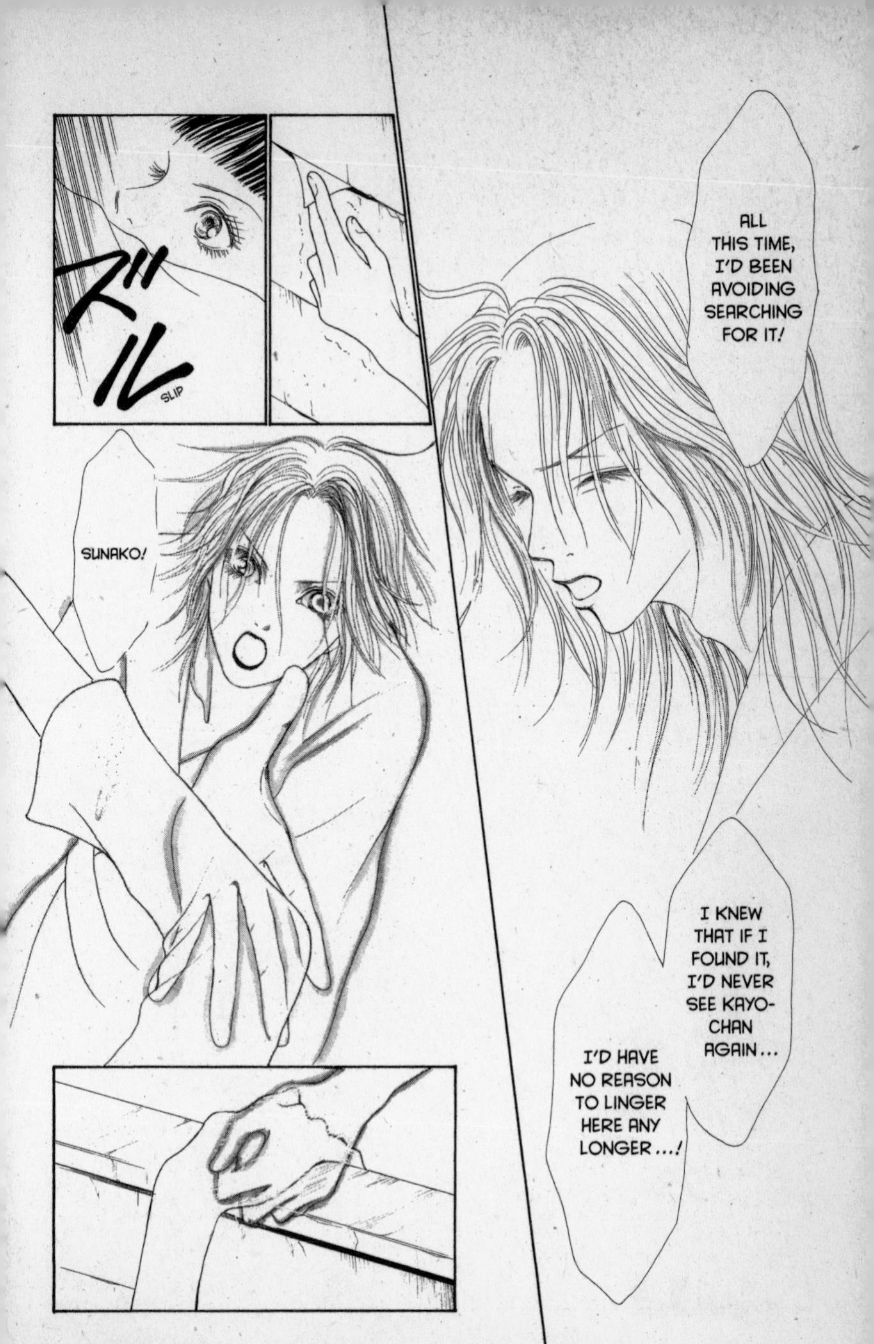
ALL THIS TIME, I'D BEEN AVOIDING SEARCHING FOR IT!
I KNEW THAT IF I FOUND IT, I'D NEVER SEE KAYO-CHAN AGAIN...
I'D HAVE NO REASON TO LINGER HERE ANY LONGER...!
ズル
SLIP
SUNAKO!

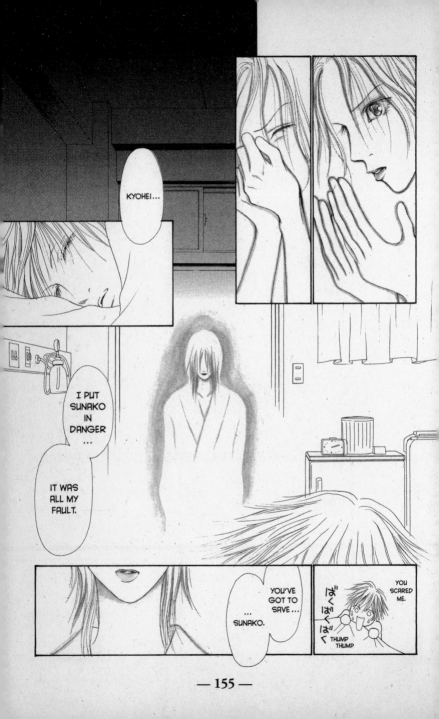

KYOHEI...

I PUT SUNAKO IN DANGER...

IT WAS ALL MY FAULT.

... SUNAKO.

YOU'VE GOT TO SAVE...

YOU SCARED ME.

THUMP THUMP

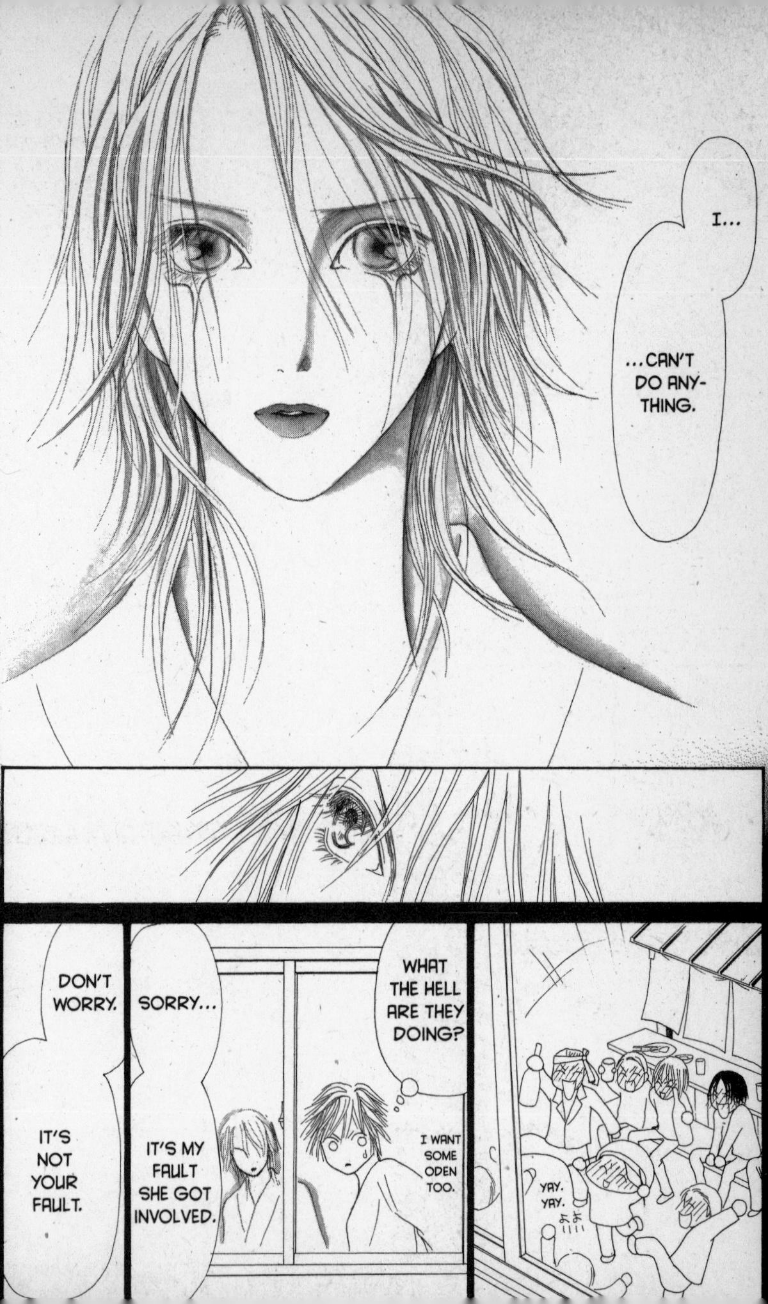
I...
...CAN'T DO ANYTHING.
YAY. YAY.
WHAT THE HELL ARE THEY DOING?
I WANT SOME ODEN TOO.
SORRY...
IT'S MY FAULT SHE GOT INVOLVED.
DON'T WORRY.
IT'S NOT YOUR FAULT.

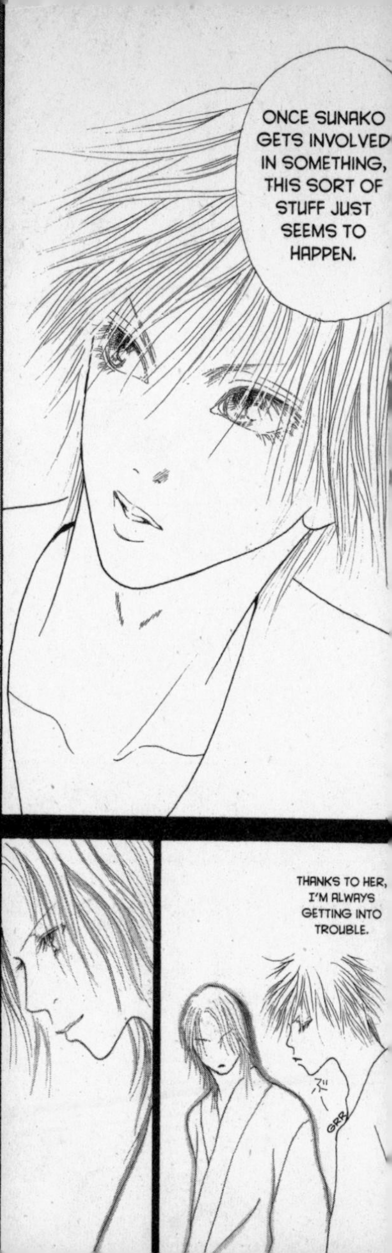
ONCE SUNAKO GETS INVOLVED IN SOMETHING, THIS SORT OF STUFF JUST SEEMS TO HAPPEN.
THANKS TO HER, I'M ALWAYS GETTING INTO TROUBLE.
ぶー
GRR
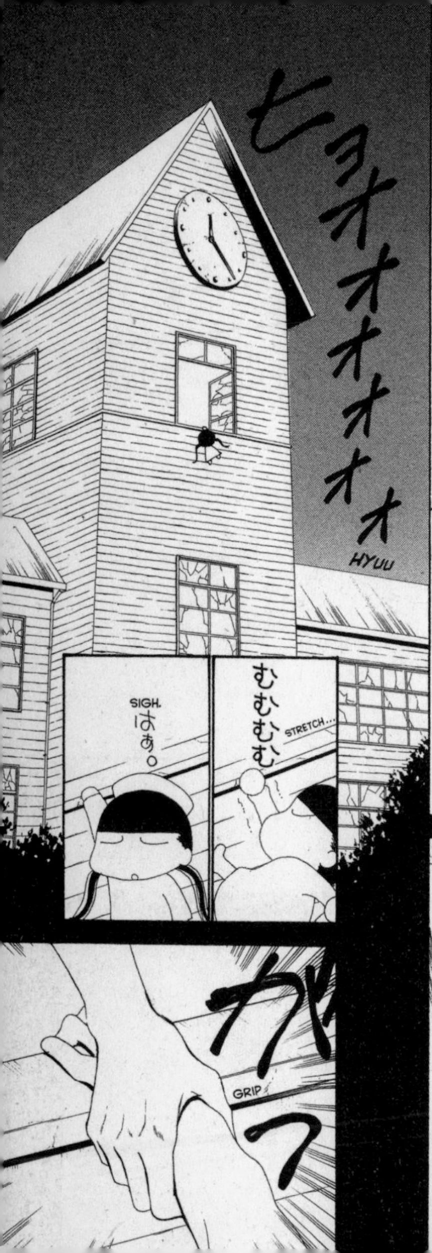
ヒョオオオオオオオ
HYUU
むむむむ
STRETCH...
SIGH.
はぁ。
ガッ
GRIP

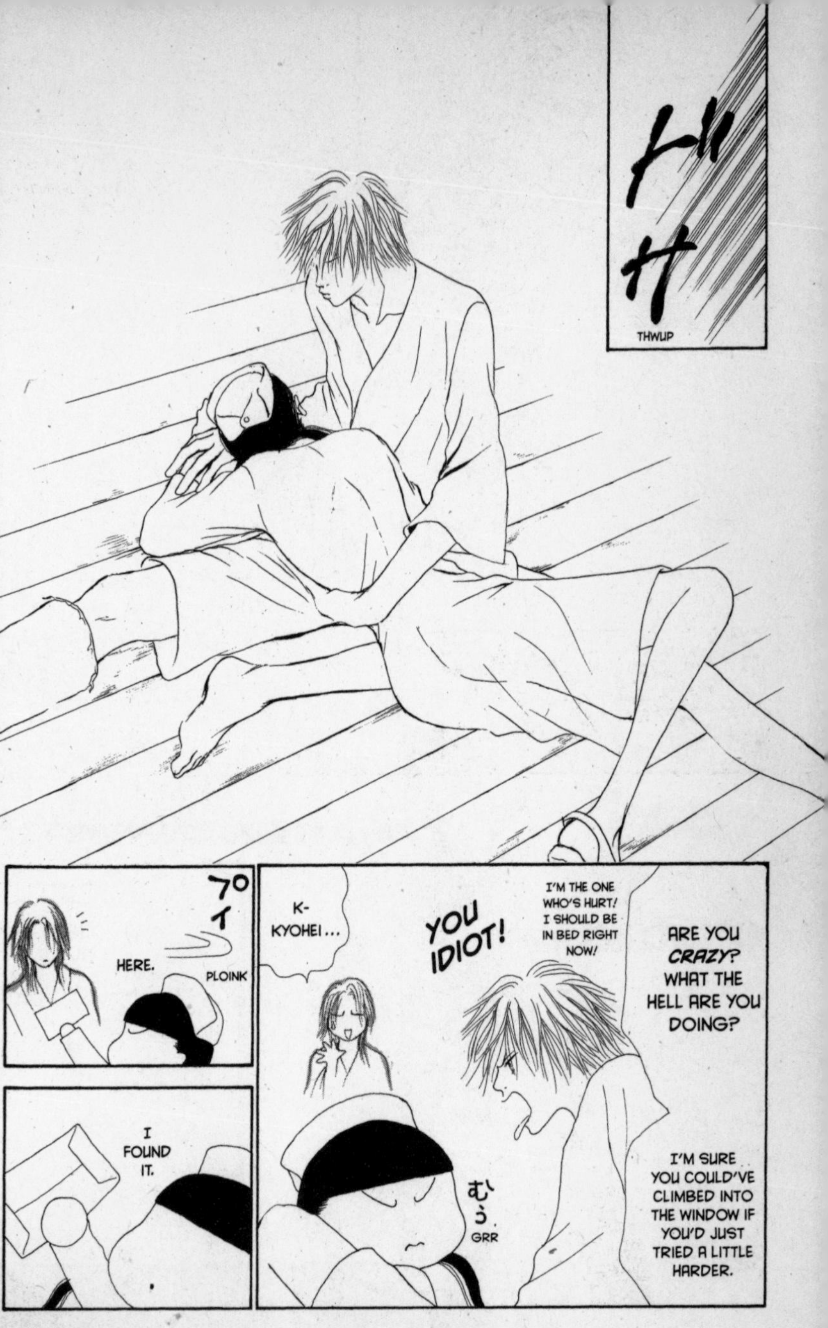
THWUP
ARE YOU CRAZY? WHAT THE HELL ARE YOU DOING?
I'M THE ONE WHO'S HURT! I SHOULD BE IN BED RIGHT NOW!
YOU IDIOT!
K-KYOHEI...
I'M SURE YOU COULD'VE CLIMBED INTO THE WINDOW IF YOU'D JUST TRIED A LITTLE HARDER.
GRR
HERE.
PLOINK
I FOUND IT.

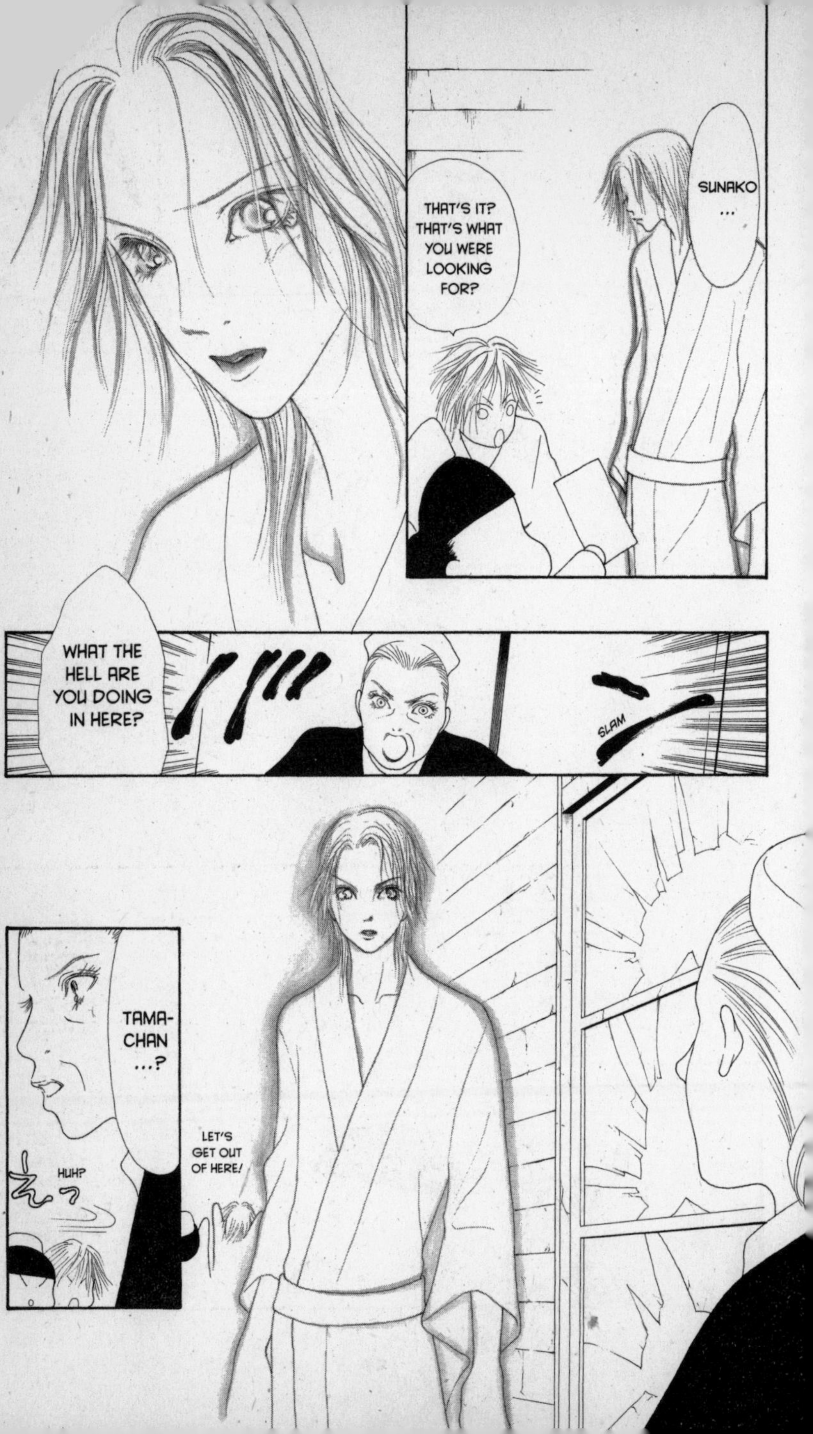
SUNAKO ...
THAT'S IT? THAT'S WHAT YOU WERE LOOKING FOR?
WHAT THE HELL ARE YOU DOING IN HERE?
SLAM
LET'S GET OUT OF HERE!
TAMA-CHAN ...?
HUH?

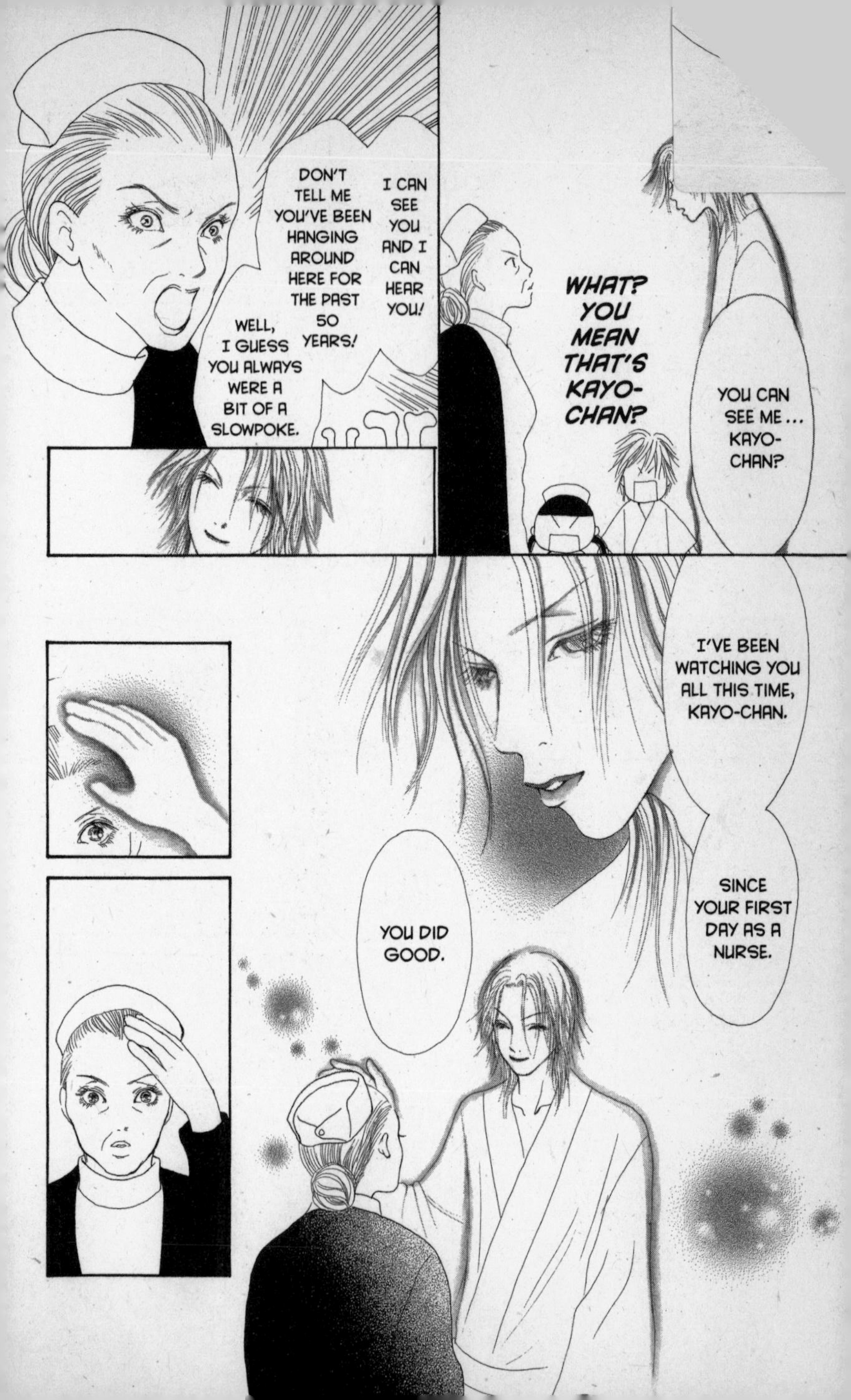
YOU CAN SEE ME... KAYO-CHAN?
WHAT? YOU MEAN THAT'S KAYO-CHAN?
I CAN SEE YOU AND I CAN HEAR YOU!
DON'T TELL ME YOU'VE BEEN HANGING AROUND HERE FOR THE PAST 50 YEARS!
WELL, I GUESS YOU ALWAYS WERE A BIT OF A SLOWPOKE.
I'VE BEEN WATCHING YOU ALL THIS TIME, KAYO-CHAN.
SINCE YOUR FIRST DAY AS A NURSE.
YOU DID GOOD.

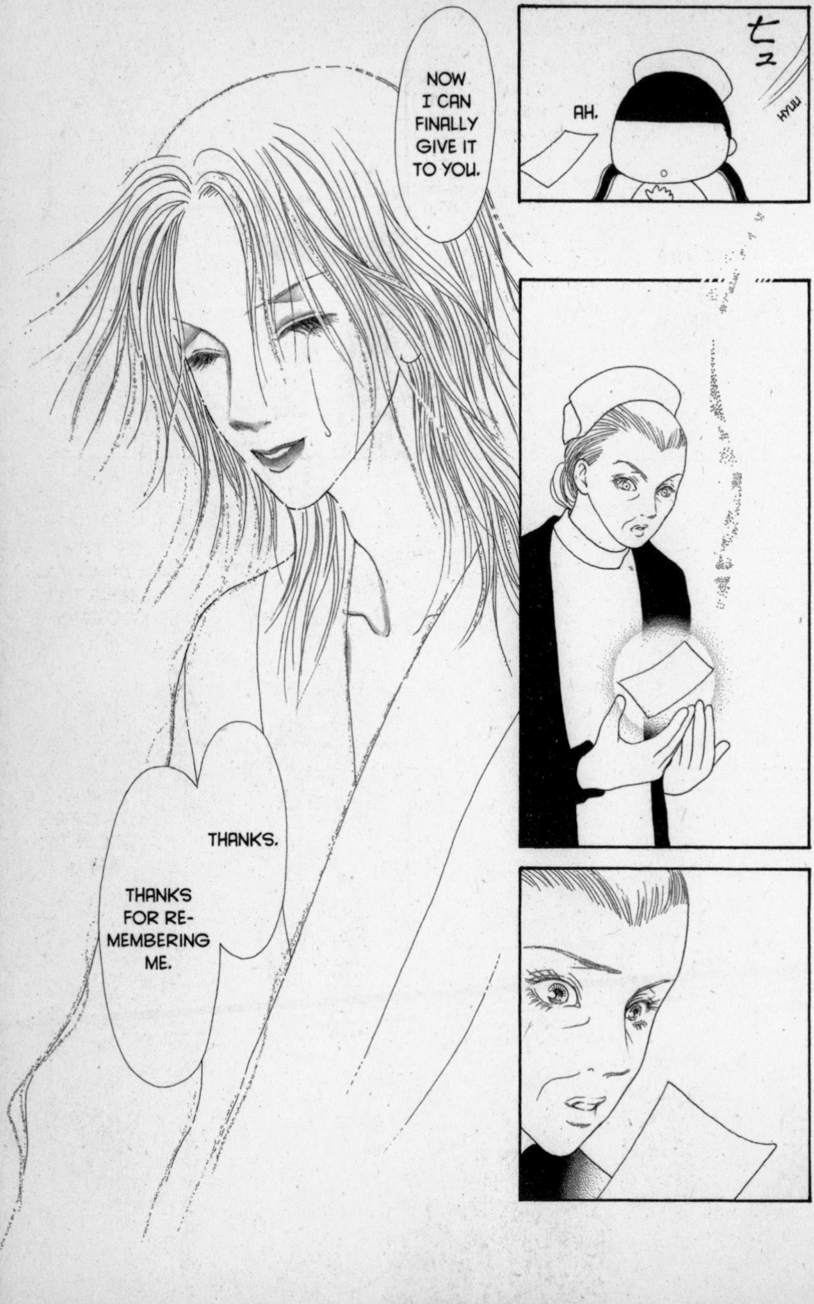
ヒュ
HYUU
AH.
NOW I CAN FINALLY GIVE IT TO YOU.
THANKS.
THANKS FOR RE-MEMBERING ME.

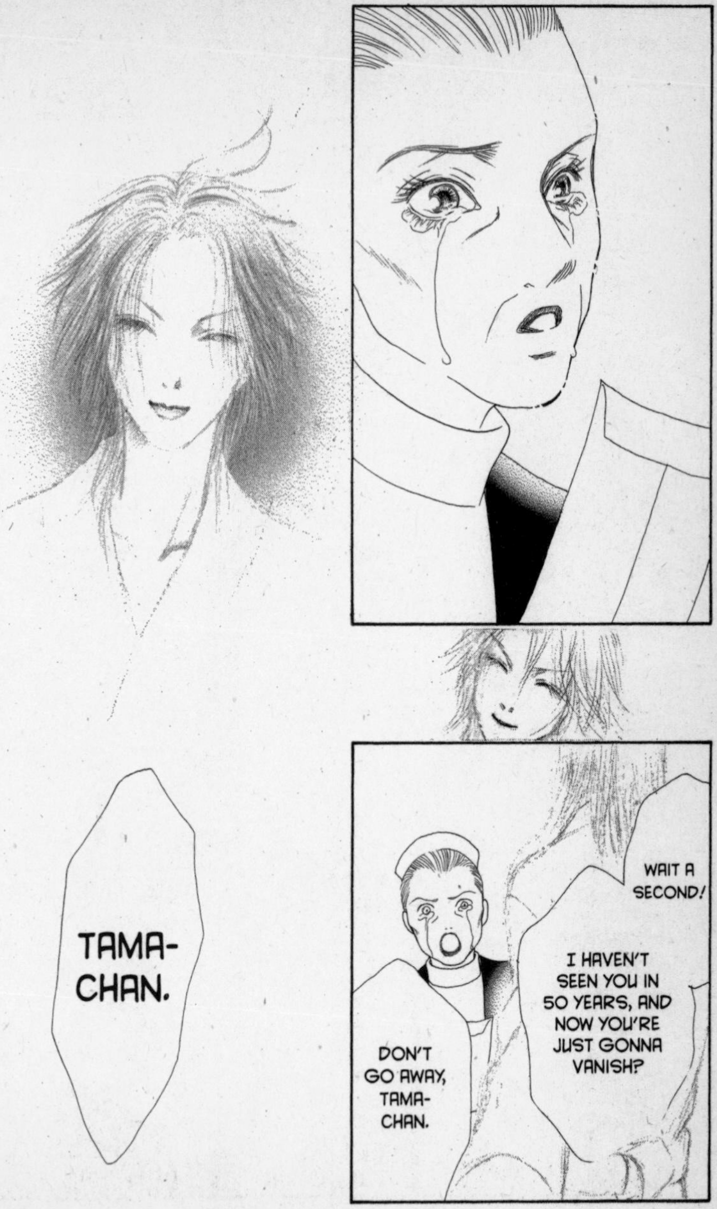
WAIT A SECOND!
I HAVEN'T SEEN YOU IN 50 YEARS, AND NOW YOU'RE JUST GONNA VANISH?
DON'T GO AWAY, TAMA-CHAN.
TAMA-CHAN.

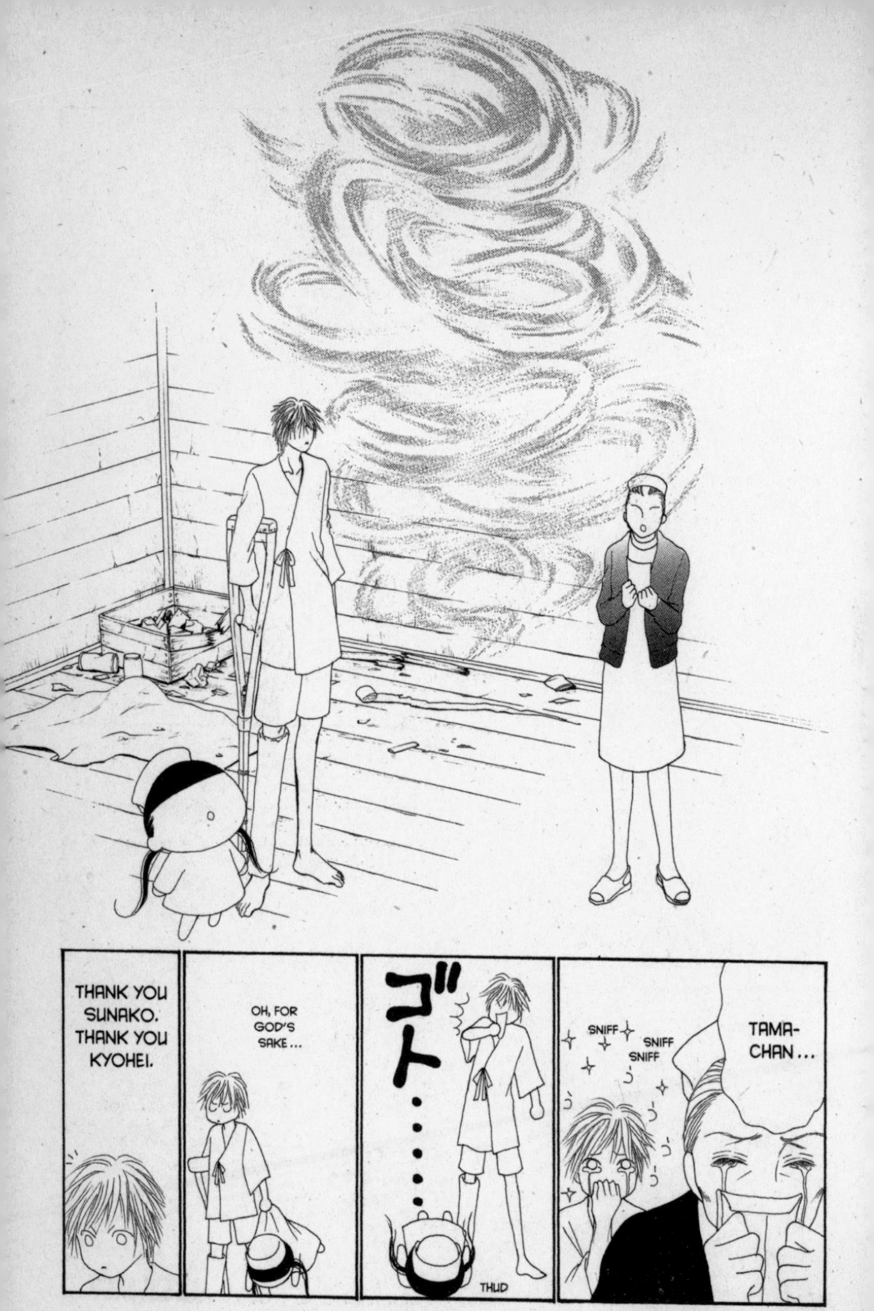
TAMA-CHAN...
SNIFF
SNIFF
SNIFF
ゴト...
THUD
OH, FOR GOD'S SAKE...
THANK YOU SUNAKO. THANK YOU KYOHEI.

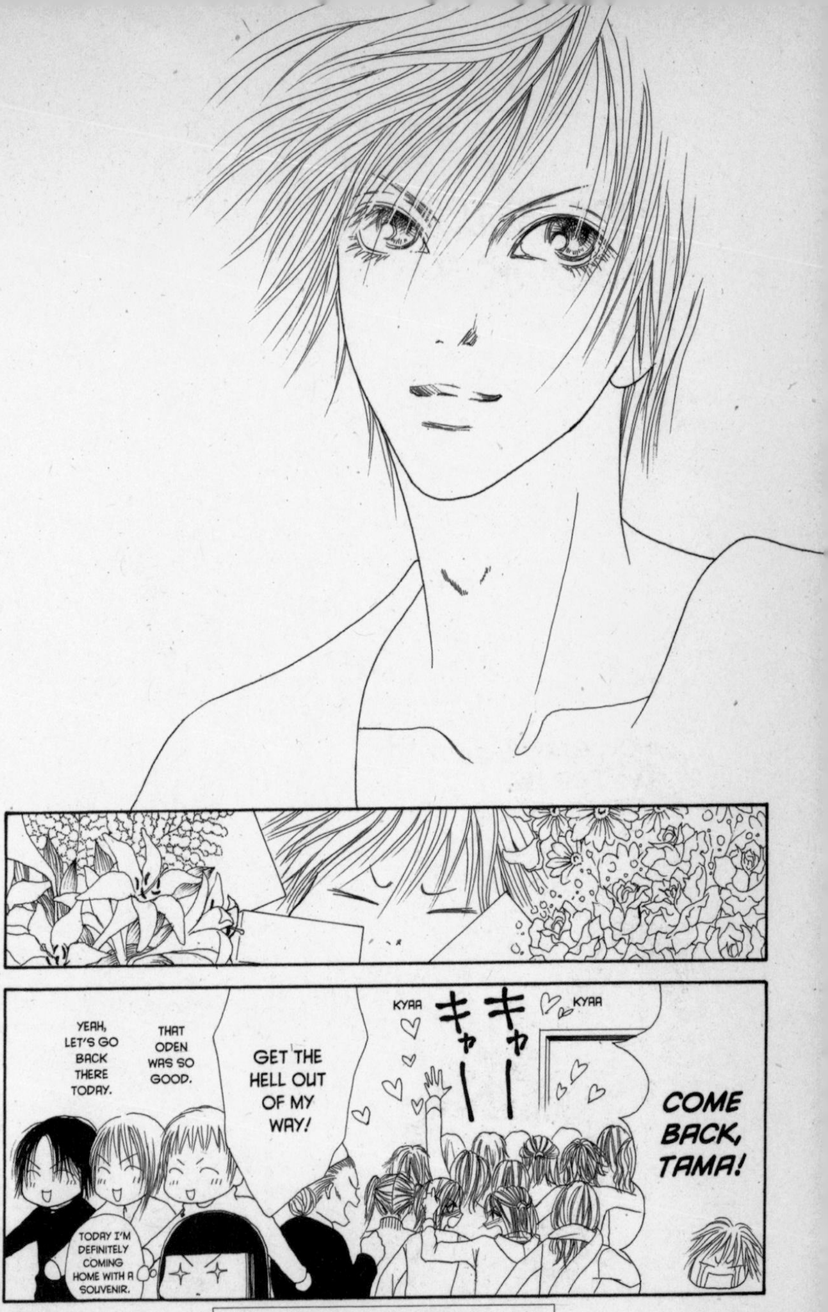
COME BACK, TAMA!
KYAA
キャー
KYAA
キャー
GET THE HELL OUT OF MY WAY!
THAT ODEN WAS SO GOOD.
YEAH, LET'S GO BACK THERE TODAY.
TODAY I'M DEFINITELY COMING HOME WITH A SOUVENIR.

CONTINUED IN WALLFLOWER BOOK 8

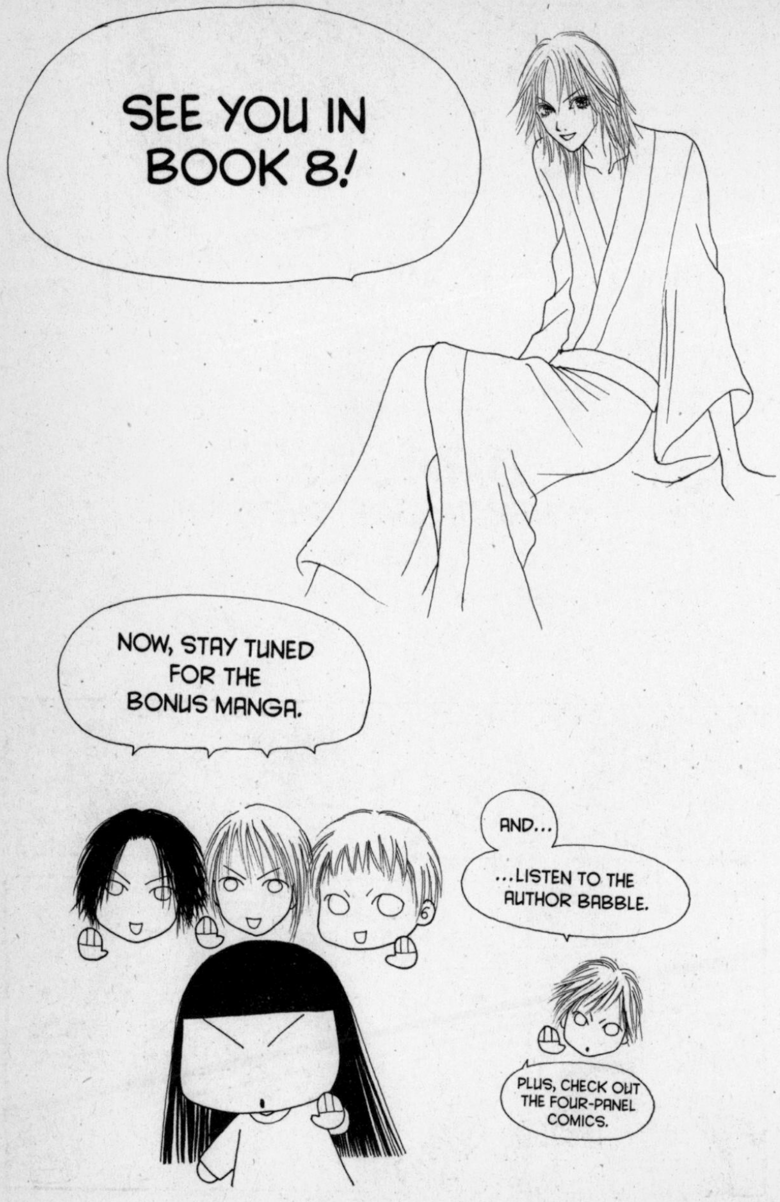
SEE YOU IN BOOK 8!
NOW, STAY TUNED FOR THE BONUS MANGA.
AND...
...LISTEN TO THE AUTHOR BABBLE.
PLUS, CHECK OUT THE FOUR-PANEL COMICS.

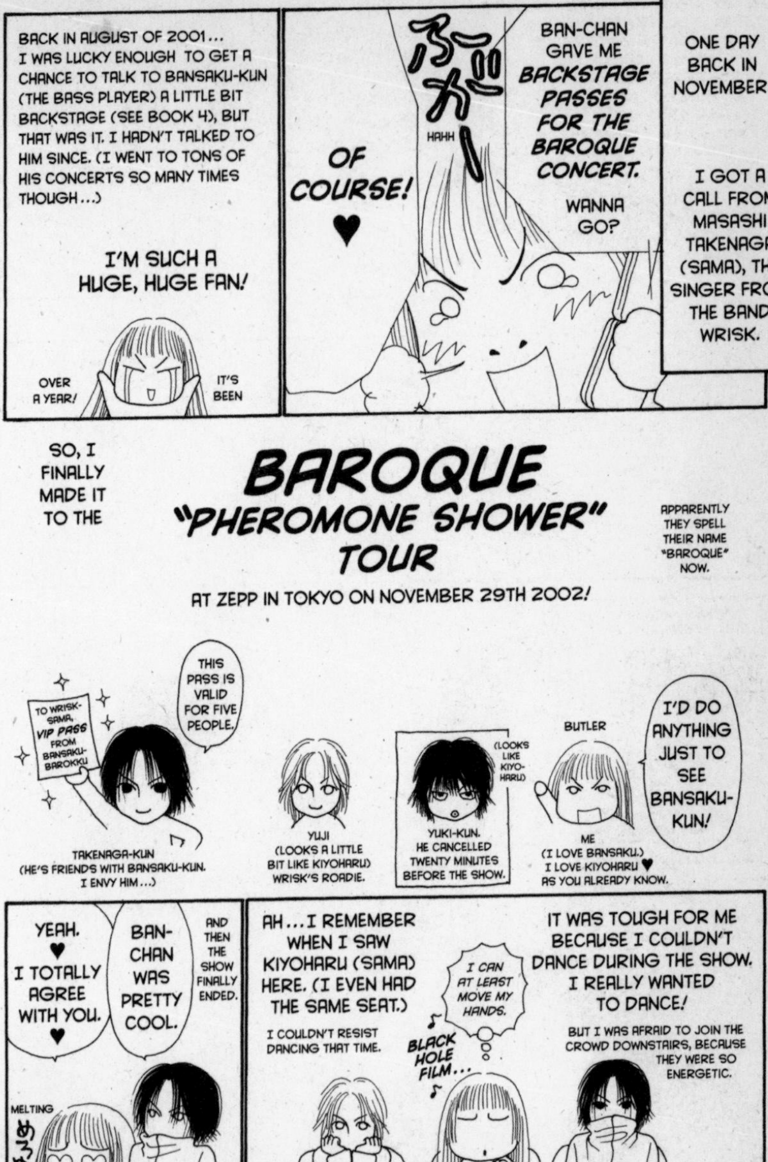
ONE DAY BACK IN NOVEMBER...
I GOT A CALL FROM MASASHI TAKENAGA (SAMA), THE SINGER FROM THE BAND WRISK.
BAN-CHAN GAVE ME BACKSTAGE PASSES FOR THE BAROQUE CONCERT.
WANNA GO?
HAHH
OF COURSE! ♥
BACK IN AUGUST OF 2001... I WAS LUCKY ENOUGH TO GET A CHANCE TO TALK TO BANSAKU-KUN (THE BASS PLAYER) A LITTLE BIT BACKSTAGE (SEE BOOK 4), BUT THAT WAS IT. I HADN'T TALKED TO HIM SINCE. (I WENT TO TONS OF HIS CONCERTS SO MANY TIMES THOUGH...)
I'M SUCH A HUGE, HUGE FAN!
IT'S BEEN
OVER A YEAR!
SO, I FINALLY MADE IT TO THE
BAROQUE
"PHEROMONE SHOWER" TOUR
AT ZEPP IN TOKYO ON NOVEMBER 29TH 2002!
APPARENTLY THEY SPELL THEIR NAME "BAROQUE" NOW.
I'D DO ANYTHING JUST TO SEE BANSAKU-KUN!
BUTLER
ME (I LOVE BANSAKU.) I LOVE KIYOHARU ♥ AS YOU ALREADY KNOW.
(LOOKS LIKE KIYO-HARU)
YUKI-KUN. HE CANCELLED TWENTY MINUTES BEFORE THE SHOW.
YUJI (LOOKS A LITTLE BIT LIKE KIYOHARU) WRISK'S ROADIE.
THIS PASS IS VALID FOR FIVE PEOPLE.
TO WRISK-SAMA, VIP PASS FROM BANSAKU-BAROKKU
TAKENAGA-KUN (HE'S FRIENDS WITH BANSAKU-KUN. I ENVY HIM...)
IT WAS TOUGH FOR ME BECAUSE I COULDN'T DANCE DURING THE SHOW. I REALLY WANTED TO DANCE!
BUT I WAS AFRAID TO JOIN THE CROWD DOWNSTAIRS, BECAUSE THEY WERE SO ENERGETIC.
I CAN AT LEAST MOVE MY HANDS.
BLACK HOLE FILM...
AH... I REMEMBER WHEN I SAW KIYOHARU (SAMA) HERE. (I EVEN HAD THE SAME SEAT.)
I COULDN'T RESIST DANCING THAT TIME.
AND THEN THE SHOW FINALLY ENDED.
BAN-CHAN WAS PRETTY COOL.
YEAH. ♥ I TOTALLY AGREE WITH YOU. ♥
MELTING

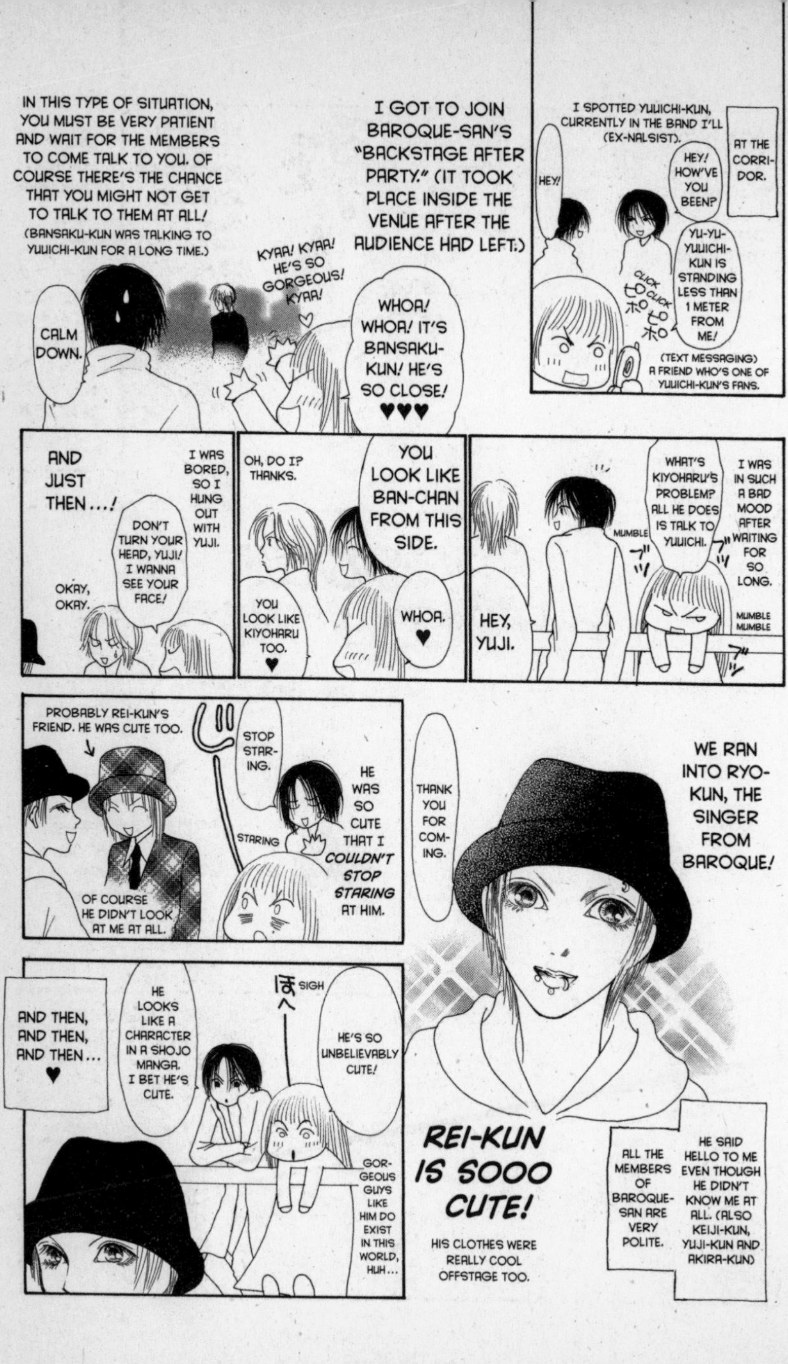
AT THE CORRIDOR.
I SPOTTED YUUICHI-KUN, CURRENTLY IN THE BAND I'LL (EX-NALSIST).
HEY! HOW'VE YOU BEEN?
HEY!
YU-YU-YUUICHI-KUN IS STANDING LESS THAN 1 METER FROM ME!
CLICK CLICK
(TEXT MESSAGING) A FRIEND WHO'S ONE OF YUUICHI-KUN'S FANS.
I GOT TO JOIN BAROQUE-SAN'S "BACKSTAGE AFTER PARTY." (IT TOOK PLACE INSIDE THE VENUE AFTER THE AUDIENCE HAD LEFT.)
WHOA! WHOA! IT'S BANSAKU-KUN! HE'S SO CLOSE! ♥♥♥
KYAA! KYAA! HE'S SO GORGEOUS! KYAA! ♥
IN THIS TYPE OF SITUATION, YOU MUST BE VERY PATIENT AND WAIT FOR THE MEMBERS TO COME TALK TO YOU. OF COURSE THERE'S THE CHANCE THAT YOU MIGHT NOT GET TO TALK TO THEM AT ALL!
(BANSAKU-KUN WAS TALKING TO YUUICHI-KUN FOR A LONG TIME.)
CALM DOWN.
I WAS IN SUCH A BAD MOOD AFTER WAITING FOR SO LONG.
WHAT'S KIYOHARU'S PROBLEM? ALL HE DOES IS TALK TO YUUICHI.
MUMBLE
MUMBLE MUMBLE
HEY, YUJI.
YOU LOOK LIKE BAN-CHAN FROM THIS SIDE.
OH, DO I? THANKS.
WHOA. ♥
YOU LOOK LIKE KIYOHARU TOO. ♥
I WAS BORED, SO I HUNG OUT WITH YUJI.
AND JUST THEN...!
DON'T TURN YOUR HEAD, YUJI! I WANNA SEE YOUR FACE!
OKAY, OKAY.
WE RAN INTO RYO-KUN, THE SINGER FROM BAROQUE!
THANK YOU FOR COMING.
REI-KUN IS SOOO CUTE!
HIS CLOTHES WERE REALLY COOL OFFSTAGE TOO.
HE SAID HELLO TO ME EVEN THOUGH HE DIDN'T KNOW ME AT ALL. (ALSO KEIJI-KUN, YUJI-KUN AND AKIRA-KUN)
ALL THE MEMBERS OF BAROQUE-SAN ARE VERY POLITE.
HE WAS SO CUTE THAT I COULDN'T STOP STARING AT HIM.
STOP STARING.
STARING
PROBABLY REI-KUN'S FRIEND. HE WAS CUTE TOO.
OF COURSE HE DIDN'T LOOK AT ME AT ALL.
HE'S SO UNBELIEVABLY CUTE!
SIGH
HE LOOKS LIKE A CHARACTER IN A SHOJO MANGA. I BET HE'S CUTE.
AND THEN, AND THEN, AND THEN... ♥
GORGEOUS GUYS LIKE HIM DO EXIST IN THIS WORLD, HUH...

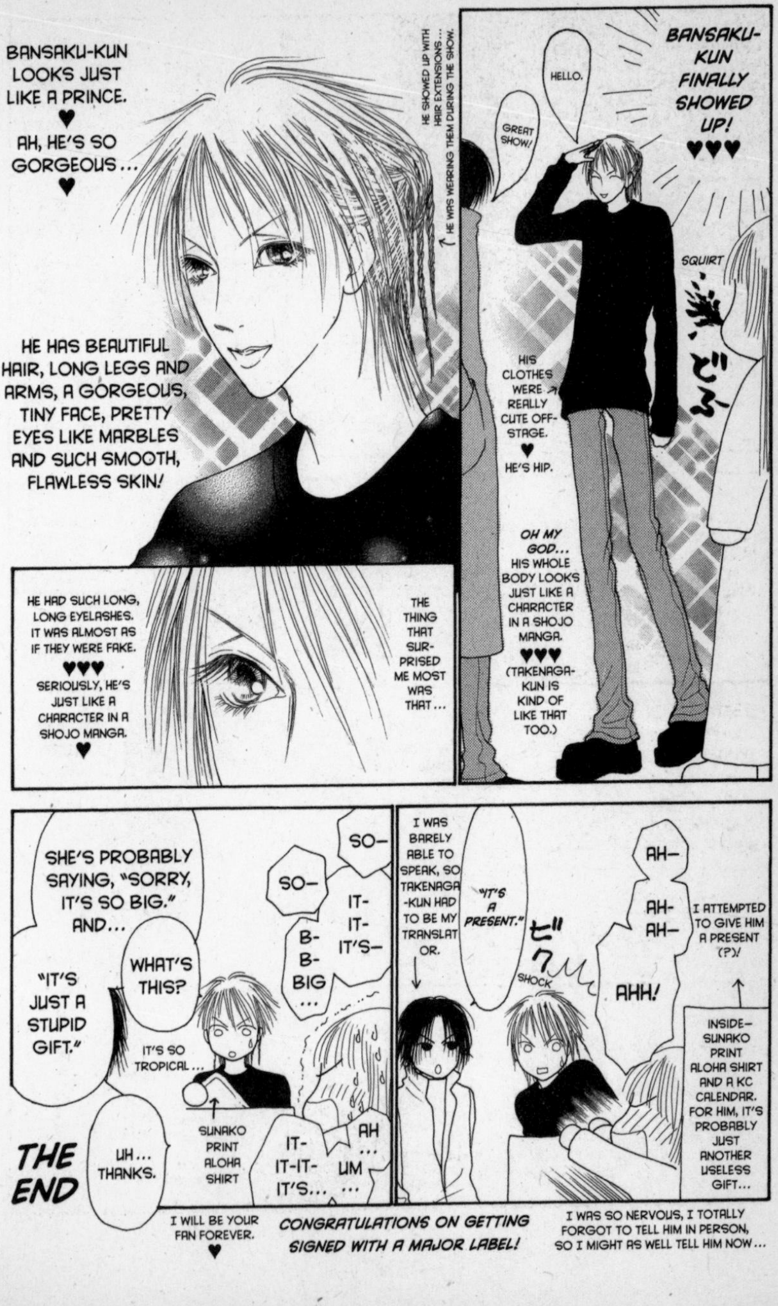

BANSAKU-KUN FINALLY SHOWED UP! ♥♥♥
HELLO.
GREAT SHOW!
SQUIRT
どふ
HIS CLOTHES WERE REALLY CUTE OFF-STAGE. ♥ HE'S HIP.
OH MY GOD... HIS WHOLE BODY LOOKS JUST LIKE A CHARACTER IN A SHOJO MANGA. ♥♥♥ (TAKENAGA-KUN IS KIND OF LIKE THAT TOO.)
HE SHOWED UP WITH HAIR EXTENSIONS... ← HE WAS WEARING THEM DURING THE SHOW.
BANSAKU-KUN LOOKS JUST LIKE A PRINCE. ♥ AH, HE'S SO GORGEOUS... ♥
HE HAS BEAUTIFUL HAIR, LONG LEGS AND ARMS, A GORGEOUS, TINY FACE, PRETTY EYES LIKE MARBLES AND SUCH SMOOTH, FLAWLESS SKIN!
THE THING THAT SUR-PRISED ME MOST WAS THAT...
HE HAD SUCH LONG, LONG EYELASHES. IT WAS ALMOST AS IF THEY WERE FAKE. ♥♥♥ SERIOUSLY, HE'S JUST LIKE A CHARACTER IN A SHOJO MANGA. ♥
I ATTEMPTED TO GIVE HIM A PRESENT (?)!
AH-
AH-AH-
AHH!
ビク
SHOCK
"IT'S A PRESENT."
I WAS BARELY ABLE TO SPEAK, SO TAKENAGA-KUN HAD TO BE MY TRANSLATOR.
INSIDE—SUNAKO PRINT ALOHA SHIRT AND A KC CALENDAR. FOR HIM, IT'S PROBABLY JUST ANOTHER USELESS GIFT...
SO-
SO-
IT-IT-IT'S-
B-B-BIG...
AH...
UM...
IT-IT-IT-IT'S...
SHE'S PROBABLY SAYING, "SORRY, IT'S SO BIG." AND...
WHAT'S THIS?
IT'S SO TROPICAL...
"IT'S JUST A STUPID GIFT."
SUNAKO PRINT ALOHA SHIRT
UH... THANKS.
THE END
I WAS SO NERVOUS, I TOTALLY FORGOT TO TELL HIM IN PERSON, SO I MIGHT AS WELL TELL HIM NOW...
CONGRATULATIONS ON GETTING SIGNED WITH A MAJOR LABEL!
I WILL BE YOUR FAN FOREVER. ♥

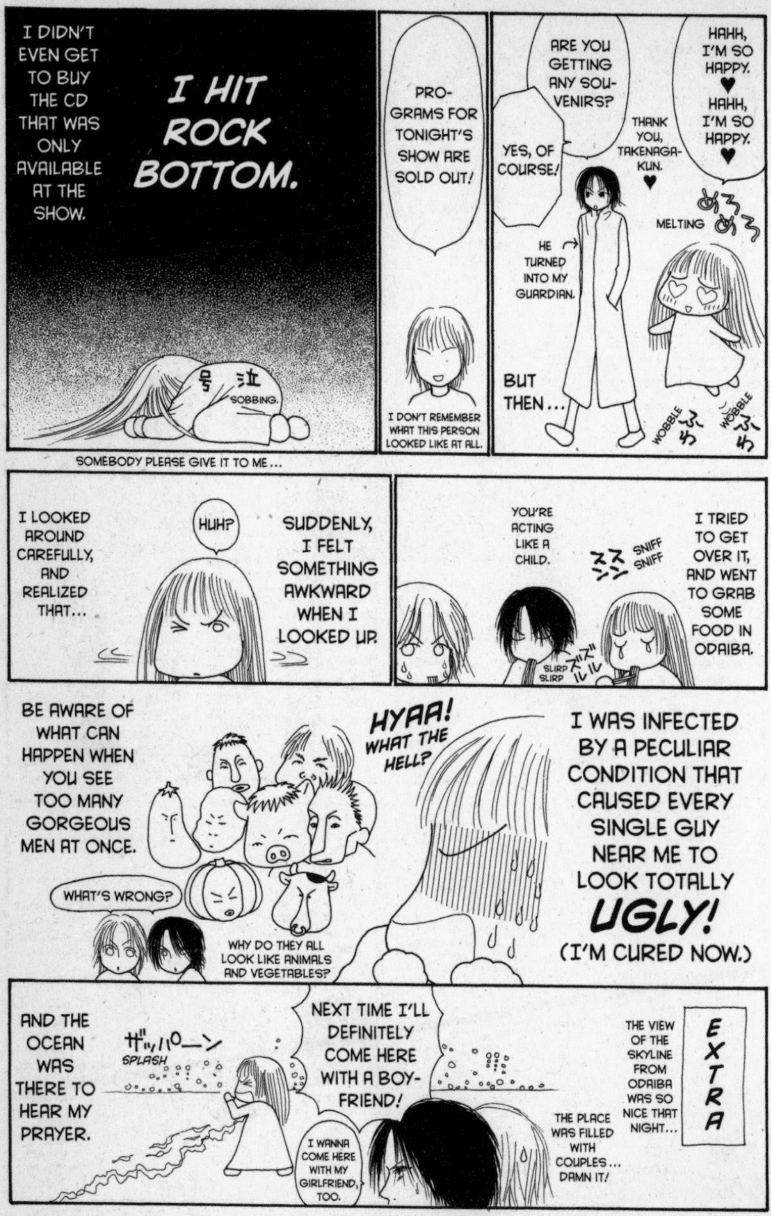
HAHH, I'M SO HAPPY. ♥ HAHH, I'M SO HAPPY. ♥
THANK YOU, TAKENAGA-KUN. ♥
ARE YOU GETTING ANY SOUVENIRS?
YES, OF COURSE!
めろめろ
MELTING
HE TURNED INTO MY GUARDIAN.
BUT THEN...
ふら WOBBLE
ふら WOBBLE
PROGRAMS FOR TONIGHT'S SHOW ARE SOLD OUT!
I DON'T REMEMBER WHAT THIS PERSON LOOKED LIKE AT ALL.
I HIT ROCK BOTTOM.
I DIDN'T EVEN GET TO BUY THE CD THAT WAS ONLY AVAILABLE AT THE SHOW.
号泣
SOBBING.
SOMEBODY PLEASE GIVE IT TO ME...
I TRIED TO GET OVER IT, AND WENT TO GRAB SOME FOOD IN ODAIBA.
ススン
SNIFF SNIFF
YOU'RE ACTING LIKE A CHILD.
ズルル
SLIRP SLIRP
SUDDENLY, I FELT SOMETHING AWKWARD WHEN I LOOKED UP.
HUH?
I LOOKED AROUND CAREFULLY, AND REALIZED THAT...
I WAS INFECTED BY A PECULIAR CONDITION THAT CAUSED EVERY SINGLE GUY NEAR ME TO LOOK TOTALLY UGLY!
(I'M CURED NOW.)
HYAA! WHAT THE HELL?
BE AWARE OF WHAT CAN HAPPEN WHEN YOU SEE TOO MANY GORGEOUS MEN AT ONCE.
WHY DO THEY ALL LOOK LIKE ANIMALS AND VEGETABLES?
WHAT'S WRONG?
EXTRA
THE VIEW OF THE SKYLINE FROM ODAIBA WAS SO NICE THAT NIGHT...
THE PLACE WAS FILLED WITH COUPLES... DAMN IT!
NEXT TIME I'LL DEFINITELY COME HERE WITH A BOY-FRIEND!
I WANNA COME HERE WITH MY GIRLFRIEND, TOO.
ザッパーン
SPLASH
AND THE OCEAN WAS THERE TO HEAR MY PRAYER.

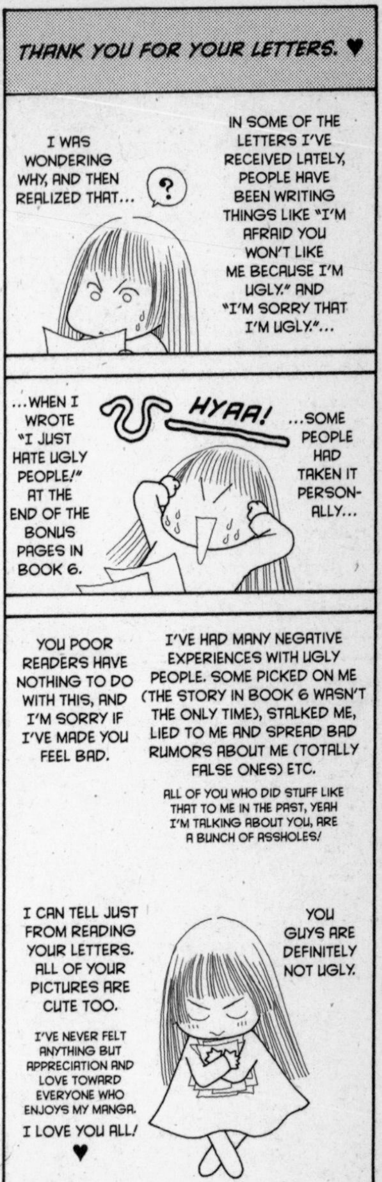
THANK YOU FOR YOUR LETTERS. ♥
IN SOME OF THE LETTERS I'VE RECEIVED LATELY, PEOPLE HAVE BEEN WRITING THINGS LIKE "I'M AFRAID YOU WON'T LIKE ME BECAUSE I'M UGLY." AND "I'M SORRY THAT I'M UGLY."...
?
I WAS WONDERING WHY, AND THEN REALIZED THAT...
...SOME PEOPLE HAD TAKEN IT PERSON-ALLY...
HYAA!
...WHEN I WROTE "I JUST HATE UGLY PEOPLE!" AT THE END OF THE BONUS PAGES IN BOOK 6.
I'VE HAD MANY NEGATIVE EXPERIENCES WITH UGLY PEOPLE. SOME PICKED ON ME (THE STORY IN BOOK 6 WASN'T THE ONLY TIME), STALKED ME, LIED TO ME AND SPREAD BAD RUMORS ABOUT ME (TOTALLY FALSE ONES) ETC.
ALL OF YOU WHO DID STUFF LIKE THAT TO ME IN THE PAST, YEAH I'M TALKING ABOUT YOU, ARE A BUNCH OF ASSHOLES!
YOU POOR READERS HAVE NOTHING TO DO WITH THIS, AND I'M SORRY IF I'VE MADE YOU FEEL BAD.
YOU GUYS ARE DEFINITELY NOT UGLY.
I CAN TELL JUST FROM READING YOUR LETTERS. ALL OF YOUR PICTURES ARE CUTE TOO.
I'VE NEVER FELT ANYTHING BUT APPRECIATION AND LOVE TOWARD EVERYONE WHO ENJOYS MY MANGA.
I LOVE YOU ALL!
♥

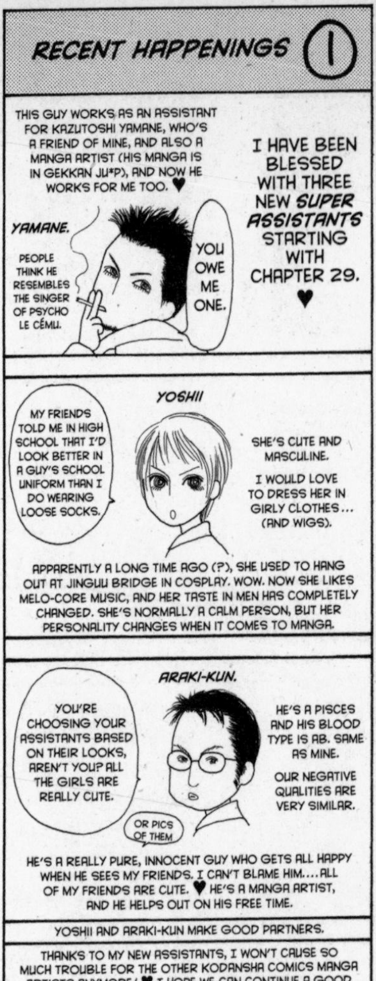
RECENT HAPPENINGS 1
I HAVE BEEN BLESSED WITH THREE NEW SUPER ASSISTANTS STARTING WITH CHAPTER 29.
♥
THIS GUY WORKS AS AN ASSISTANT FOR KAZUTOSHI YAMANE, WHO'S A FRIEND OF MINE, AND ALSO A MANGA ARTIST (HIS MANGA IS IN GEKKAN JU*P), AND NOW HE WORKS FOR ME TOO. ♥
YOU OWE ME ONE.
YAMANE.
PEOPLE THINK HE RESEMBLES THE SINGER OF PSYCHO LE CÉMU.
YOSHII
SHE'S CUTE AND MASCULINE.
I WOULD LOVE TO DRESS HER IN GIRLY CLOTHES... (AND WIGS).
MY FRIENDS TOLD ME IN HIGH SCHOOL THAT I'D LOOK BETTER IN A GUY'S SCHOOL UNIFORM THAN I DO WEARING LOOSE SOCKS.
APPARENTLY A LONG TIME AGO (?), SHE USED TO HANG OUT AT JINGUU BRIDGE IN COSPLAY. WOW. NOW SHE LIKES MELO-CORE MUSIC, AND HER TASTE IN MEN HAS COMPLETELY CHANGED. SHE'S NORMALLY A CALM PERSON, BUT HER PERSONALITY CHANGES WHEN IT COMES TO MANGA.
ARAKI-KUN.
HE'S A PISCES AND HIS BLOOD TYPE IS AB. SAME AS MINE.
OUR NEGATIVE QUALITIES ARE VERY SIMILAR.
YOU'RE CHOOSING YOUR ASSISTANTS BASED ON THEIR LOOKS, AREN'T YOU? ALL THE GIRLS ARE REALLY CUTE.
OR PICS OF THEM
HE'S A REALLY PURE, INNOCENT GUY WHO GETS ALL HAPPY WHEN HE SEES MY FRIENDS. I CAN'T BLAME HIM.... ALL OF MY FRIENDS ARE CUTE. ♥ HE'S A MANGA ARTIST, AND HE HELPS OUT ON HIS FREE TIME.
YOSHII AND ARAKI-KUN MAKE GOOD PARTNERS.
THANKS TO MY NEW ASSISTANTS, I WON'T CAUSE SO MUCH TROUBLE FOR THE OTHER KODANSHA COMICS MANGA ARTISTS ANYMORE! ♥ I HOPE WE CAN CONTINUE A GOOD WORKING RELATIONSHIP FOR A LONG TIME.
I HAVE THE BEST ASSISTANTS IN THE WHOLE WORLD... THAT INCLUDES HANA-CHAN!
RIGHT!
IS THERE ANYONE WHO CAN DRAW MOBU?
OH, WHAT'RE WE GONNA DO ABOUT MOBU?
*MOBU = PEOPLE IN THE BACKGROUND

RECENT HAPPENINGS ②

I WAS IN SAPPORO FOR CHRISTMAS, AND KABUKI-CHO FOR NEW YEAR'S. (I WAS IN SHIBUYA RIGHT BEFORE THAT.)

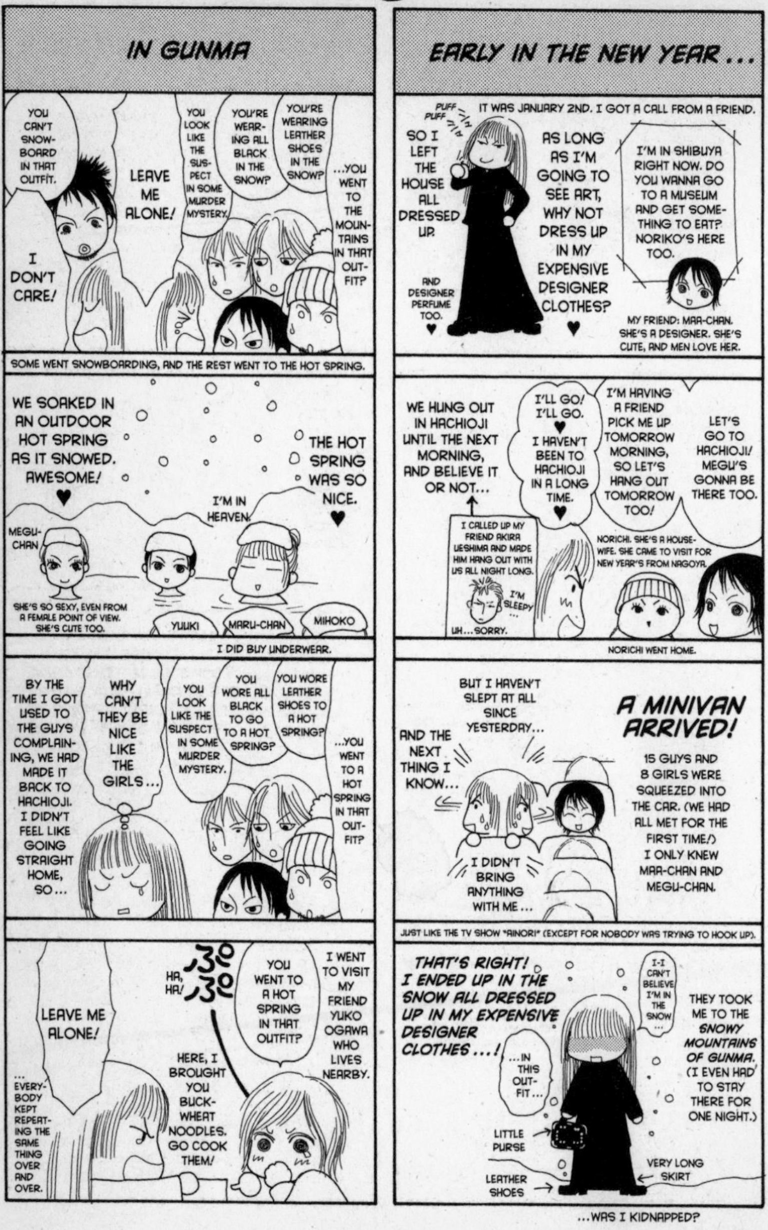
EARLY IN THE NEW YEAR...
IT WAS JANUARY 2ND. I GOT A CALL FROM A FRIEND.
I'M IN SHIBUYA RIGHT NOW. DO YOU WANNA GO TO A MUSEUM AND GET SOMETHING TO EAT? NORIKO'S HERE TOO.
MY FRIEND: MAA-CHAN. SHE'S A DESIGNER. SHE'S CUTE, AND MEN LOVE HER.
AS LONG AS I'M GOING TO SEE ART, WHY NOT DRESS UP IN MY EXPENSIVE DESIGNER CLOTHES? ♥
PUFF PUFF
SO I LEFT THE HOUSE ALL DRESSED UP.
AND DESIGNER PERFUME TOO. ♥
LET'S GO TO HACHIOJI! MEGU'S GONNA BE THERE TOO.
I'M HAVING A FRIEND PICK ME UP TOMORROW MORNING, SO LET'S HANG OUT TOMORROW TOO!
I'LL GO! I'LL GO. ♥ I HAVEN'T BEEN TO HACHIOJI IN A LONG TIME. ♥
WE HUNG OUT IN HACHIOJI UNTIL THE NEXT MORNING, AND BELIEVE IT OR NOT...
I CALLED UP MY FRIEND AKIRA UESHIMA AND MADE HIM HANG OUT WITH US ALL NIGHT LONG.
I'M SLEEPY...
UH...SORRY.
NORICHI. SHE'S A HOUSEWIFE. SHE CAME TO VISIT FOR NEW YEAR'S FROM NAGOYA.
NORICHI WENT HOME.
A MINIVAN ARRIVED!
15 GUYS AND 8 GIRLS WERE SQUEEZED INTO THE CAR. (WE HAD ALL MET FOR THE FIRST TIME!) I ONLY KNEW MAA-CHAN AND MEGU-CHAN.
BUT I HAVEN'T SLEPT AT ALL SINCE YESTERDAY...
AND THE NEXT THING I KNOW...
I DIDN'T BRING ANYTHING WITH ME...
JUST LIKE THE TV SHOW "AINORI" (EXCEPT FOR NOBODY WAS TRYING TO HOOK UP).
THEY TOOK ME TO THE SNOWY MOUNTAINS OF GUNMA. (I EVEN HAD TO STAY THERE FOR ONE NIGHT.)
I-I CAN'T BELIEVE I'M IN THE SNOW...
THAT'S RIGHT! I ENDED UP IN THE SNOW ALL DRESSED UP IN MY EXPENSIVE DESIGNER CLOTHES...!
...IN THIS OUTFIT...
LITTLE PURSE
VERY LONG SKIRT
LEATHER SHOES
...WAS I KIDNAPPED?
IN GUNMA
YOU'RE WEARING LEATHER SHOES IN THE SNOW?
...YOU WENT TO THE MOUNTAINS IN THAT OUTFIT?
YOU'RE WEARING ALL BLACK IN THE SNOW?
YOU LOOK LIKE THE SUSPECT IN SOME MURDER MYSTERY.
LEAVE ME ALONE!
YOU CAN'T SNOWBOARD IN THAT OUTFIT.
I DON'T CARE!
SOME WENT SNOWBOARDING, AND THE REST WENT TO THE HOT SPRING.
THE HOT SPRING WAS SO NICE. ♥
I'M IN HEAVEN.
WE SOAKED IN AN OUTDOOR HOT SPRING AS IT SNOWED. AWESOME! ♥
MEGU-CHAN
SHE'S SO SEXY, EVEN FROM A FEMALE POINT OF VIEW. SHE'S CUTE TOO.
MIHOKO
MARU-CHAN
YUUKI
I DID BUY UNDERWEAR.
YOU WORE LEATHER SHOES TO A HOT SPRING?
...YOU WENT TO A HOT SPRING IN THAT OUTFIT?
YOU WORE ALL BLACK TO GO TO A HOT SPRING?
YOU LOOK LIKE THE SUSPECT IN SOME MURDER MYSTERY.
WHY CAN'T THEY BE NICE LIKE THE GIRLS...
BY THE TIME I GOT USED TO THE GUYS COMPLAINING, WE HAD MADE IT BACK TO HACHIOJI. I DIDN'T FEEL LIKE GOING STRAIGHT HOME, SO...
I WENT TO VISIT MY FRIEND YUKO OGAWA WHO LIVES NEARBY.
YOU WENT TO A HOT SPRING IN THAT OUTFIT?
ぷっ ぷっ
HA, HA!
HERE, I BROUGHT YOU BUCKWHEAT NOODLES. GO COOK THEM!
LEAVE ME ALONE!
...EVERYBODY KEPT REPEATING THE SAME THING OVER AND OVER.

I WENT TO VISIT SOME FRIENDS OF MINE WITH KOTA-SAMA ON THE WAY BACK (?) FROM BAROQUE'S "ZEKKO KAMEN" TOUR. ♥

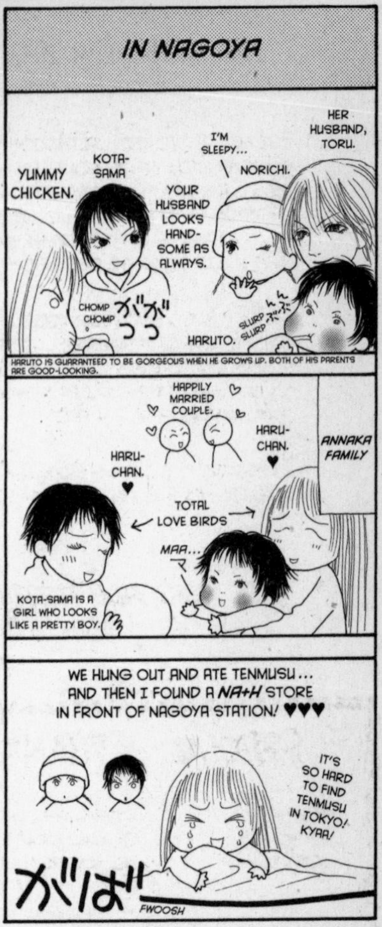
IN NAGOYA
HER HUSBAND, TORU.
I'M SLEEPY...
NORICHI.
KOTA-SAMA
YOUR HUSBAND LOOKS HANDSOME AS ALWAYS.
YUMMY CHICKEN.
SLURP SLURP
HARUTO.
CHOMP CHOMP
HARUTO IS GUARANTEED TO BE GORGEOUS WHEN HE GROWS UP. BOTH OF HIS PARENTS ARE GOOD-LOOKING.
ANNAKA FAMILY
HARU-CHAN. ♥
HAPPILY MARRIED COUPLE.
HARU-CHAN. ♥
TOTAL LOVE BIRDS
MAA...
マ
KOTA-SAMA IS A GIRL WHO LOOKS LIKE A PRETTY BOY.
WE HUNG OUT AND ATE TENMUSU... AND THEN I FOUND A NA+H STORE IN FRONT OF NAGOYA STATION! ♥♥♥
IT'S SO HARD TO FIND TENMUSU IN TOKYO! KYAA!
FWOOSH

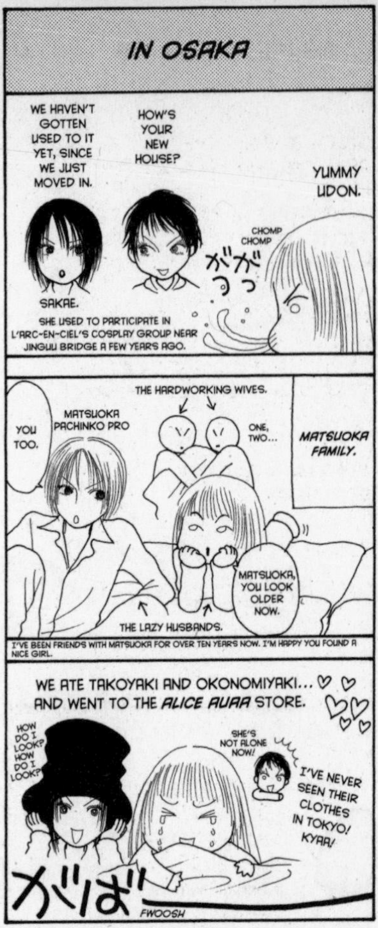
IN OSAKA
YUMMY UDON.
HOW'S YOUR NEW HOUSE?
WE HAVEN'T GOTTEN USED TO IT YET, SINCE WE JUST MOVED IN.
CHOMP CHOMP
SAKAE.
SHE USED TO PARTICIPATE IN L'ARC-EN-CIEL'S COSPLAY GROUP NEAR JINGUU BRIDGE A FEW YEARS AGO.
MATSUOKA FAMILY.
ONE, TWO...
THE HARDWORKING WIVES.
MATSUOKA PACHINKO PRO
YOU TOO.
MATSUOKA, YOU LOOK OLDER NOW.
THE LAZY HUSBANDS.
I'VE BEEN FRIENDS WITH MATSUOKA FOR OVER TEN YEARS NOW. I'M HAPPY YOU FOUND A NICE GIRL.
WE ATE TAKOYAKI AND OKONOMIYAKI... ♥ ♥ AND WENT TO THE ALICE AUAA STORE.
I'VE NEVER SEEN THEIR CLOTHES IN TOKYO! KYAA!
SHE'S NOT ALONE NOW!
HOW DO I LOOK? HOW DO I LOOK?
FWOOSH

IT WAS SUCH A WONDERFUL TRIP (?)!

THE SHOWS WERE AWESOME ♥ AND THE FOOD WAS GREAT! ♥ AND I FINALLY BOUGHT THE CLOTHES I'D BEEN WANTING FOR SO LONG! ♥ ABOVE ALL, I GOT TO SEE MY OLD FRIENDS! ♥

ACTUALLY, I EVEN RAN INTO A FRIEND AT A VENUE IN NAGOYA (YUKA-CHAN WHO LIVES IN NAGOYA)! WHAT A SURPRISE!

I WAS SO HAPPY. ♥

AND ... AS SOON AS I CAME BACK TO TOKYO, I WENT ON A SHOPPING SPREE AT JEAN PAUL GAULTIER IN OMOTESANDO AND H.NAOTO IN LAFORLET. AND THEN I WENT TO SEE BAROQUE'S "ZEKKO KAMEN" TOUR AGAIN, ONLY IN TOKYO THIS TIME....

I END UP DOING THE SAME THINGS, NO MATTER WHERE I AM.

THANKS TO KOSHIRO-KUN'S IMPRESSIVE SALES TECHNIQUE (?), I'VE BEEN BUYING A LOT OF CLOTHES FROM H.NAOTO IN LAFORLET LATELY.... WE'VE BEEN FRIENDS FOR OVER TEN YEARS NOW.

THANKS FOR STICKING AROUND! ♥

I'VE FINALLY MOVED ... ALTHOUGH MY ROOM IS STILL MESSY.
I WASN'T CONFIDENT ENOUGH IN MY ABILITY TO TAKE CARE OF ANIMALS,
SO I GAVE UP ON GETTING A PET. SNIFF ...
MY ROOM IS TRANSFORMING INTO A WEIRD PLACE WITH MY SANTA CHAIR,
SKULL CHAIR, THIRTY DIFFERENT SKELETON ITEMS AND TWO TORSOS.
THAT'S RIGHT. I'M THE ONE WHO'S CHASING THE GUYS AWAY ... SIGH.

THANK YOU SO MUCH FOR YOUR LETTERS. ♥
YOU GUYS GIVE ME ENERGY ... THAT MAKES ME A MILLION TIMES STRONGER!
SORRY FOR MAKING YOU WORRY EVER SINCE I WROTE THAT I WAS
"EMOTIONALLY IMBALANCED." THANKS FOR YOUR KINDNESS. I'M OKAY
NOW ... PROBABLY ⟶ HEY!

I'M SORRY IT'S TAKING SO MUCH TIME TO WRITE YOU BACK.
I REALLY HOPE I CAN RESPOND SOMEDAY SOON ...!

SEE YOU ALL AGAIN IN BOOK 8! ♥

SEE YOU LATER! OKAY?

SPECIAL THANKS

HANA-CHAN,
ARAKI-KUN,
YOSHII.

AYUAYU WATANABE,
ATSUKO NAMBA,
IYU KOZAKURA.

MINE-SAMA,
SHIOZAWA-SAMA,
INO-SAMA,
EVERYONE IN THE
EDITORIAL DEPARTMENT.

CREDITS FOR
THE BONUS
PAGES ...

MASASHI
TAKENAGA-SAMA,
YUJI,
BAROQUE-SAMA

MA-CHAN, MEGU-CHAN,
NORICHI, KOTAKI-CHAN,
SAKAE, AN-CHAN,
TAKA MATSUOKA, YUKO NEO ...
                WHAT DO YOU MEAN NEO?
KAI-CHAN, CHISATO-CHAN,
TORU-SAN, MAKO, KOSHIRO-KUN,
YUKA-CHAN AND HER FRIENDS,
EVERYONE WHO SENT ME LETTERS.

About the Creator

Tomoko Hayakawa was born on March 4.

Since her debut as a manga creator, Tomoko Hayakawa has worked on many shojo titles with the theme of romantic love—only to realize that she could write about other subjects as well. She decided to pack her newest story with the things she likes most, which led to her current, enormously popular series, *The Wallflower*.

Her favorite things are: Tim Burton's *The Nightmare Before Christmas*, Jean-Paul Gaultier, and samurai dramas on TV. Her hobbies are collecting items with skull designs and watching *bishonen* (beautiful boys). Her dream is to build a mansion like the one that the Addams family lives in. Her favorite pastime is to lie around at home with her cat, Ten (whose full name is Tennosuke).

Her zodiac sign is Pisces, and her blood group is AB.

Translation Notes

Japanese is a tricky language for most Westerners, and translation is often more art than science. For your edification and reading pleasure, here are notes on some of the places where we could have gone in a different direction in our translation of the work, or where a Japanese cultural reference is used.

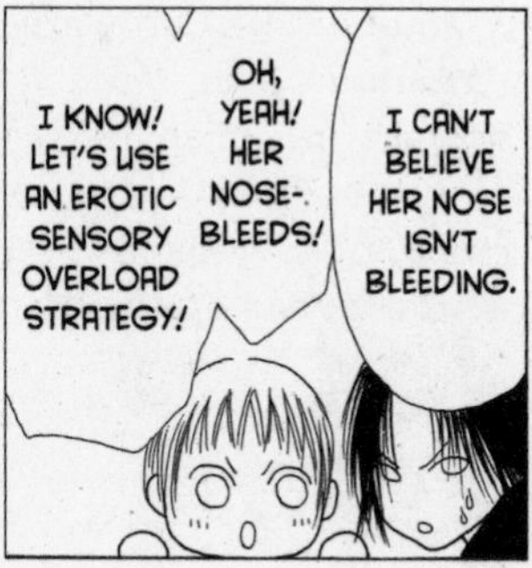
I CAN'T BELIEVE HER NOSE ISN'T BLEEDING.
OH, YEAH! HER NOSE-BLEEDS!
I KNOW! LET'S USE AN EROTIC SENSORY OVERLOAD STRATEGY!

Nosebleeds (page 27)

In Japan, nosebleeds are said to be caused by sudden sexual arousal. That's why Sunako often gets nosebleeds when she has a close encounter with one of the guys.

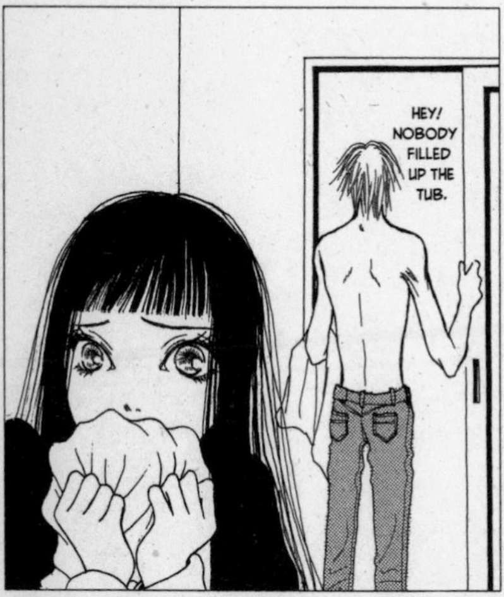
HEY! NOBODY FILLED UP THE TUB.

Rub-a-dub-dub (page 33)

Japanese families usually fill the bathtub once and share the same bath water. It's customary to wash your hair and body in the shower first before soaking in the tub. You never use soap in the tub itself.

Lone Wolf (page 51)

Ranmaru is imagining himself as the famous character in the popular TV series/manga *Kozure Ookami* (Lone Wolf and Cub). "Shito shito picchan" is part of the show's theme song. The series is about a samurai who travels with his baby.

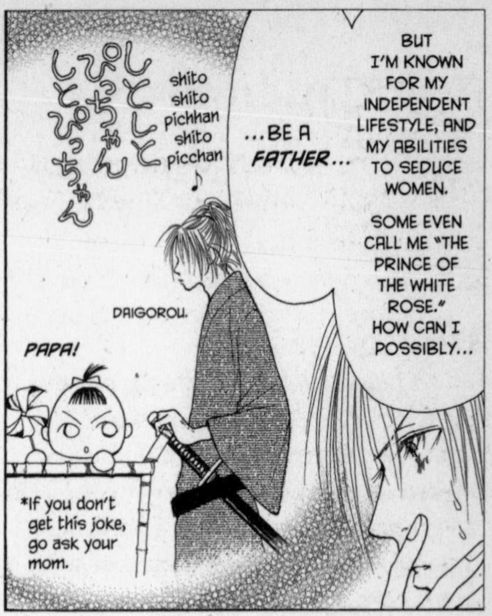
BUT I'M KNOWN FOR MY INDEPENDENT LIFESTYLE, AND MY ABILITIES TO SEDUCE WOMEN.
SOME EVEN CALL ME "THE PRINCE OF THE WHITE ROSE." HOW CAN I POSSIBLY...
...BE A FATHER...
しとしとぴっちゃん しとぴっちゃん
shito shito pichhan shito picchan ♪
DAIGOROU.
PAPA!
*If you don't get this joke, go ask your mom.

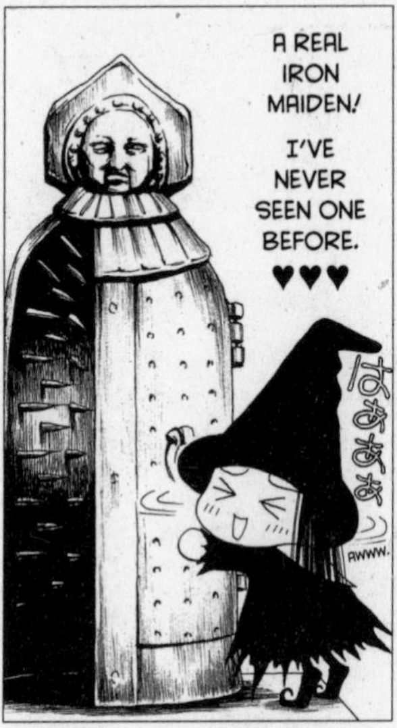
A REAL IRON MAIDEN!
I'VE NEVER SEEN ONE BEFORE. ♥♥♥
はあああ
AWWW.

Iron maiden (page 92)

The iron maiden, also known as the Virgin of Nuremberg, was a torture device used during the Middle Ages. The prisoner was shut inside and then pierced with numerous metal spikes.

Emperor Nero (page 92)

Nero was a Roman emperor from 54 A.D. to 68 A.D. Sunako-chan really knows her history.

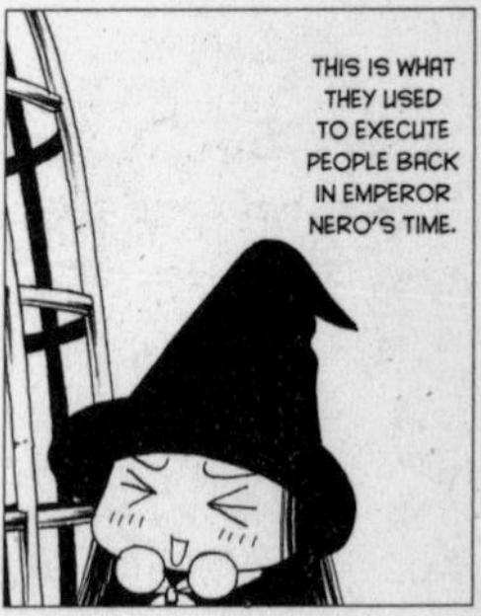
THIS IS WHAT THEY USED TO EXECUTE PEOPLE BACK IN EMPEROR NERO'S TIME.

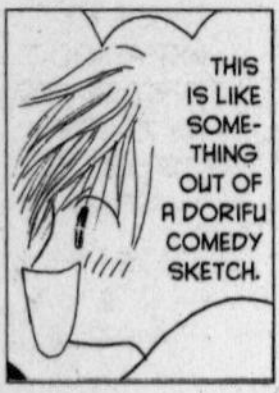
THIS IS LIKE SOMETHING OUT OF A DORIFU COMEDY SKETCH.

Dorifu (page 131)

Dorifu, or "The Drifters," is a famous comedy troupe.

Oden (page 138)

Oden is a tasty dish made up of various ingredients boiled in soup stock. Common ingredients include daikon radish, hardboiled eggs, *konyaku* (yam cake) and various types of fishcake. Oden food stalls are a common sight in urban areas.

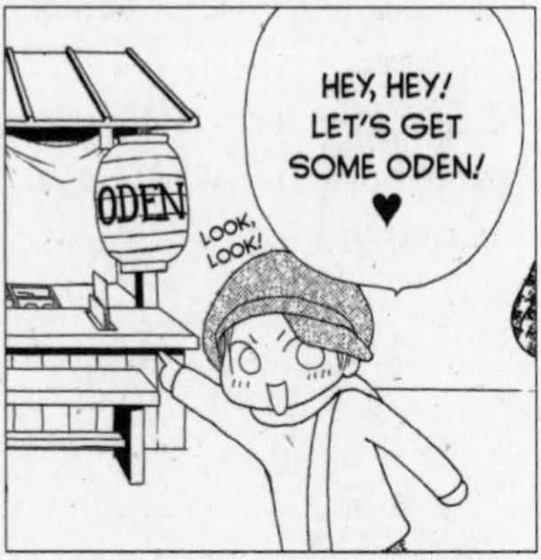
HEY, HEY! LET'S GET SOME ODEN! ♥
LOOK, LOOK!
ODEN

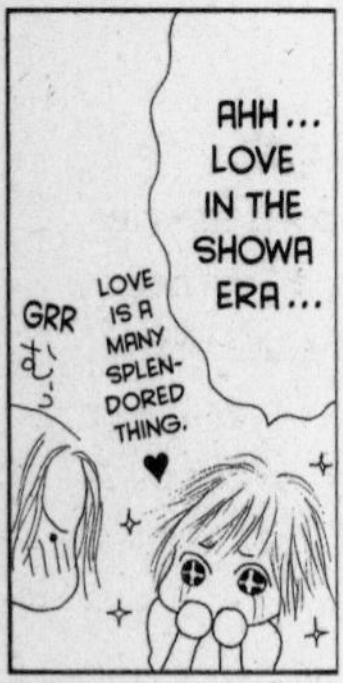
AHH... LOVE IN THE SHOWA ERA...
LOVE IS A MANY SPLENDORED THING. ♥
GRR

Showa period (page 141)

The Showa period of Japanese history lasted from 1926–1989. The current period is called Heisei.

Loose Socks (page 170)

Loose socks are a type of white kneesock that schoolgirls wear with their uniforms.

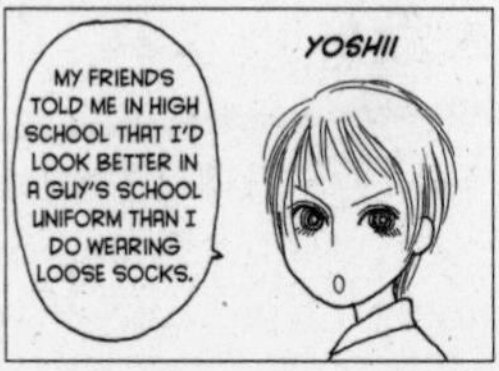
YOSHI!
MY FRIENDS TOLD ME IN HIGH SCHOOL THAT I'D LOOK BETTER IN A GUY'S SCHOOL UNIFORM THAN I DO WEARING LOOSE SOCKS.

Tenmusu (page 172)

An *onigiri* (rice ball) stuffed with tempura.

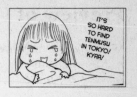

IT'S SO HARD TO FIND TENMUSU IN TOKYO! KYAA!

Takoyaki (page 172)

Takoyaki are octopus fritters. *Okonomiyaki* is a sort of pancake stuffed with meat and veggies.

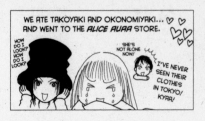

WE ATE TAKOYAKI AND OKONOMIYAKI... AND WENT TO THE *ALICE AUAA* STORE.
I'VE NEVER SEEN THEIR CLOTHES IN TOKYO! KYAA!
SHE'S NOT ALONE NOW!
HOW DO I LOOK? HOW DO I LOOK?

Preview of Volume 8

We're pleased to present you a preview from Volume 8. This volume will be available in English on June 27, 2006, but for now you'll have to make do with Japanese!

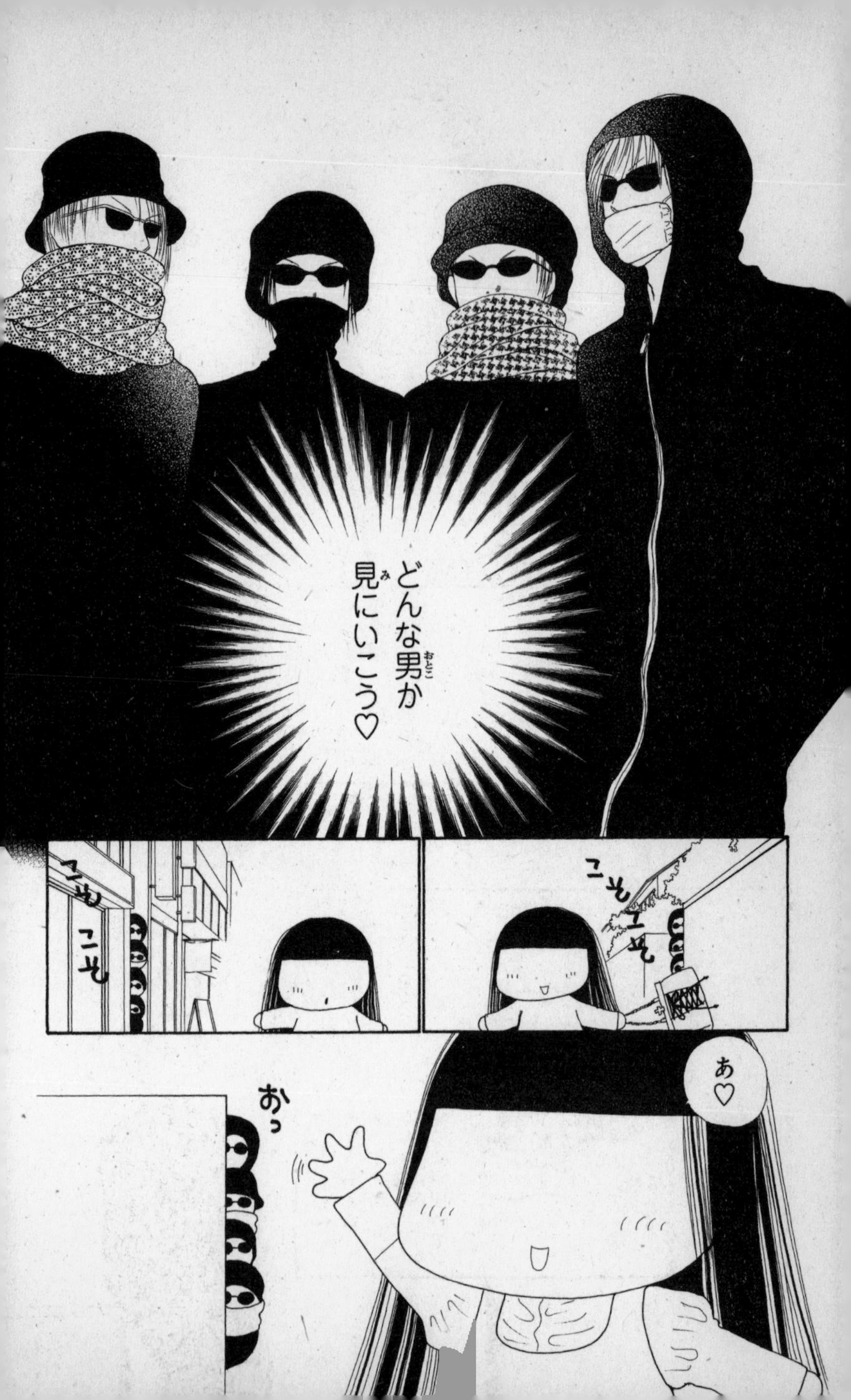
どんな男か見にいこう♡
こそこそ
こそこそ
あ♡
おっ

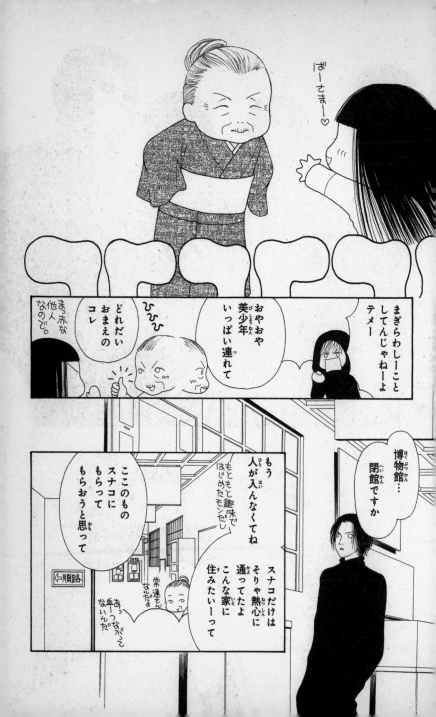

ぼーさまー♡

まぎらわしーこと
してんじゃねーよ
テメー

おやおや
美少年
いっぱい連れて

どれだい
おまえの
コレ

ひひひ

まっ赤な
他人
なのど。

博物館…
閉館ですか

もう
人が入んなくてね

もともと趣味で
はじめたモンだし

スナコだけは
そりゃ熱心に
通ってたよ

こんな家に
住みたいって

ここのもの
スナコに
もらって
もらおうと思って

常連さん
なんだよ

あっ
つながって
ないんだ

←順路

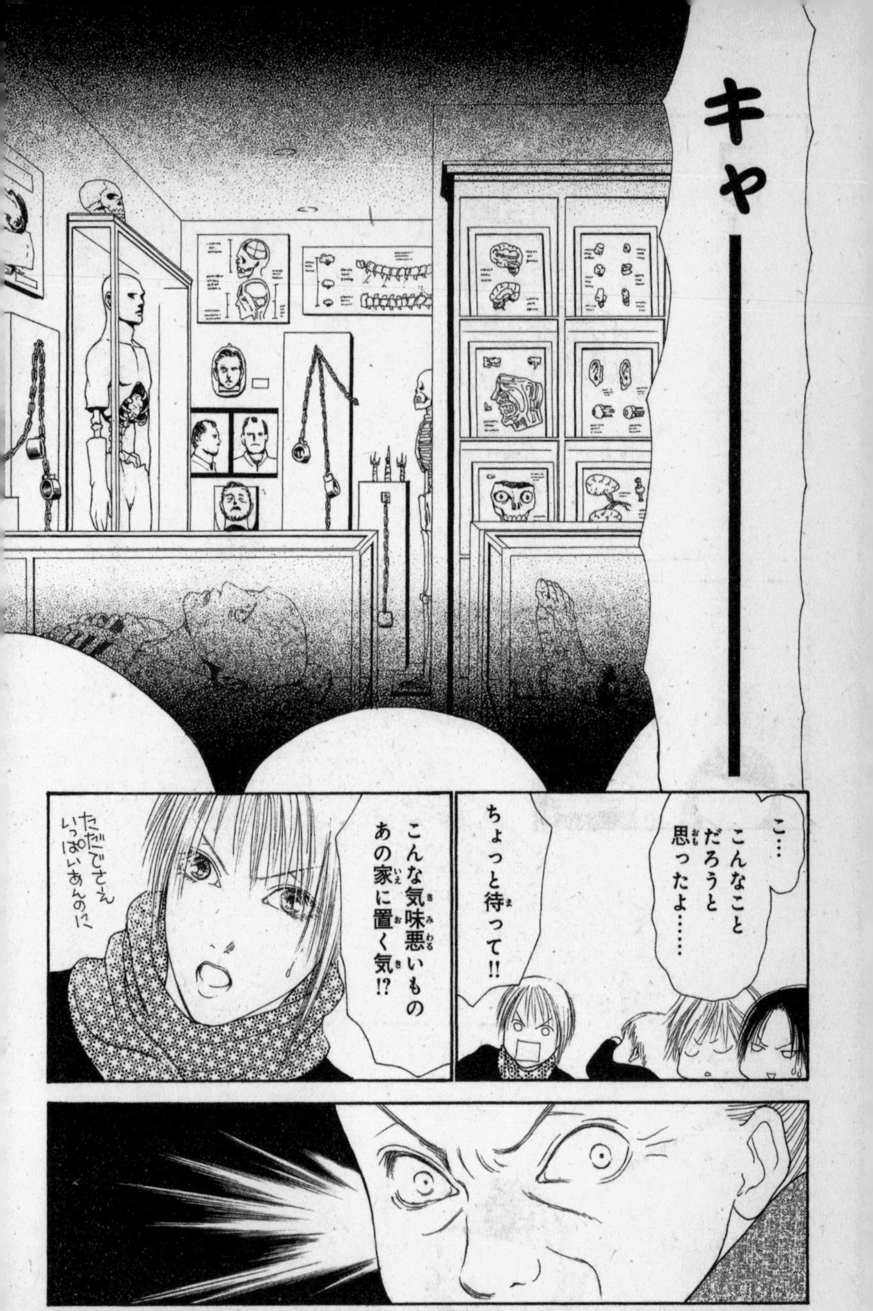
キャーー
こ…こんなことだろうと思ったよ……
ちょっと待って!!
こんな気味悪いものあの家に置く気!?
ただでさえいっぱいあんのに

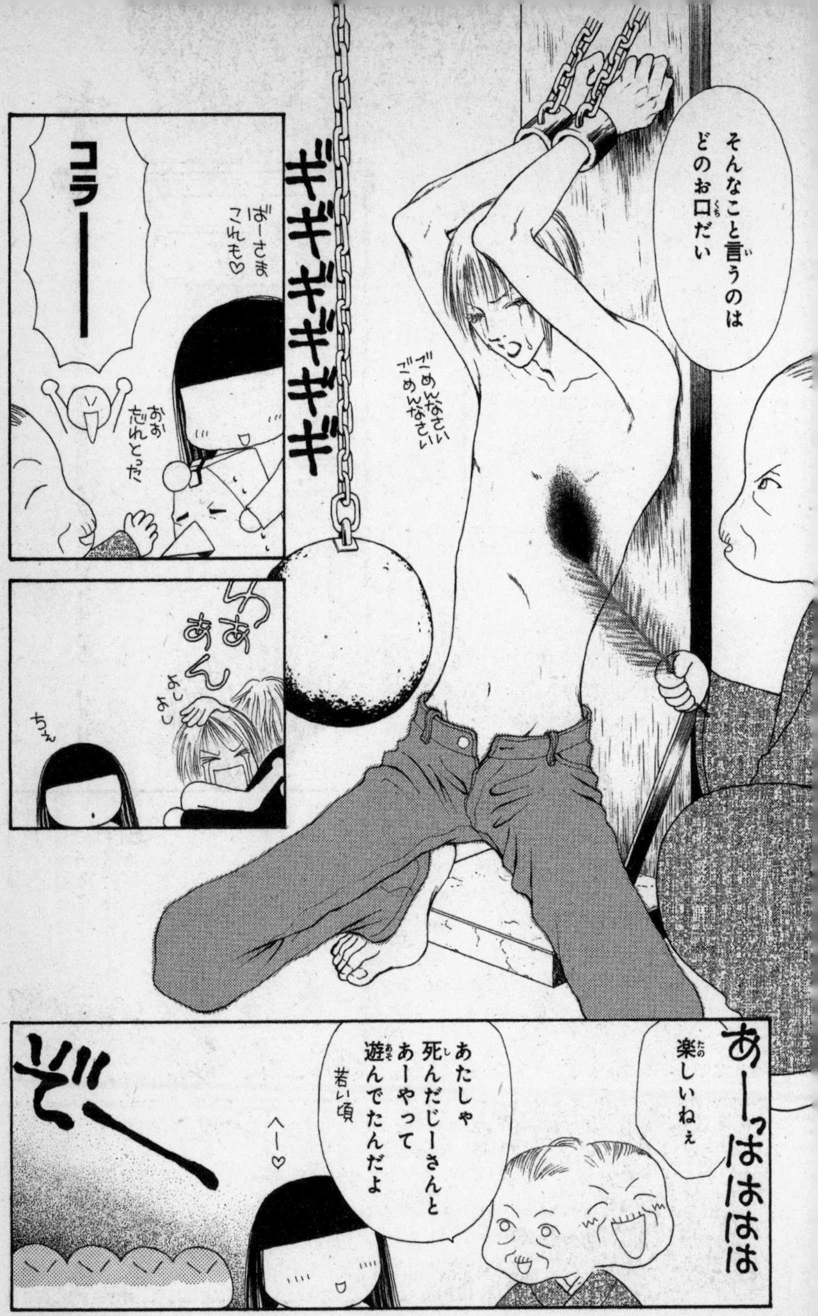

そんなこと言うのはどのお口だい
ごめんなさいごめんなさい
ギギギギギギ
ばーさまこれも♡
コラーーー
おお忘れとった
わあああん
よしよし
ちぇ
あーっははは
楽しいねぇ
あたしゃ死んだじーさんとあーやって遊んでたんだよ
若い頃
へー♡
ぞ〜〜

LOVE ROMA

BY MINORU TOYODA

"We have been telling all the people we meet to read this manga!"
—CLAMP, creators of Tsubasa

LOVE ROMA
1
MINORU TOYODA

A fun, romantic comedy, Love Roma is about the simple kind of relationships we all longed for when we were young. It's a story of love at first sight—literally. When Hoshino sees Negishi for the first time, he asks her to be his girlfriend. Shocked, Negishi nevertheless agrees to allow Hoshino to walk her home, while he explains why he is in love with her. Touched, Negishi begins to feel something for this strange young boy from her school.

Ages: 16+

Special extras in each volume! Read them all!

DEL REY

VISIT WWW.DELREYMANGA.COM TO:
- View release date calendars for upcoming volumes
- Sign up for Del Rey's free manga e-newsletter
- Find out the latest about new Del Rey Manga series

School Rumble

BY JIN KOBAYASHI

SUBTLETY IS FOR WIMPS!

She . . . is a second-year high school student with a single all-consuming question: Will the boy she likes ever really notice her?

He . . . is the school's most notorious juvenile delinquent, and he's suddenly come to a shocking realization: He's got a huge crush, and now he must tell her how he feels.

Life-changing obsessions, colossal foul-ups, grand schemes, deep-seated anxieties, and raging hormones—School Rumble portrays high school as it really is: over-the-top comedy!

Ages: 16 +

Special extras in each volume! Read them all!

VISIT WWW.DELREYMANGA.COM TO:
- Read sample pages
- View release date calendars for upcoming volumes
- Sign up for Del Rey's free manga e-newsletter
- Find out the latest about new Del Rey Manga series

TOMARE!

[STOP!]

You're going the wrong way!

Manga is a completely different type of reading experience.

To start at the beginning, go to the end!

That's right! Authentic manga is read the traditional Japanese way—from right to left. Exactly the opposite of how American books are read. It's easy to follow: Just go to the other end of the book, and read each page—and each panel—from right side to left side, starting at the top right. Now you're experiencing manga as it was meant to be!